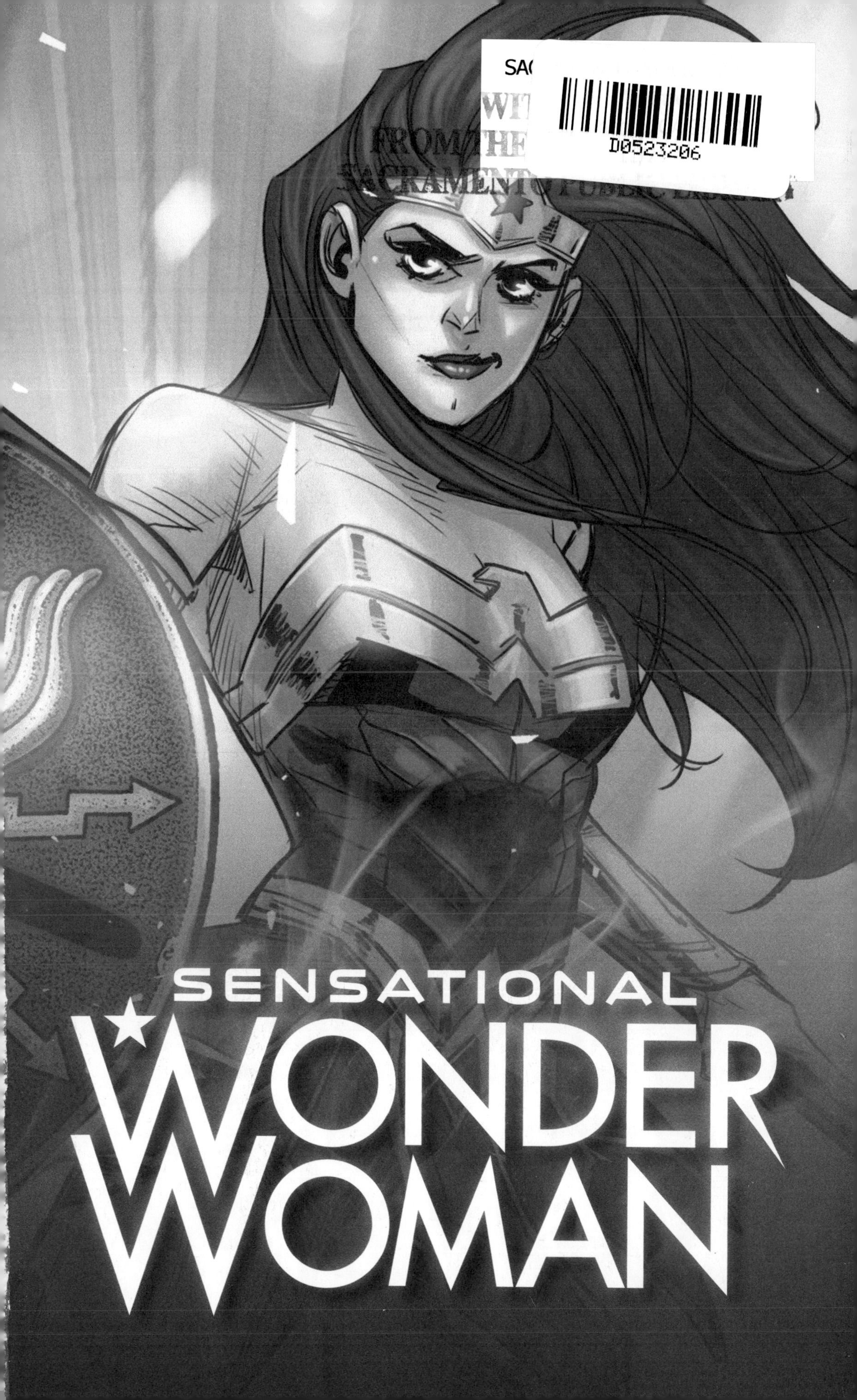
SENSATIONAL
WONDER
WOMAN

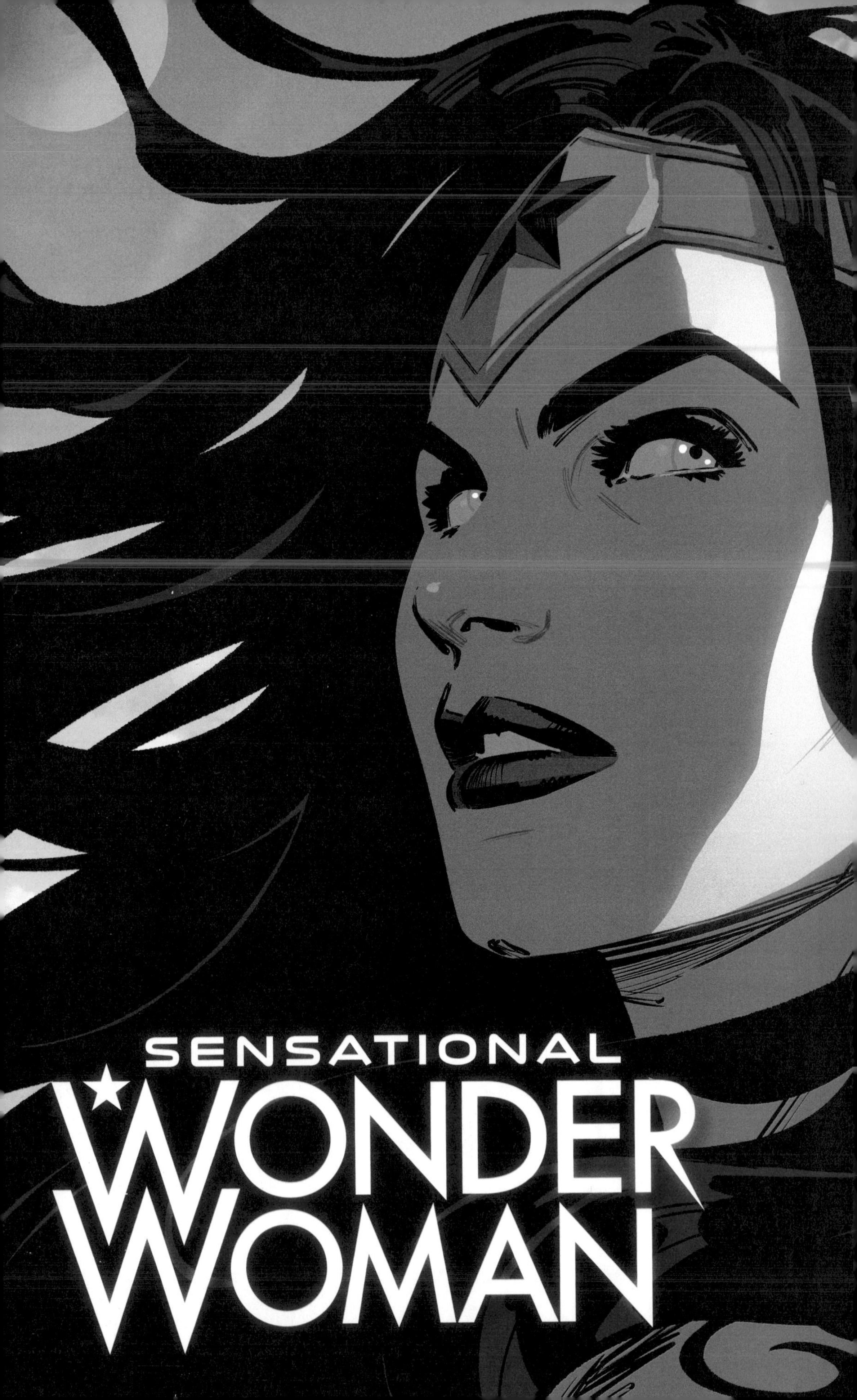
SENSATIONAL
WONDER
WOMAN

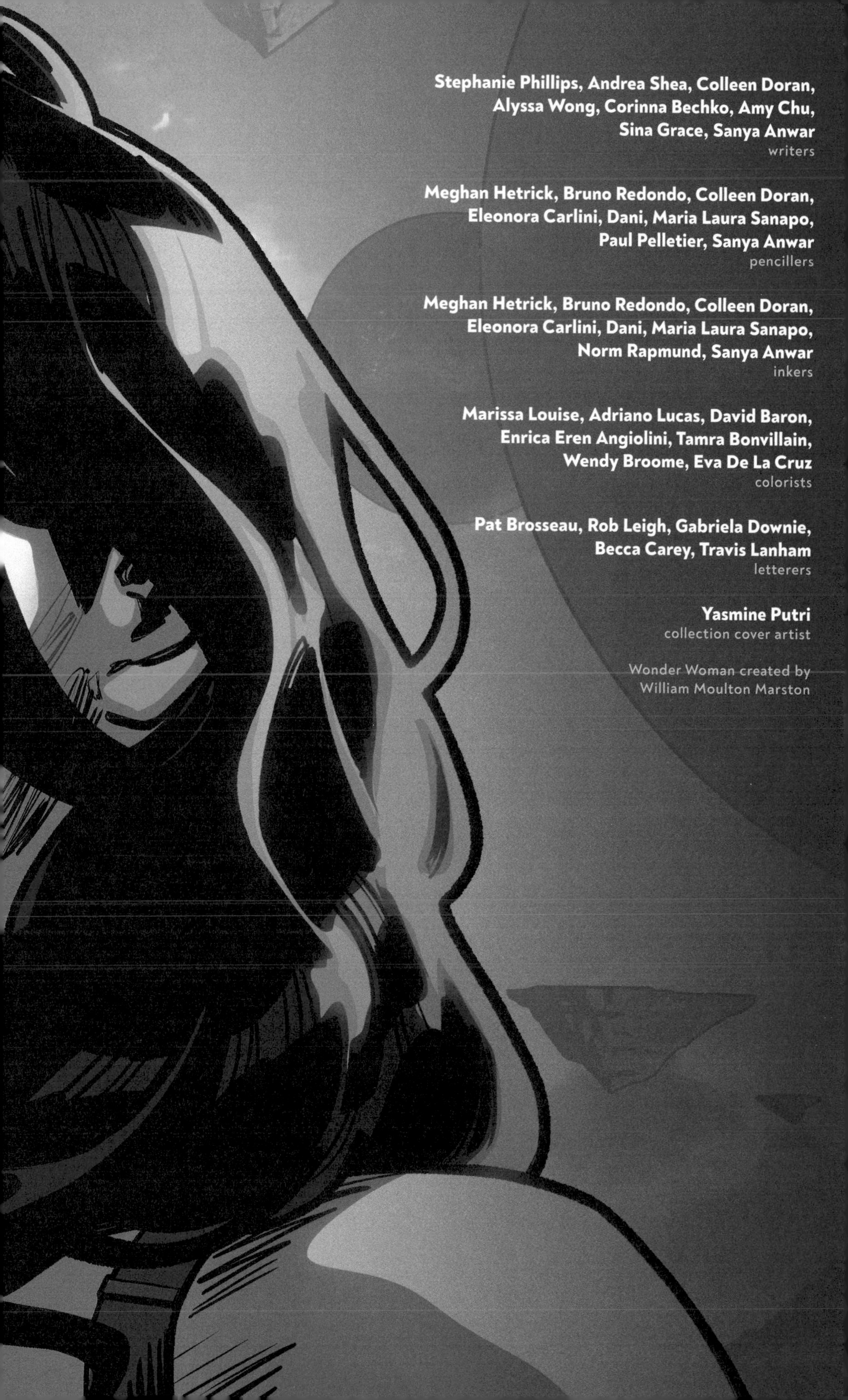

Stephanie Phillips, Andrea Shea, Colleen Doran,
Alyssa Wong, Corinna Bechko, Amy Chu,
Sina Grace, Sanya Anwar
writers

Meghan Hetrick, Bruno Redondo, Colleen Doran,
Eleonora Carlini, Dani, Maria Laura Sanapo,
Paul Pelletier, Sanya Anwar
pencillers

Meghan Hetrick, Bruno Redondo, Colleen Doran,
Eleonora Carlini, Dani, Maria Laura Sanapo,
Norm Rapmund, Sanya Anwar
inkers

Marissa Louise, Adriano Lucas, David Baron,
Enrica Eren Angiolini, Tamra Bonvillain,
Wendy Broome, Eva De La Cruz
colorists

Pat Brosseau, Rob Leigh, Gabriela Downie,
Becca Carey, Travis Lanham
letterers

Yasmine Putri
collection cover artist

Wonder Woman created by
William Moulton Marston

Michael McCalister
Editor – Original Series & Collected Edition

Liz Erickson
Editor – Original Series

Steve Cook
Design Director – Books

Megen Bellersen
Publication Design

Erin Vanover
Publication Production

Marie Javins
Editor-in-Chief, DC Comics

Daniel Cherry III
Senior VP – General Manager

Jim Lee
Publisher & Chief Creative Officer

Joen Choe
VP – Global Brand & Creative Services

Don Falletti
VP – Manufacturing Operations & Workflow Management

Lawrence Ganem
VP – Talent Services

Alison Gill
Senior VP – Manufacturing & Operations

Nick J. Napolitano
VP – Manufacturing Administration & Design

Nancy Spears
VP – Revenue

SENSATIONAL WONDER WOMAN VOL. 1

DC Comics, 2900 West Alameda Ave., Burbank, CA 91505
Printed by LSC Communications, Owensville, MO, USA. 8/27/21. First Printing.
ISBN: 978-1-77951-266-6

Library of Congress Cataloging-in-Publication Data is available.

PEFC Certified

This product is from sustainably managed forests and controlled sources

PEFC/29-31-337   www.pefc.org

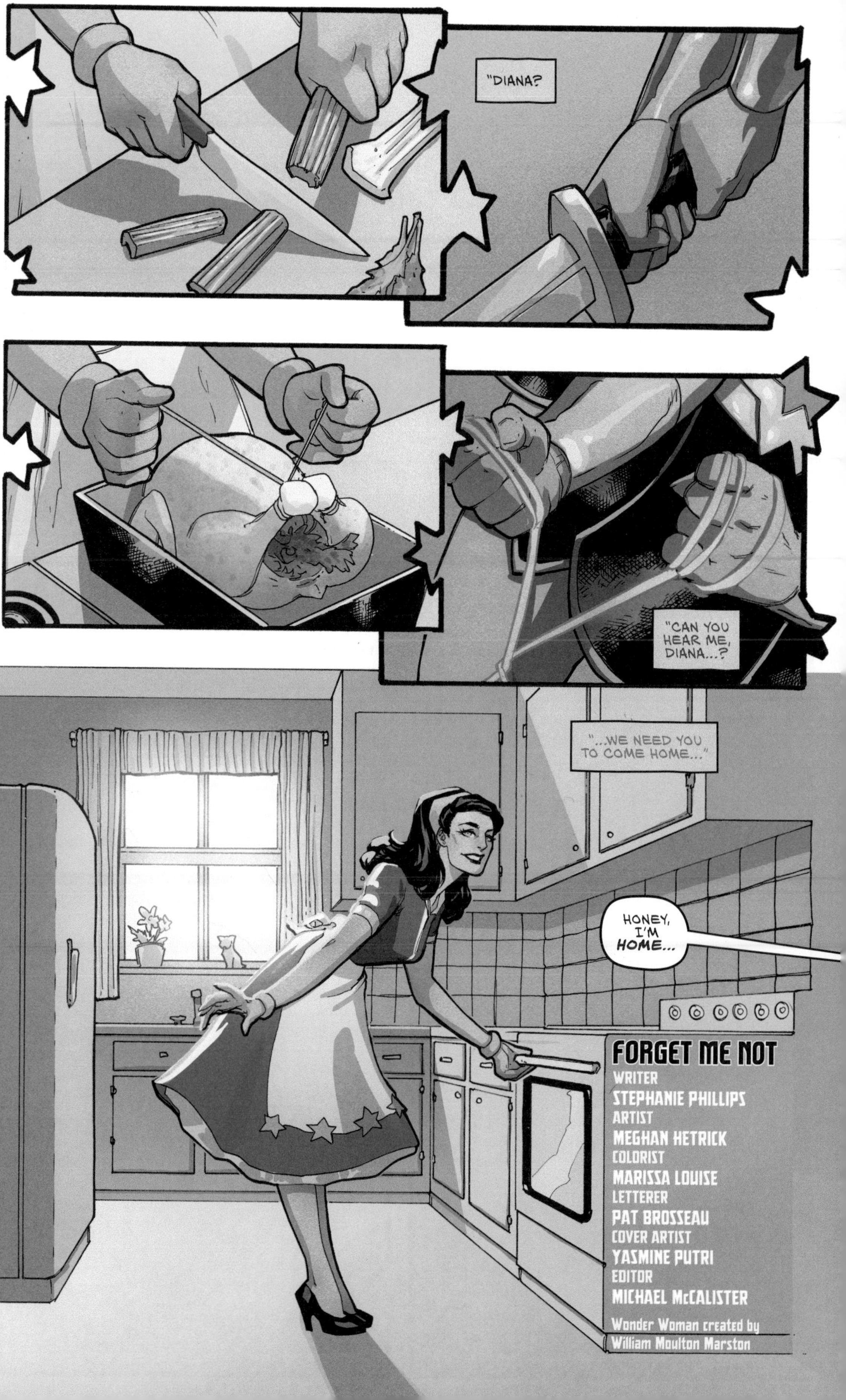
"DIANA?
"CAN YOU HEAR ME, DIANA...?
"...WE NEED YOU TO COME HOME..."
HONEY, I'M HOME...
FORGET ME NOT
WRITER
STEPHANIE PHILLIPS
ARTIST
MEGHAN HETRICK
COLORIST
MARISSA LOUISE
LETTERER
PAT BROSSEAU
COVER ARTIST
YASMINE PUTRI
EDITOR
MICHAEL McCALISTER
Wonder Woman created by
William Moulton Marston

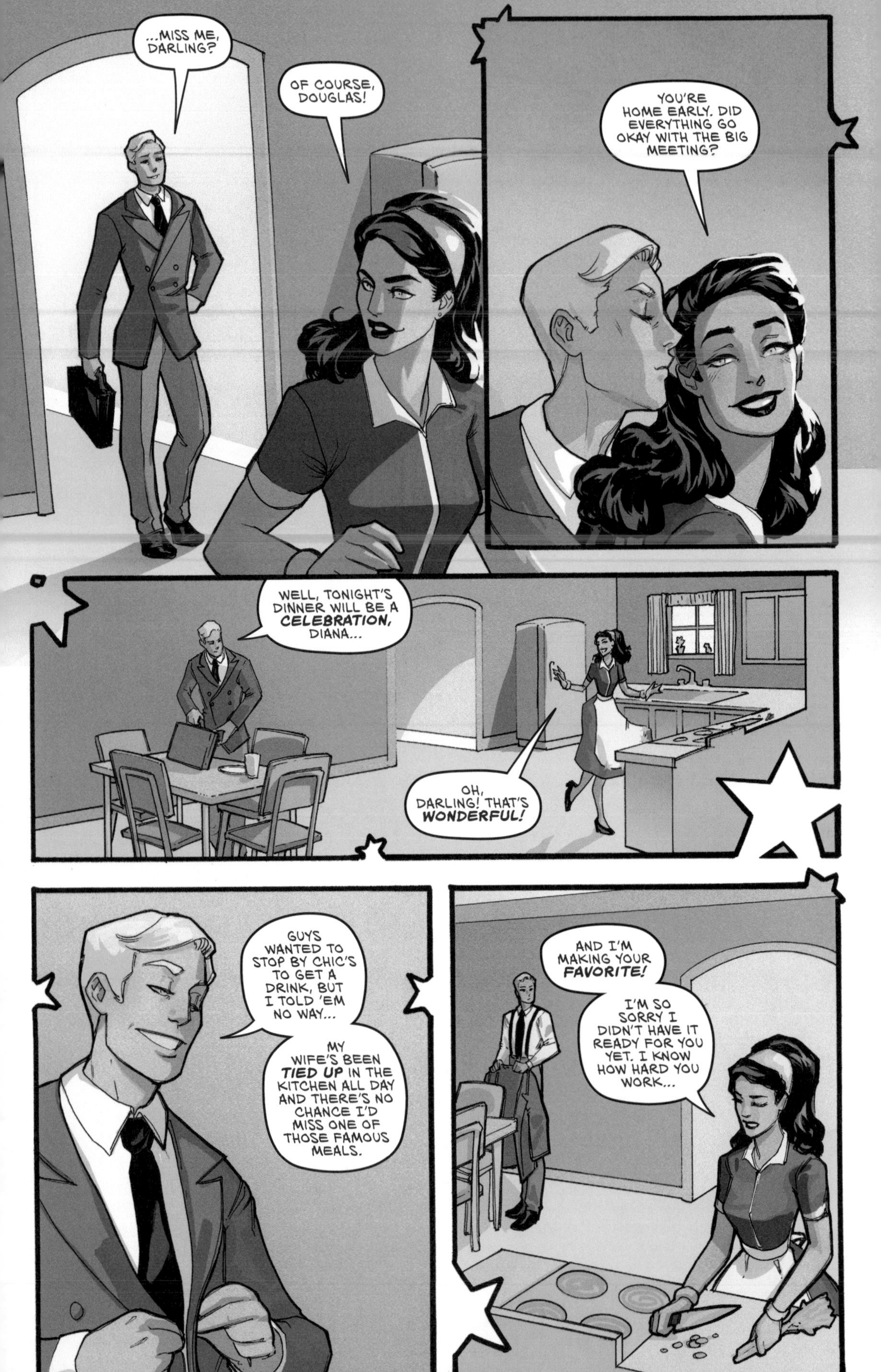
...MISS ME, DARLING?
OF COURSE, DOUGLAS!
YOU'RE HOME EARLY. DID EVERYTHING GO OKAY WITH THE BIG MEETING?
WELL, TONIGHT'S DINNER WILL BE A CELEBRATION, DIANA...
OH, DARLING! THAT'S WONDERFUL!
GUYS WANTED TO STOP BY CHIC'S TO GET A DRINK, BUT I TOLD 'EM NO WAY...
MY WIFE'S BEEN TIED UP IN THE KITCHEN ALL DAY AND THERE'S NO CHANCE I'D MISS ONE OF THOSE FAMOUS MEALS.
AND I'M MAKING YOUR FAVORITE!
I'M SO SORRY I DIDN'T HAVE IT READY FOR YOU YET. I KNOW HOW HARD YOU WORK...

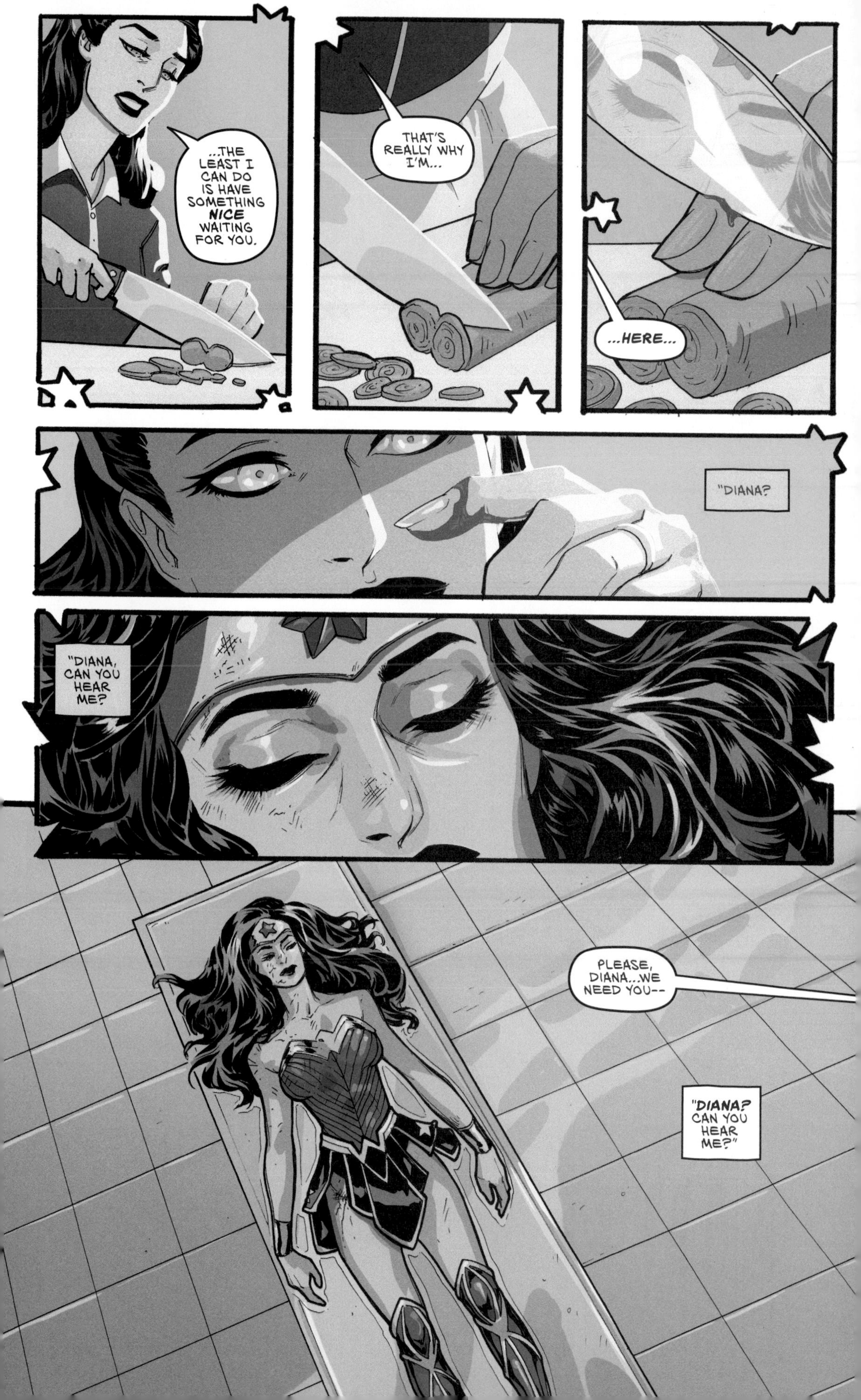
...THE LEAST I CAN DO IS HAVE SOMETHING NICE WAITING FOR YOU.
THAT'S REALLY WHY I'M...
...HERE...
"DIANA?
"DIANA, CAN YOU HEAR ME?
PLEASE, DIANA...WE NEED YOU--
"DIANA? CAN YOU HEAR ME?"

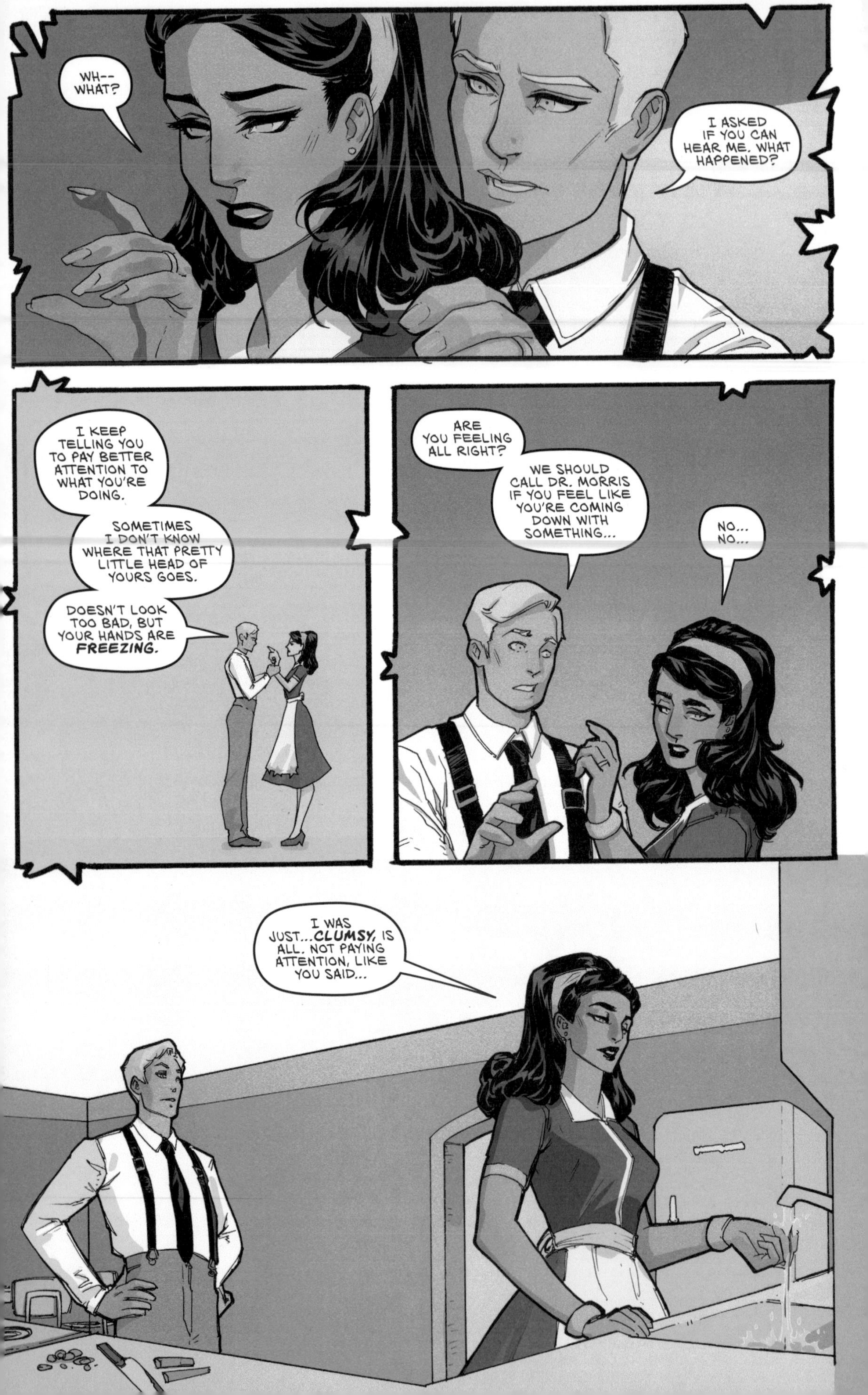
WH-- WHAT?
I ASKED IF YOU CAN HEAR ME. WHAT HAPPENED?
I KEEP TELLING YOU TO PAY BETTER ATTENTION TO WHAT YOU'RE DOING.
SOMETIMES I DON'T KNOW WHERE THAT PRETTY LITTLE HEAD OF YOURS GOES.
DOESN'T LOOK TOO BAD, BUT YOUR HANDS ARE **FREEZING.**
ARE YOU FEELING ALL RIGHT?
WE SHOULD CALL DR. MORRIS IF YOU FEEL LIKE YOU'RE COMING DOWN WITH SOMETHING...
NO... NO...
I WAS JUST...**CLUMSY,** IS ALL. NOT PAYING ATTENTION, LIKE YOU SAID...

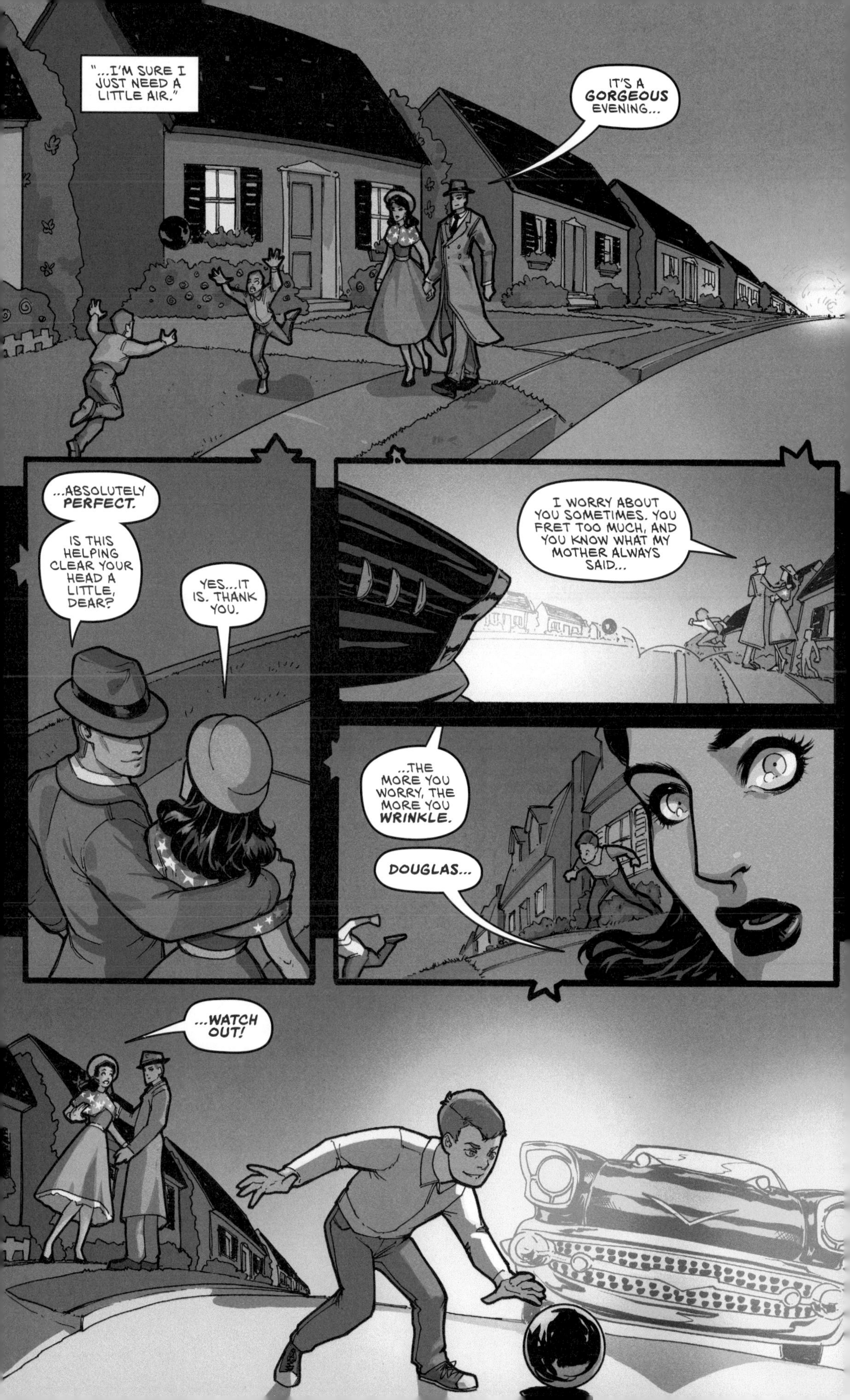
"...I'M SURE I JUST NEED A LITTLE AIR."
IT'S A GORGEOUS EVENING...
...ABSOLUTELY PERFECT.
IS THIS HELPING CLEAR YOUR HEAD A LITTLE, DEAR?
YES...IT IS. THANK YOU.
I WORRY ABOUT YOU SOMETIMES. YOU FRET TOO MUCH, AND YOU KNOW WHAT MY MOTHER ALWAYS SAID...
...THE MORE YOU WORRY, THE MORE YOU WRINKLE.
DOUGLAS...
...WATCH OUT!

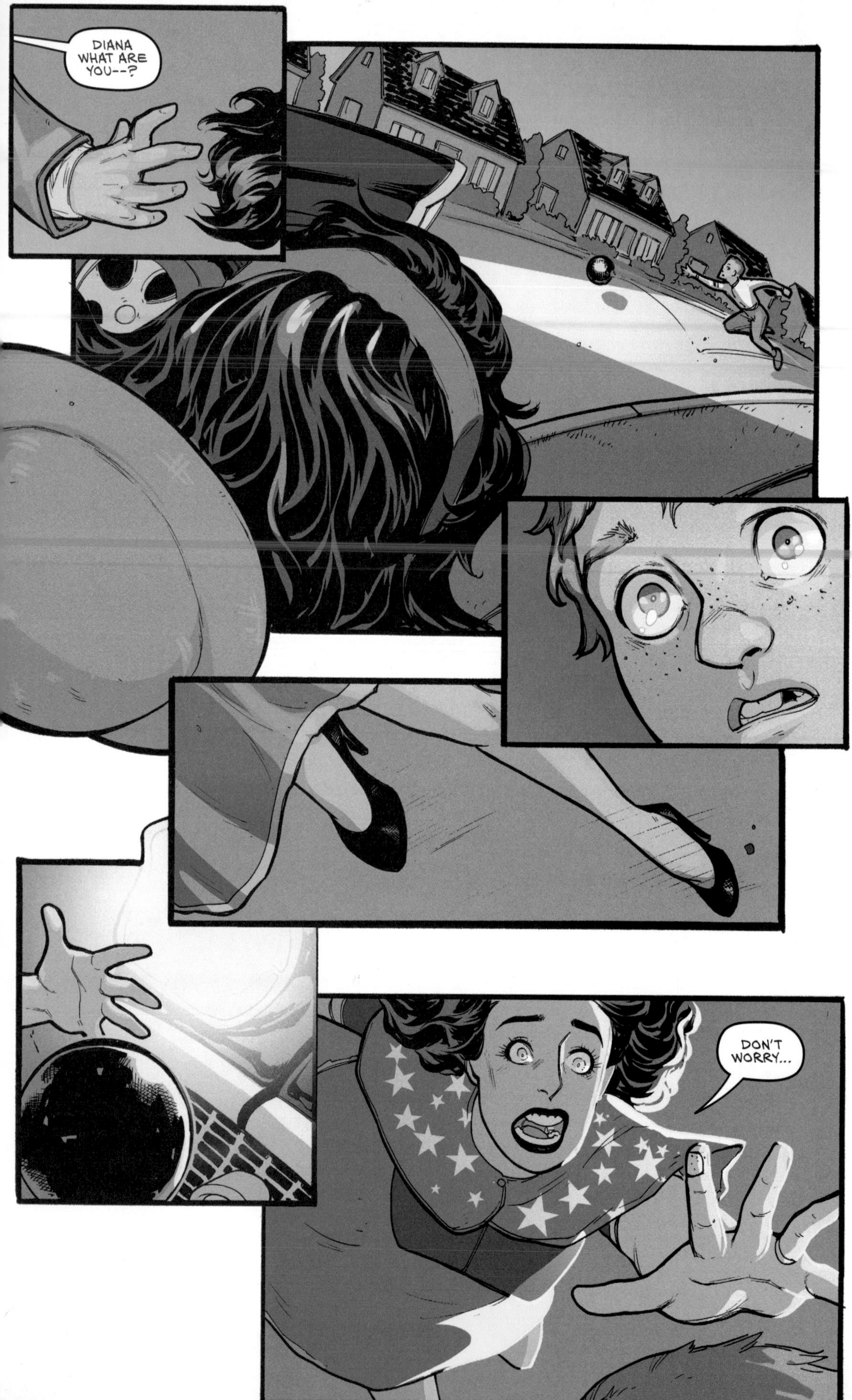
DIANA WHAT ARE YOU--?
DON'T WORRY...

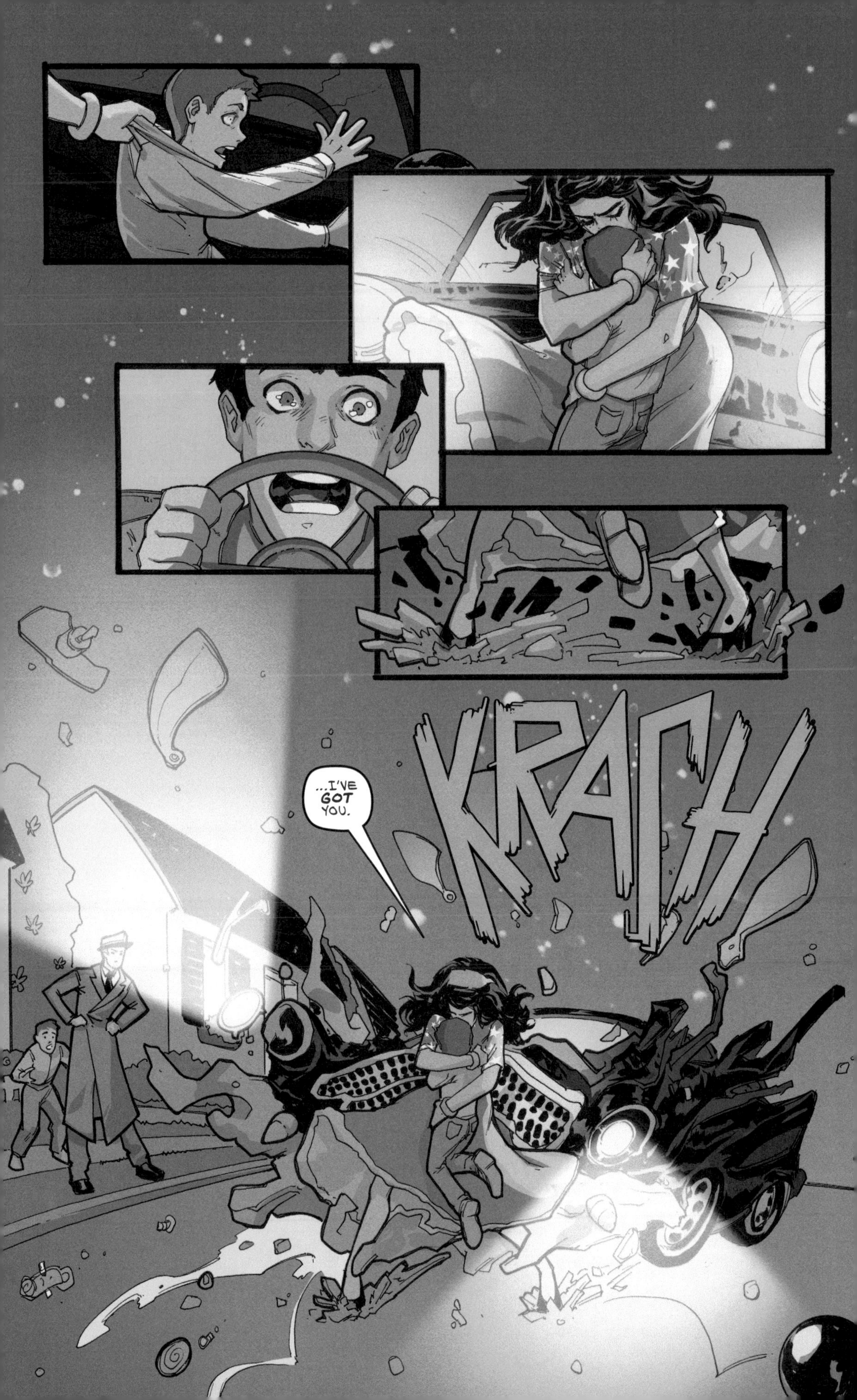
KRASH
...I'VE GOT YOU.

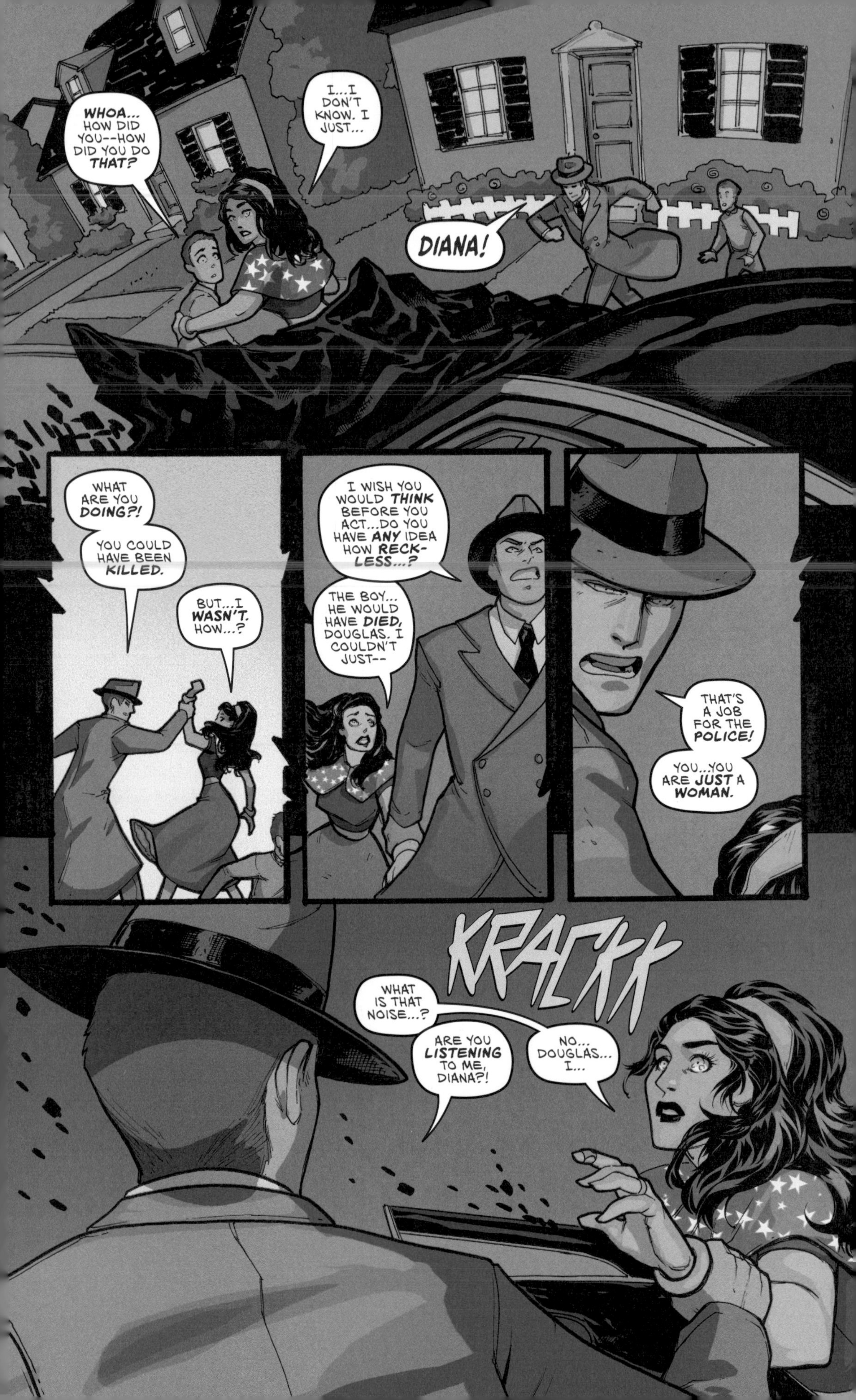
WHOA... HOW DID YOU--HOW DID YOU DO THAT?
I...I DON'T KNOW. I JUST...
DIANA!
WHAT ARE YOU DOING?!
YOU COULD HAVE BEEN KILLED.
BUT...I WASN'T. HOW...?
I WISH YOU WOULD THINK BEFORE YOU ACT...DO YOU HAVE ANY IDEA HOW RECK-LESS...?
THE BOY... HE WOULD HAVE DIED, DOUGLAS. I COULDN'T JUST--
THAT'S A JOB FOR THE POLICE!
YOU...YOU ARE JUST A WOMAN.
KRACKK
WHAT IS THAT NOISE...?
ARE YOU LISTENING TO ME, DIANA?!
NO... DOUGLAS... I...

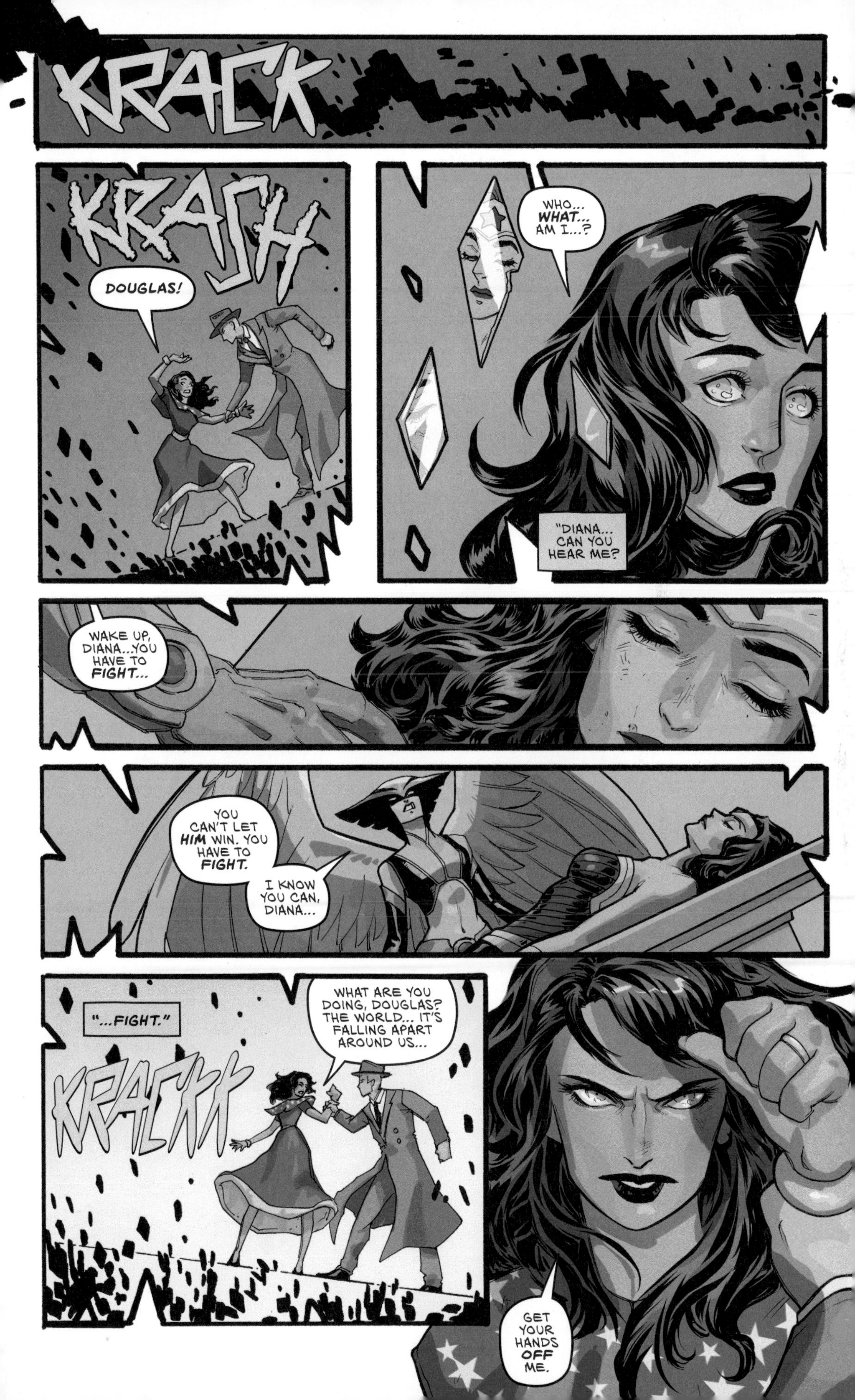
KRACK
KRASH
DOUGLAS!
WHO... WHAT... AM I...?
"DIANA... CAN YOU HEAR ME?
WAKE UP, DIANA...YOU HAVE TO FIGHT...
YOU CAN'T LET HIM WIN. YOU HAVE TO FIGHT.
I KNOW YOU CAN, DIANA...
"...FIGHT."
KRAKK
WHAT ARE YOU DOING, DOUGLAS? THE WORLD... IT'S FALLING APART AROUND US...
GET YOUR HANDS OFF ME.

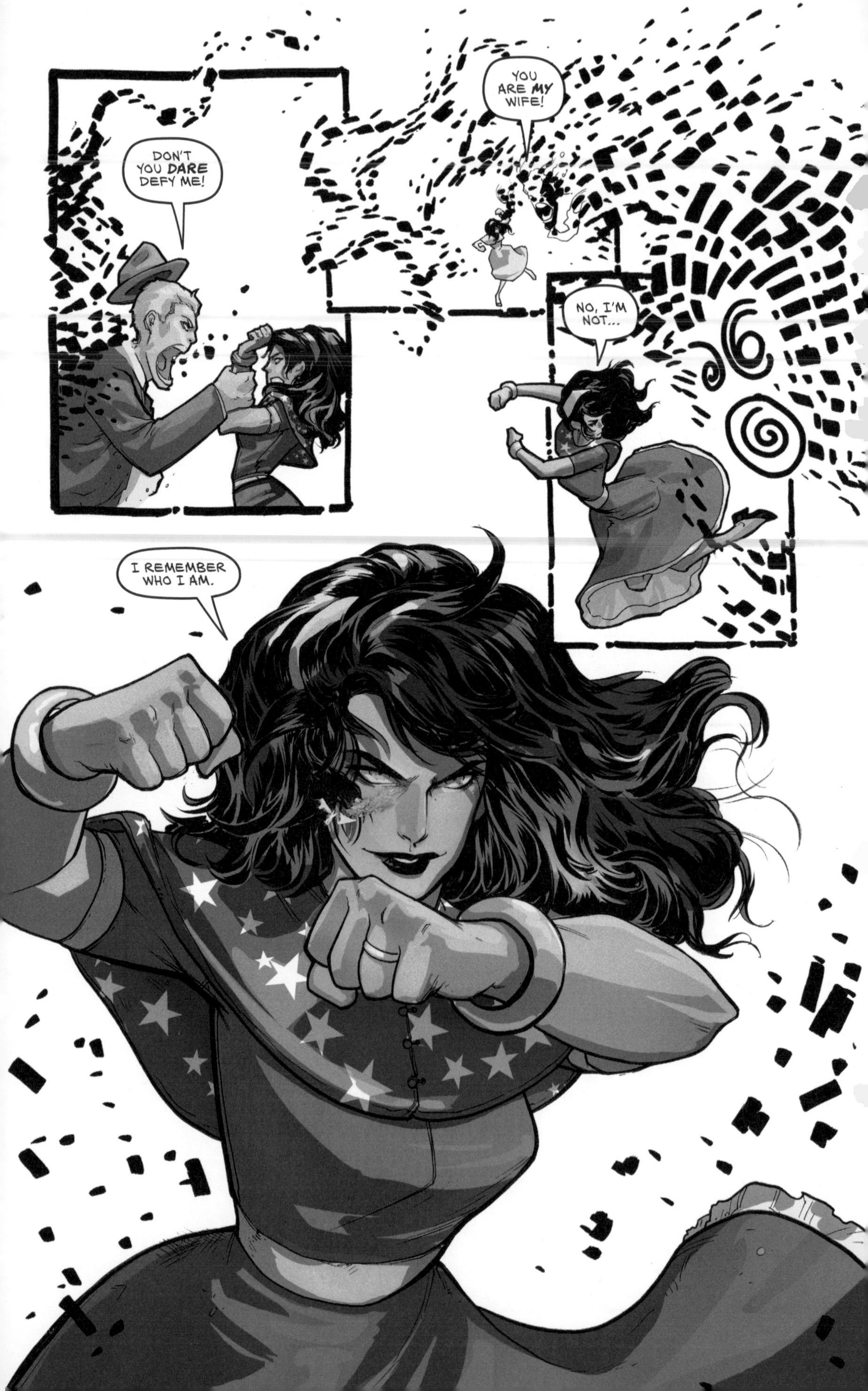
DON'T YOU DARE DEFY ME!
YOU ARE MY WIFE!
NO, I'M NOT...
I REMEMBER WHO I AM.

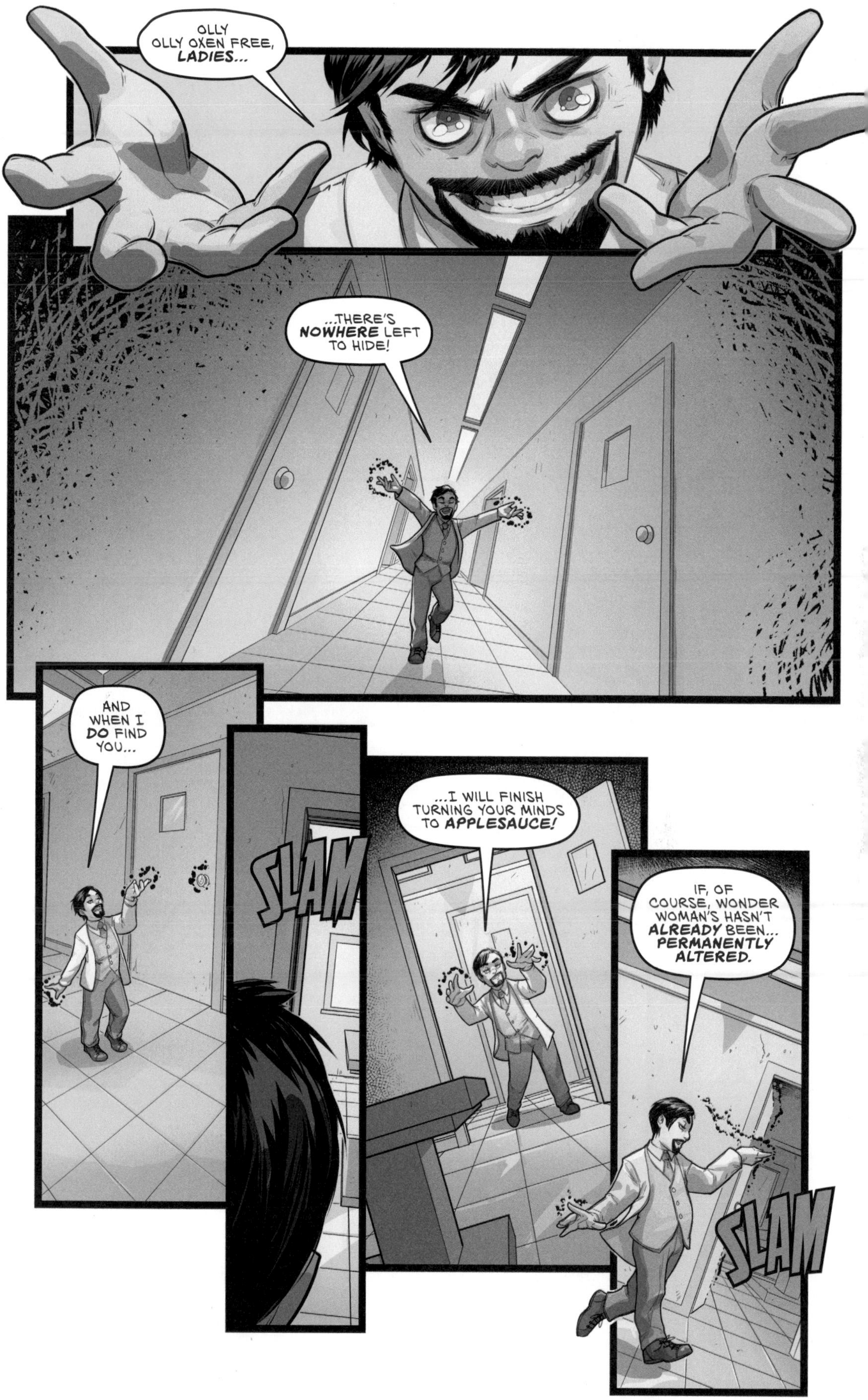
OLLY OLLY OXEN FREE, LADIES...
...THERE'S NOWHERE LEFT TO HIDE!
AND WHEN I DO FIND YOU...
SLAM
...I WILL FINISH TURNING YOUR MINDS TO APPLESAUCE!
IF, OF COURSE, WONDER WOMAN'S HASN'T ALREADY BEEN... PERMANENTLY ALTERED.
SLAM

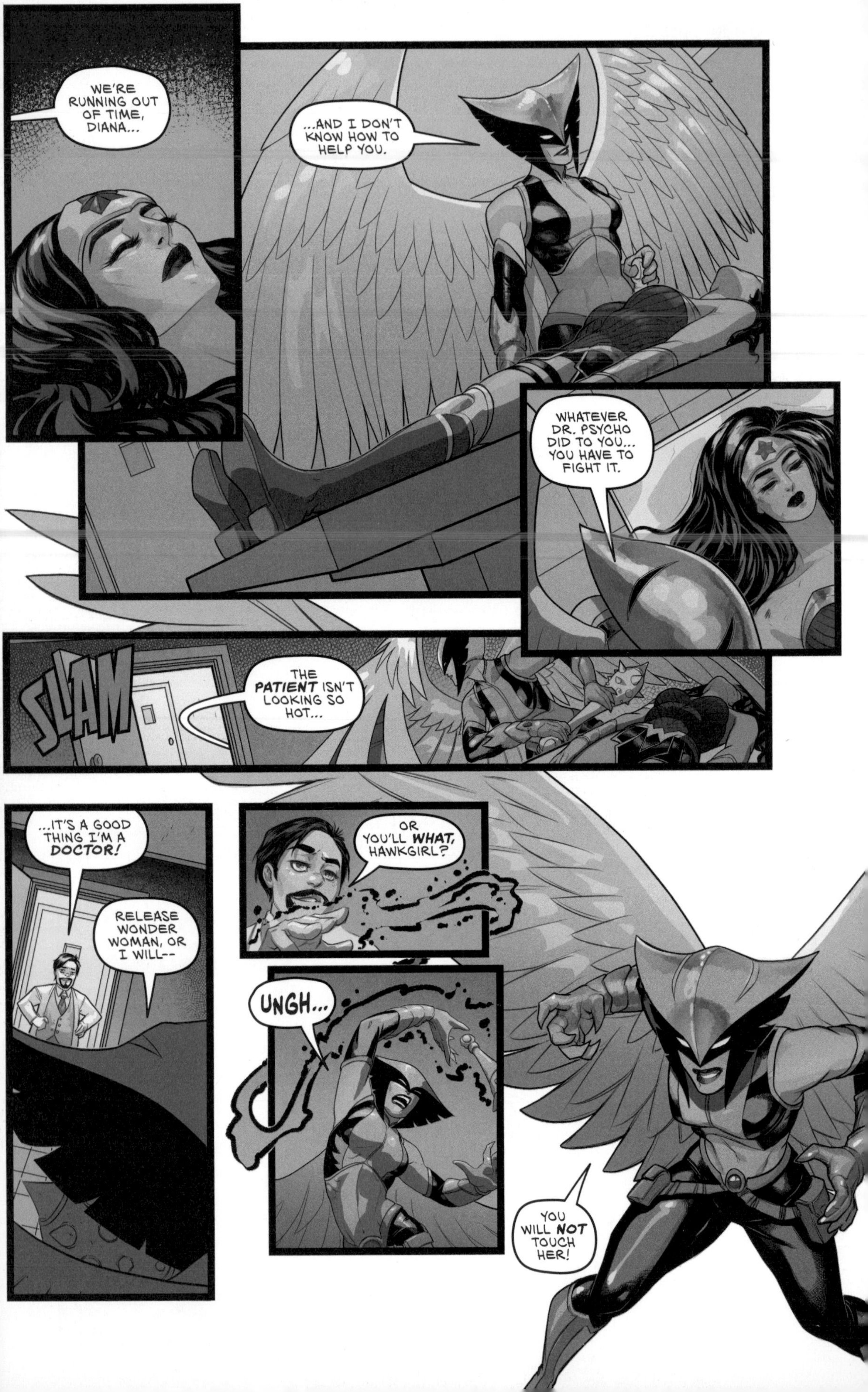
WE'RE RUNNING OUT OF TIME, DIANA...
...AND I DON'T KNOW HOW TO HELP YOU.
WHATEVER DR. PSYCHO DID TO YOU... YOU HAVE TO FIGHT IT.
SLAM
THE **PATIENT** ISN'T LOOKING SO HOT...
...IT'S A GOOD THING I'M A ***DOCTOR!***
RELEASE WONDER WOMAN, OR I WILL--
OR YOU'LL **WHAT,** HAWKGIRL?
UNGH...
YOU WILL **NOT** TOUCH HER!

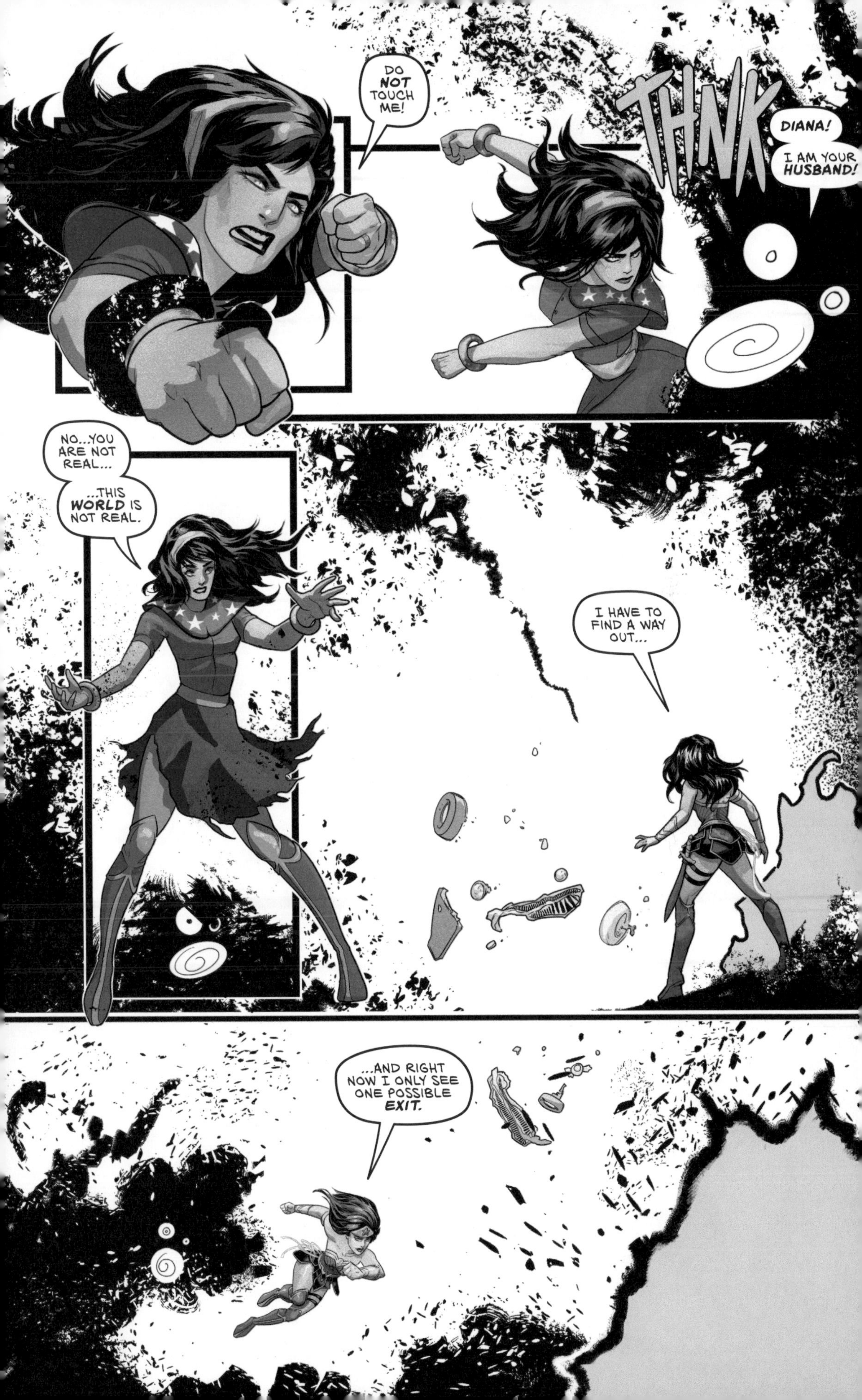
DO NOT TOUCH ME!
THNK
DIANA!
I AM YOUR HUSBAND!
NO...YOU ARE NOT REAL...
...THIS WORLD IS NOT REAL.
I HAVE TO FIND A WAY OUT...
...AND RIGHT NOW I ONLY SEE ONE POSSIBLE EXIT.

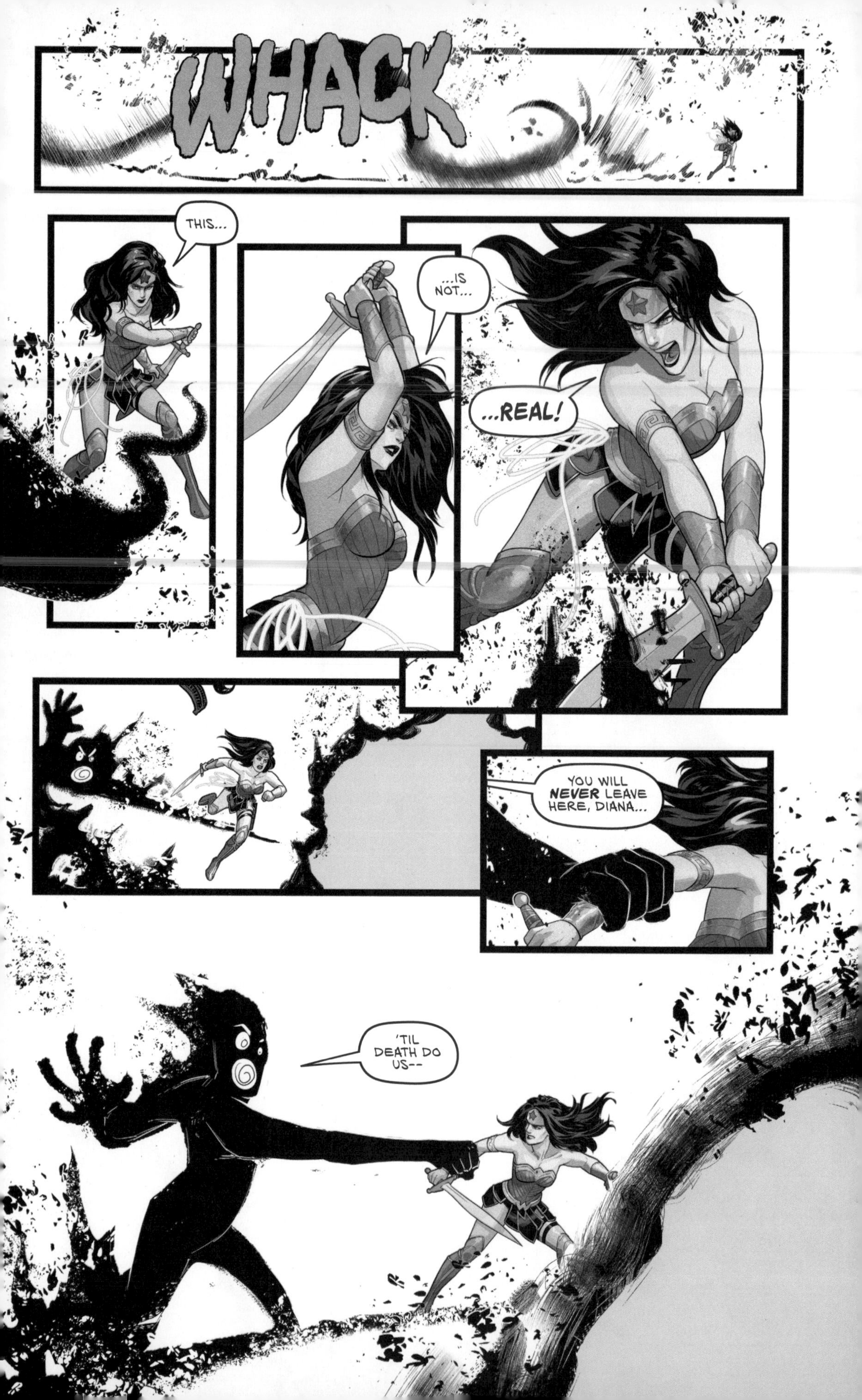
WHACK
THIS...
...IS NOT...
...REAL!
YOU WILL NEVER LEAVE HERE, DIANA...
'TIL DEATH DO US--

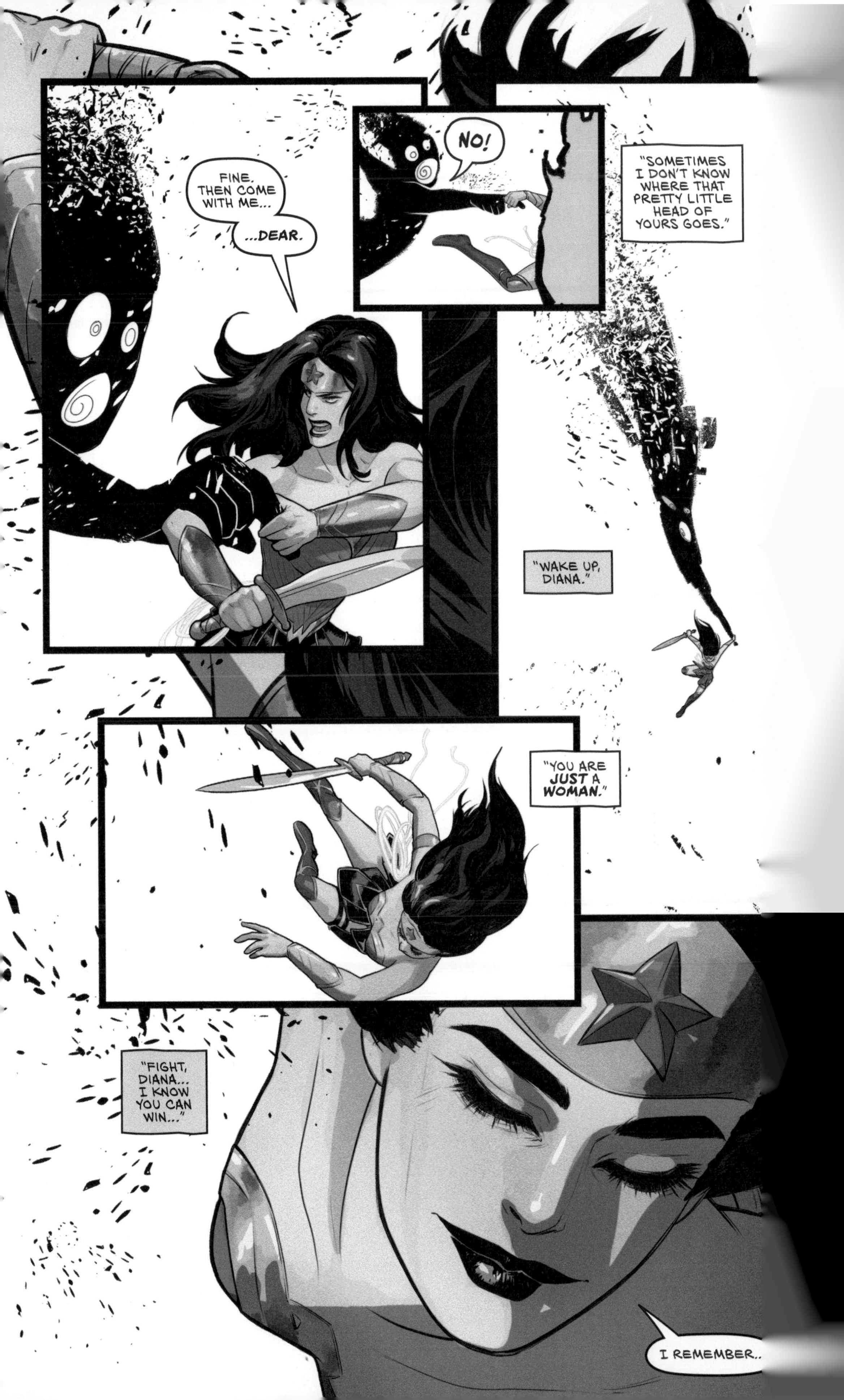
FINE. THEN COME WITH ME...
...DEAR.
NO!
"SOMETIMES I DON'T KNOW WHERE THAT PRETTY LITTLE HEAD OF YOURS GOES."
"WAKE UP, DIANA."
"YOU ARE JUST A WOMAN."
"FIGHT, DIANA... I KNOW YOU CAN WIN..."
I REMEMBER..

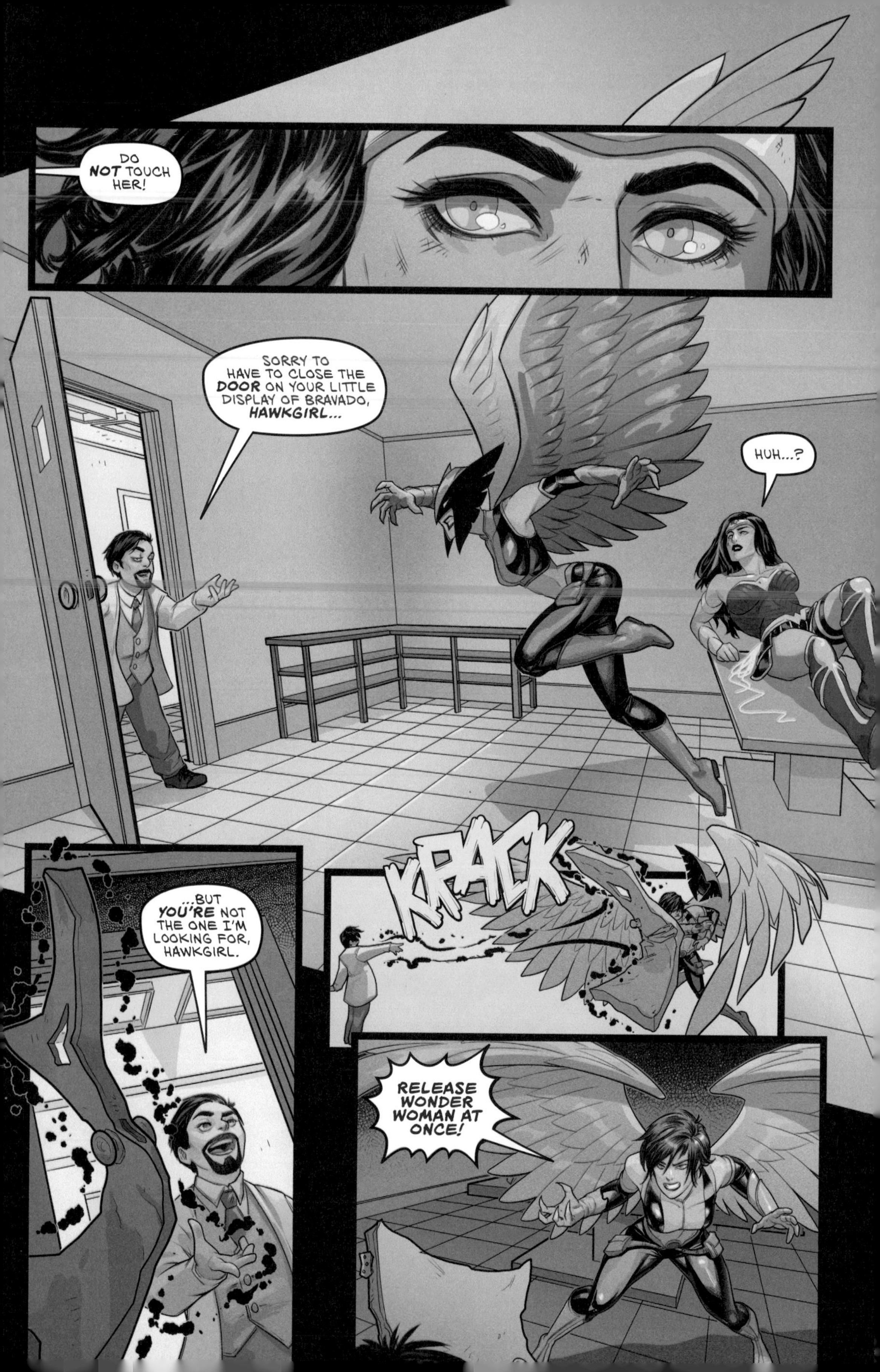
DO NOT TOUCH HER!
SORRY TO HAVE TO CLOSE THE DOOR ON YOUR LITTLE DISPLAY OF BRAVADO, HAWKGIRL...
HUH...?
KRACK
...BUT YOU'RE NOT THE ONE I'M LOOKING FOR, HAWKGIRL.
RELEASE WONDER WOMAN AT ONCE!

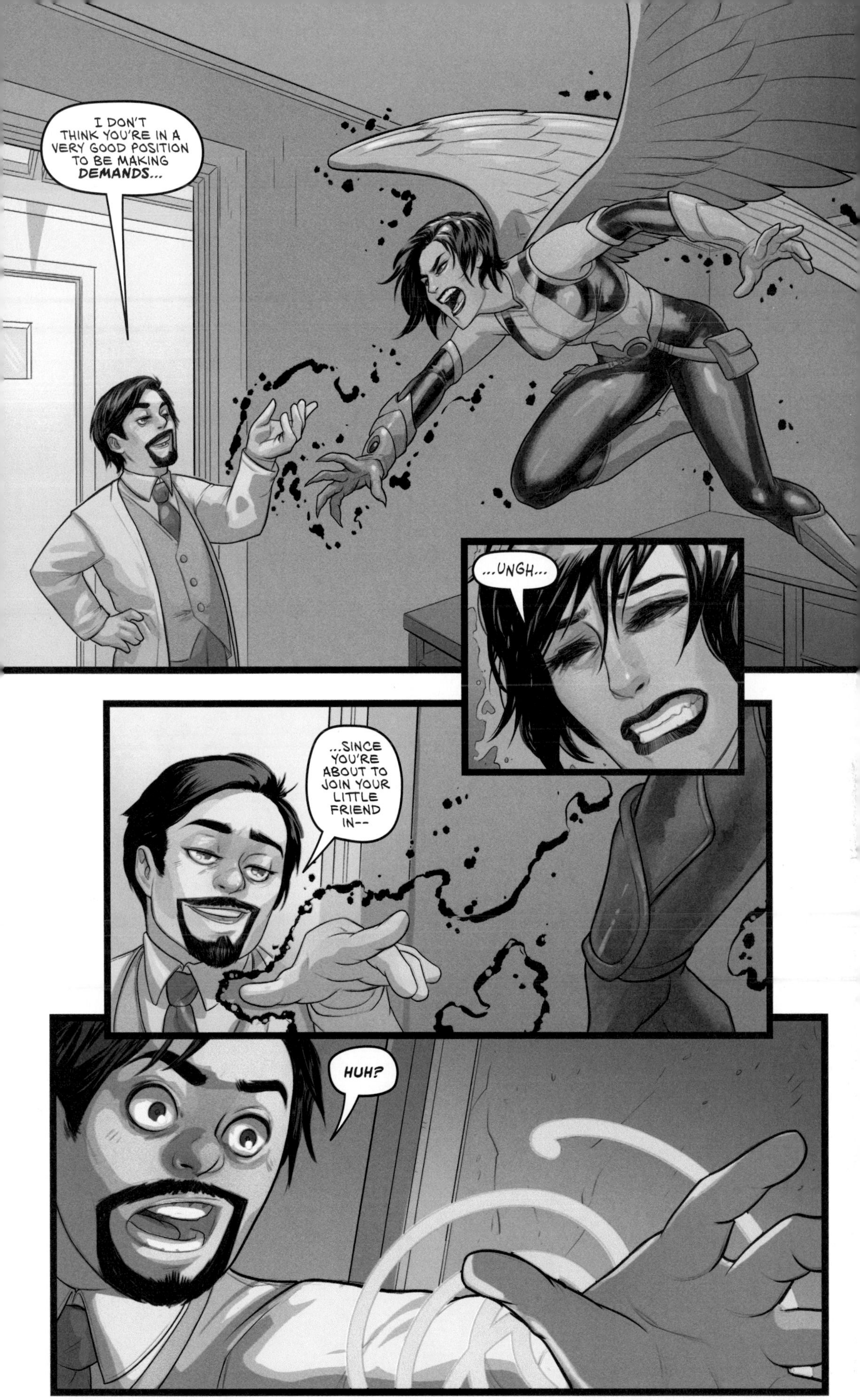
I DON'T THINK YOU'RE IN A VERY GOOD POSITION TO BE MAKING DEMANDS...
...UNGH...
...SINCE YOU'RE ABOUT TO JOIN YOUR LITTLE FRIEND IN--
HUH?

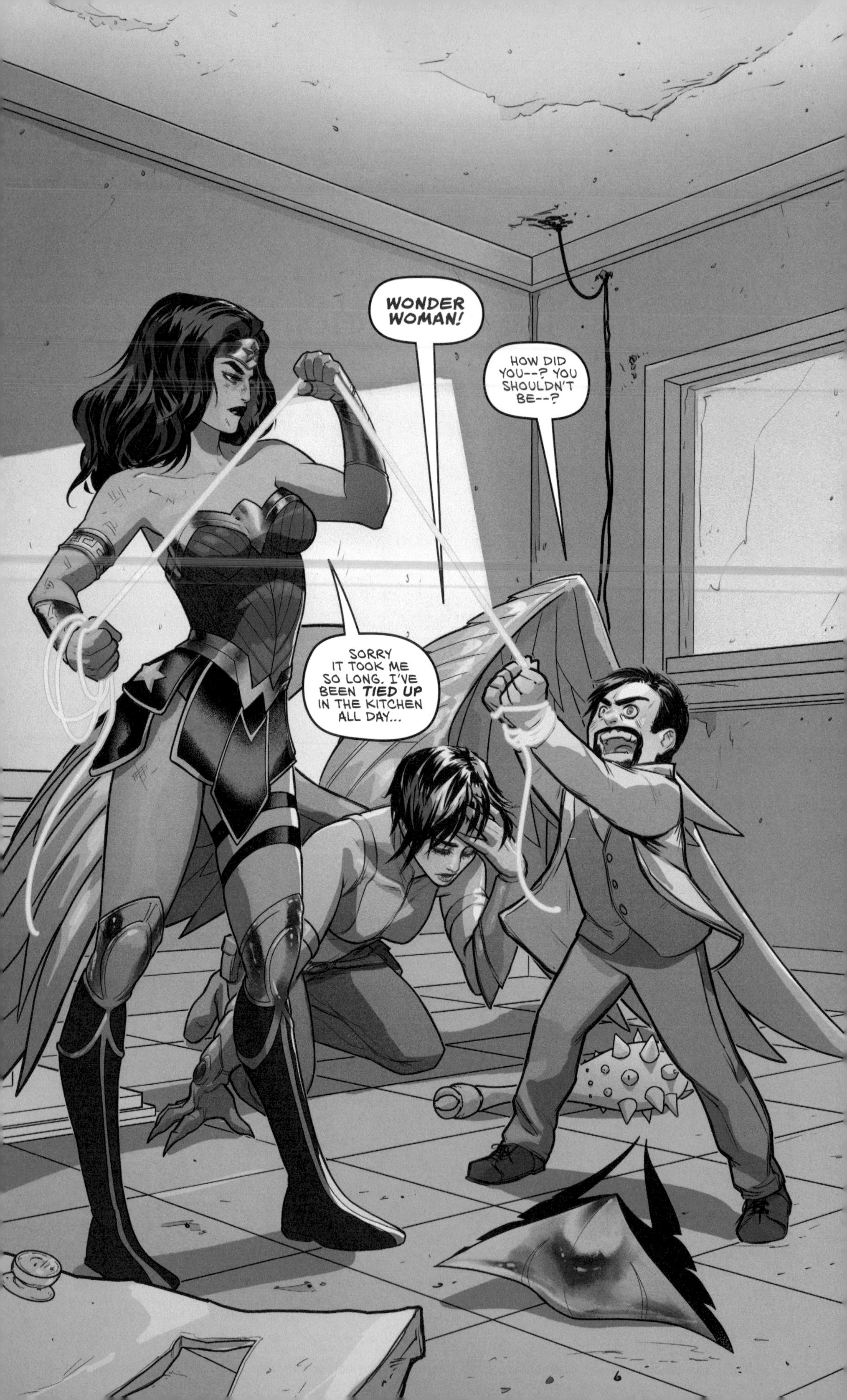
WONDER WOMAN!
HOW DID YOU--? YOU SHOULDN'T BE--?
SORRY IT TOOK ME SO LONG. I'VE BEEN TIED UP IN THE KITCHEN ALL DAY...

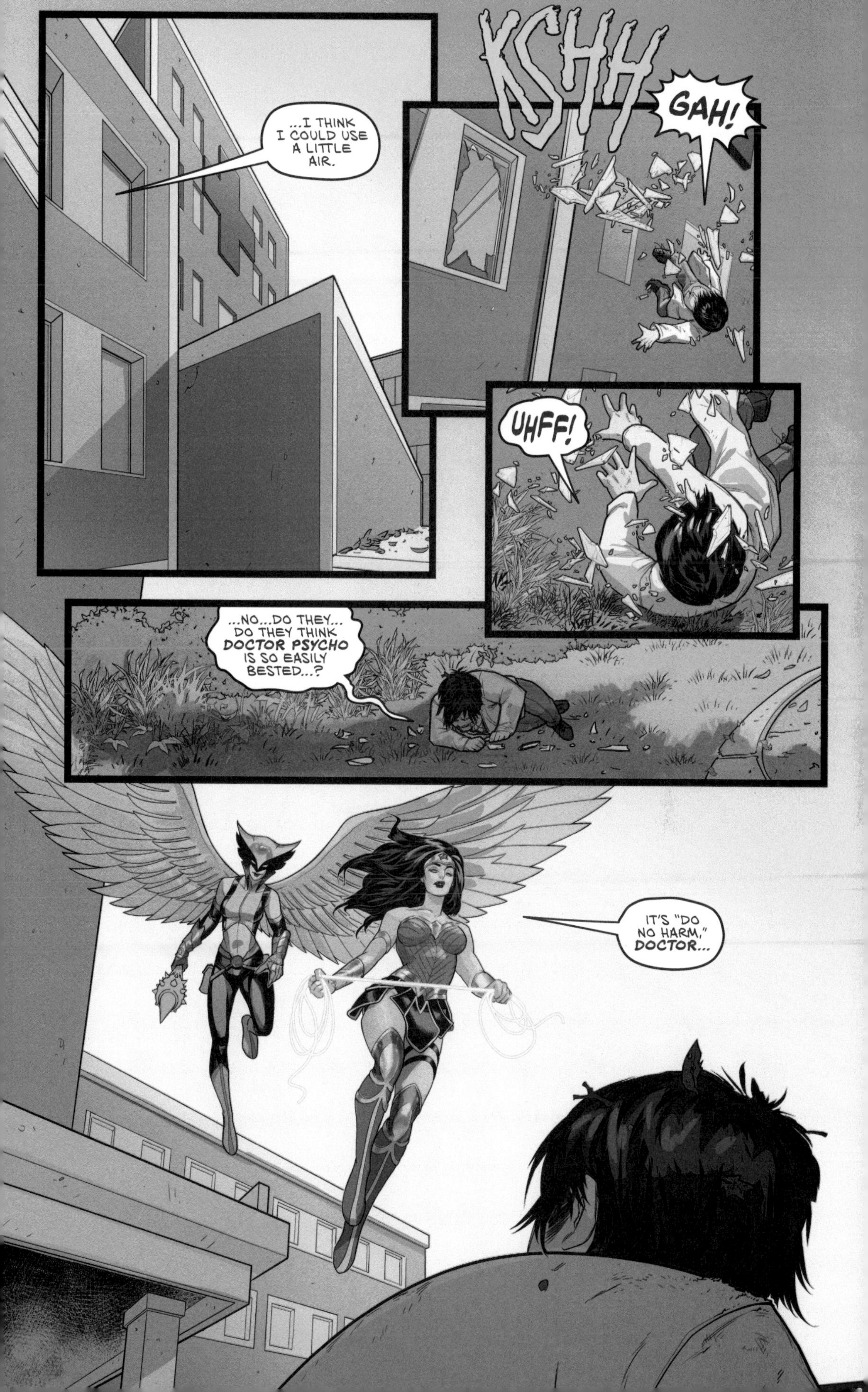
...I THINK I COULD USE A LITTLE AIR.
KSHH
GAH!
UHFF!
...NO...DO THEY... DO THEY THINK DOCTOR PSYCHO IS SO EASILY BESTED...?
IT'S "DO NO HARM," DOCTOR...

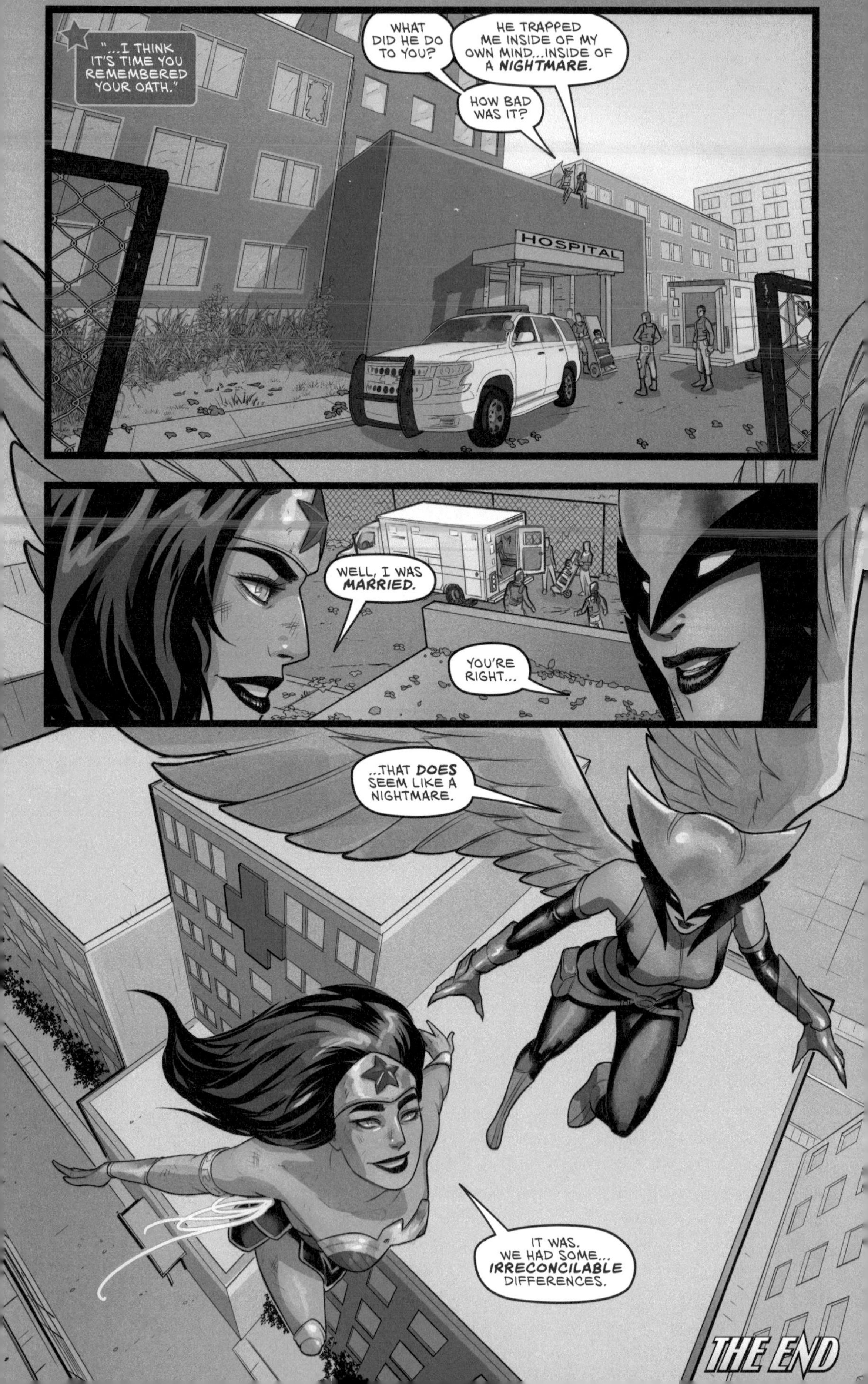

"...I THINK IT'S TIME YOU REMEMBERED YOUR OATH."
WHAT DID HE DO TO YOU?
HE TRAPPED ME INSIDE OF MY OWN MIND...INSIDE OF A **NIGHTMARE.**
HOW BAD WAS IT?
HOSPITAL
WELL, I WAS **MARRIED.**
YOU'RE RIGHT...
...THAT **DOES** SEEM LIKE A NIGHTMARE.
IT WAS. WE HAD SOME... **IRRECONCILABLE** DIFFERENCES.
THE END

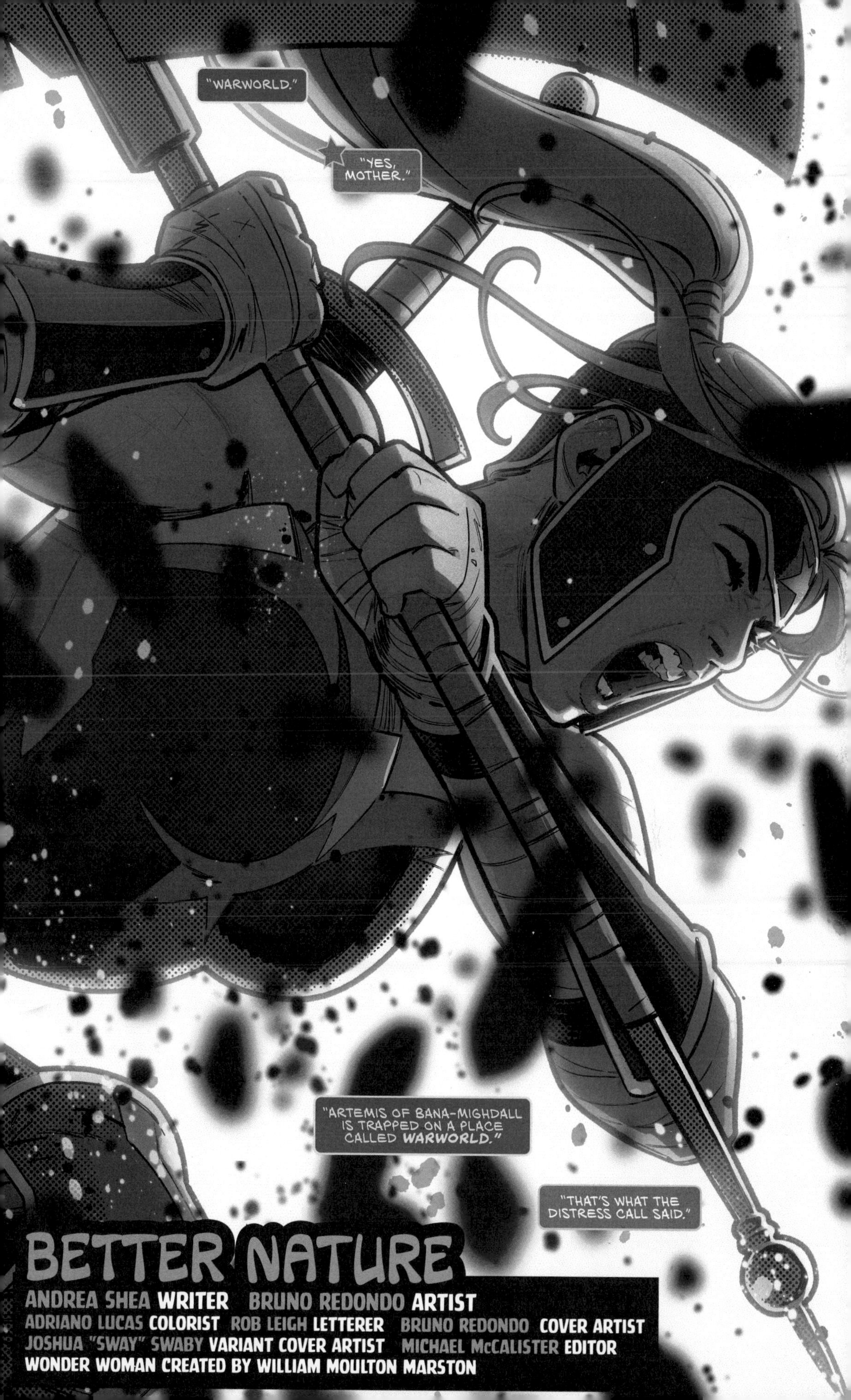
"WARWORLD."
"YES, MOTHER."
"ARTEMIS OF BANA-MIGHDALL IS TRAPPED ON A PLACE CALLED WARWORLD."
"THAT'S WHAT THE DISTRESS CALL SAID."
BETTER NATURE
ANDREA SHEA WRITER BRUNO REDONDO ARTIST
ADRIANO LUCAS COLORIST ROB LEIGH LETTERER BRUNO REDONDO COVER ARTIST
JOSHUA "SWAY" SWABY VARIANT COVER ARTIST MICHAEL McCALISTER EDITOR
WONDER WOMAN CREATED BY WILLIAM MOULTON MARSTON

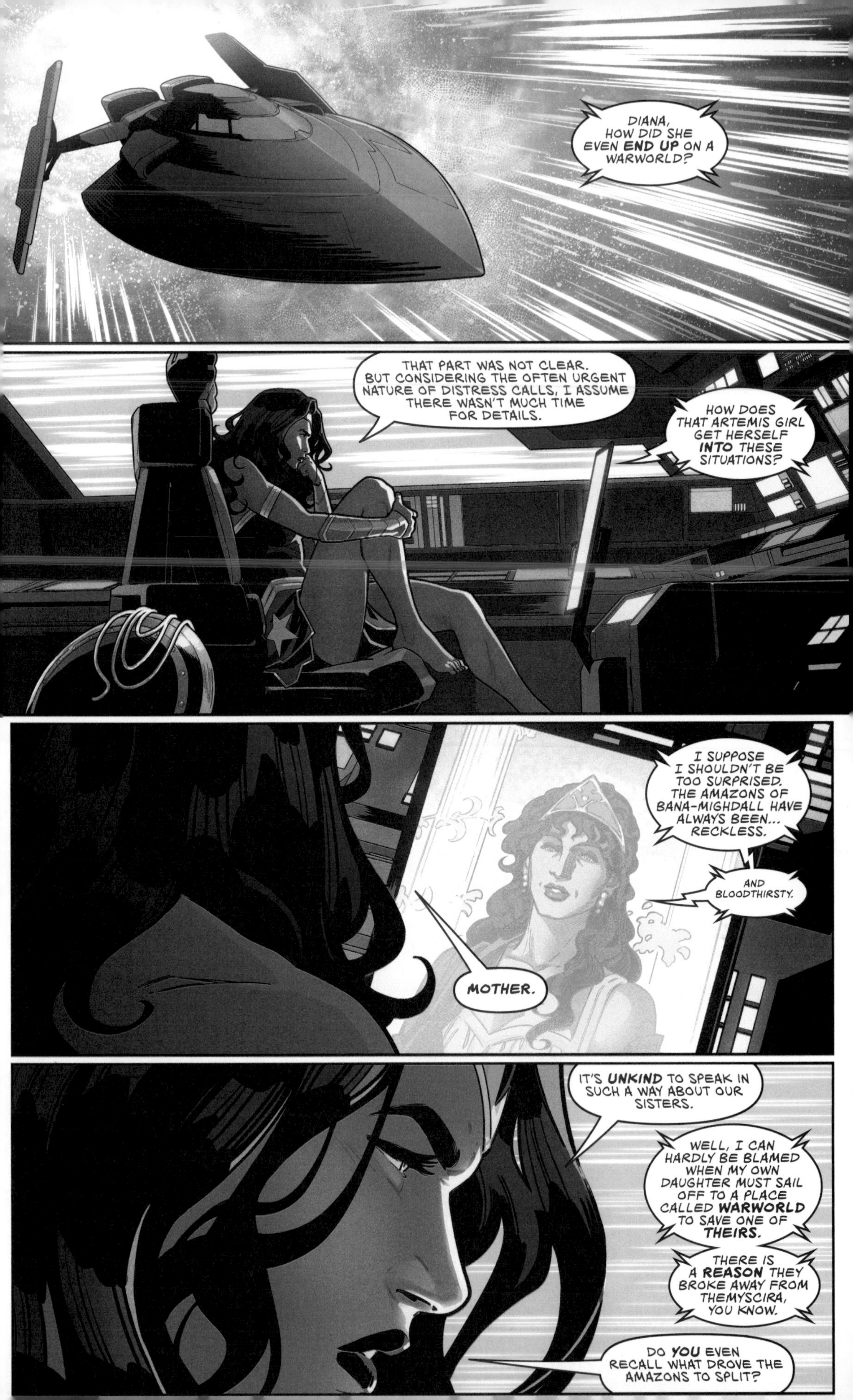

DIANA, HOW DID SHE EVEN END UP ON A WARWORLD?
THAT PART WAS NOT CLEAR. BUT CONSIDERING THE OFTEN URGENT NATURE OF DISTRESS CALLS, I ASSUME THERE WASN'T MUCH TIME FOR DETAILS.
HOW DOES THAT ARTEMIS GIRL GET HERSELF INTO THESE SITUATIONS?
I SUPPOSE I SHOULDN'T BE TOO SURPRISED. THE AMAZONS OF BANA-MIGHDALL HAVE ALWAYS BEEN... RECKLESS.
AND BLOODTHIRSTY.
MOTHER.
IT'S UNKIND TO SPEAK IN SUCH A WAY ABOUT OUR SISTERS.
WELL, I CAN HARDLY BE BLAMED WHEN MY OWN DAUGHTER MUST SAIL OFF TO A PLACE CALLED WARWORLD TO SAVE ONE OF THEIRS.
THERE IS A REASON THEY BROKE AWAY FROM THEMYSCIRA, YOU KNOW.
DO YOU EVEN RECALL WHAT DROVE THE AMAZONS TO SPLIT?

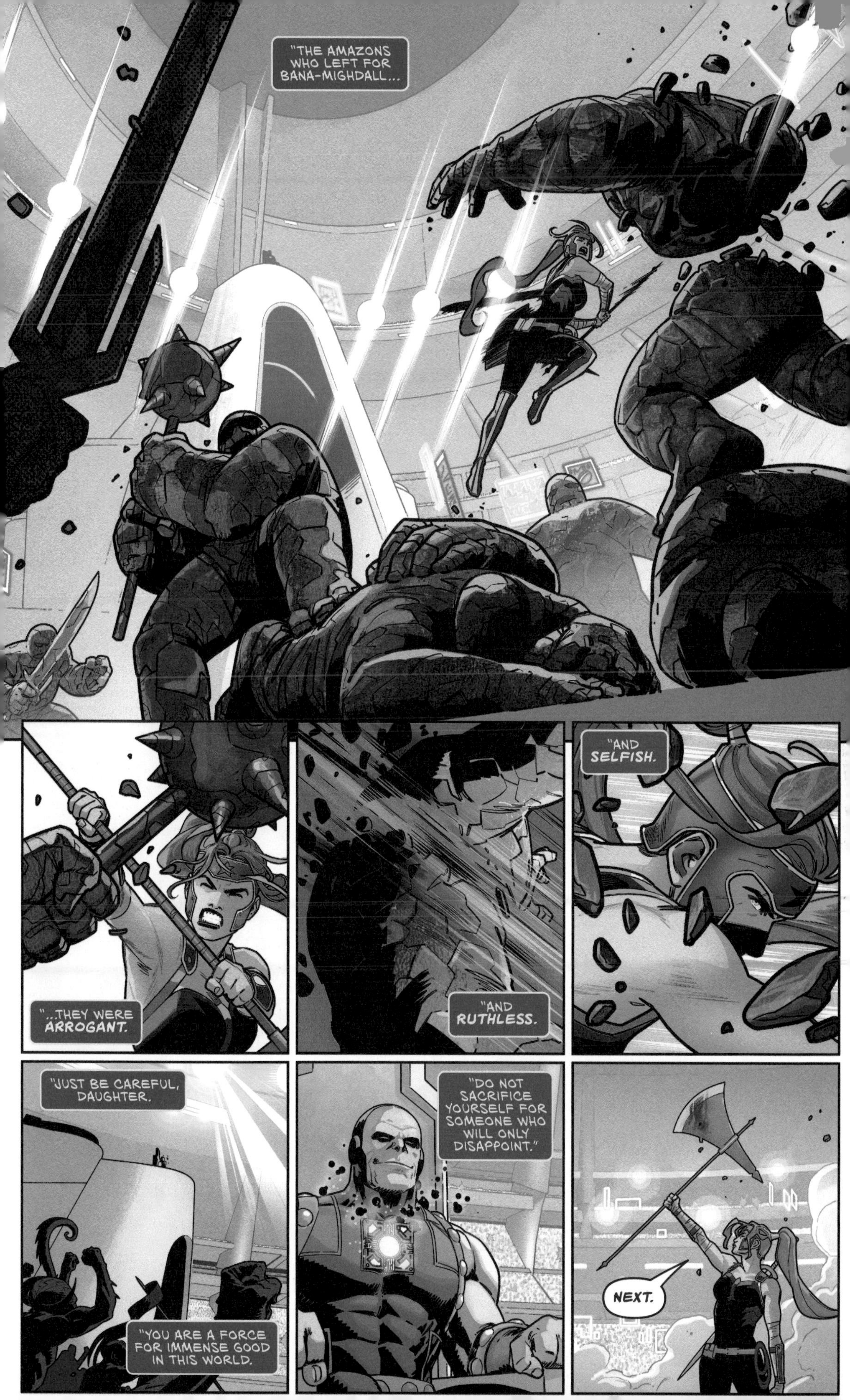
"THE AMAZONS WHO LEFT FOR BANA-MIGHDALL...
"...THEY WERE ARROGANT.
"AND RUTHLESS.
"AND SELFISH.
"JUST BE CAREFUL, DAUGHTER.
"YOU ARE A FORCE FOR IMMENSE GOOD IN THIS WORLD.
"DO NOT SACRIFICE YOURSELF FOR SOMEONE WHO WILL ONLY DISAPPOINT."
NEXT.

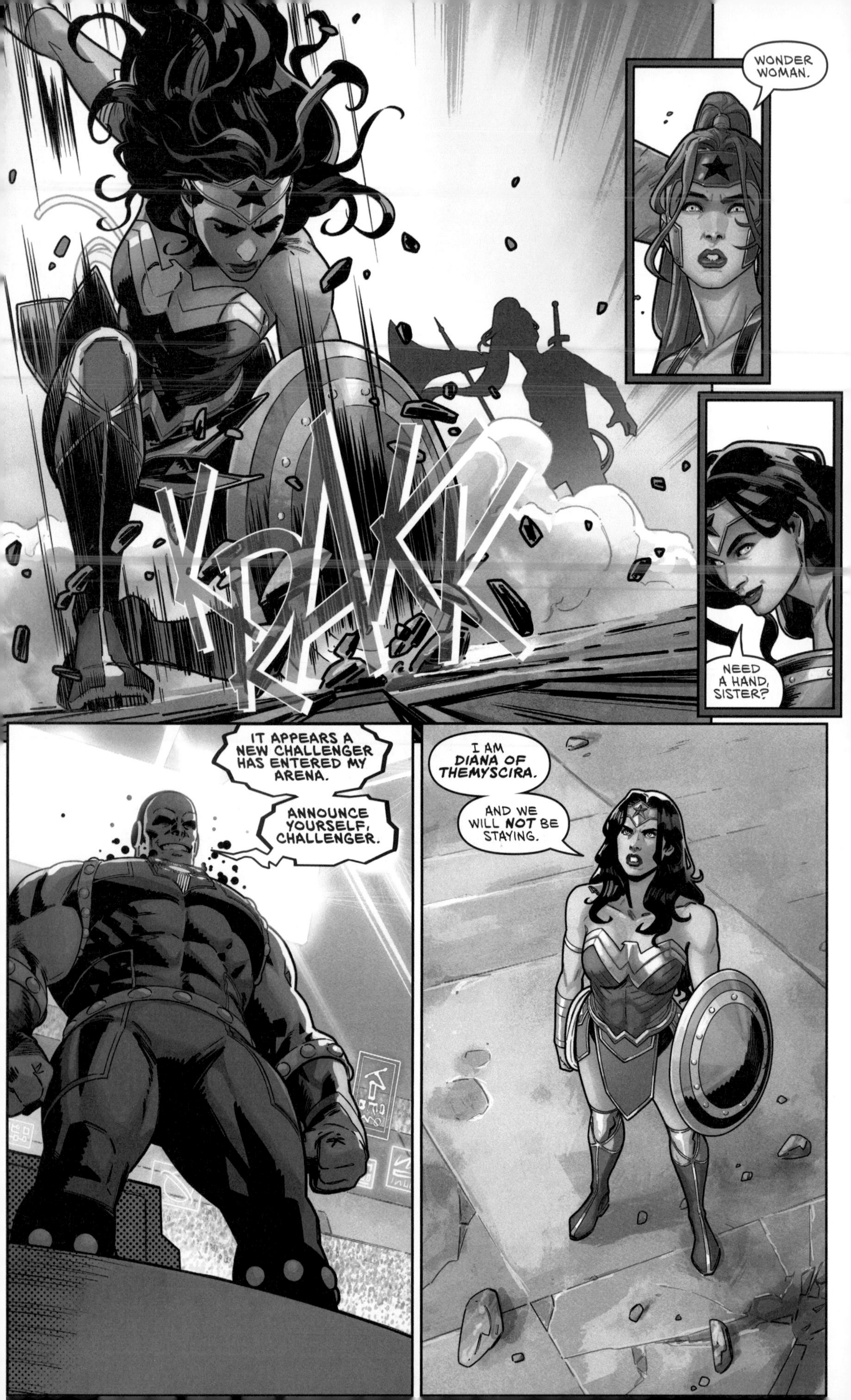

KRAKK
WONDER WOMAN.
NEED A HAND, SISTER?
IT APPEARS A NEW CHALLENGER HAS ENTERED MY ARENA.
ANNOUNCE YOURSELF, CHALLENGER.
I AM DIANA OF THEMYSCIRA.
AND WE WILL NOT BE STAYING.

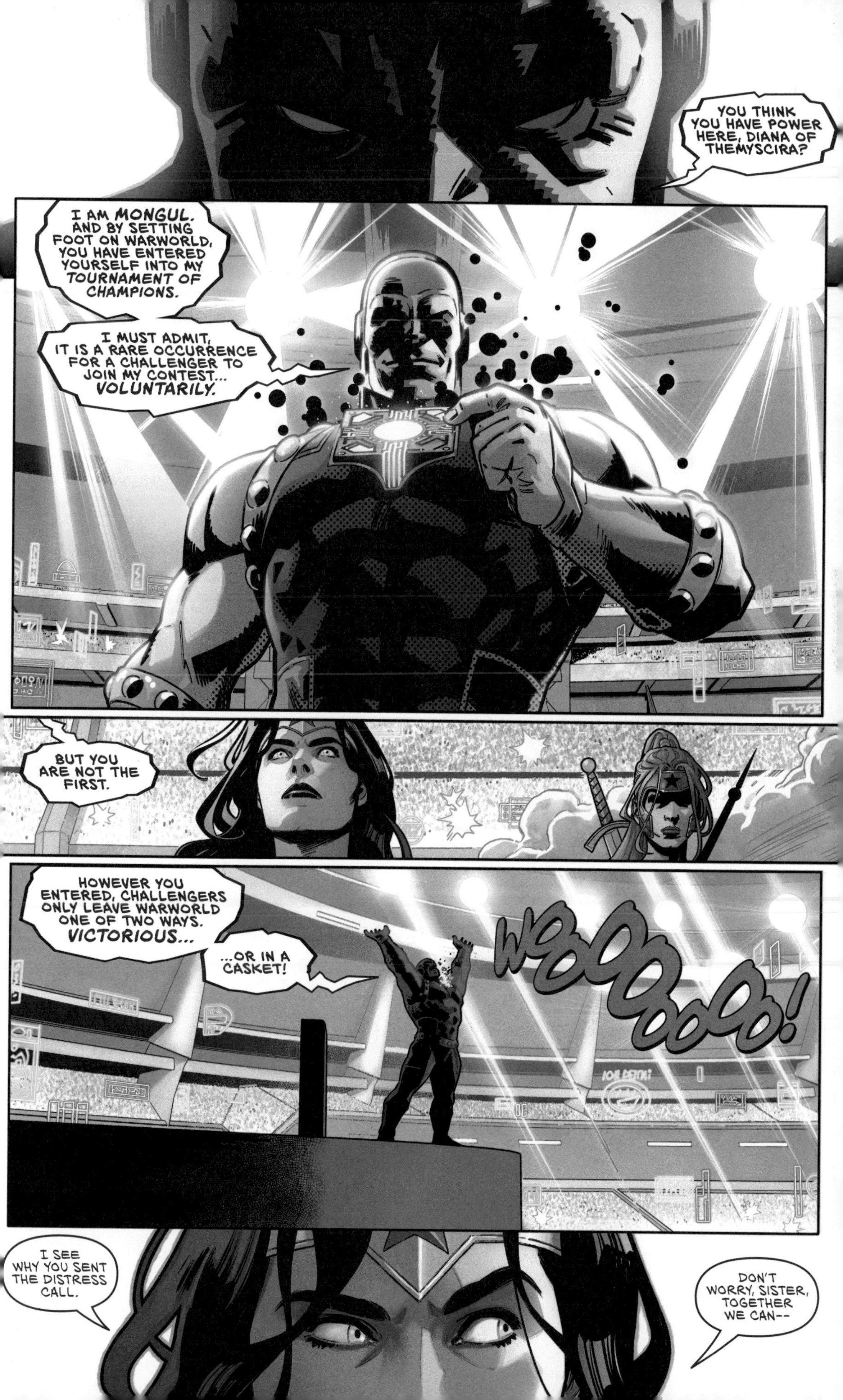
YOU THINK YOU HAVE POWER HERE, DIANA OF THEMYSCIRA?
I AM MONGUL. AND BY SETTING FOOT ON WARWORLD, YOU HAVE ENTERED YOURSELF INTO MY TOURNAMENT OF CHAMPIONS.
I MUST ADMIT, IT IS A RARE OCCURRENCE FOR A CHALLENGER TO JOIN MY CONTEST... VOLUNTARILY.
BUT YOU ARE NOT THE FIRST.
HOWEVER YOU ENTERED, CHALLENGERS ONLY LEAVE WARWORLD ONE OF TWO WAYS. VICTORIOUS...
...OR IN A CASKET!
WOOOOOOOOO!
I SEE WHY YOU SENT THE DISTRESS CALL.
DON'T WORRY, SISTER, TOGETHER WE CAN--

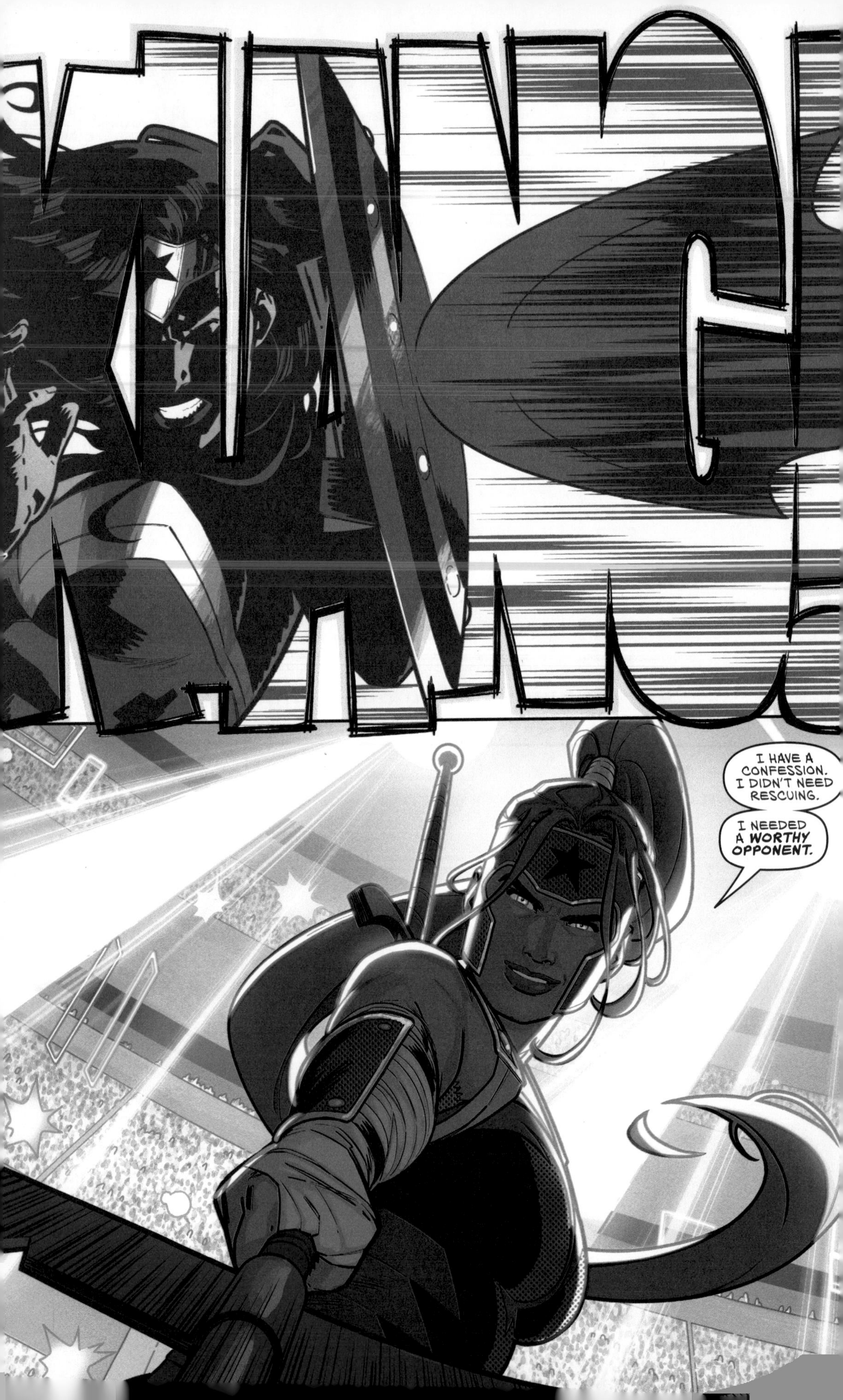
I HAVE A CONFESSION. I DIDN'T NEED RESCUING.
I NEEDED A WORTHY OPPONENT.

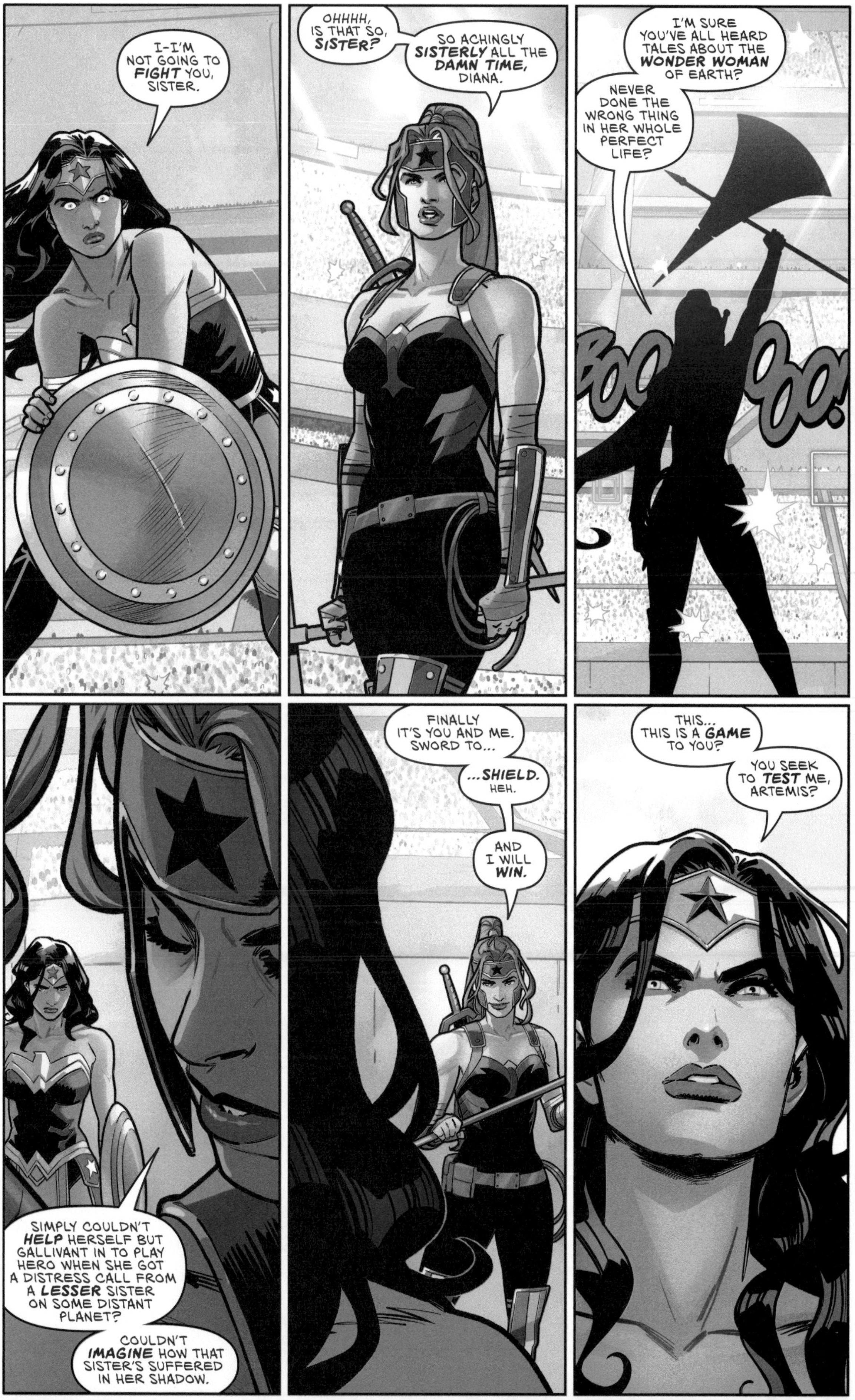

I-I'M NOT GOING TO FIGHT YOU, SISTER.
OHHHH, IS THAT SO, SISTER?
SO ACHINGLY SISTERLY ALL THE DAMN TIME, DIANA.
I'M SURE YOU'VE ALL HEARD TALES ABOUT THE WONDER WOMAN OF EARTH?
NEVER DONE THE WRONG THING IN HER WHOLE PERFECT LIFE?
BOOOOOO!
SIMPLY COULDN'T HELP HERSELF BUT GALLIVANT IN TO PLAY HERO WHEN SHE GOT A DISTRESS CALL FROM A LESSER SISTER ON SOME DISTANT PLANET?
COULDN'T IMAGINE HOW THAT SISTER'S SUFFERED IN HER SHADOW.
FINALLY IT'S YOU AND ME. SWORD TO...
...SHIELD. HEH.
AND I WILL WIN.
THIS... THIS IS A GAME TO YOU?
YOU SEEK TO TEST ME, ARTEMIS?

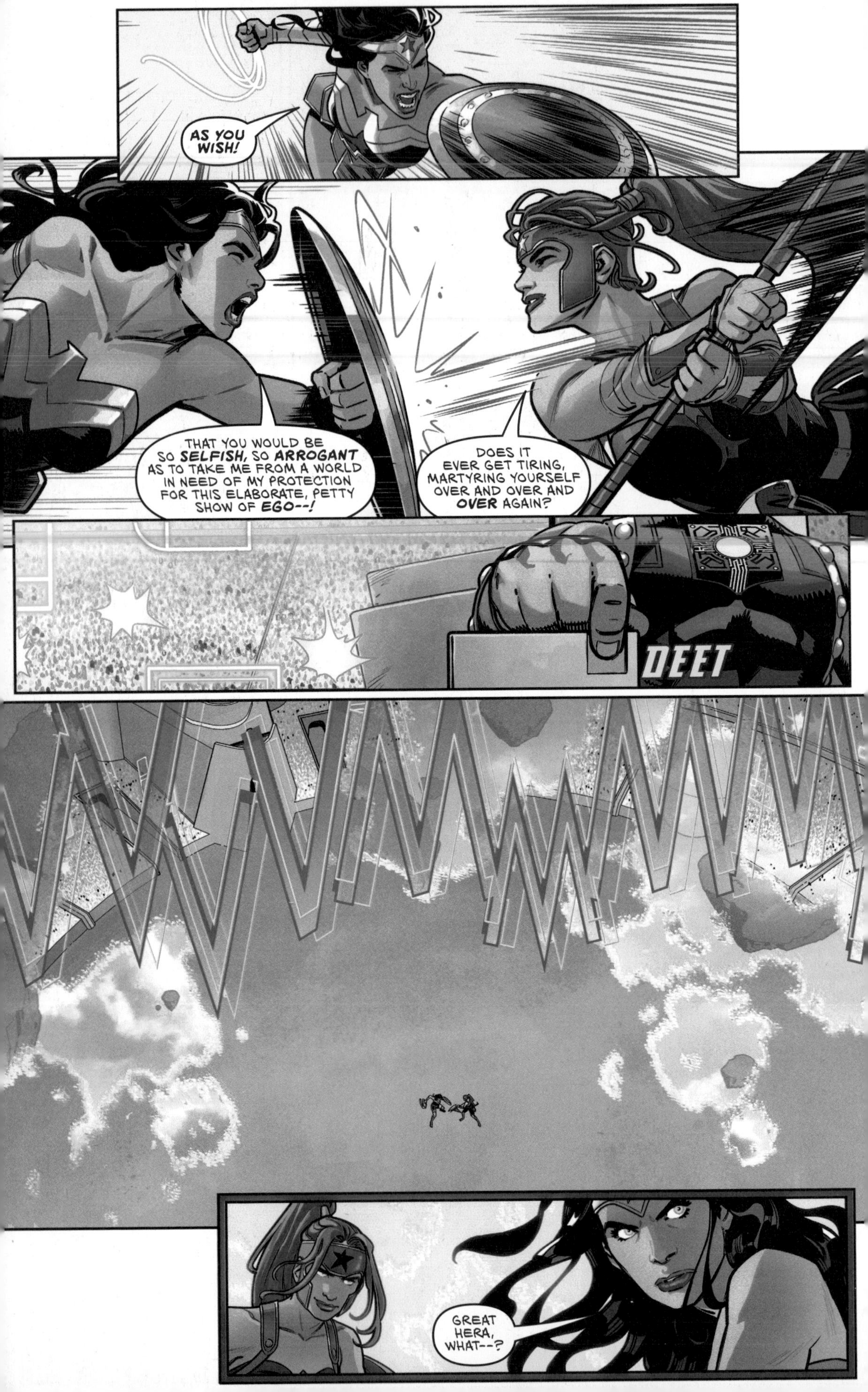
AS YOU WISH!
THAT YOU WOULD BE SO SELFISH, SO ARROGANT AS TO TAKE ME FROM A WORLD IN NEED OF MY PROTECTION FOR THIS ELABORATE, PETTY SHOW OF EGO--!
DOES IT EVER GET TIRING, MARTYRING YOURSELF OVER AND OVER AND OVER AGAIN?
DEET
GREAT HERA, WHAT--?

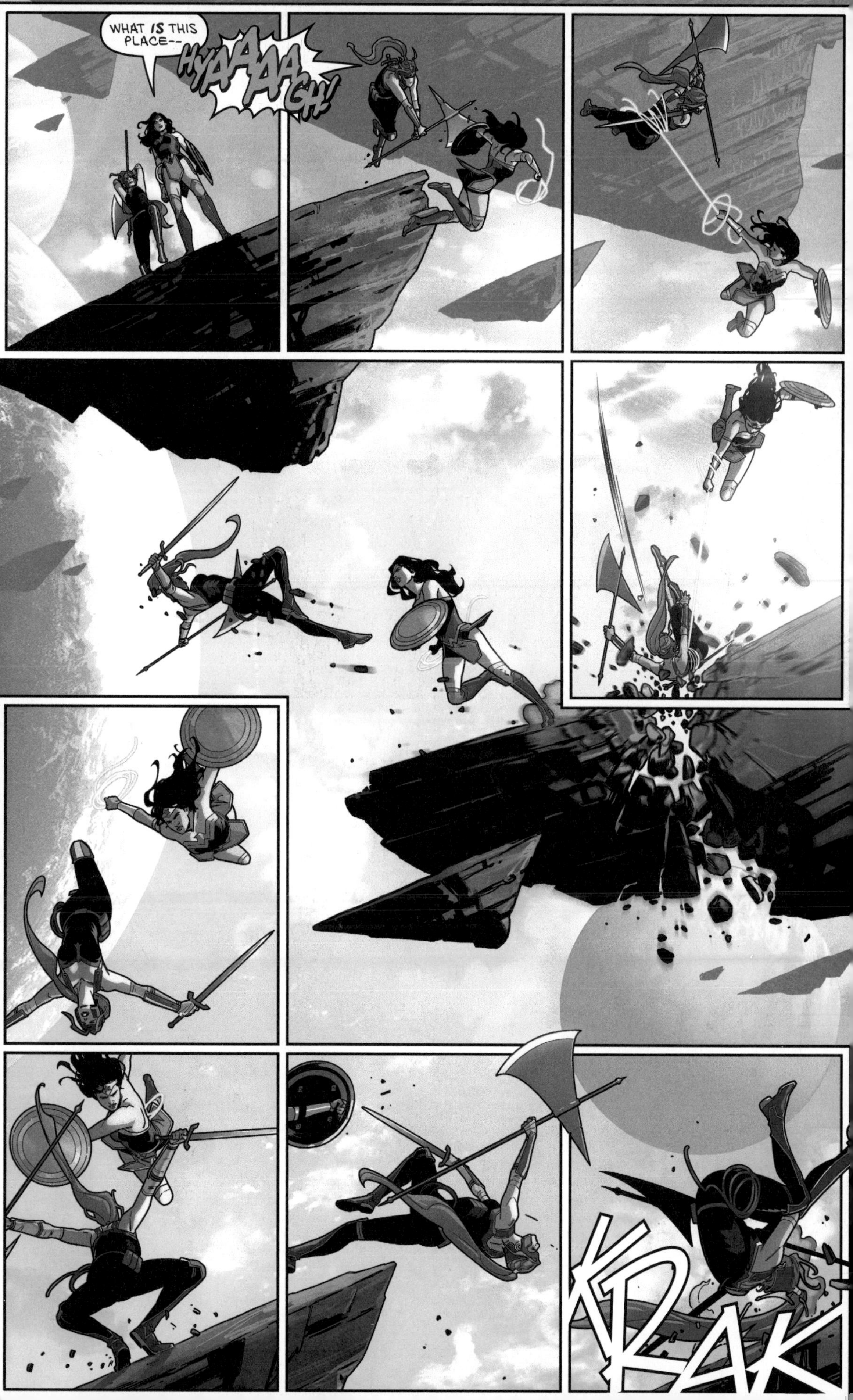

WHAT IS THIS PLACE--
HYAAAAAGH!
KRAK!

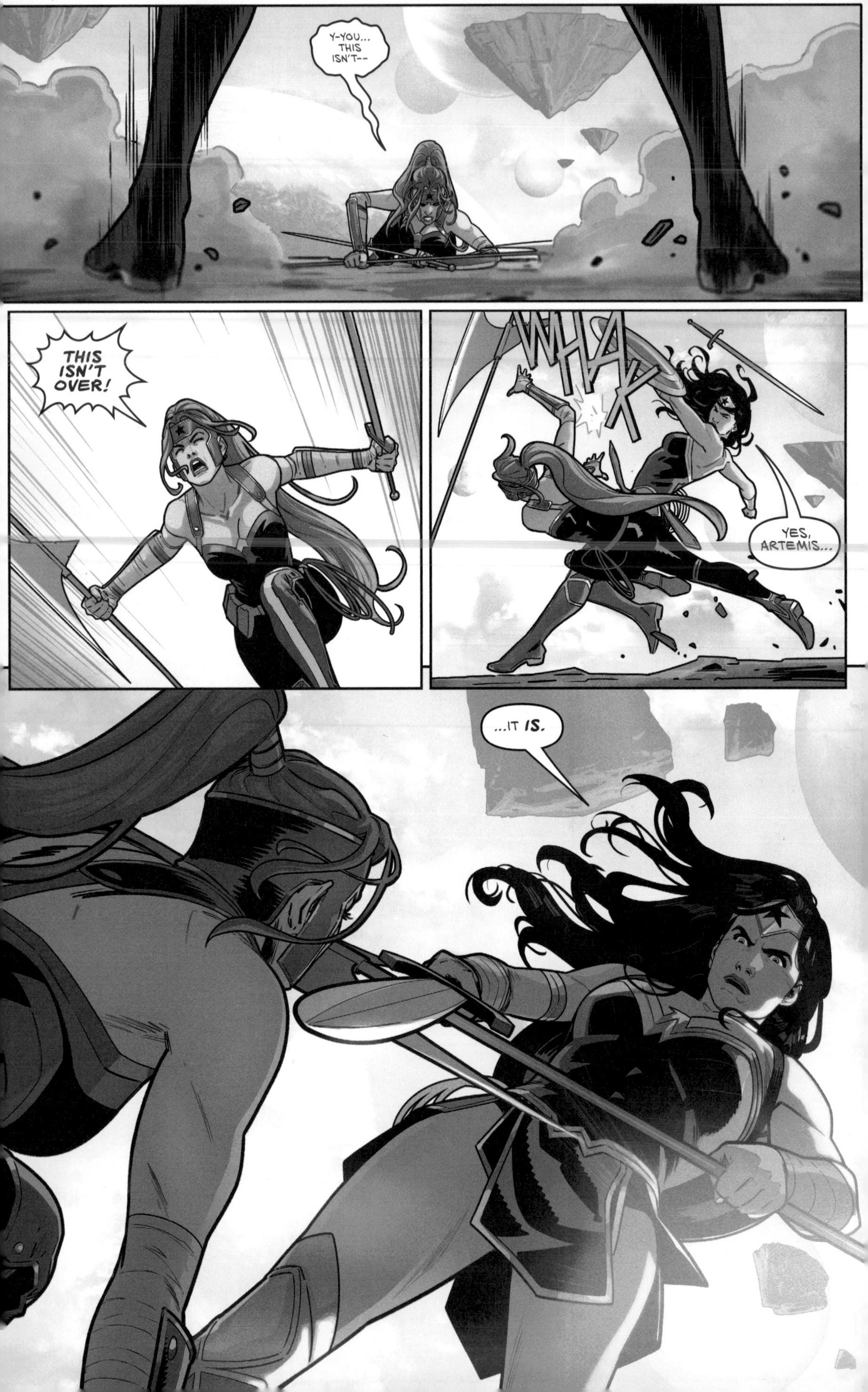

Y-YOU... THIS ISN'T--
THIS ISN'T OVER!
WHAK
YES, ARTEMIS...
...IT IS.

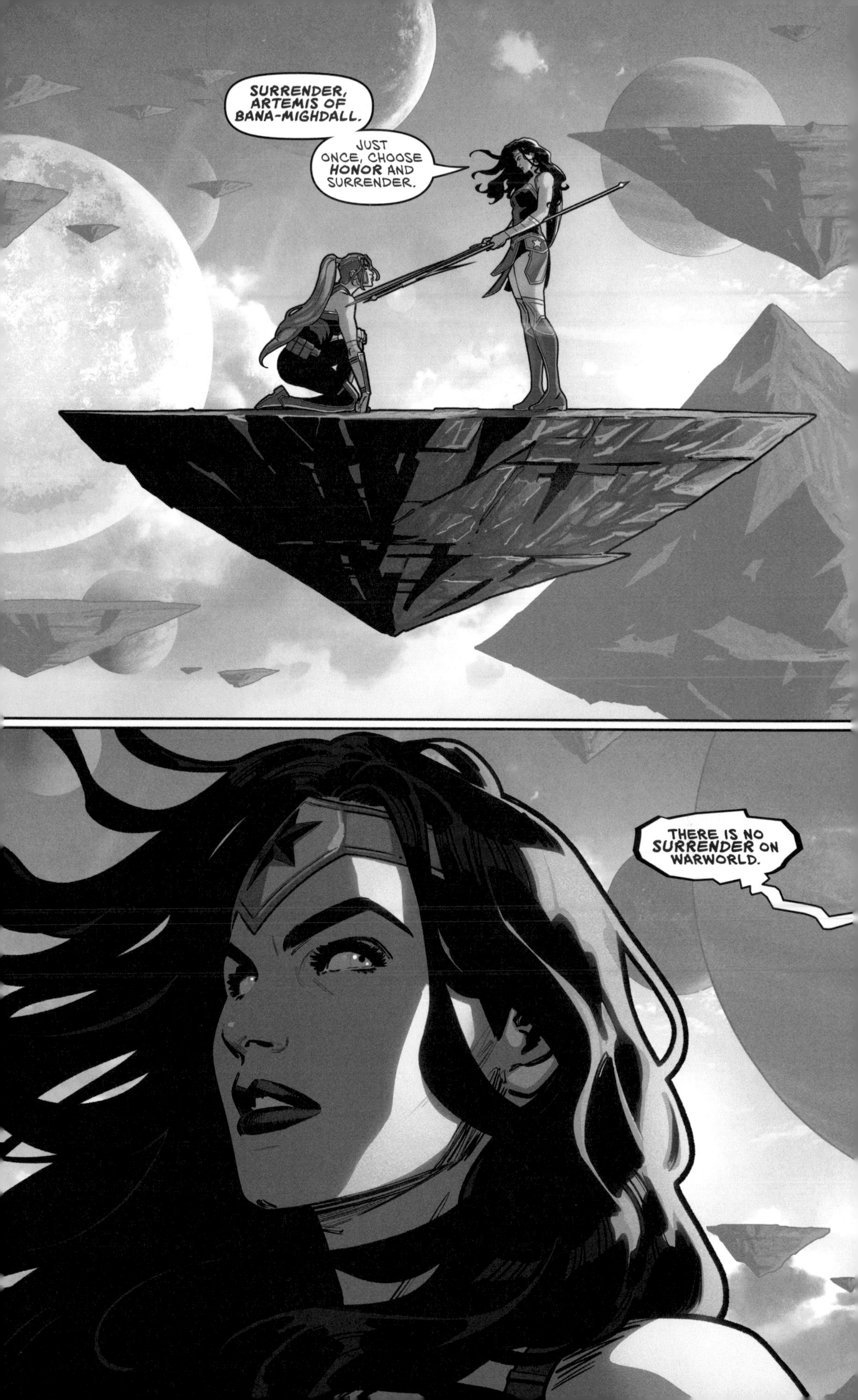
SURRENDER, ARTEMIS OF BANA-MIGHDALL.
JUST ONCE, CHOOSE HONOR AND SURRENDER.
THERE IS NO SURRENDER ON WARWORLD.

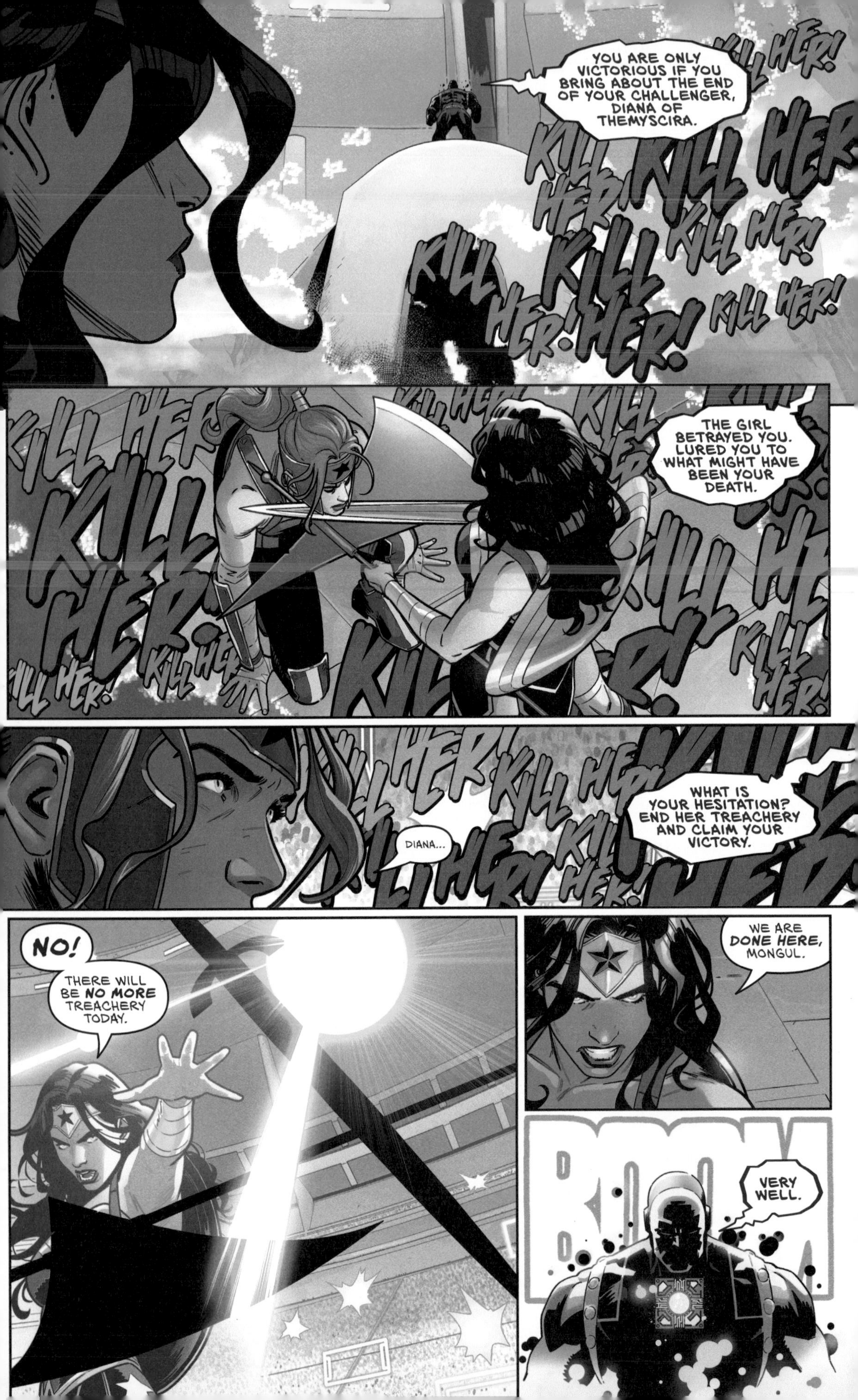

YOU ARE ONLY VICTORIOUS IF YOU BRING ABOUT THE END OF YOUR CHALLENGER, DIANA OF THEMYSCIRA.
KILL HER! KILL HER! KILL HER! KILL HER! KILL HER! KILL HER!
THE GIRL BETRAYED YOU. LURED YOU TO WHAT MIGHT HAVE BEEN YOUR DEATH.
KILL HER! KILL HER! KILL HER! KILL HER!
DIANA...
WHAT IS YOUR HESITATION? END HER TREACHERY AND CLAIM YOUR VICTORY.
NO!
THERE WILL BE NO MORE TREACHERY TODAY.
WE ARE DONE HERE, MONGUL.
VERY WELL.

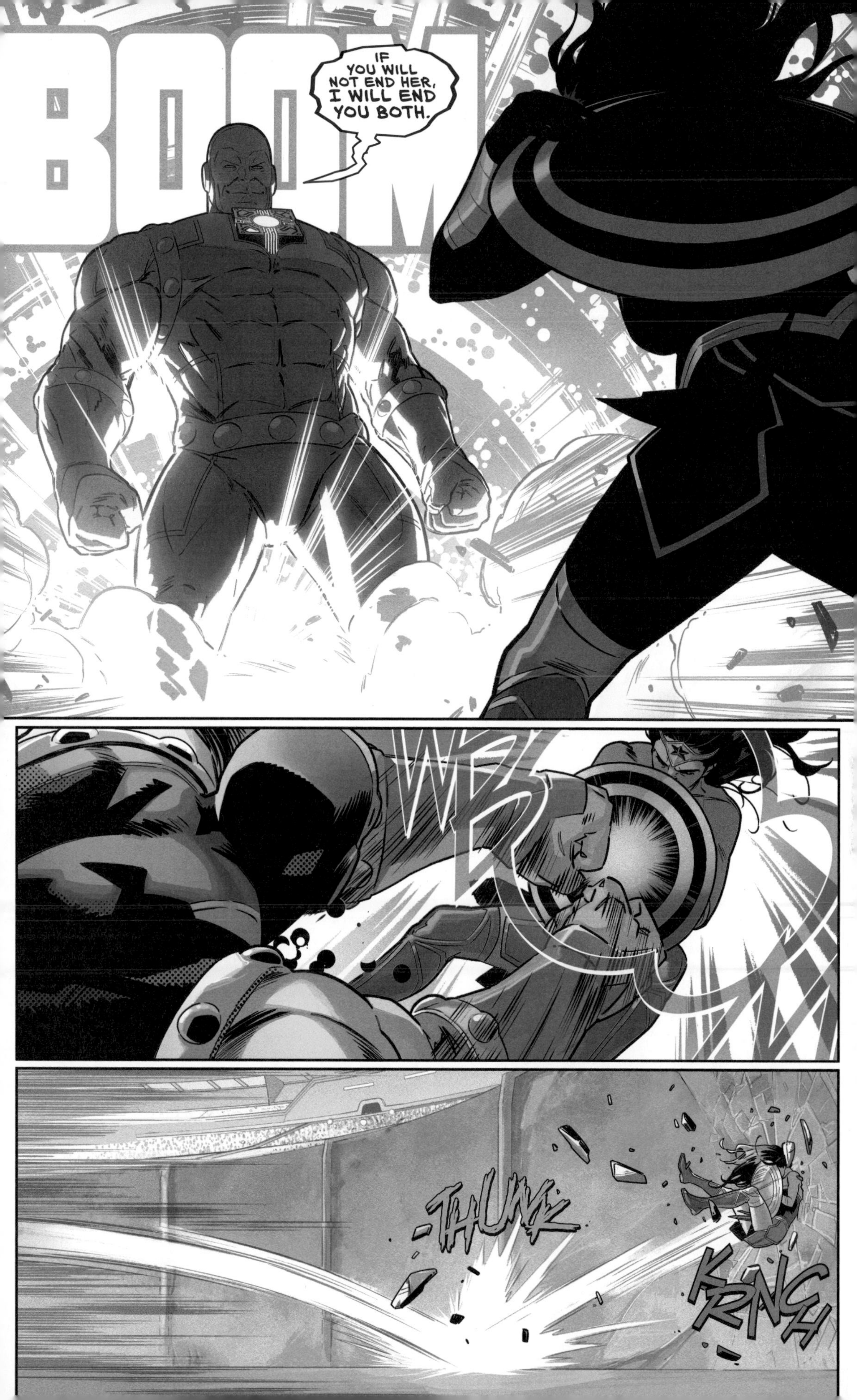
BOOM
IF YOU WILL NOT END HER, I WILL END YOU BOTH.
THUNK
KRNCH

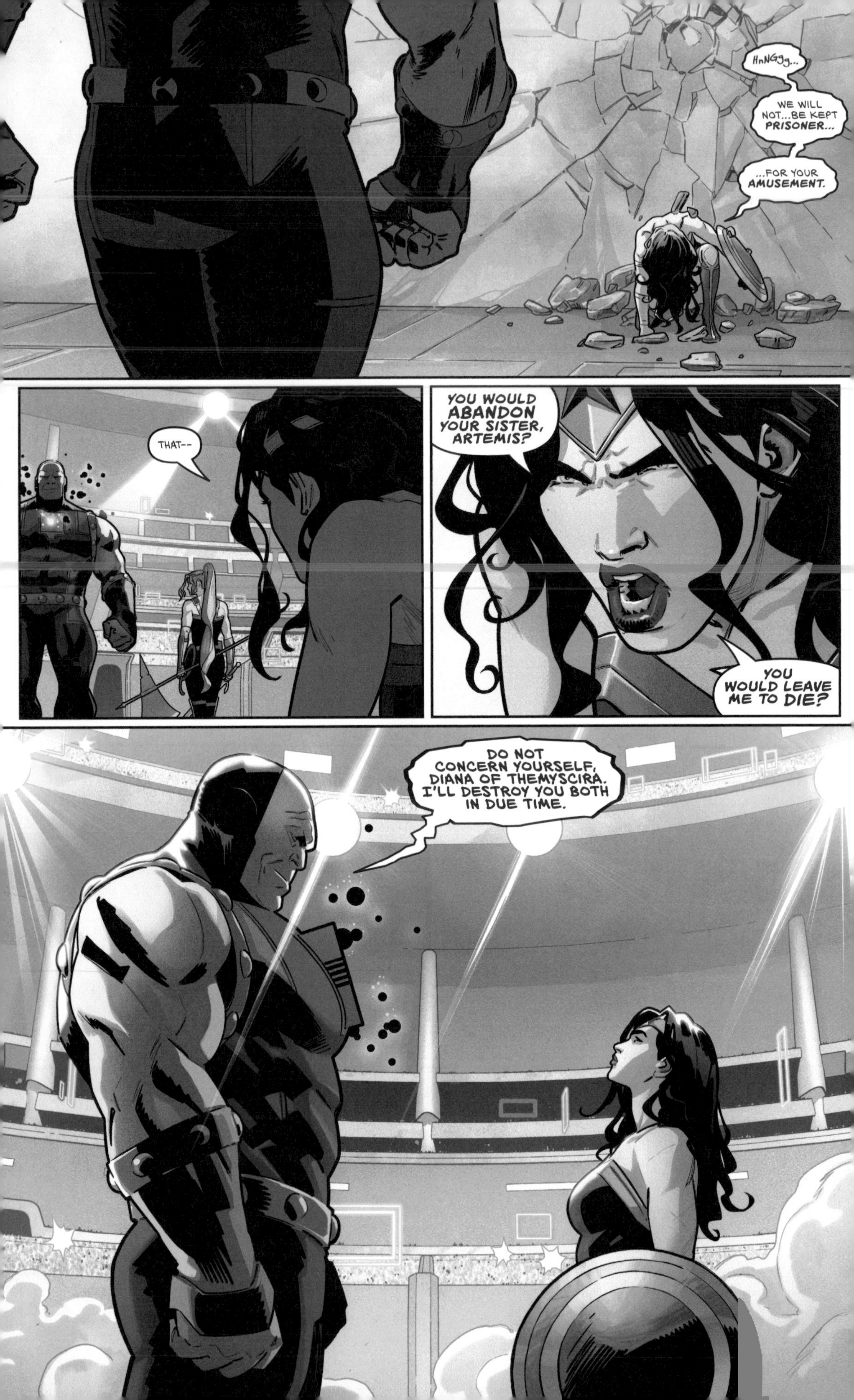
HnNGgg...
WE WILL NOT...BE KEPT PRISONER...
...FOR YOUR AMUSEMENT.
THAT--
YOU WOULD ABANDON YOUR SISTER, ARTEMIS?
YOU WOULD LEAVE ME TO DIE?
DO NOT CONCERN YOURSELF, DIANA OF THEMYSCIRA. I'LL DESTROY YOU BOTH IN DUE TIME.

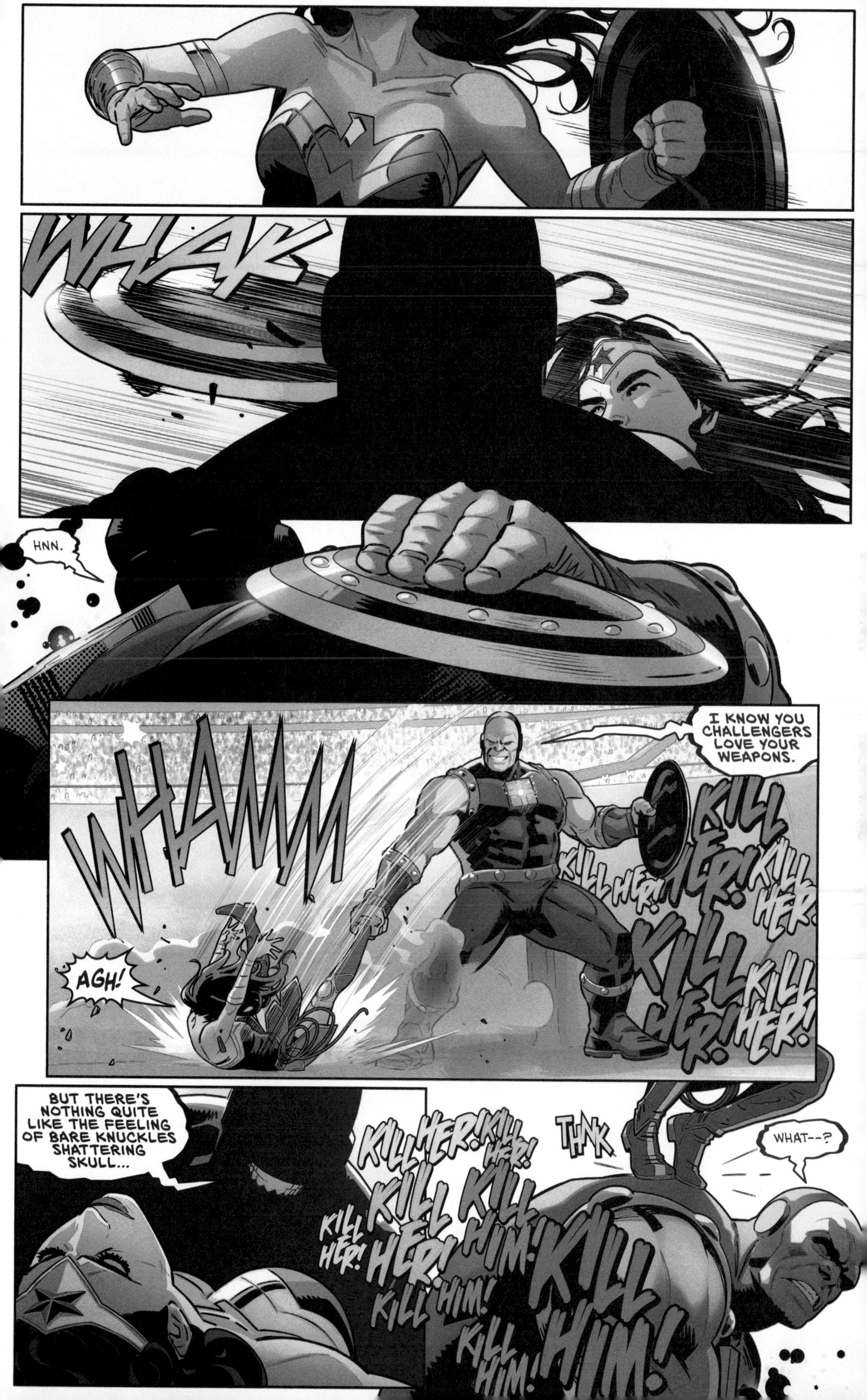
WHAK
HNN.
WHAMM
I KNOW YOU CHALLENGERS LOVE YOUR WEAPONS.
AGH!
KILL HER! KILL HER! KILL HER! KILL HER! KILL HER!
BUT THERE'S NOTHING QUITE LIKE THE FEELING OF BARE KNUCKLES SHATTERING SKULL...
THNK
WHAT--?
KILL HER! KILL HER! KILL HER! KILL HER! KILL HIM! KILL HIM! KILL HIM! KILL HIM!

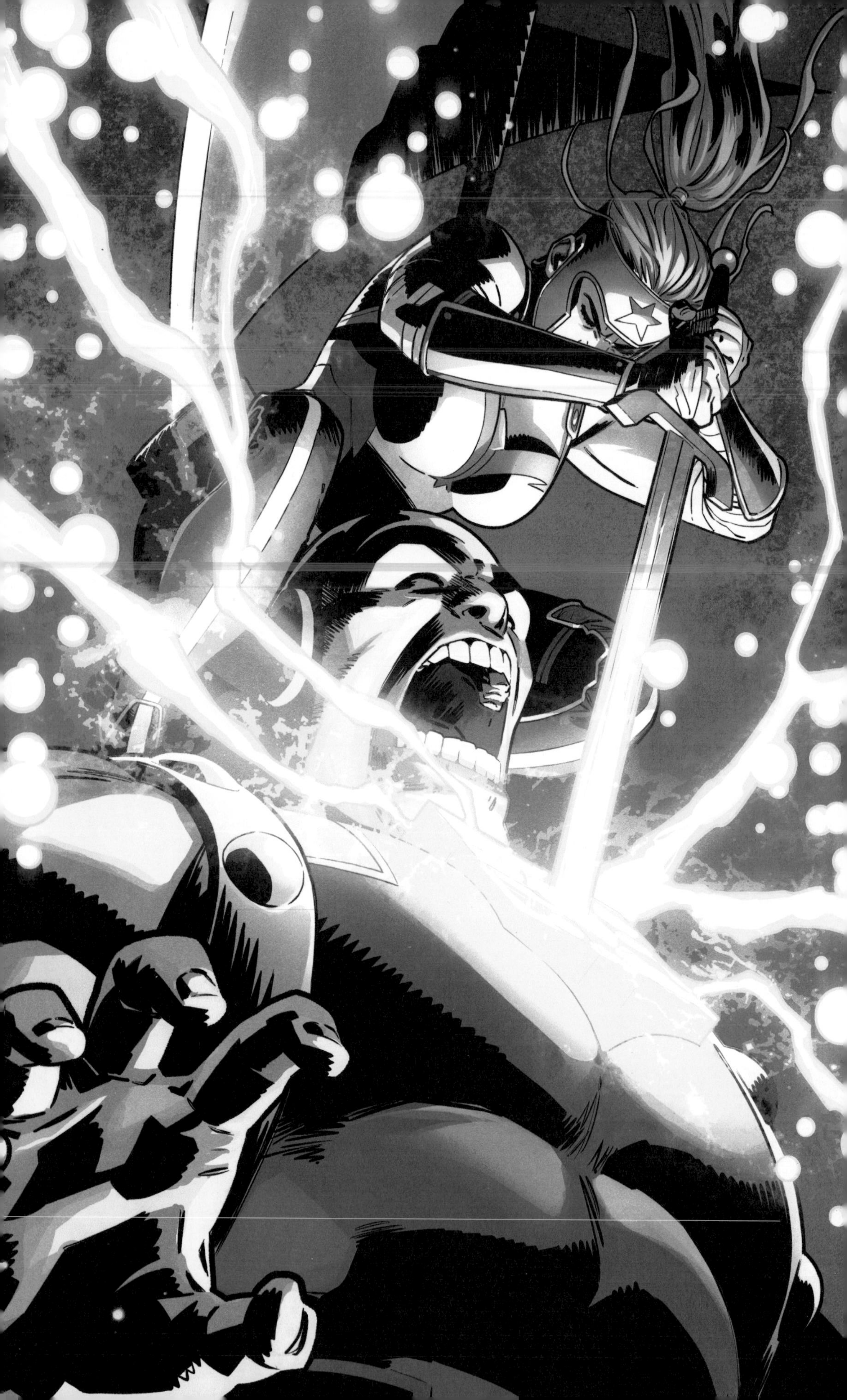

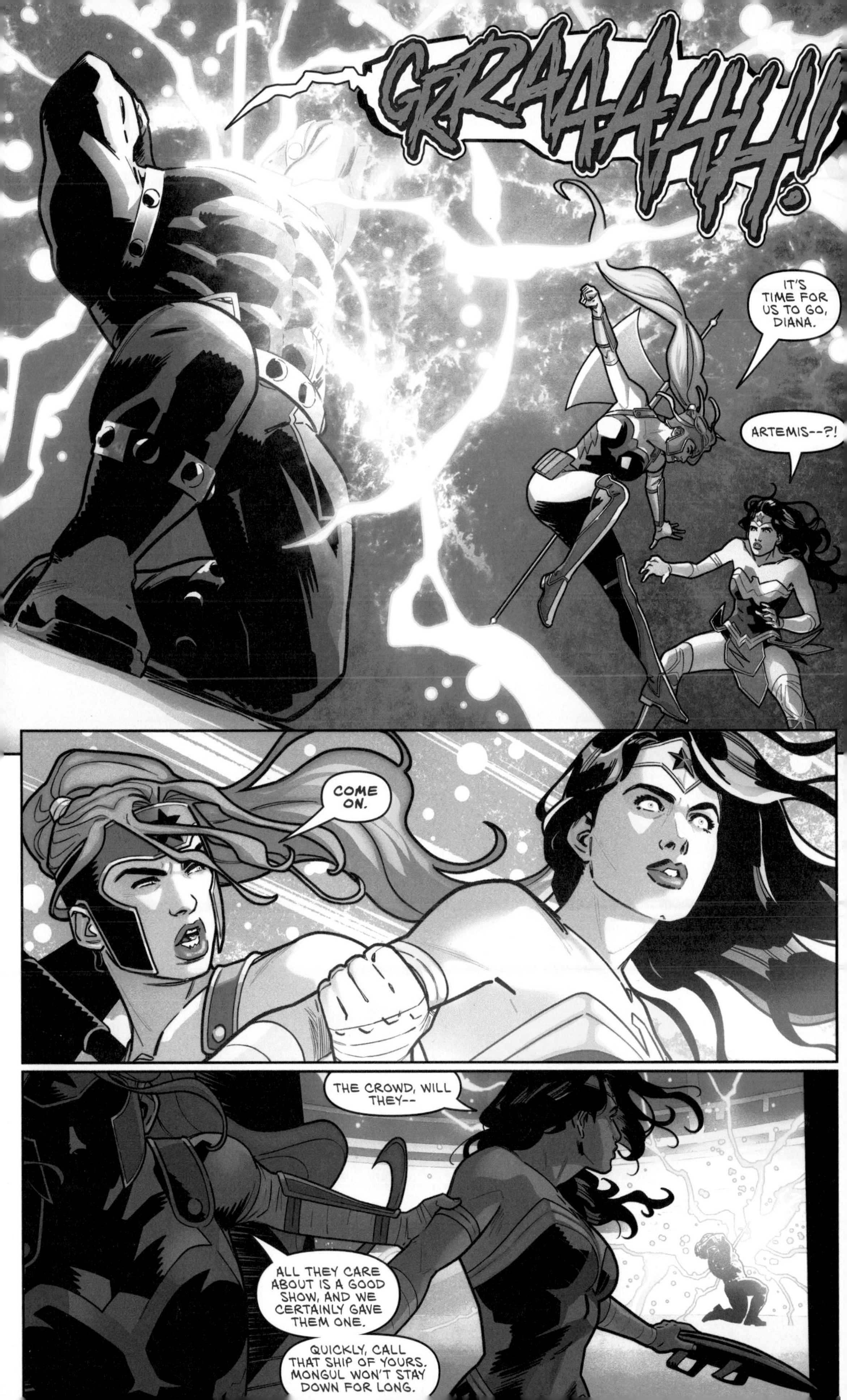
GRRAAAAHH!
IT'S TIME FOR US TO GO, DIANA.
ARTEMIS--?!
COME ON.
THE CROWD, WILL THEY--
ALL THEY CARE ABOUT IS A GOOD SHOW, AND WE CERTAINLY GAVE THEM ONE.
QUICKLY, CALL THAT SHIP OF YOURS. MONGUL WON'T STAY DOWN FOR LONG.

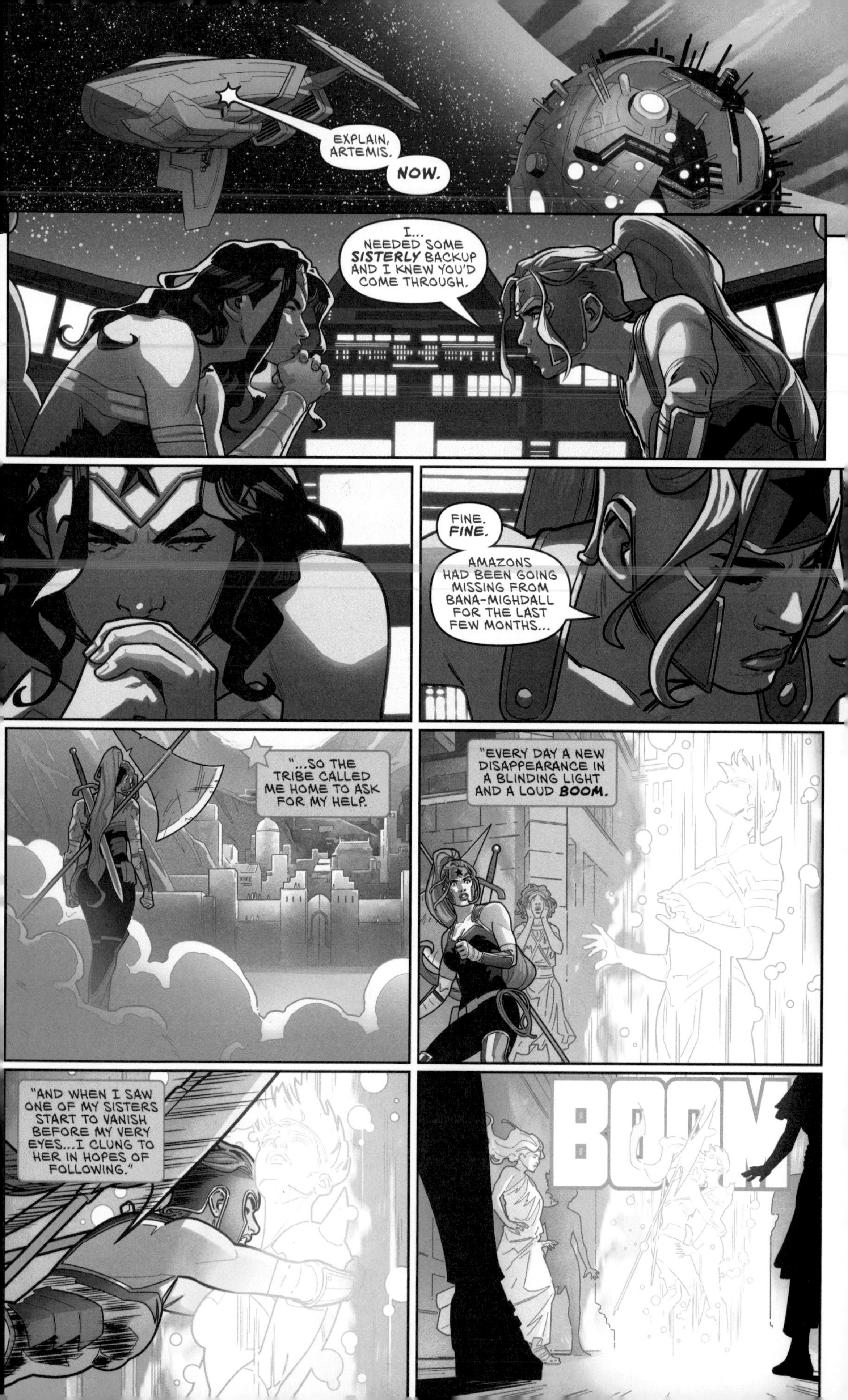

EXPLAIN, ARTEMIS.
NOW.
I... NEEDED SOME SISTERLY BACKUP AND I KNEW YOU'D COME THROUGH.
FINE. FINE.
AMAZONS HAD BEEN GOING MISSING FROM BANA-MIGHDALL FOR THE LAST FEW MONTHS...
"...SO THE TRIBE CALLED ME HOME TO ASK FOR MY HELP.
"EVERY DAY A NEW DISAPPEARANCE IN A BLINDING LIGHT AND A LOUD BOOM.
"AND WHEN I SAW ONE OF MY SISTERS START TO VANISH BEFORE MY VERY EYES...I CLUNG TO HER IN HOPES OF FOLLOWING."
BOOM

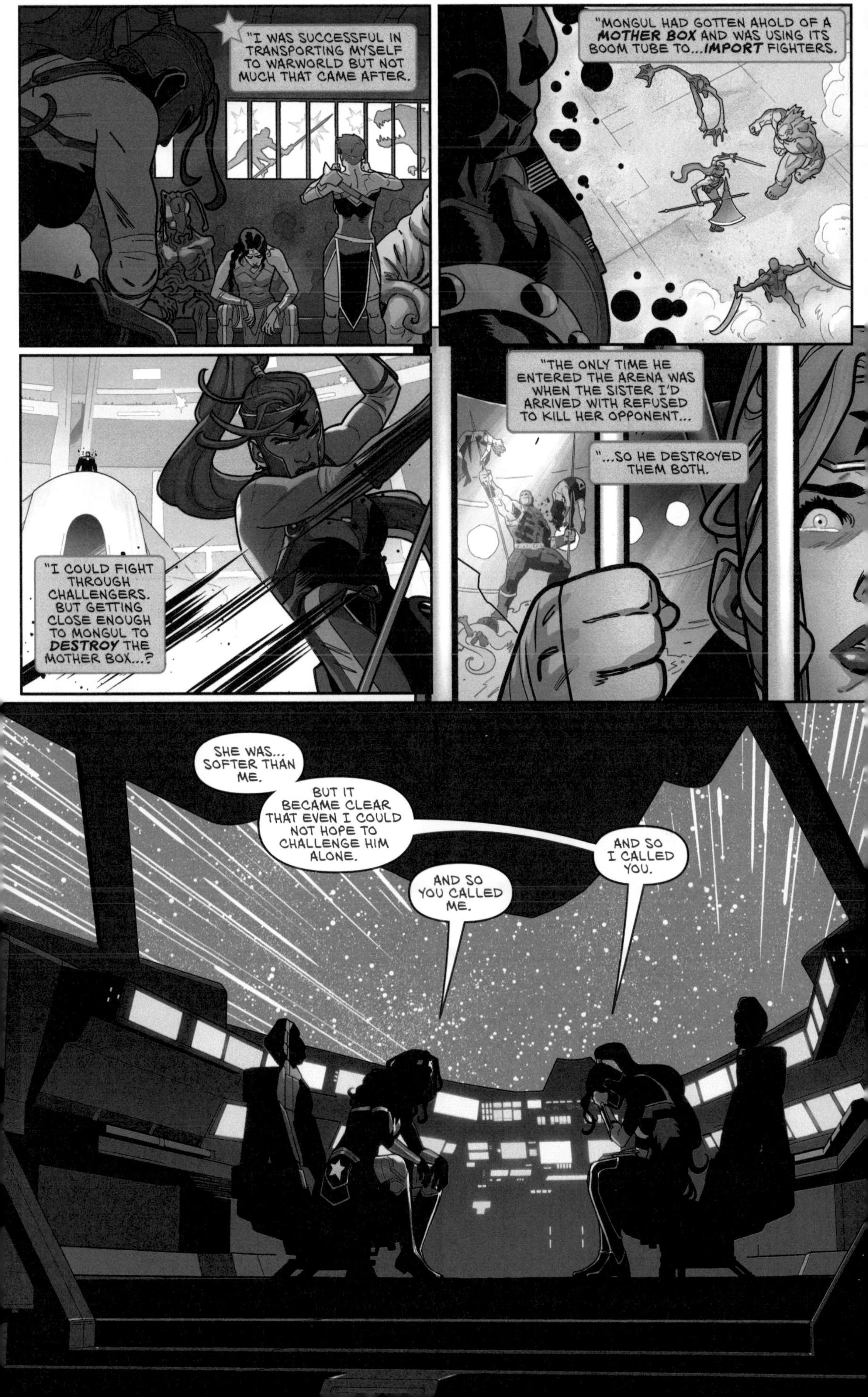

"I WAS SUCCESSFUL IN TRANSPORTING MYSELF TO WARWORLD BUT NOT MUCH THAT CAME AFTER.
"MONGUL HAD GOTTEN AHOLD OF A **MOTHER BOX** AND WAS USING ITS BOOM TUBE TO...***IMPORT*** FIGHTERS.
"I COULD FIGHT THROUGH CHALLENGERS. BUT GETTING CLOSE ENOUGH TO MONGUL TO ***DESTROY*** THE MOTHER BOX...?
"THE ONLY TIME HE ENTERED THE ARENA WAS WHEN THE SISTER I'D ARRIVED WITH REFUSED TO KILL HER OPPONENT...
"...SO HE DESTROYED THEM BOTH.
SHE WAS... SOFTER THAN ME.
BUT IT BECAME CLEAR THAT EVEN I COULD NOT HOPE TO CHALLENGE HIM ALONE.
AND SO YOU CALLED ME.
AND SO I CALLED YOU.

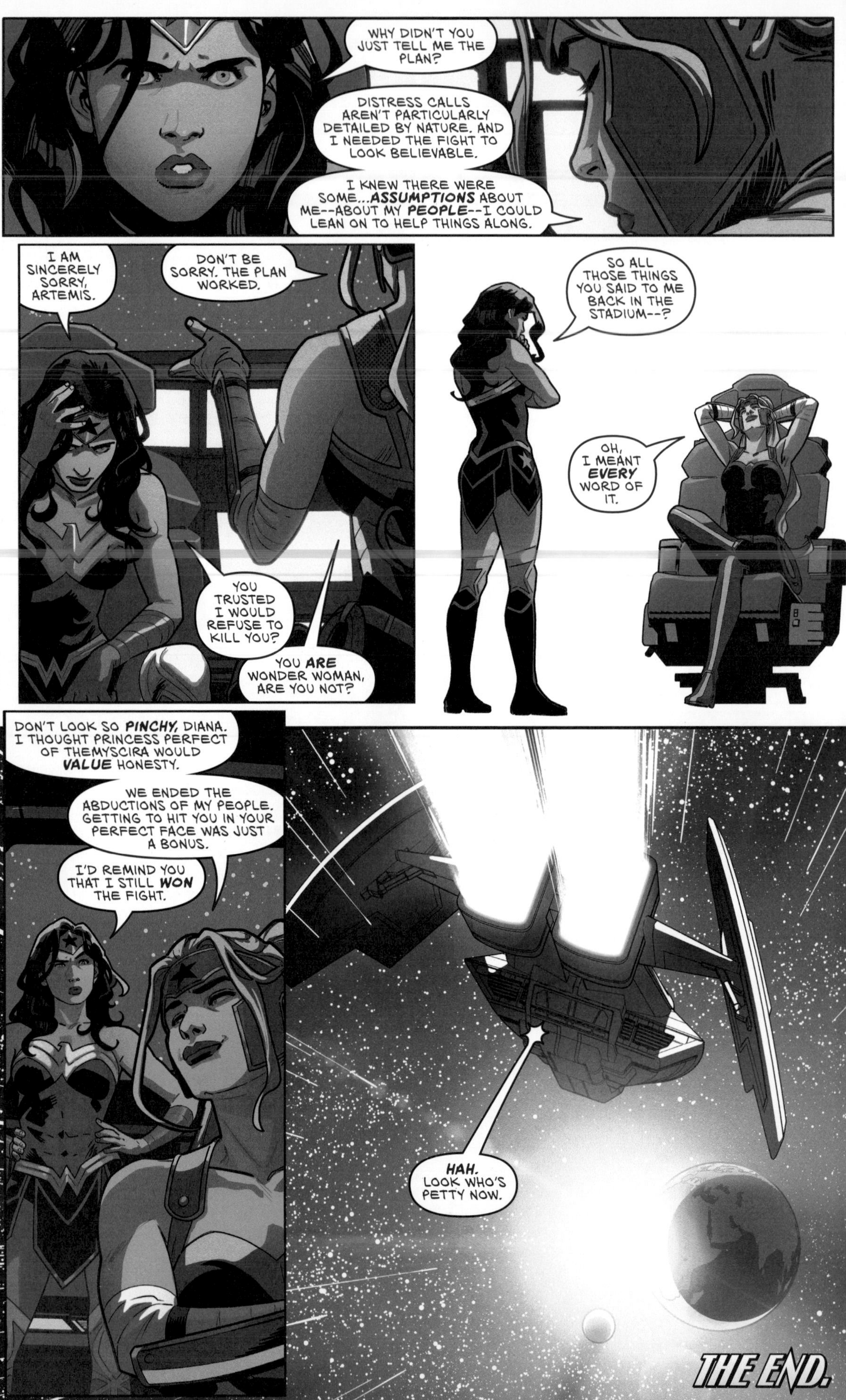
WHY DIDN'T YOU JUST TELL ME THE PLAN?
DISTRESS CALLS AREN'T PARTICULARLY DETAILED BY NATURE. AND I NEEDED THE FIGHT TO LOOK BELIEVABLE.
I KNEW THERE WERE SOME...ASSUMPTIONS ABOUT ME--ABOUT MY PEOPLE--I COULD LEAN ON TO HELP THINGS ALONG.
I AM SINCERELY SORRY, ARTEMIS.
DON'T BE SORRY. THE PLAN WORKED.
YOU TRUSTED I WOULD REFUSE TO KILL YOU?
YOU ARE WONDER WOMAN, ARE YOU NOT?
SO ALL THOSE THINGS YOU SAID TO ME BACK IN THE STADIUM--?
OH, I MEANT EVERY WORD OF IT.
DON'T LOOK SO PINCHY, DIANA. I THOUGHT PRINCESS PERFECT OF THEMYSCIRA WOULD VALUE HONESTY.
WE ENDED THE ABDUCTIONS OF MY PEOPLE. GETTING TO HIT YOU IN YOUR PERFECT FACE WAS JUST A BONUS.
I'D REMIND YOU THAT I STILL WON THE FIGHT.
HAH. LOOK WHO'S PETTY NOW.
THE END.

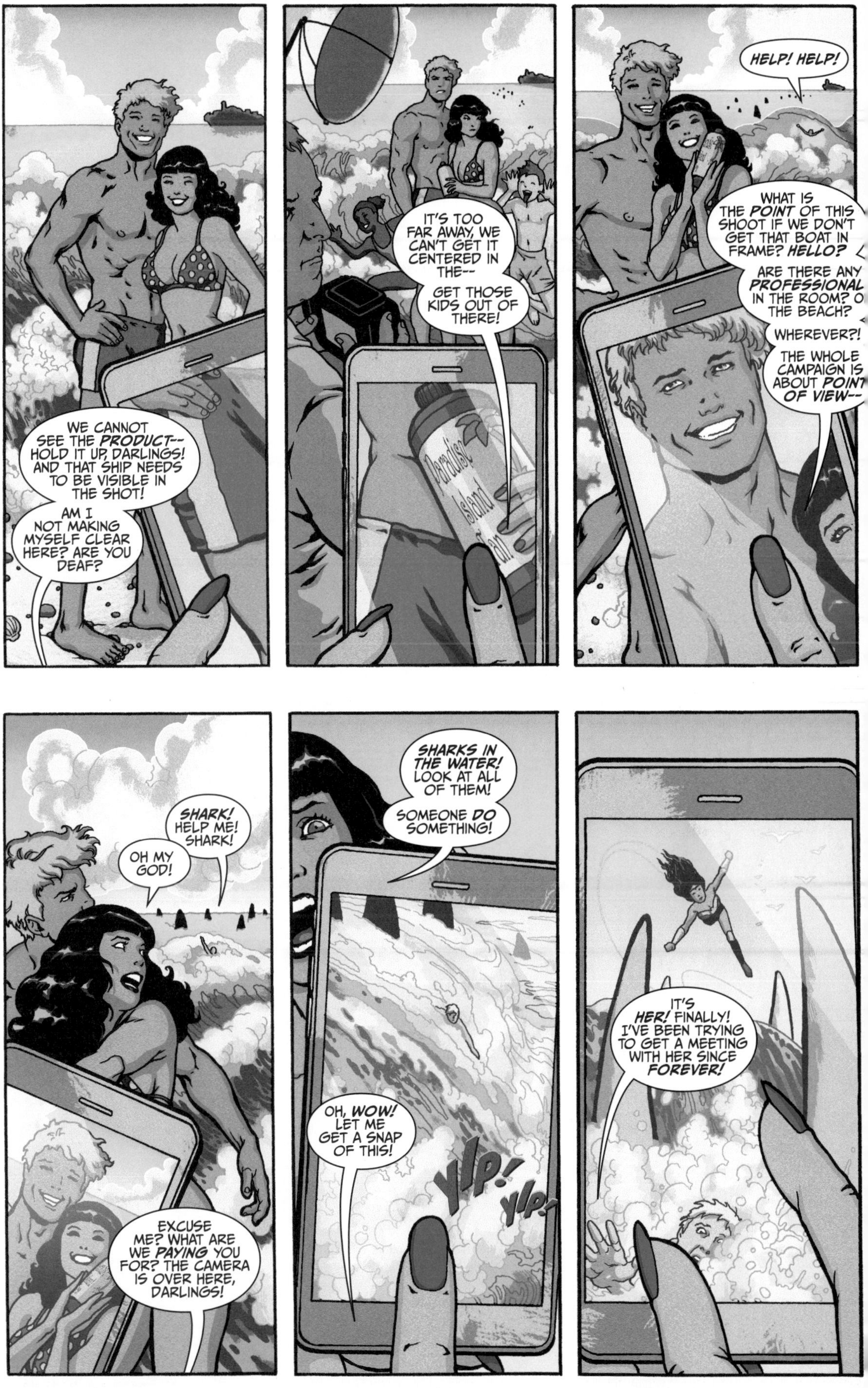
WE CANNOT SEE THE PRODUCT-- HOLD IT UP, DARLINGS! AND THAT SHIP NEEDS TO BE VISIBLE IN THE SHOT!
AM I NOT MAKING MYSELF CLEAR HERE? ARE YOU DEAF?
IT'S TOO FAR AWAY, WE CAN'T GET IT CENTERED IN THE--
GET THOSE KIDS OUT OF THERE!
Paradise Island Tan
HELP! HELP!
WHAT IS THE POINT OF THIS SHOOT IF WE DON'T GET THAT BOAT IN FRAME? HELLO?
ARE THERE ANY PROFESSIONAL IN THE ROOM? O THE BEACH?
WHEREVER?!
THE WHOLE CAMPAIGN IS ABOUT POINT OF VIEW--
SHARK! HELP ME! SHARK!
OH MY GOD!
EXCUSE ME? WHAT ARE WE PAYING YOU FOR? THE CAMERA IS OVER HERE, DARLINGS!
SHARKS IN THE WATER! LOOK AT ALL OF THEM!
SOMEONE DO SOMETHING!
OH, WOW! LET ME GET A SNAP OF THIS!
YIP! YIP!
IT'S HER! FINALLY! I'VE BEEN TRYING TO GET A MEETING WITH HER SINCE FOREVER!

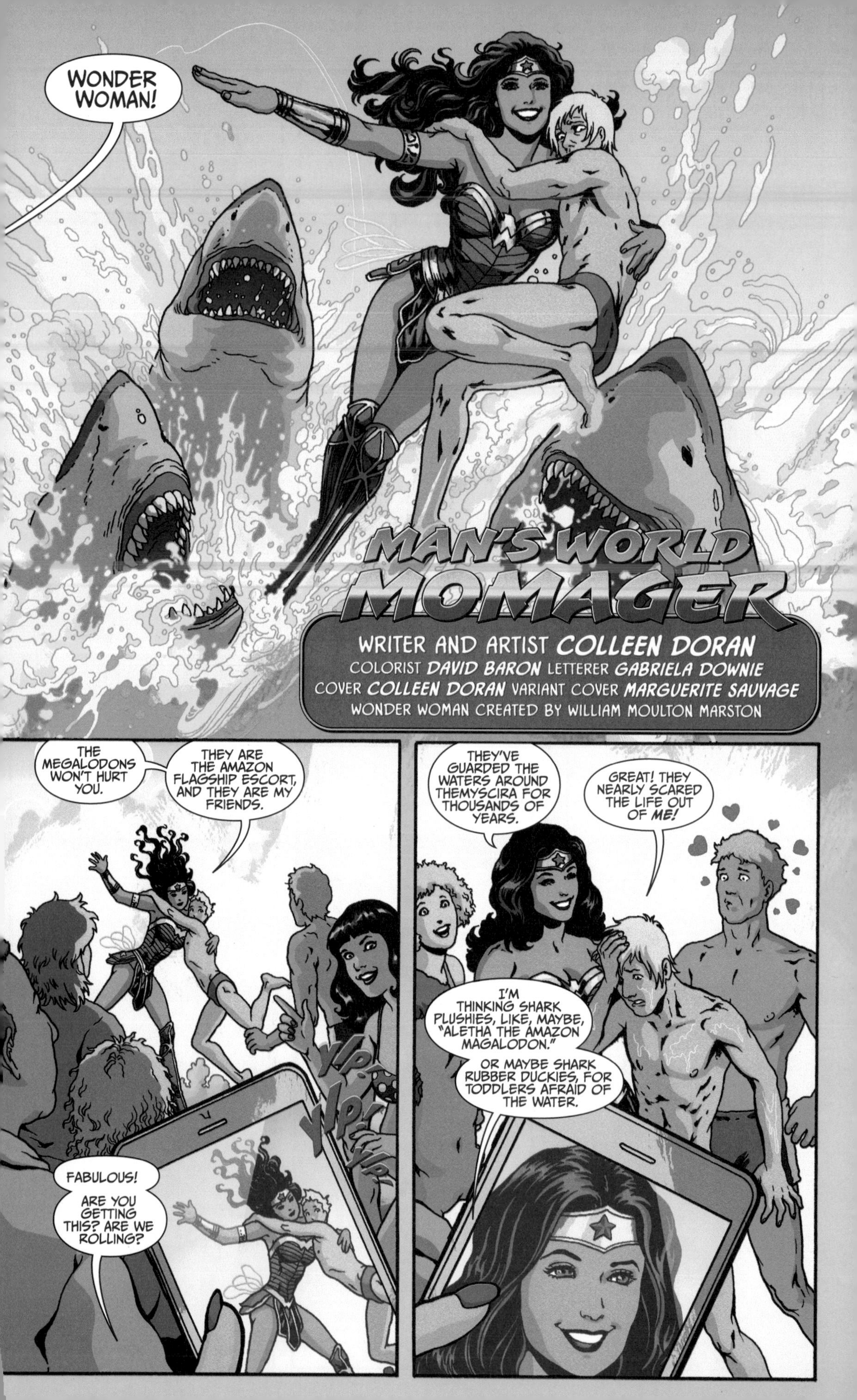
WONDER WOMAN!
MAN'S WORLD MOMAGER
WRITER AND ARTIST COLLEEN DORAN
COLORIST DAVID BARON LETTERER GABRIELA DOWNIE
COVER COLLEEN DORAN VARIANT COVER MARGUERITE SAUVAGE
WONDER WOMAN CREATED BY WILLIAM MOULTON MARSTON
THE MEGALODONS WON'T HURT YOU.
THEY ARE THE AMAZON FLAGSHIP ESCORT, AND THEY ARE MY FRIENDS.
YIP! YIP! YIP!
FABULOUS!
ARE YOU GETTING THIS? ARE WE ROLLING?
THEY'VE GUARDED THE WATERS AROUND THEMYSCIRA FOR THOUSANDS OF YEARS.
GREAT! THEY NEARLY SCARED THE LIFE OUT OF ME!
I'M THINKING SHARK PLUSHIES, LIKE, MAYBE, "ALETHA THE AMAZON MAGALODON."
OR MAYBE SHARK RUBBER DUCKIES, FOR TODDLERS AFRAID OF THE WATER.

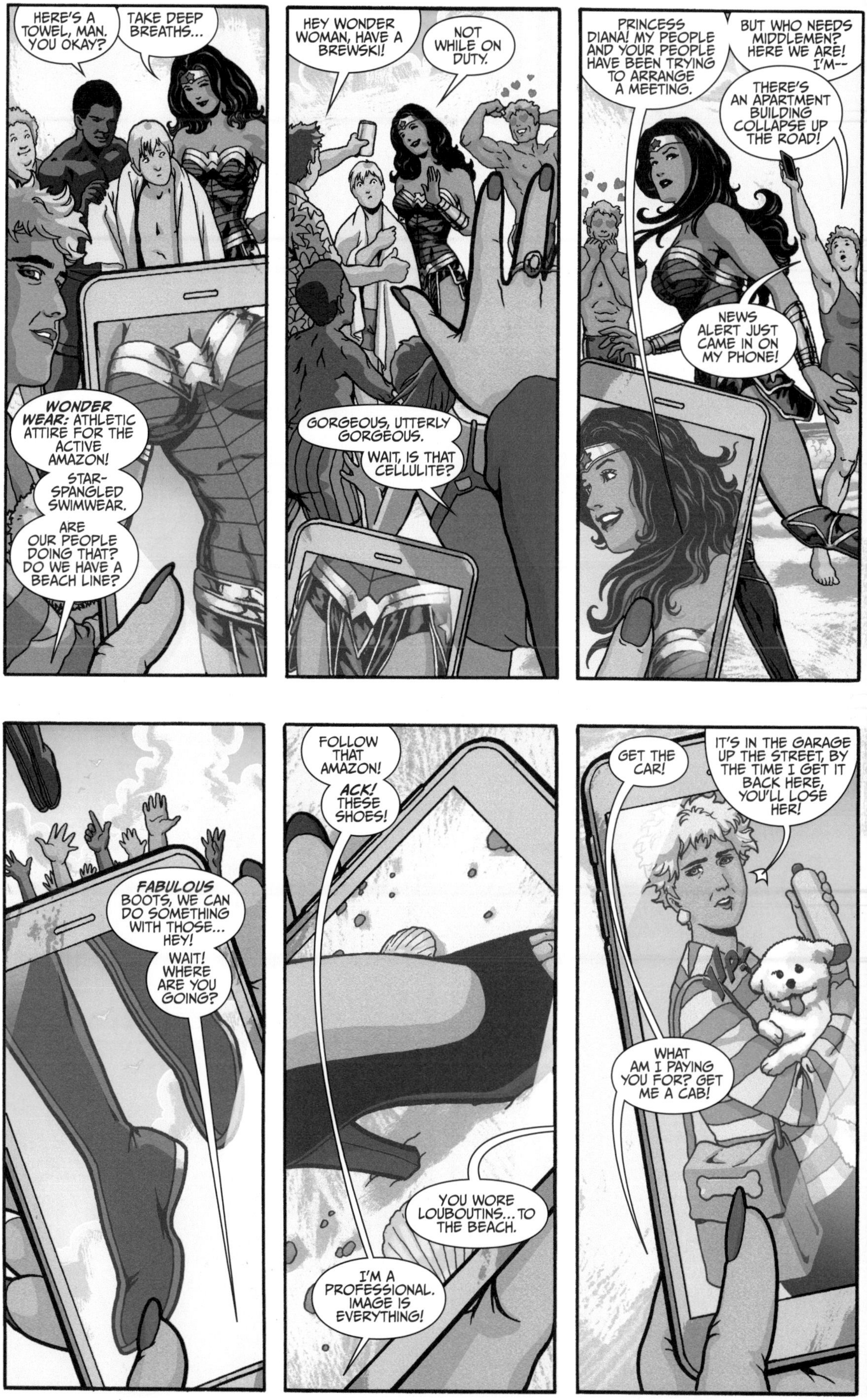
HERE'S A TOWEL, MAN. YOU OKAY?
TAKE DEEP BREATHS...
WONDER WEAR: ATHLETIC ATTIRE FOR THE ACTIVE AMAZON!
STAR-SPANGLED SWIMWEAR.
ARE OUR PEOPLE DOING THAT? DO WE HAVE A BEACH LINE?
HEY WONDER WOMAN, HAVE A BREWSKI!
NOT WHILE ON DUTY.
GORGEOUS, UTTERLY GORGEOUS.
WAIT, IS THAT CELLULITE?
PRINCESS DIANA! MY PEOPLE AND YOUR PEOPLE HAVE BEEN TRYING TO ARRANGE A MEETING.
BUT WHO NEEDS MIDDLEMEN? HERE WE ARE! I'M--
THERE'S AN APARTMENT BUILDING COLLAPSE UP THE ROAD!
NEWS ALERT JUST CAME IN ON MY PHONE!
FABULOUS BOOTS, WE CAN DO SOMETHING WITH THOSE... HEY!
WAIT! WHERE ARE YOU GOING?
FOLLOW THAT AMAZON!
ACK! THESE SHOES!
YOU WORE LOUBOUTINS... TO THE BEACH.
I'M A PROFESSIONAL. IMAGE IS EVERYTHING!
GET THE CAR!
IT'S IN THE GARAGE UP THE STREET, BY THE TIME I GET IT BACK HERE, YOU'LL LOSE HER!
WHAT AM I PAYING YOU FOR? GET ME A CAB!

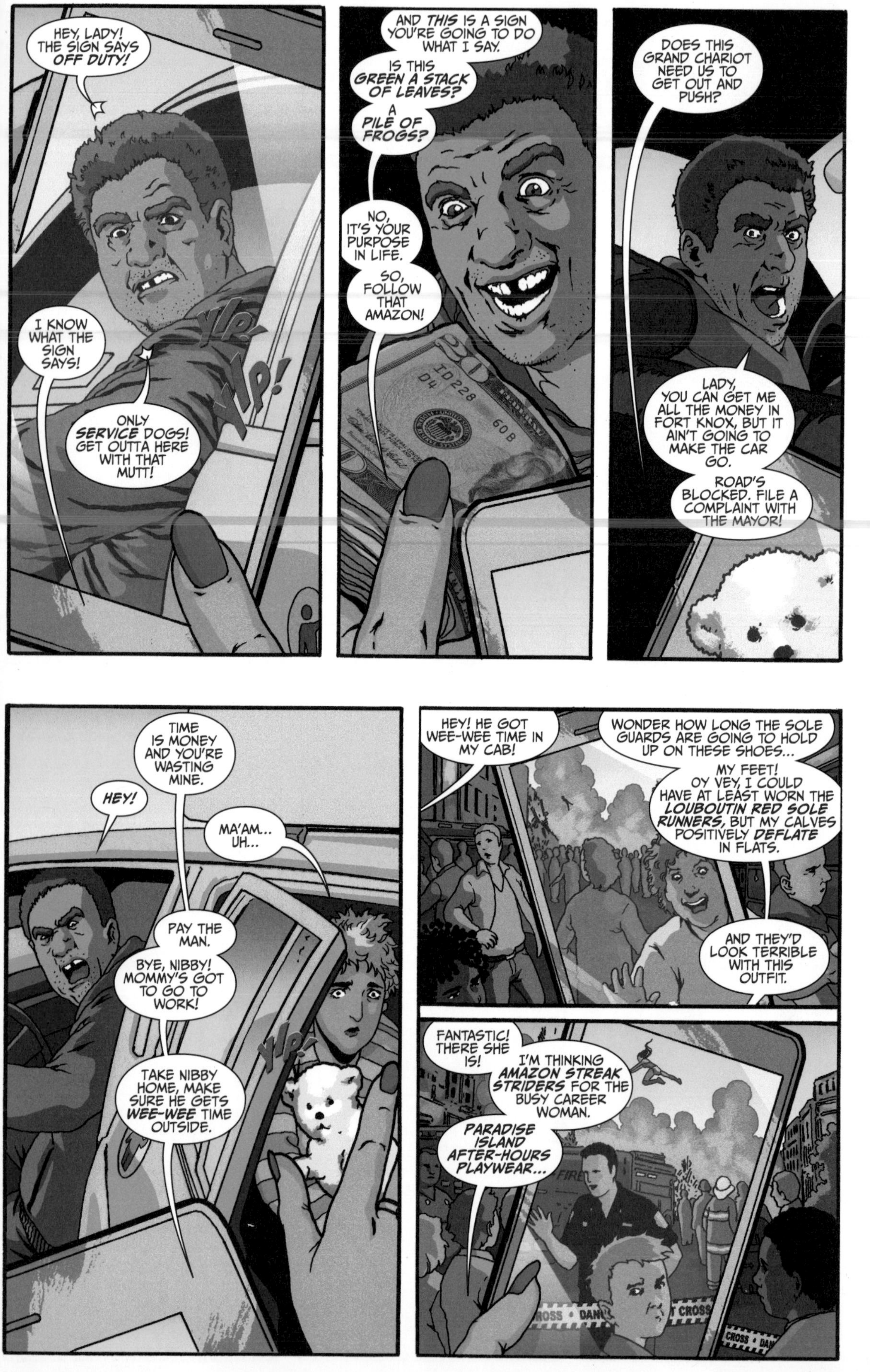
HEY, LADY! THE SIGN SAYS OFF DUTY!
I KNOW WHAT THE SIGN SAYS!
Y!P!
Y!P!
ONLY SERVICE DOGS! GET OUTTA HERE WITH THAT MUTT!
AND THIS IS A SIGN YOU'RE GOING TO DO WHAT I SAY.
IS THIS GREEN A STACK OF LEAVES?
A PILE OF FROGS?
NO, IT'S YOUR PURPOSE IN LIFE.
SO, FOLLOW THAT AMAZON!
DOES THIS GRAND CHARIOT NEED US TO GET OUT AND PUSH?
LADY, YOU CAN GET ME ALL THE MONEY IN FORT KNOX, BUT IT AIN'T GOING TO MAKE THE CAR GO.
ROAD'S BLOCKED. FILE A COMPLAINT WITH THE MAYOR!
TIME IS MONEY AND YOU'RE WASTING MINE.
HEY!
MA'AM... UH...
PAY THE MAN.
BYE, NIBBY! MOMMY'S GOT TO GO TO WORK!
TAKE NIBBY HOME, MAKE SURE HE GETS WEE-WEE TIME OUTSIDE.
Y!P!
HEY! HE GOT WEE-WEE TIME IN MY CAB!
WONDER HOW LONG THE SOLE GUARDS ARE GOING TO HOLD UP ON THESE SHOES...
MY FEET! OY VEY, I COULD HAVE AT LEAST WORN THE LOUBOUTIN RED SOLE RUNNERS, BUT MY CALVES POSITIVELY DEFLATE IN FLATS.
AND THEY'D LOOK TERRIBLE WITH THIS OUTFIT.
FANTASTIC! THERE SHE IS!
I'M THINKING AMAZON STREAK STRIDERS FOR THE BUSY CAREER WOMAN.
PARADISE ISLAND AFTER-HOURS PLAYWEAR...

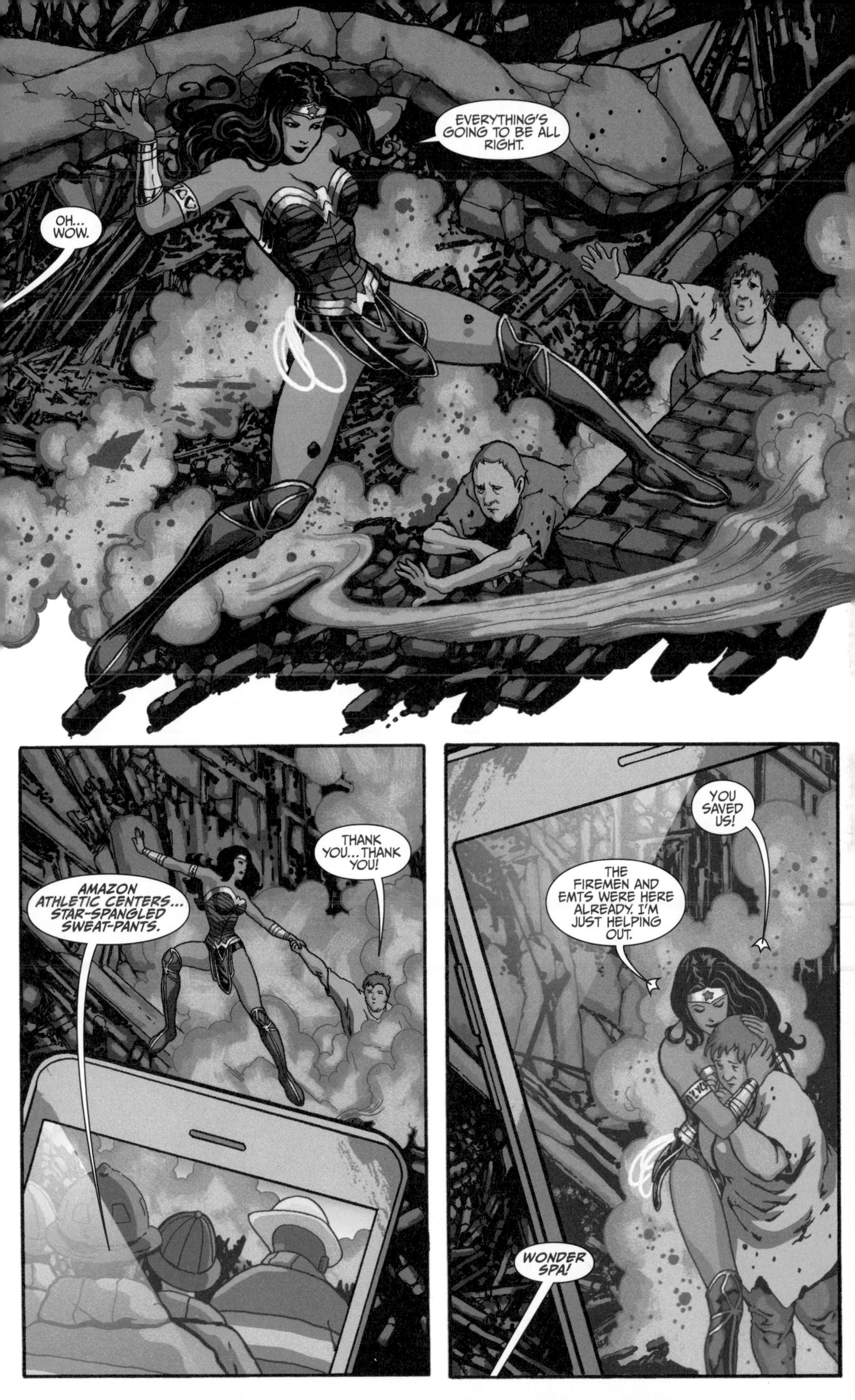
EVERYTHING'S GOING TO BE ALL RIGHT.
OH... WOW.
THANK YOU...THANK YOU!
AMAZON ATHLETIC CENTERS... STAR-SPANGLED SWEAT-PANTS.
YOU SAVED US!
THE FIREMEN AND EMTS WERE HERE ALREADY. I'M JUST HELPING OUT.
WONDER SPA!

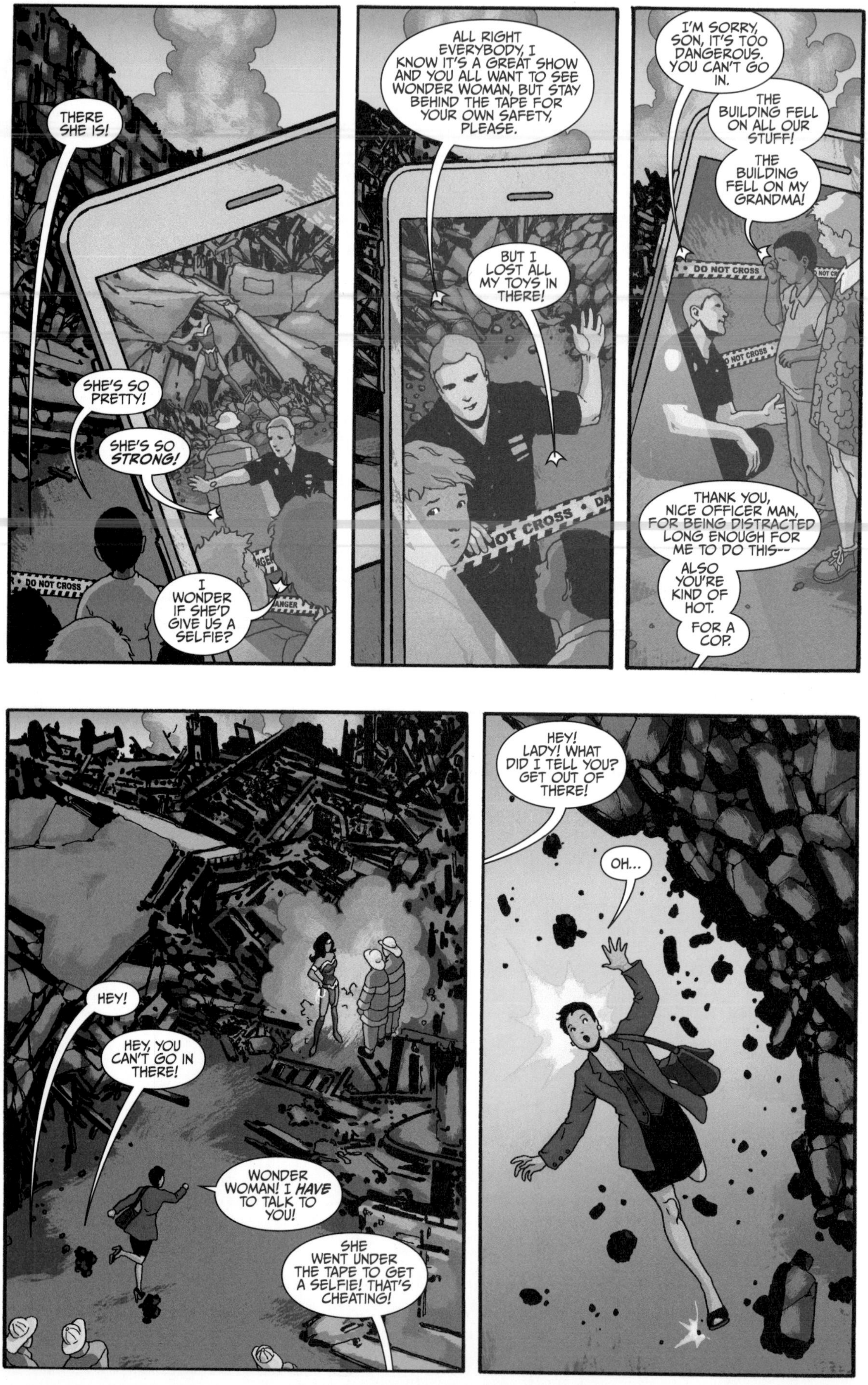
THERE SHE IS!
SHE'S SO PRETTY!
SHE'S SO STRONG!
I WONDER IF SHE'D GIVE US A SELFIE?
DO NOT CROSS
ALL RIGHT EVERYBODY, I KNOW IT'S A GREAT SHOW AND YOU ALL WANT TO SEE WONDER WOMAN, BUT STAY BEHIND THE TAPE FOR YOUR OWN SAFETY, PLEASE.
BUT I LOST ALL MY TOYS IN THERE!
I'M SORRY, SON, IT'S TOO DANGEROUS. YOU CAN'T GO IN.
THE BUILDING FELL ON ALL OUR STUFF!
THE BUILDING FELL ON MY GRANDMA!
DO NOT CROSS
THANK YOU, NICE OFFICER MAN, FOR BEING DISTRACTED LONG ENOUGH FOR ME TO DO THIS--
ALSO YOU'RE KIND OF HOT.
FOR A COP.
HEY!
HEY, YOU CAN'T GO IN THERE!
WONDER WOMAN! I HAVE TO TALK TO YOU!
SHE WENT UNDER THE TAPE TO GET A SELFIE! THAT'S CHEATING!
HEY! LADY! WHAT DID I TELL YOU? GET OUT OF THERE!
OH...

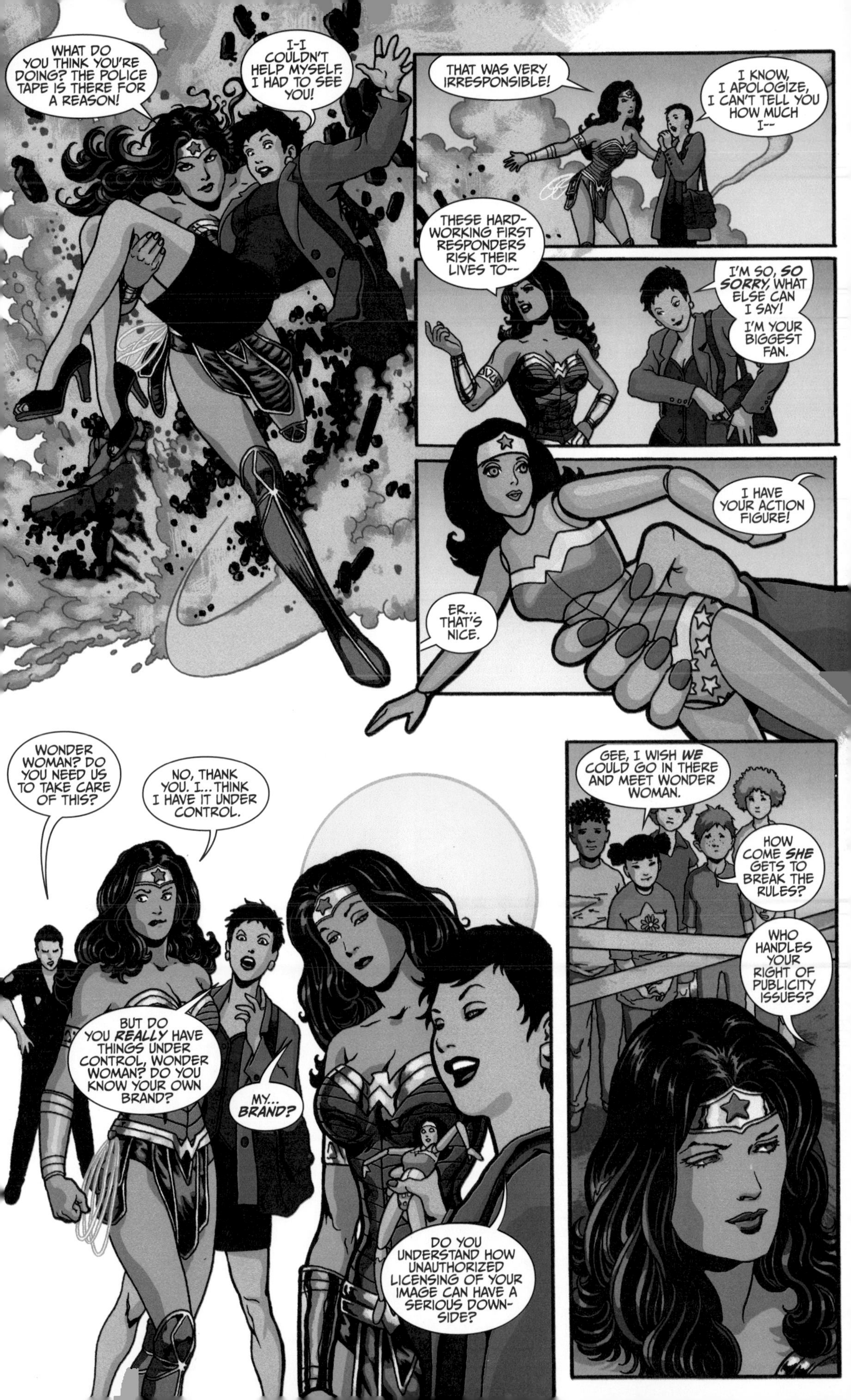
WHAT DO YOU THINK YOU'RE DOING? THE POLICE TAPE IS THERE FOR A REASON!
I-I COULDN'T HELP MYSELF. I HAD TO SEE YOU!
THAT WAS VERY IRRESPONSIBLE!
I KNOW, I APOLOGIZE, I CAN'T TELL YOU HOW MUCH I--
THESE HARD-WORKING FIRST RESPONDERS RISK THEIR LIVES TO--
I'M SO, SO SORRY, WHAT ELSE CAN I SAY!
I'M YOUR BIGGEST FAN.
I HAVE YOUR ACTION FIGURE!
ER... THAT'S NICE.
WONDER WOMAN? DO YOU NEED US TO TAKE CARE OF THIS?
NO, THANK YOU. I... THINK I HAVE IT UNDER CONTROL.
BUT DO YOU REALLY HAVE THINGS UNDER CONTROL, WONDER WOMAN? DO YOU KNOW YOUR OWN BRAND?
MY... BRAND?
DO YOU UNDERSTAND HOW UNAUTHORIZED LICENSING OF YOUR IMAGE CAN HAVE A SERIOUS DOWN-SIDE?
GEE, I WISH WE COULD GO IN THERE AND MEET WONDER WOMAN.
HOW COME SHE GETS TO BREAK THE RULES?
WHO HANDLES YOUR RIGHT OF PUBLICITY ISSUES?

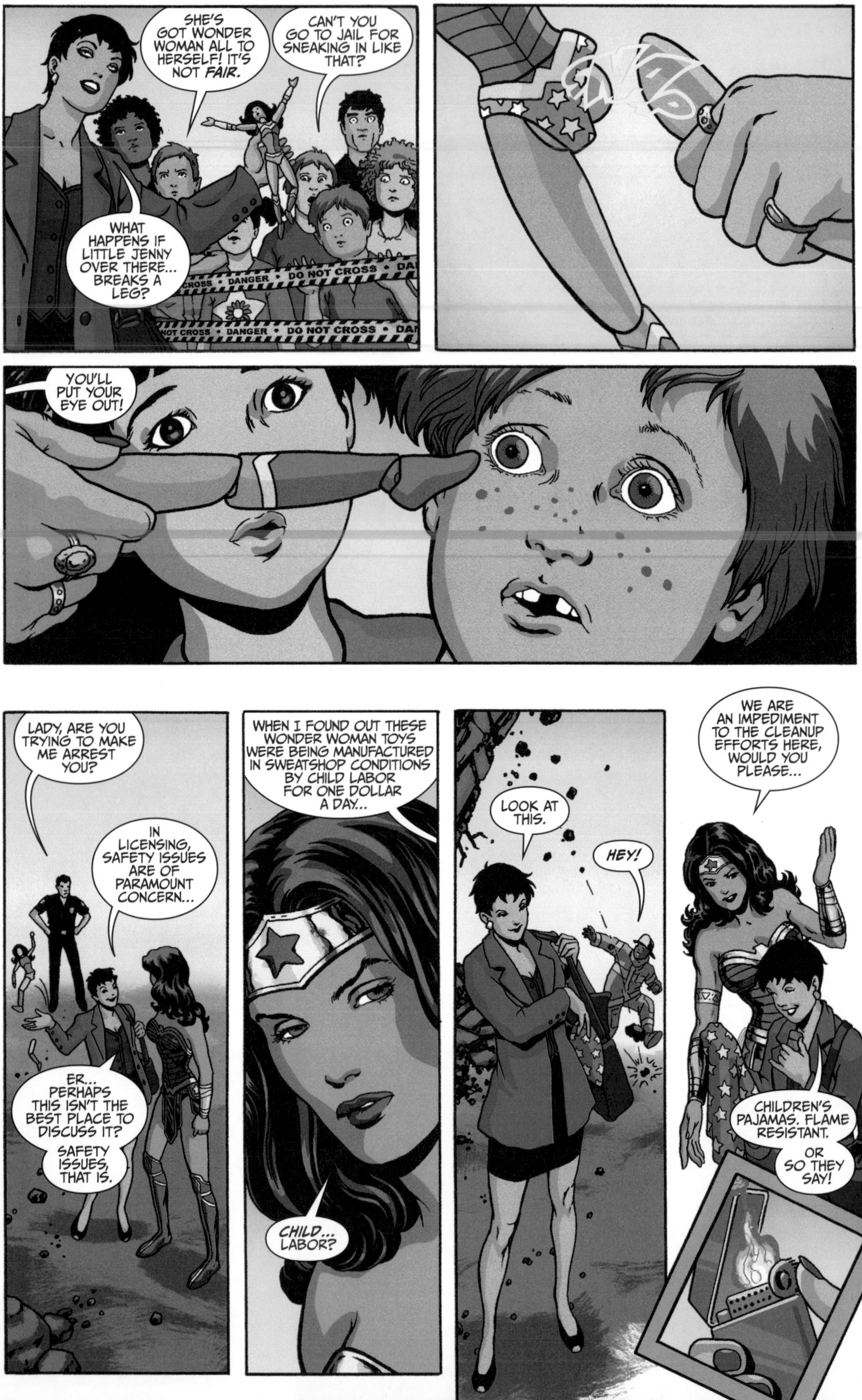
SHE'S GOT WONDER WOMAN ALL TO HERSELF! IT'S NOT FAIR.
CAN'T YOU GO TO JAIL FOR SNEAKING IN LIKE THAT?
WHAT HAPPENS IF LITTLE JENNY OVER THERE... BREAKS A LEG?
DANGER • DO NOT CROSS
YOU'LL PUT YOUR EYE OUT!
LADY, ARE YOU TRYING TO MAKE ME ARREST YOU?
IN LICENSING, SAFETY ISSUES ARE OF PARAMOUNT CONCERN...
ER... PERHAPS THIS ISN'T THE BEST PLACE TO DISCUSS IT?
SAFETY ISSUES, THAT IS.
WHEN I FOUND OUT THESE WONDER WOMAN TOYS WERE BEING MANUFACTURED IN SWEATSHOP CONDITIONS BY CHILD LABOR FOR ONE DOLLAR A DAY...
CHILD... LABOR?
LOOK AT THIS.
HEY!
WE ARE AN IMPEDIMENT TO THE CLEANUP EFFORTS HERE, WOULD YOU PLEASE...
CHILDREN'S PAJAMAS. FLAME RESISTANT.
OR SO THEY SAY!

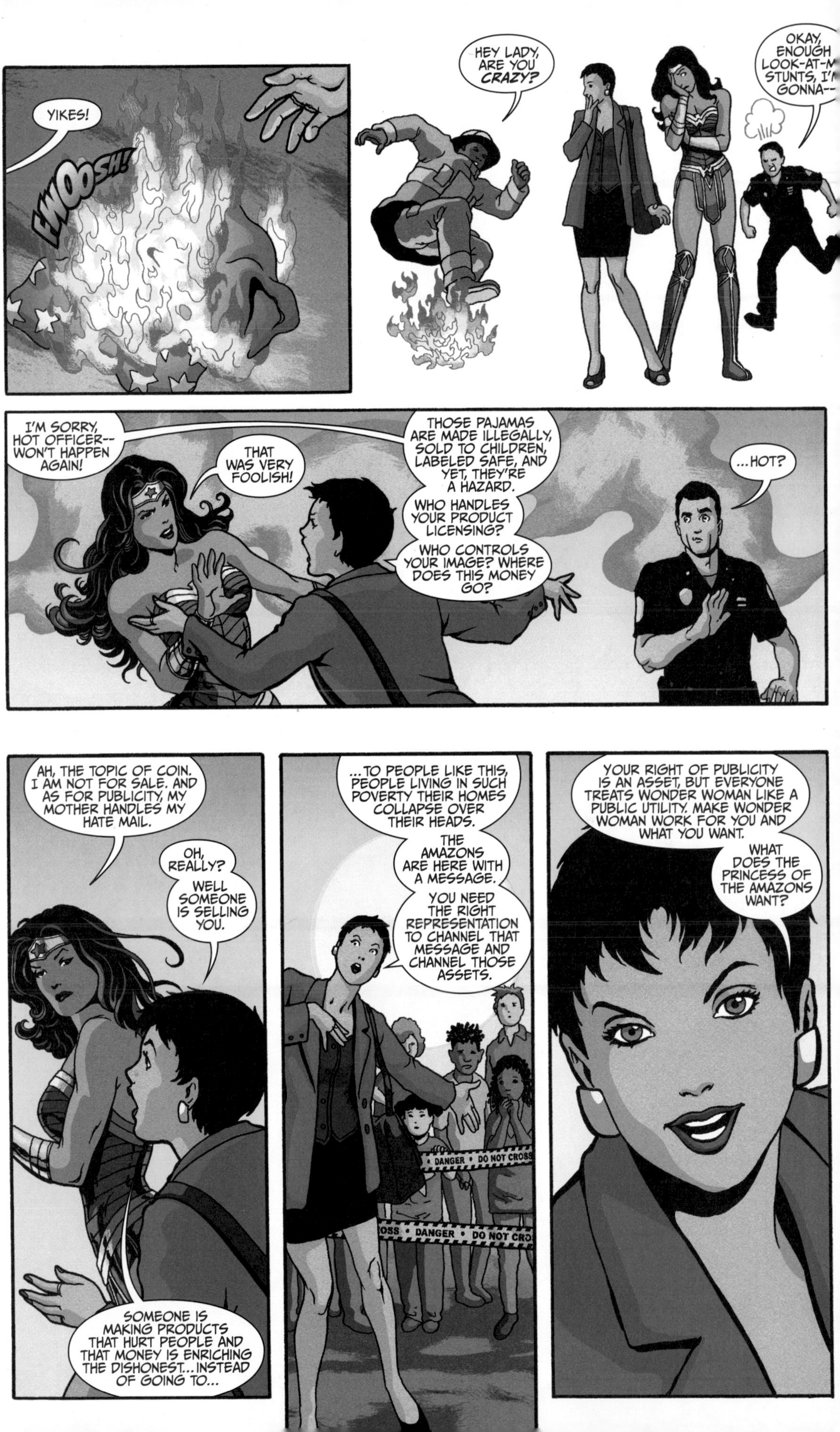
YIKES!
FWOOSH!
HEY LADY, ARE YOU CRAZY?
OKAY, ENOUGH LOOK-AT-M STUNTS, I' GONNA--
I'M SORRY, HOT OFFICER-- WON'T HAPPEN AGAIN!
THAT WAS VERY FOOLISH!
THOSE PAJAMAS ARE MADE ILLEGALLY, SOLD TO CHILDREN, LABELED SAFE, AND YET, THEY'RE A HAZARD.
WHO HANDLES YOUR PRODUCT LICENSING?
WHO CONTROLS YOUR IMAGE? WHERE DOES THIS MONEY GO?
...HOT?
AH, THE TOPIC OF COIN. I AM NOT FOR SALE. AND AS FOR PUBLICITY, MY MOTHER HANDLES MY HATE MAIL.
OH, REALLY?
WELL SOMEONE IS SELLING YOU.
SOMEONE IS MAKING PRODUCTS THAT HURT PEOPLE AND THAT MONEY IS ENRICHING THE DISHONEST... INSTEAD OF GOING TO...
...TO PEOPLE LIKE THIS, PEOPLE LIVING IN SUCH POVERTY THEIR HOMES COLLAPSE OVER THEIR HEADS.
THE AMAZONS ARE HERE WITH A MESSAGE.
YOU NEED THE RIGHT REPRESENTATION TO CHANNEL THAT MESSAGE AND CHANNEL THOSE ASSETS.
DANGER DO NOT CROSS
OSS DANGER DO NOT CRO
YOUR RIGHT OF PUBLICITY IS AN ASSET, BUT EVERYONE TREATS WONDER WOMAN LIKE A PUBLIC UTILITY. MAKE WONDER WOMAN WORK FOR YOU AND WHAT YOU WANT.
WHAT DOES THE PRINCESS OF THE AMAZONS WANT?

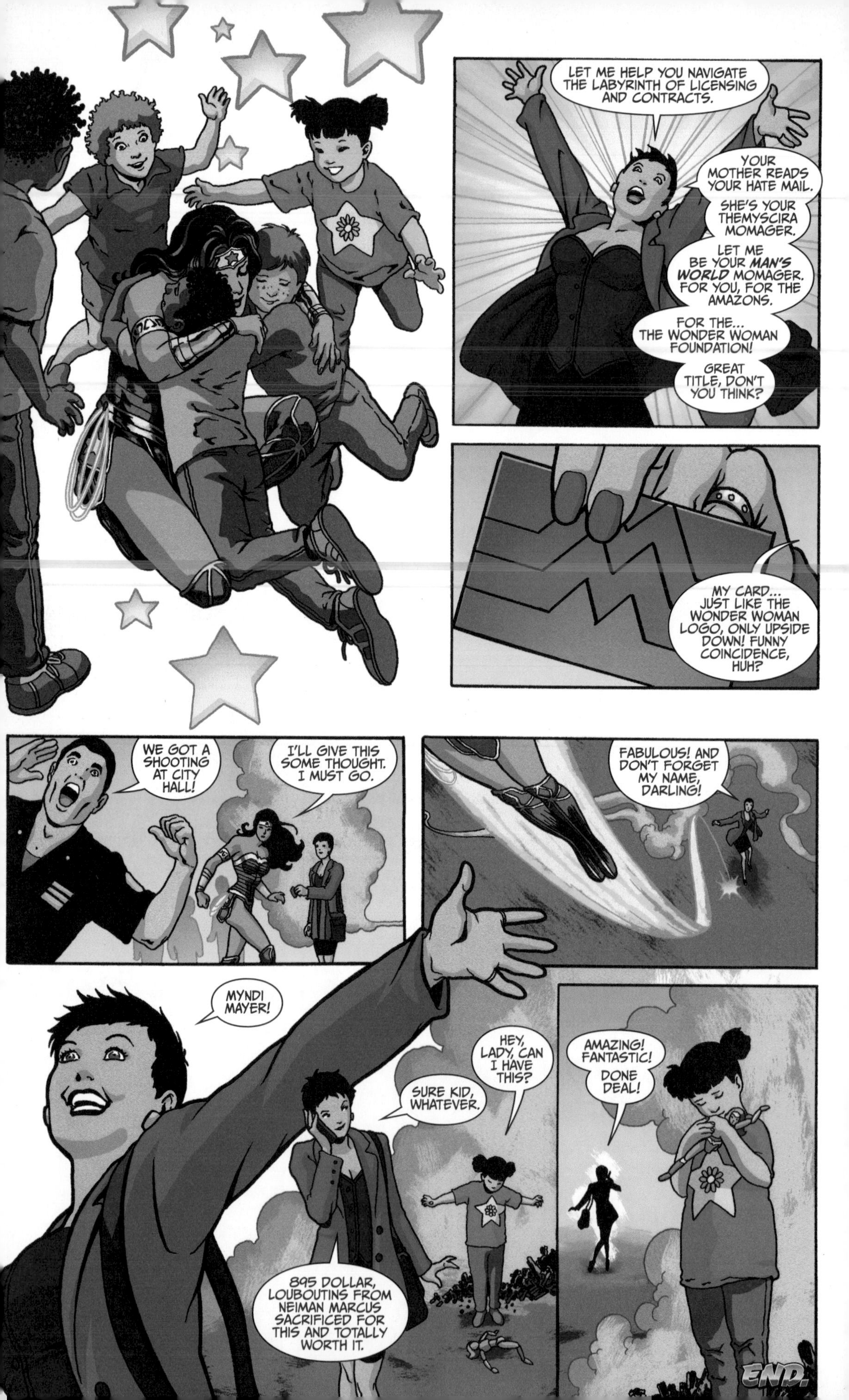
LET ME HELP YOU NAVIGATE THE LABYRINTH OF LICENSING AND CONTRACTS.
YOUR MOTHER READS YOUR HATE MAIL.
SHE'S YOUR THEMYSCIRA MOMAGER.
LET ME BE YOUR *MAN'S WORLD* MOMAGER. FOR YOU, FOR THE AMAZONS.
FOR THE... THE WONDER WOMAN FOUNDATION!
GREAT TITLE, DON'T YOU THINK?
MY CARD... JUST LIKE THE WONDER WOMAN LOGO, ONLY UPSIDE DOWN! FUNNY COINCIDENCE, HUH?
WE GOT A SHOOTING AT CITY HALL!
I'LL GIVE THIS SOME THOUGHT. I MUST GO.
FABULOUS! AND DON'T FORGET MY NAME, DARLING!
MYNDI MAYER!
SURE KID, WHATEVER.
HEY, LADY, CAN I HAVE THIS?
895 DOLLAR, LOUBOUTINS FROM NEIMAN MARCUS SACRIFICED FOR THIS AND TOTALLY WORTH IT.
AMAZING! FANTASTIC!
DONE DEAL!
END.

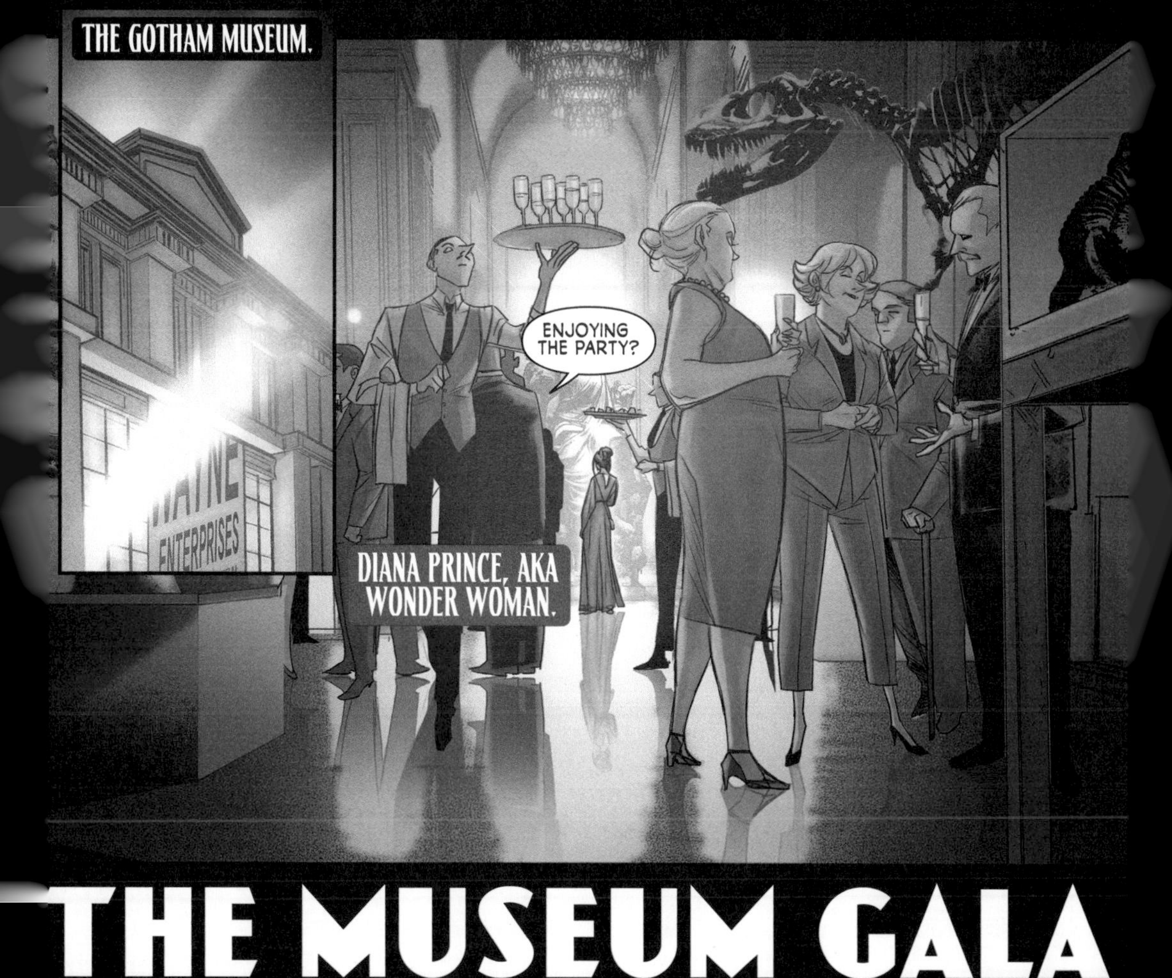
THE GOTHAM MUSEUM.
ENTERPRISES
ENJOYING THE PARTY?
DIANA PRINCE, AKA WONDER WOMAN.

THE MUSEUM GALA

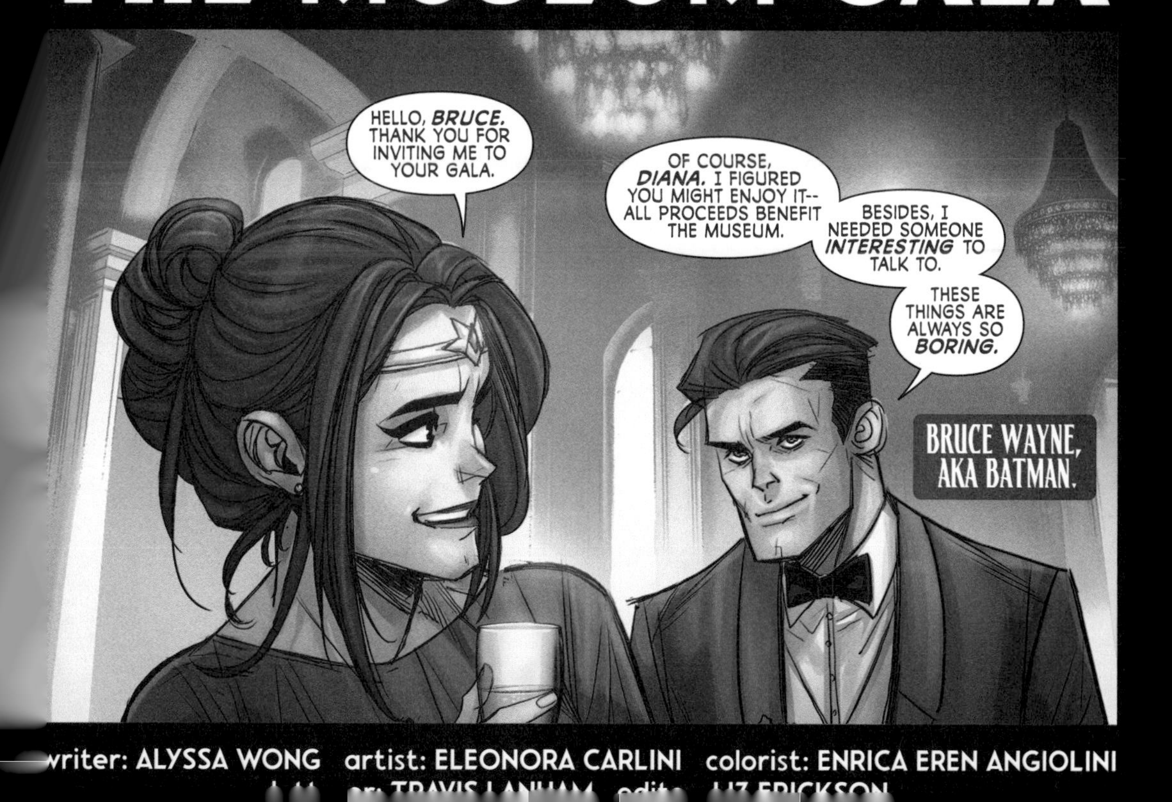
HELLO, *BRUCE.* THANK YOU FOR INVITING ME TO YOUR GALA.
OF COURSE, *DIANA.* I FIGURED YOU MIGHT ENJOY IT-- ALL PROCEEDS BENEFIT THE MUSEUM.
BESIDES, I NEEDED SOMEONE *INTERESTING* TO TALK TO.
THESE THINGS ARE ALWAYS SO *BORING.*
BRUCE WAYNE, AKA BATMAN.

writer: ALYSSA WONG artist: ELEONORA CARLINI colorist: ENRICA EREN ANGIOLINI

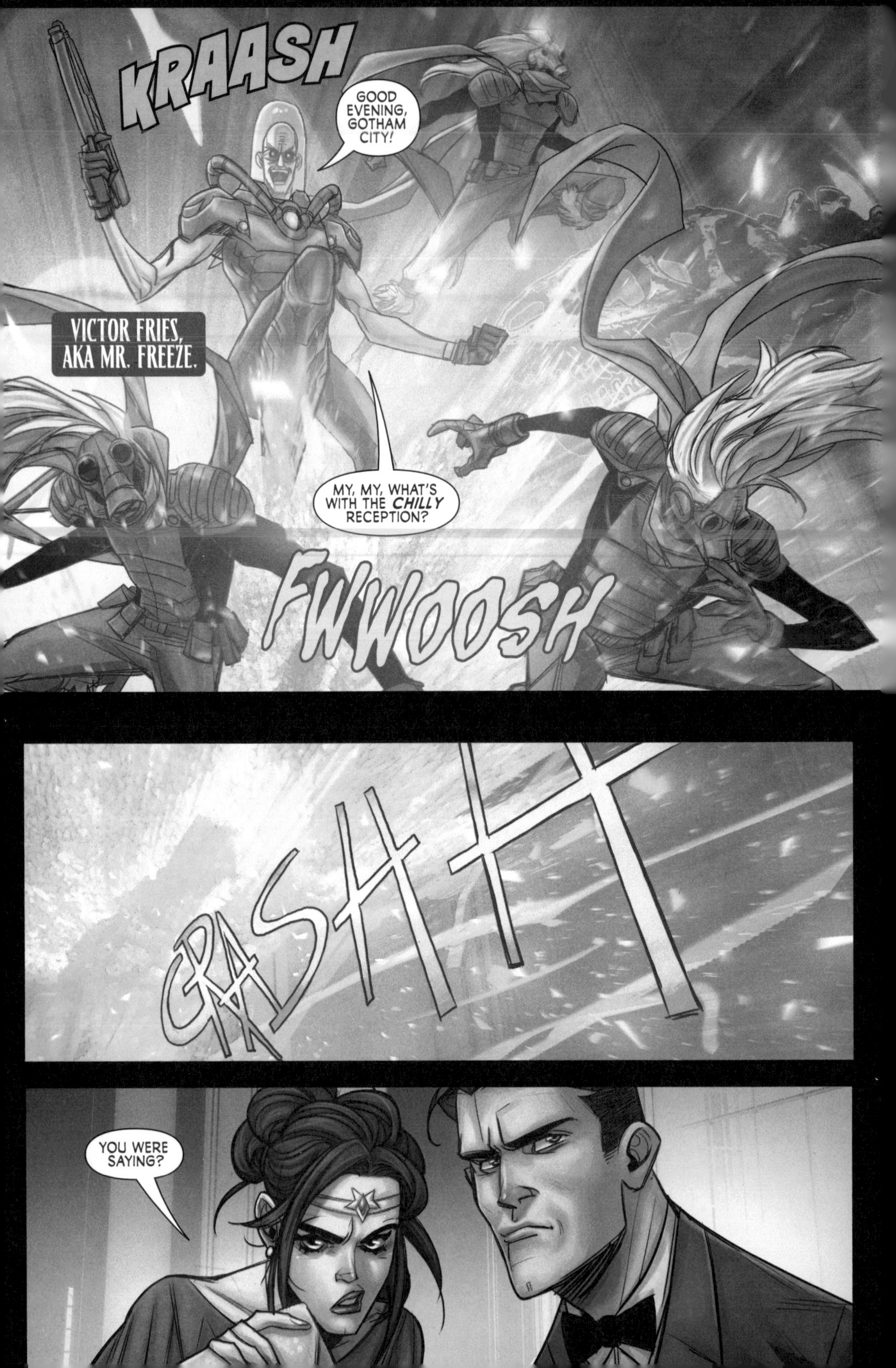
KRAASH
GOOD EVENING, GOTHAM CITY!
VICTOR FRIES, AKA MR. FREEZE.
MY, MY, WHAT'S WITH THE CHILLY RECEPTION?
FWWOOSH
CRASHHH
YOU WERE SAYING?

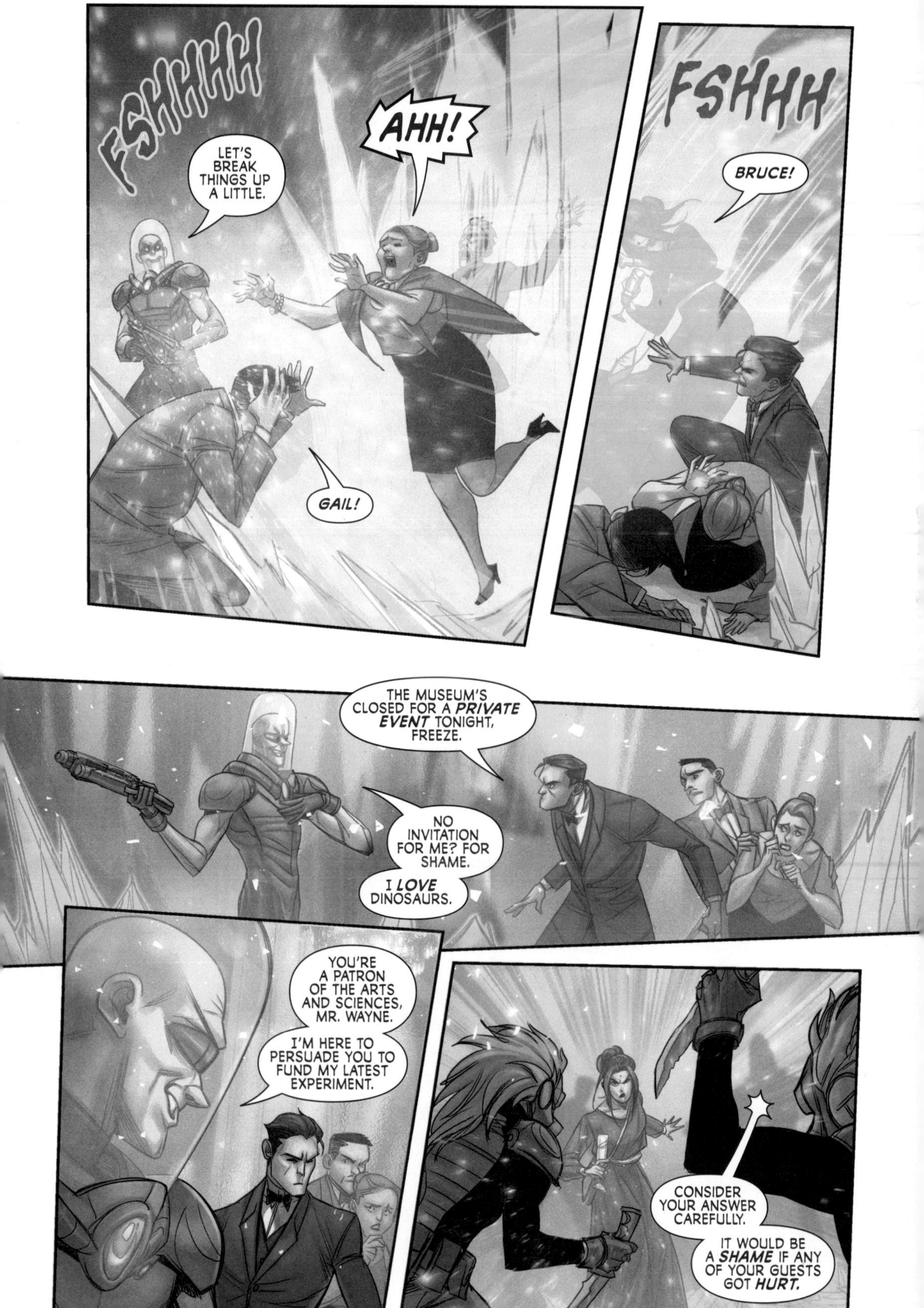
FSHHHH
LET'S BREAK THINGS UP A LITTLE.
AHH!
GAIL!
FSHHH
BRUCE!
THE MUSEUM'S CLOSED FOR A PRIVATE EVENT TONIGHT, FREEZE.
NO INVITATION FOR ME? FOR SHAME.
I LOVE DINOSAURS.
YOU'RE A PATRON OF THE ARTS AND SCIENCES, MR. WAYNE.
I'M HERE TO PERSUADE YOU TO FUND MY LATEST EXPERIMENT.
CONSIDER YOUR ANSWER CAREFULLY.
IT WOULD BE A SHAME IF ANY OF YOUR GUESTS GOT HURT.

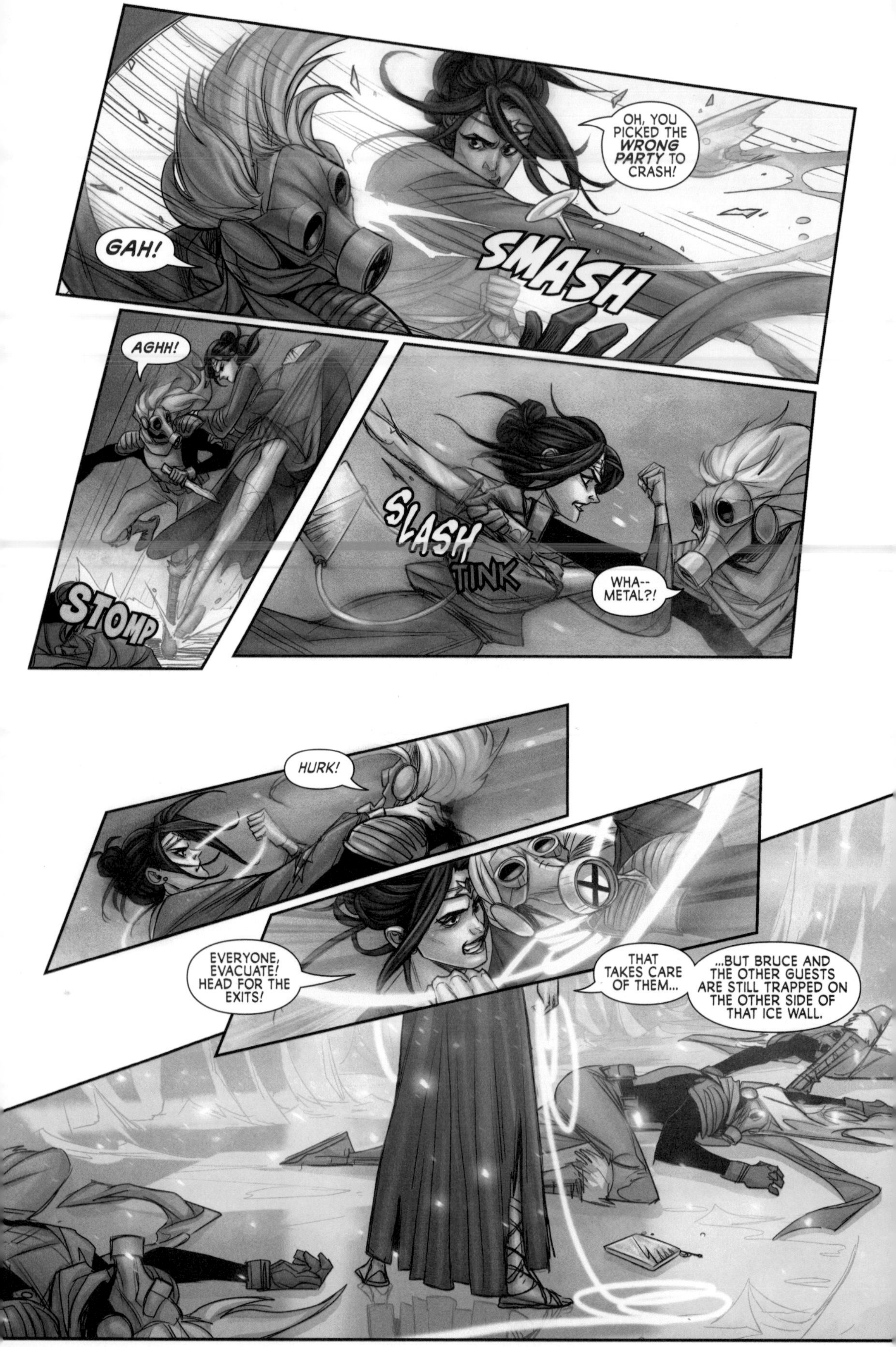
OH, YOU PICKED THE WRONG PARTY TO CRASH!
GAH!
SMASH
AGHH!
STOMP
SLASH
TINK
WHA-- METAL?!
HURK!
EVERYONE, EVACUATE! HEAD FOR THE EXITS!
THAT TAKES CARE OF THEM...
...BUT BRUCE AND THE OTHER GUESTS ARE STILL TRAPPED ON THE OTHER SIDE OF THAT ICE WALL.

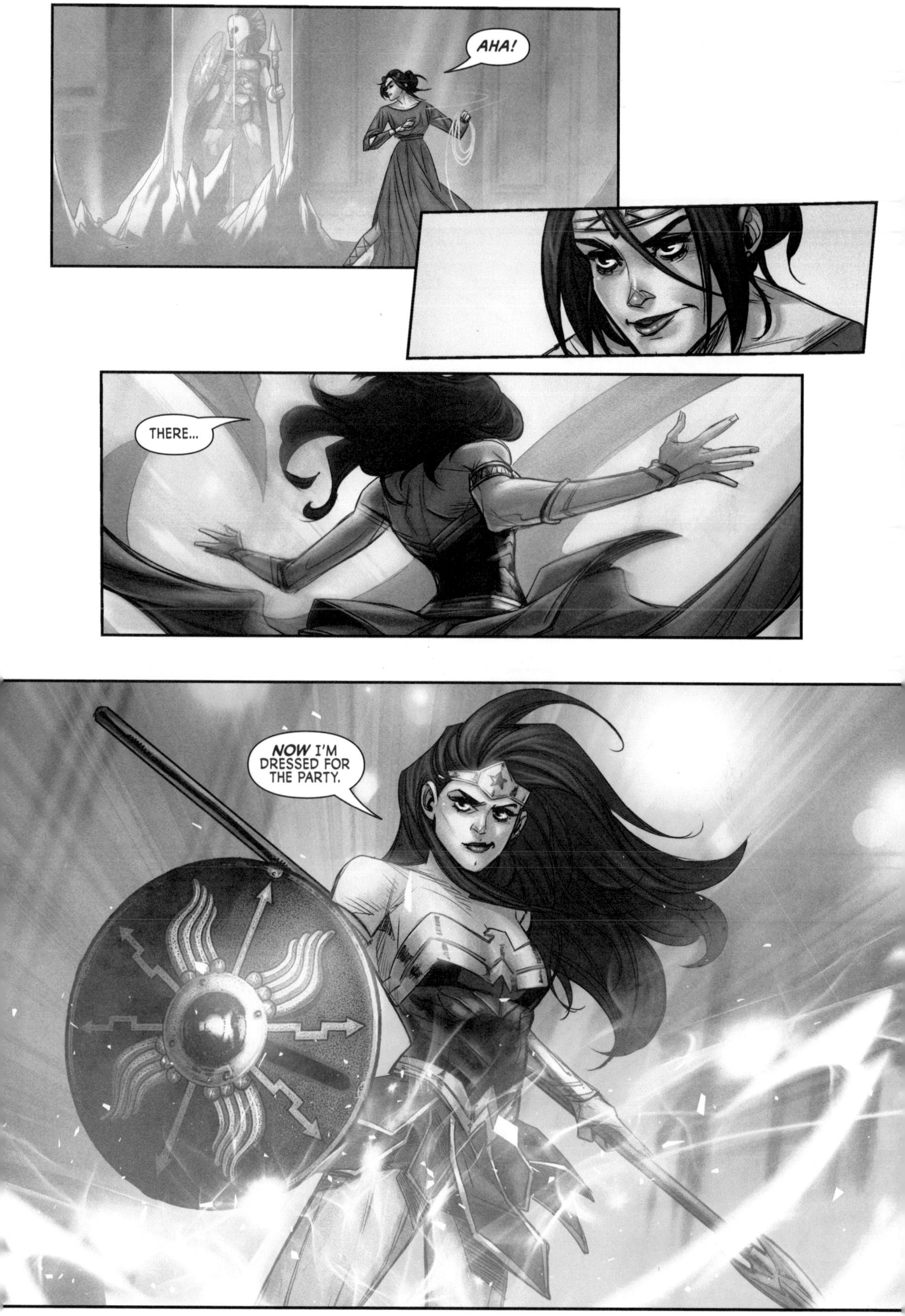
AHA!
THERE...
NOW I'M DRESSED FOR THE PARTY.

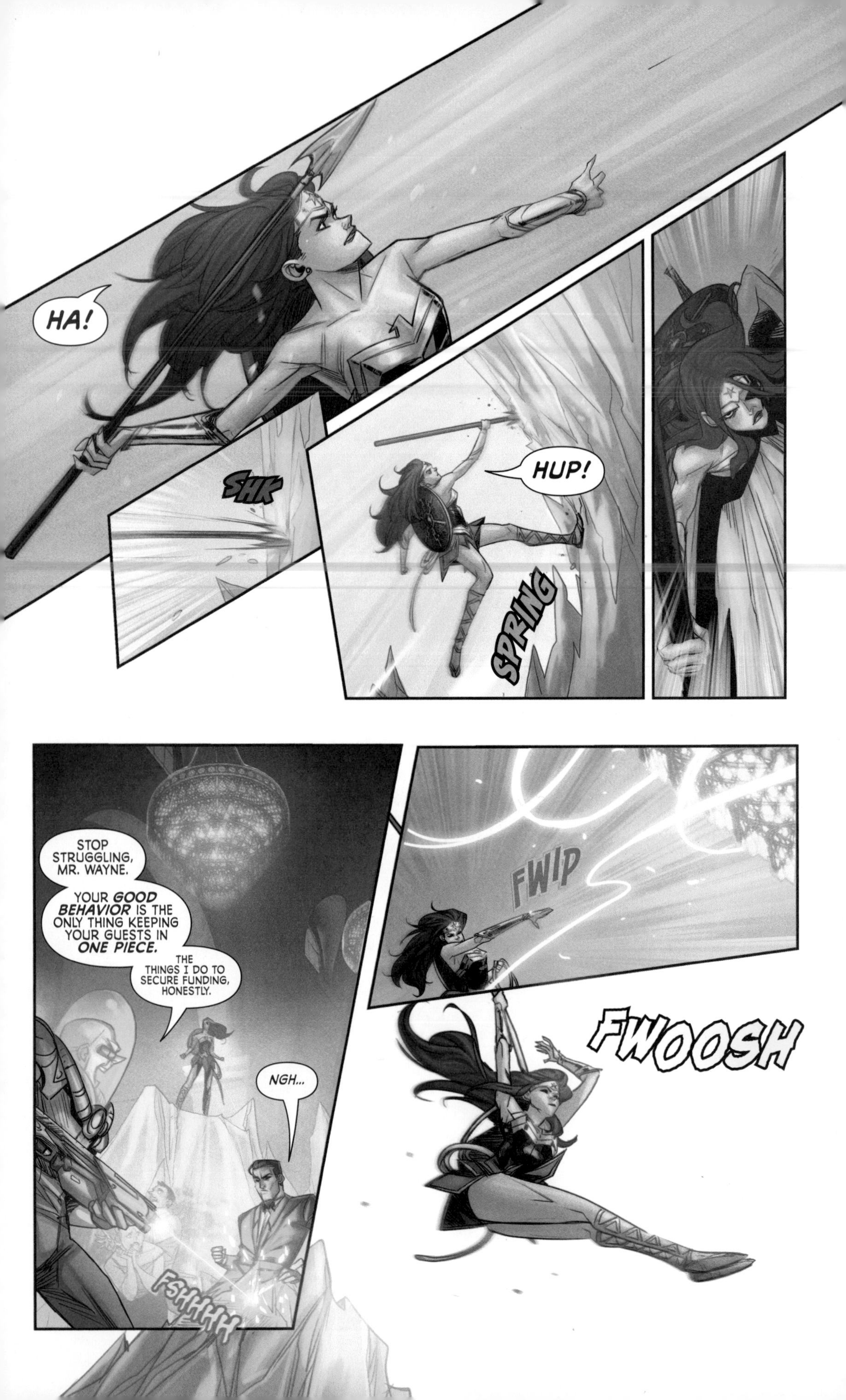
HA!
SHK
HUP!
SPRING
STOP STRUGGLING, MR. WAYNE.
YOUR GOOD BEHAVIOR IS THE ONLY THING KEEPING YOUR GUESTS IN ONE PIECE.
THE THINGS I DO TO SECURE FUNDING, HONESTLY.
NGH...
FSHHHH
FWIP
FWOOSH

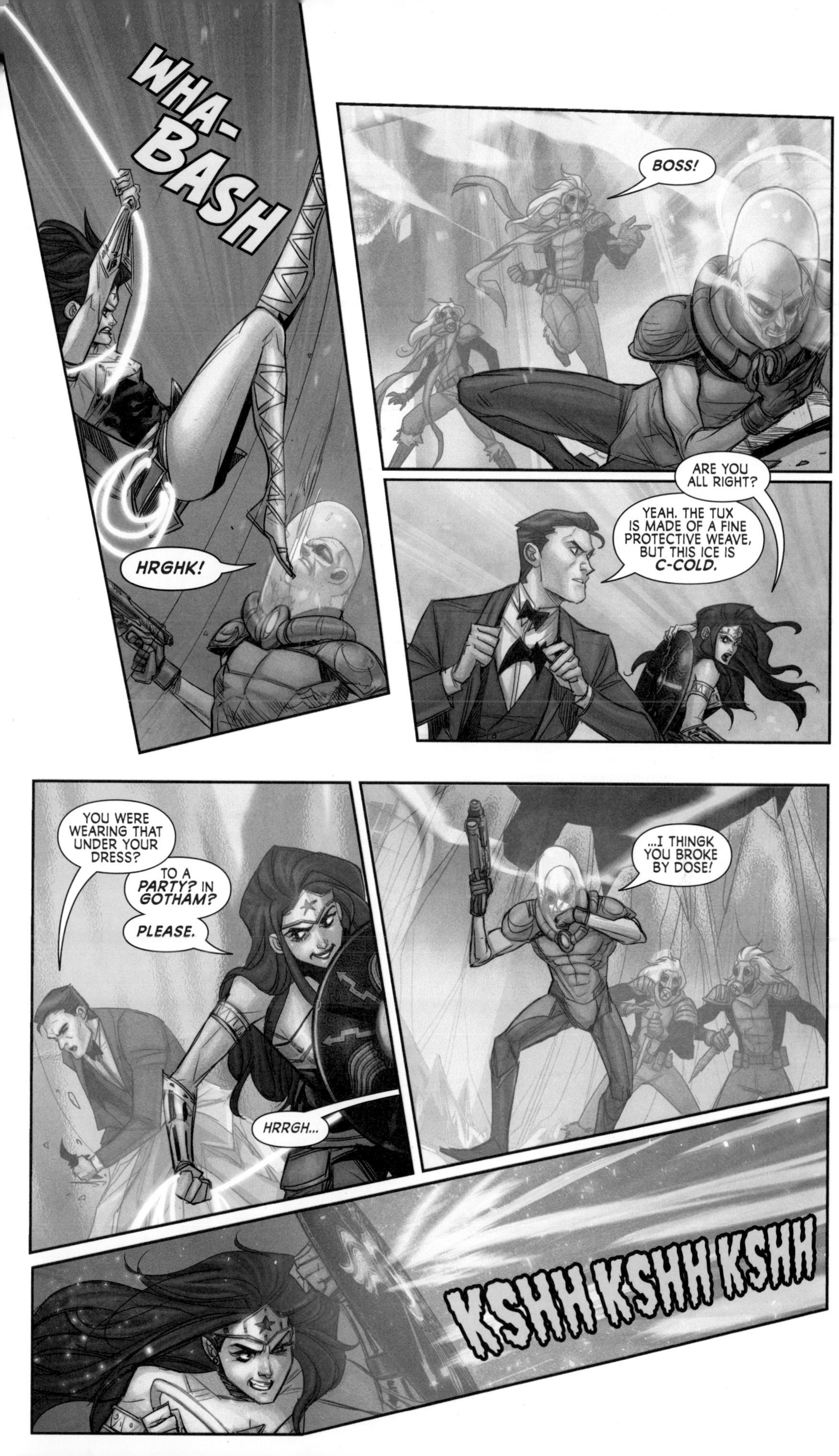
WHA-BASH
HRGHK!
BOSS!
ARE YOU ALL RIGHT?
YEAH. THE TUX IS MADE OF A FINE PROTECTIVE WEAVE, BUT THIS ICE IS C-COLD.
YOU WERE WEARING THAT UNDER YOUR DRESS?
TO A PARTY? IN GOTHAM?
PLEASE.
HRRGH...
...I THINGK YOU BROKE BY DOSE!
KSHH KSHH KSHH

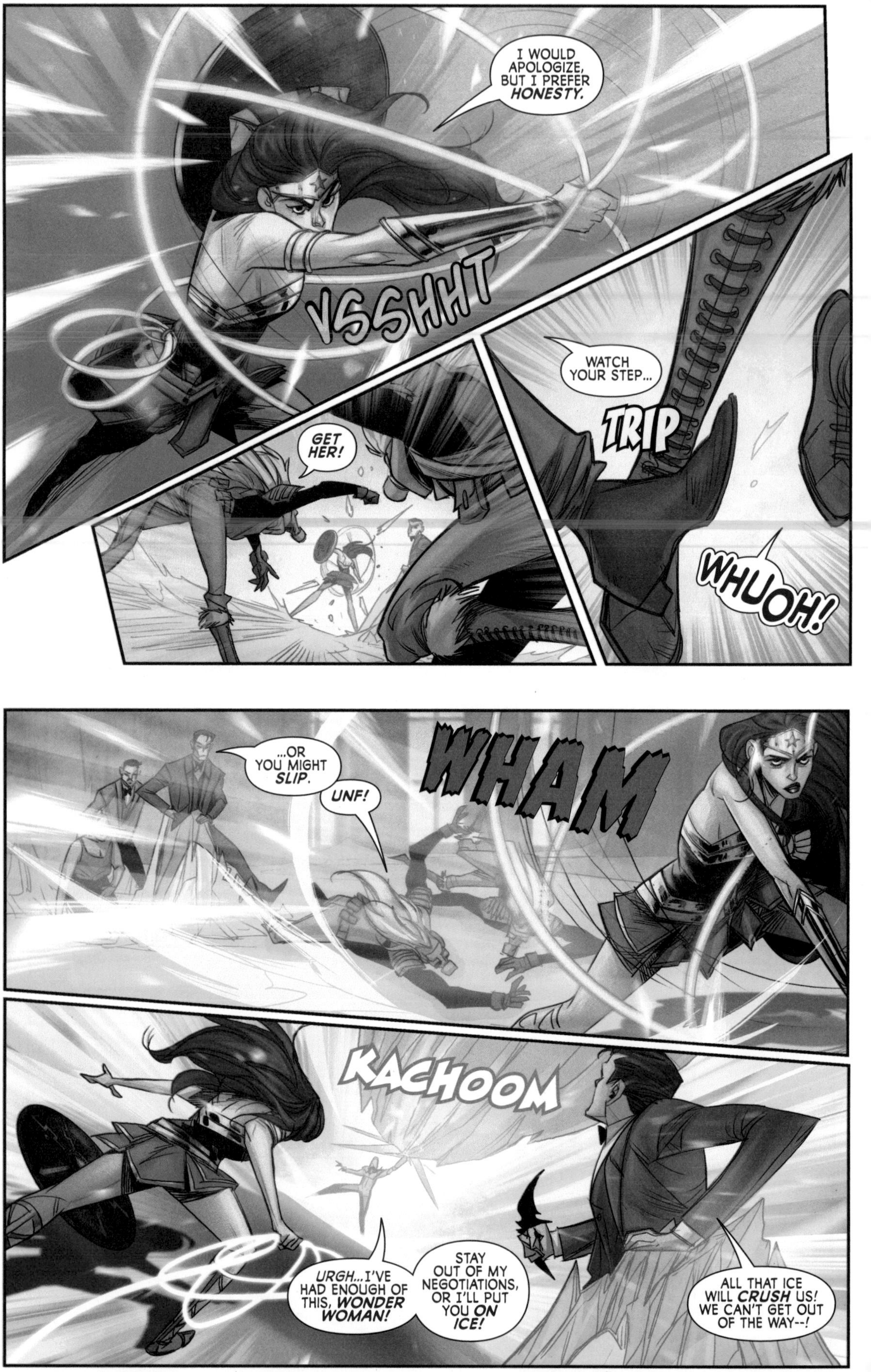
I WOULD APOLOGIZE, BUT I PREFER HONESTY.
VSSHHT
GET HER!
WATCH YOUR STEP...
TRIP
WHUOH!
...OR YOU MIGHT SLIP.
UNF!
WHAM
KACHOOM
URGH... I'VE HAD ENOUGH OF THIS, WONDER WOMAN!
STAY OUT OF MY NEGOTIATIONS, OR I'LL PUT YOU ON ICE!
ALL THAT ICE WILL CRUSH US! WE CAN'T GET OUT OF THE WAY--!

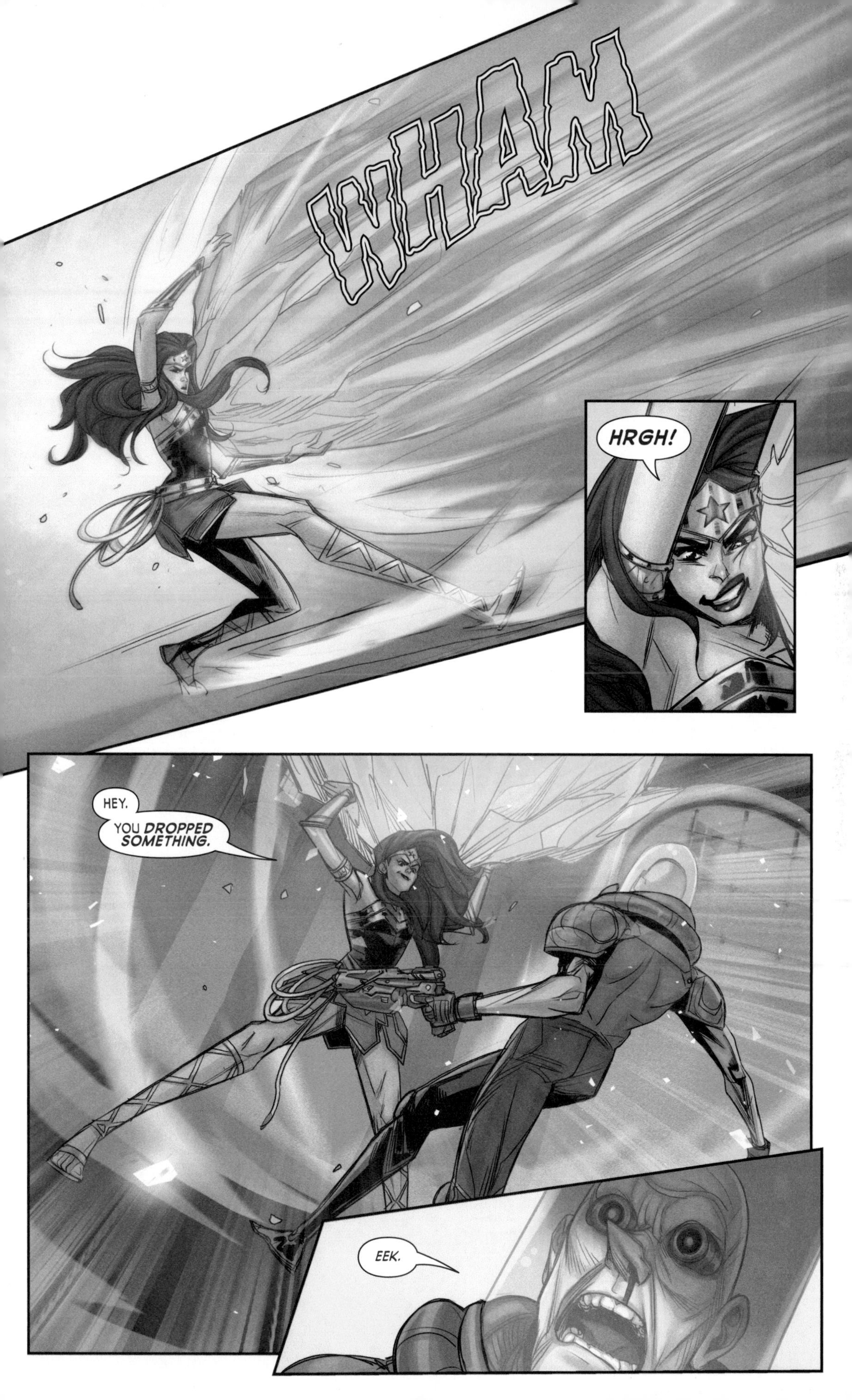
WHAM
HRGH!
HEY.
YOU DROPPED SOMETHING.
EEK.

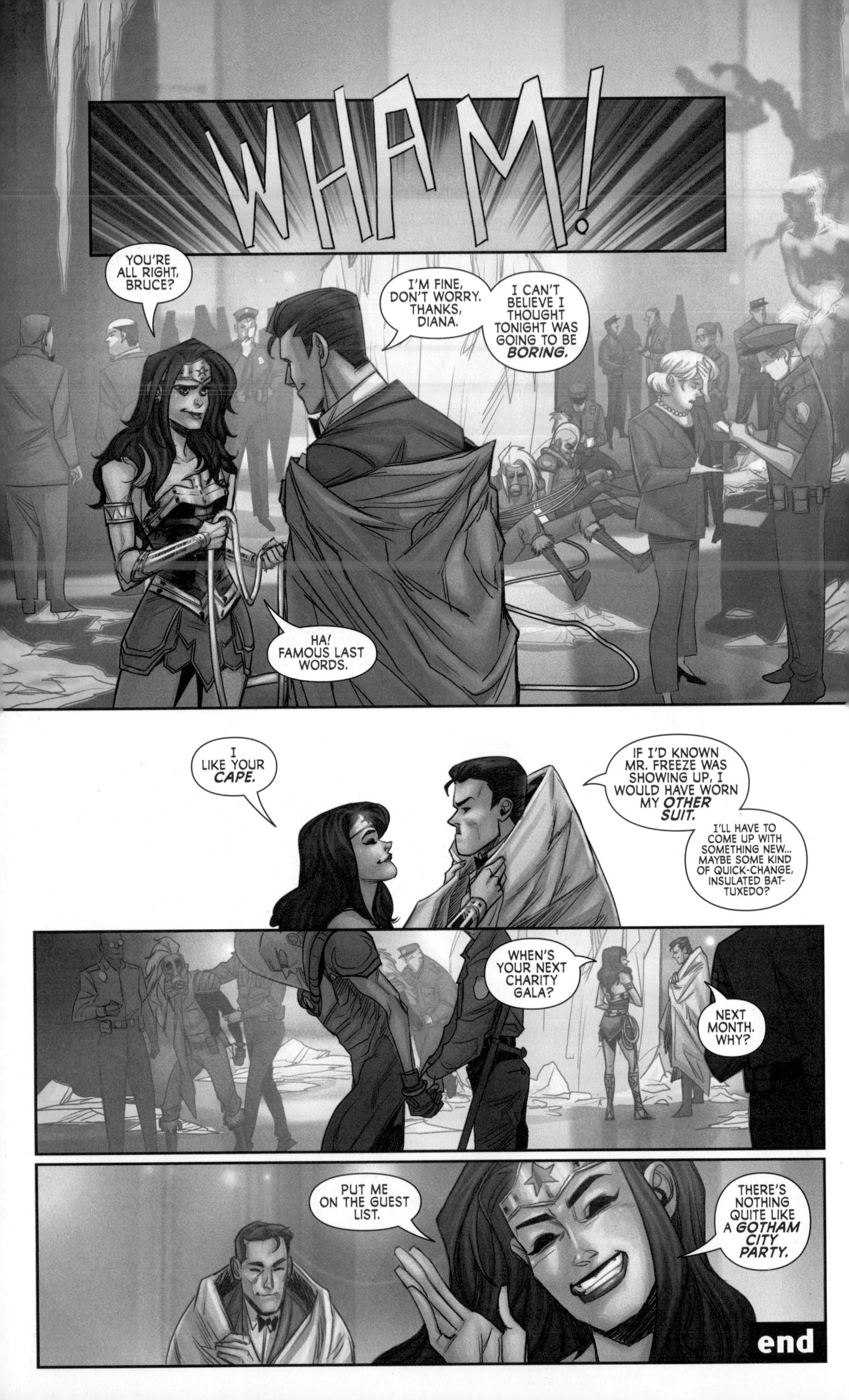
WHAM!
YOU'RE ALL RIGHT, BRUCE?
I'M FINE, DON'T WORRY. THANKS, DIANA.
I CAN'T BELIEVE I THOUGHT TONIGHT WAS GOING TO BE BORING.
HA! FAMOUS LAST WORDS.
I LIKE YOUR CAPE.
IF I'D KNOWN MR. FREEZE WAS SHOWING UP, I WOULD HAVE WORN MY OTHER SUIT.
I'LL HAVE TO COME UP WITH SOMETHING NEW... MAYBE SOME KIND OF QUICK-CHANGE, INSULATED BAT-TUXEDO?
WHEN'S YOUR NEXT CHARITY GALA?
NEXT MONTH. WHY?
PUT ME ON THE GUEST LIST.
THERE'S NOTHING QUITE LIKE A GOTHAM CITY PARTY.
end

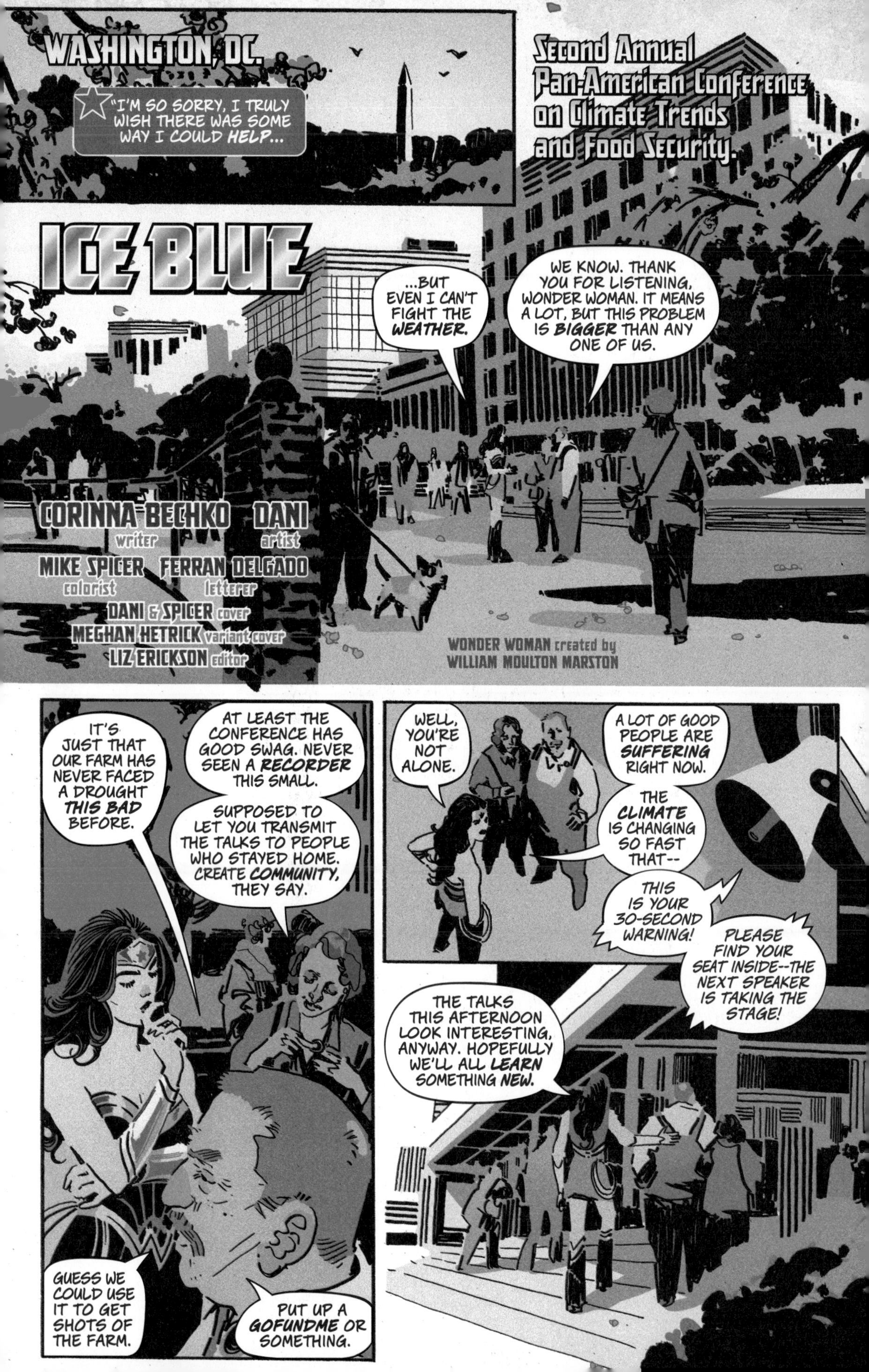
WASHINGTON, DC.
"I'M SO SORRY, I TRULY WISH THERE WAS SOME WAY I COULD HELP...
Second Annual Pan-American Conference on Climate Trends and Food Security.
ICE BLUE
...BUT EVEN I CAN'T FIGHT THE WEATHER.
WE KNOW. THANK YOU FOR LISTENING, WONDER WOMAN. IT MEANS A LOT, BUT THIS PROBLEM IS BIGGER THAN ANY ONE OF US.
CORINNA BECHKO writer DANI artist
MIKE SPICER colorist FERRAN DELGADO letterer
DANI & SPICER cover
MEGHAN HETRICK variant cover
LIZ ERICKSON editor
WONDER WOMAN created by WILLIAM MOULTON MARSTON
IT'S JUST THAT OUR FARM HAS NEVER FACED A DROUGHT THIS BAD BEFORE.
AT LEAST THE CONFERENCE HAS GOOD SWAG. NEVER SEEN A RECORDER THIS SMALL.
SUPPOSED TO LET YOU TRANSMIT THE TALKS TO PEOPLE WHO STAYED HOME. CREATE COMMUNITY, THEY SAY.
GUESS WE COULD USE IT TO GET SHOTS OF THE FARM.
PUT UP A GOFUNDME OR SOMETHING.
WELL, YOU'RE NOT ALONE.
A LOT OF GOOD PEOPLE ARE SUFFERING RIGHT NOW.
THE CLIMATE IS CHANGING SO FAST THAT--
THIS IS YOUR 30-SECOND WARNING!
PLEASE FIND YOUR SEAT INSIDE--THE NEXT SPEAKER IS TAKING THE STAGE!
THE TALKS THIS AFTERNOON LOOK INTERESTING, ANYWAY. HOPEFULLY WE'LL ALL LEARN SOMETHING NEW.

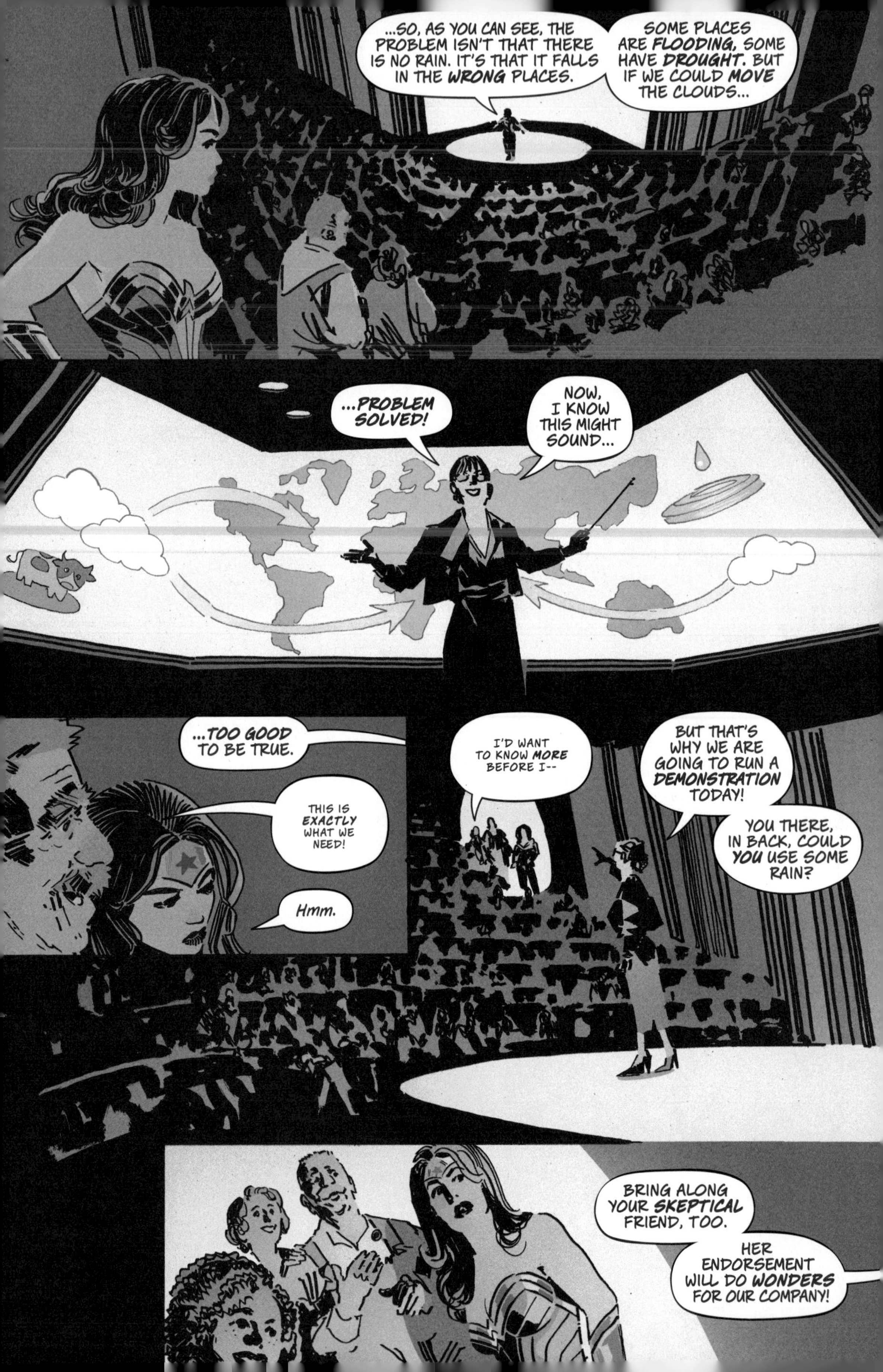
...SO, AS YOU CAN SEE, THE PROBLEM ISN'T THAT THERE IS NO RAIN. IT'S THAT IT FALLS IN THE WRONG PLACES.
SOME PLACES ARE FLOODING, SOME HAVE DROUGHT. BUT IF WE COULD MOVE THE CLOUDS...
...PROBLEM SOLVED!
NOW, I KNOW THIS MIGHT SOUND...
...TOO GOOD TO BE TRUE.
THIS IS EXACTLY WHAT WE NEED!
Hmm.
I'D WANT TO KNOW MORE BEFORE I--
BUT THAT'S WHY WE ARE GOING TO RUN A DEMONSTRATION TODAY!
YOU THERE, IN BACK, COULD YOU USE SOME RAIN?
BRING ALONG YOUR SKEPTICAL FRIEND, TOO.
HER ENDORSEMENT WILL DO WONDERS FOR OUR COMPANY!

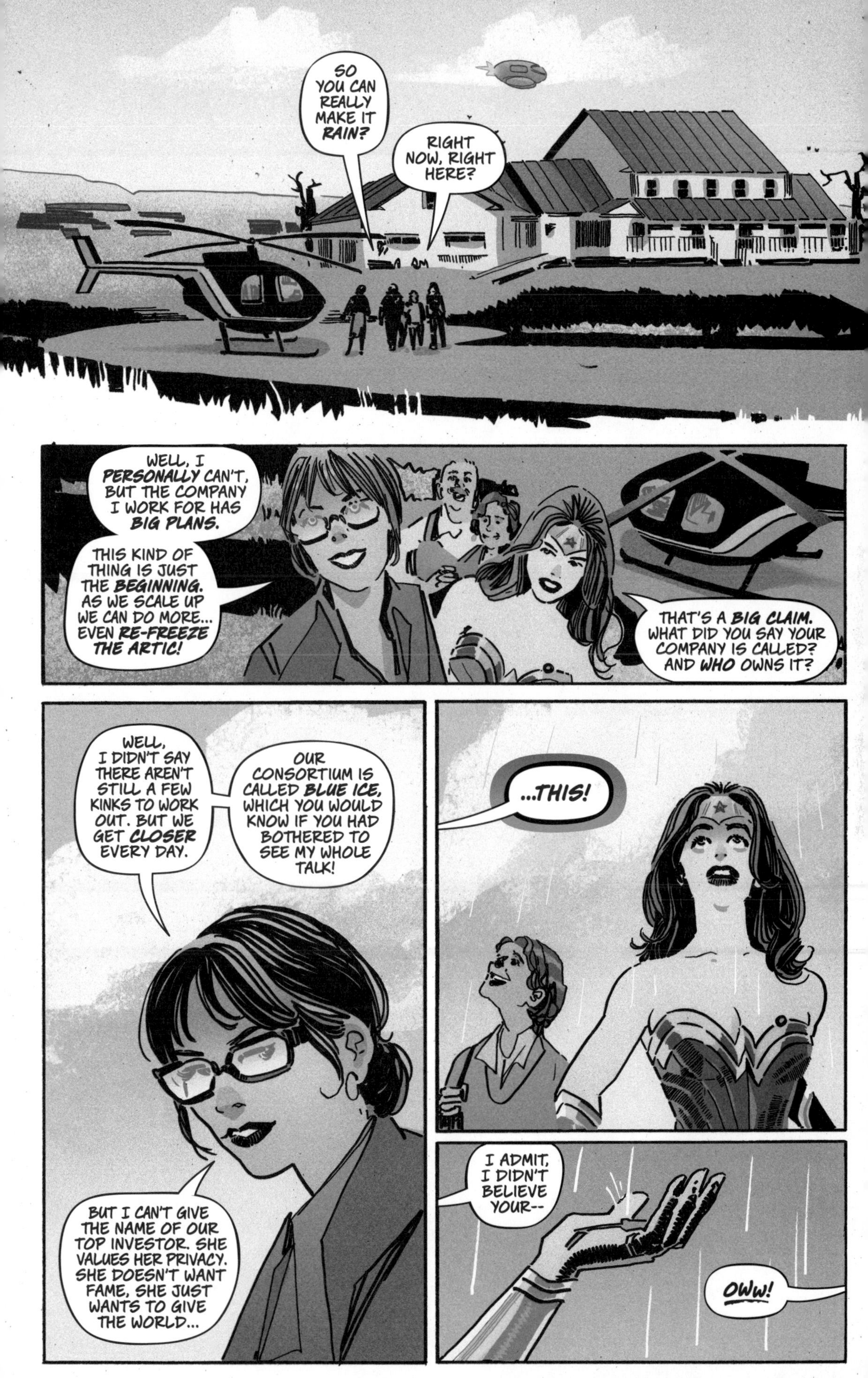

SO YOU CAN REALLY MAKE IT RAIN?
RIGHT NOW, RIGHT HERE?
WELL, I PERSONALLY CAN'T, BUT THE COMPANY I WORK FOR HAS BIG PLANS.
THIS KIND OF THING IS JUST THE BEGINNING. AS WE SCALE UP WE CAN DO MORE... EVEN RE-FREEZE THE ARTIC!
THAT'S A BIG CLAIM. WHAT DID YOU SAY YOUR COMPANY IS CALLED? AND WHO OWNS IT?
WELL, I DIDN'T SAY THERE AREN'T STILL A FEW KINKS TO WORK OUT. BUT WE GET CLOSER EVERY DAY.
OUR CONSORTIUM IS CALLED BLUE ICE, WHICH YOU WOULD KNOW IF YOU HAD BOTHERED TO SEE MY WHOLE TALK!
BUT I CAN'T GIVE THE NAME OF OUR TOP INVESTOR. SHE VALUES HER PRIVACY. SHE DOESN'T WANT FAME, SHE JUST WANTS TO GIVE THE WORLD...
...THIS!
I ADMIT, I DIDN'T BELIEVE YOUR--
OWW!

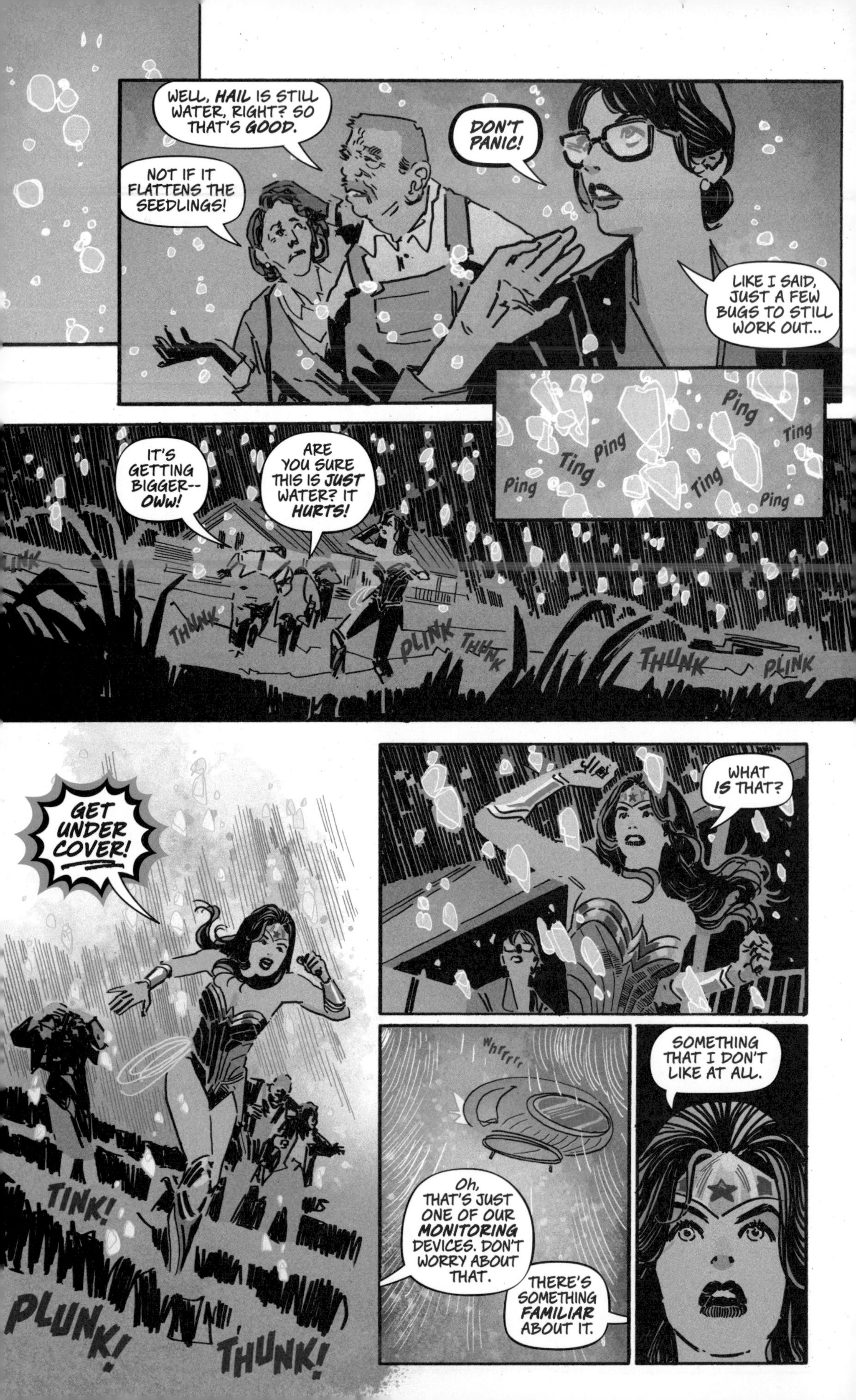
WELL, HAIL IS STILL WATER, RIGHT? SO THAT'S GOOD.
NOT IF IT FLATTENS THE SEEDLINGS!
DON'T PANIC!
LIKE I SAID, JUST A FEW BUGS TO STILL WORK OUT...
Ping
Ting
Ping
Ting
Ping
Ting
Ping
IT'S GETTING BIGGER-- OWW!
ARE YOU SURE THIS IS JUST WATER? IT HURTS!
THUNK
PLINK
THUNK
THUNK
PLINK
GET UNDER COVER!
TINK!
PLUNK!
THUNK!
WHAT IS THAT?
Whrrrr
Oh, THAT'S JUST ONE OF OUR MONITORING DEVICES. DON'T WORRY ABOUT THAT.
THERE'S SOMETHING FAMILIAR ABOUT IT.
SOMETHING THAT I DON'T LIKE AT ALL.

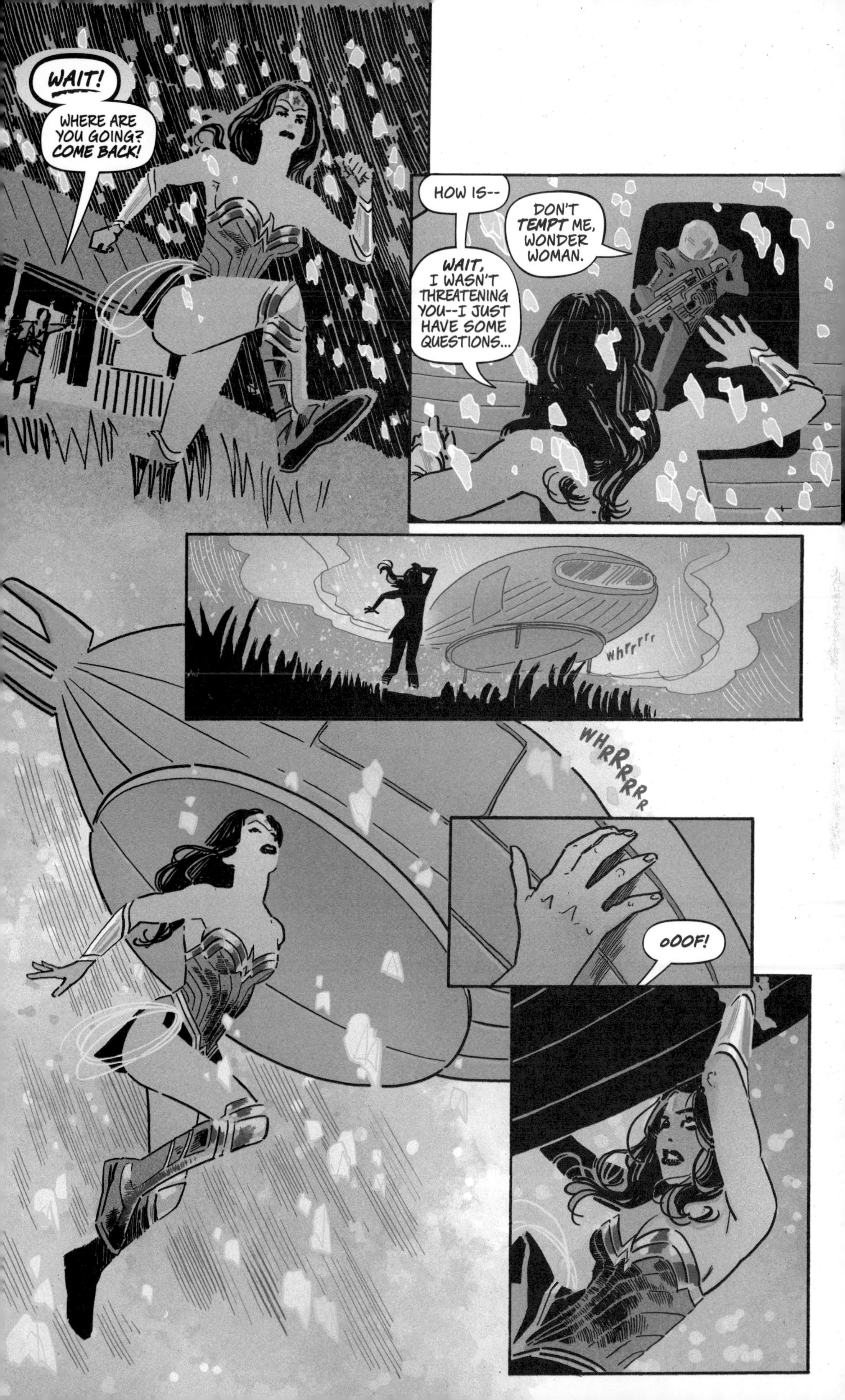
WAIT!
WHERE ARE YOU GOING? COME BACK!
HOW IS--
DON'T TEMPT ME, WONDER WOMAN.
WAIT, I WASN'T THREATENING YOU--I JUST HAVE SOME QUESTIONS...
Whrrrrr
WHRRRRRR
oOOF!

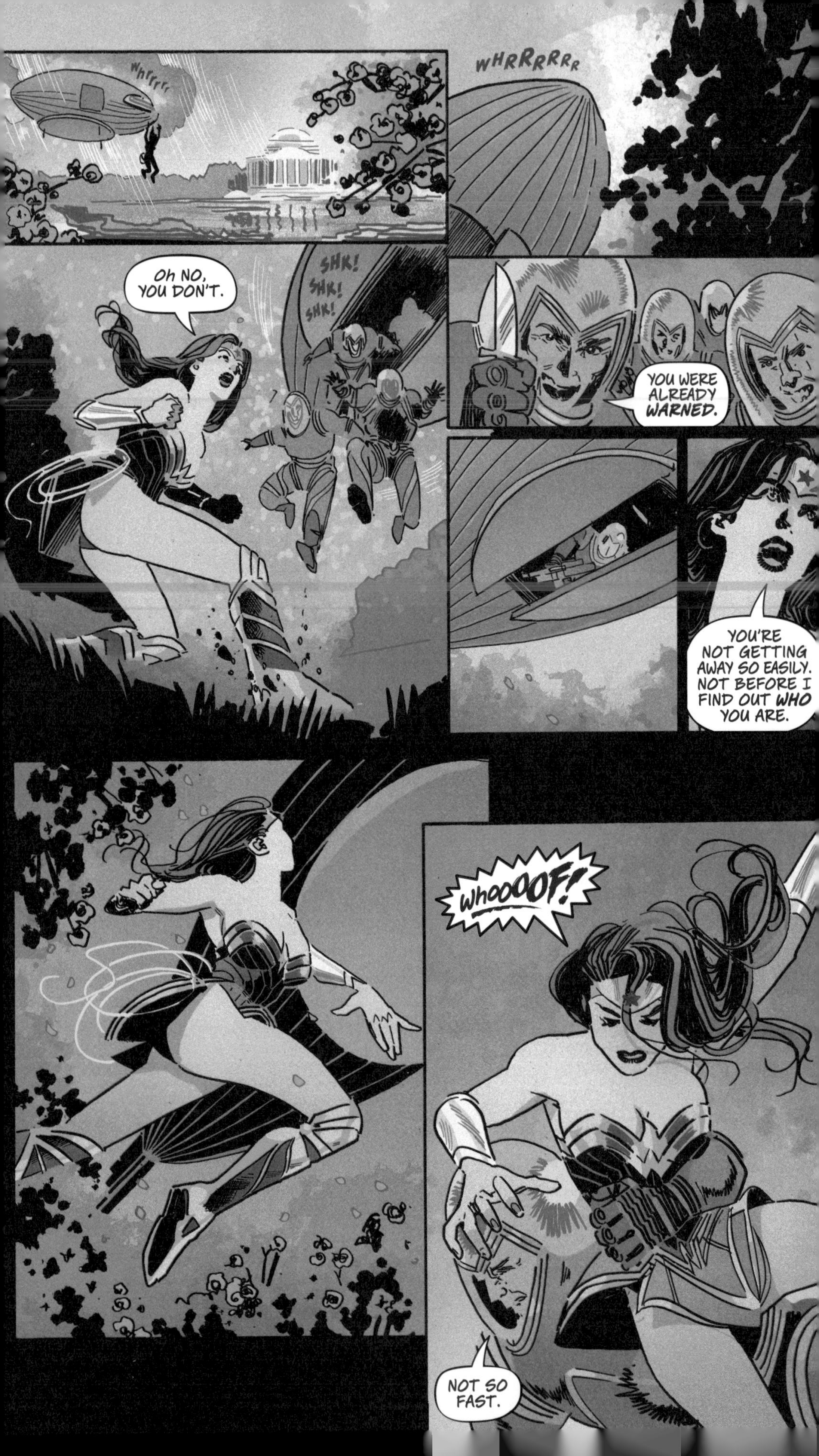
Whrrrr
WHRRRRRR
Oh NO, YOU DON'T.
SHK! SHK! SHK!
YOU WERE ALREADY WARNED.
YOU'RE NOT GETTING AWAY SO EASILY. NOT BEFORE I FIND OUT WHO YOU ARE.
WhoOOOF!
NOT SO FAST.

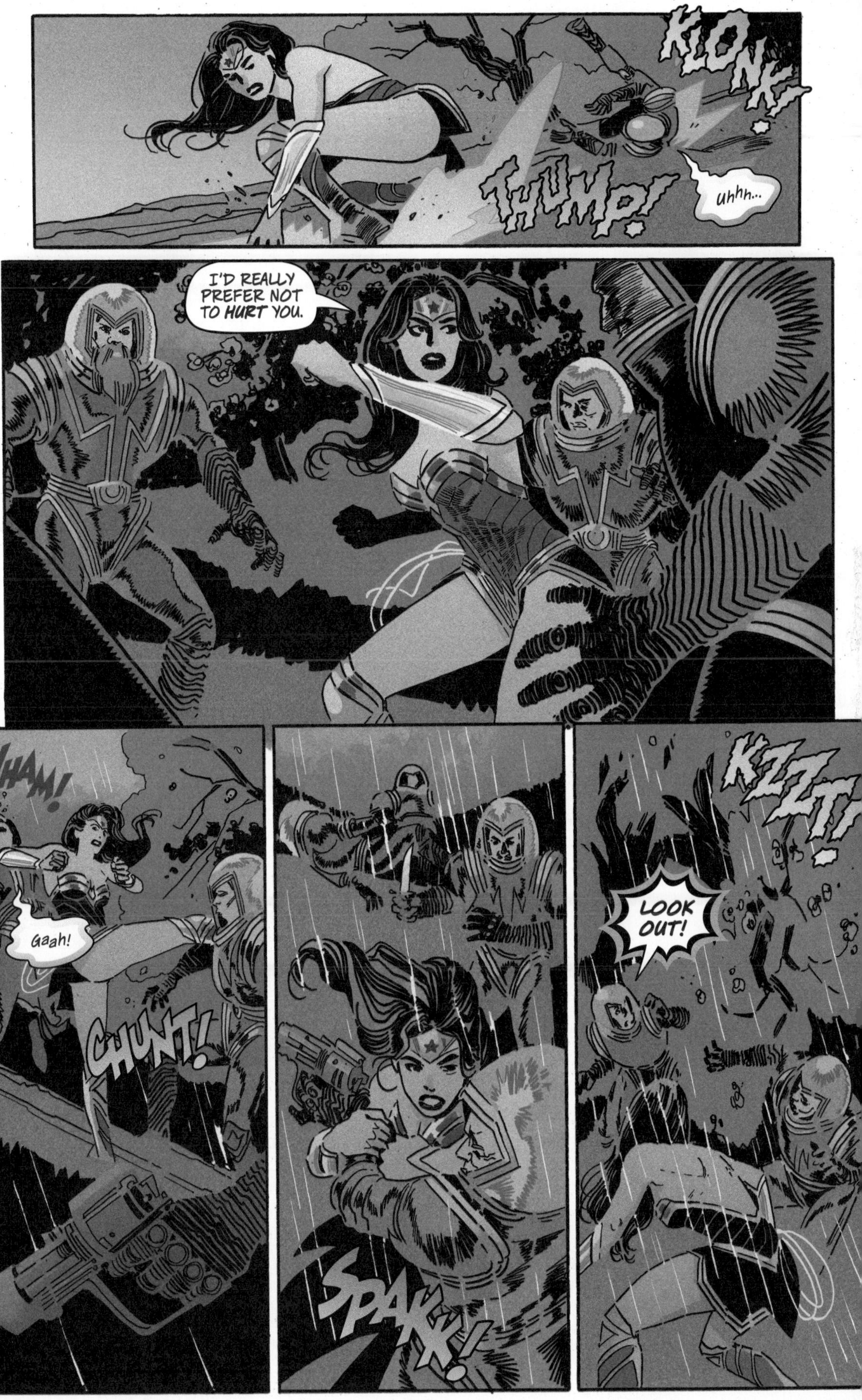
KLONK!
THUMP!
uhhh...
I'D REALLY PREFER NOT TO HURT YOU.
WHAM!
Gaah!
CHUNT!
SPAKK!
KZZT!
LOOK OUT!

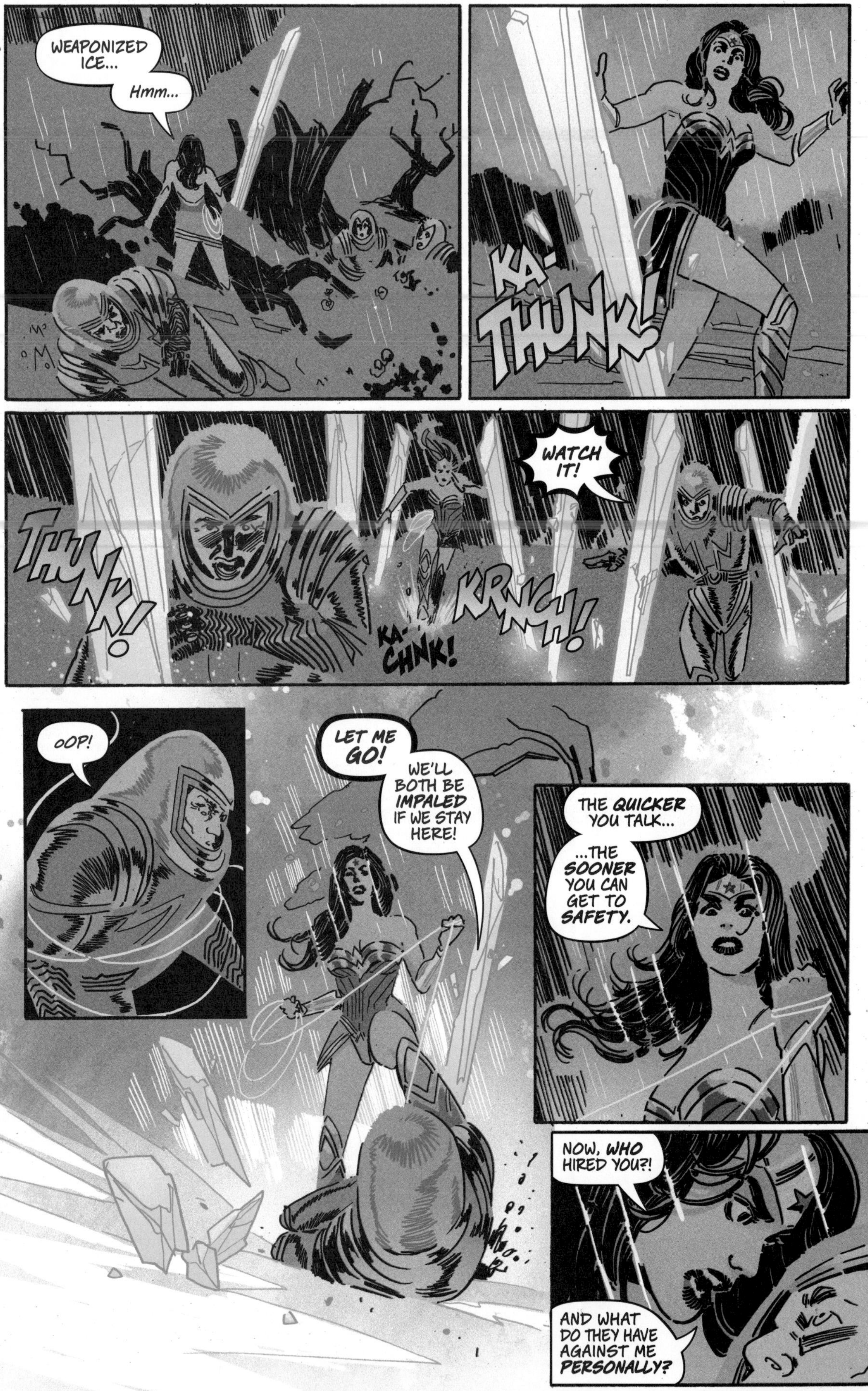

WEAPONIZED ICE...
Hmm...
KA-THUNK!
THUNK!
WATCH IT!
KA-CHNK!
KRNCH!
OOP!
LET ME GO!
WE'LL BOTH BE IMPALED IF WE STAY HERE!
THE QUICKER YOU TALK...
...THE SOONER YOU CAN GET TO SAFETY.
NOW, WHO HIRED YOU?!
AND WHAT DO THEY HAVE AGAINST ME PERSONALLY?

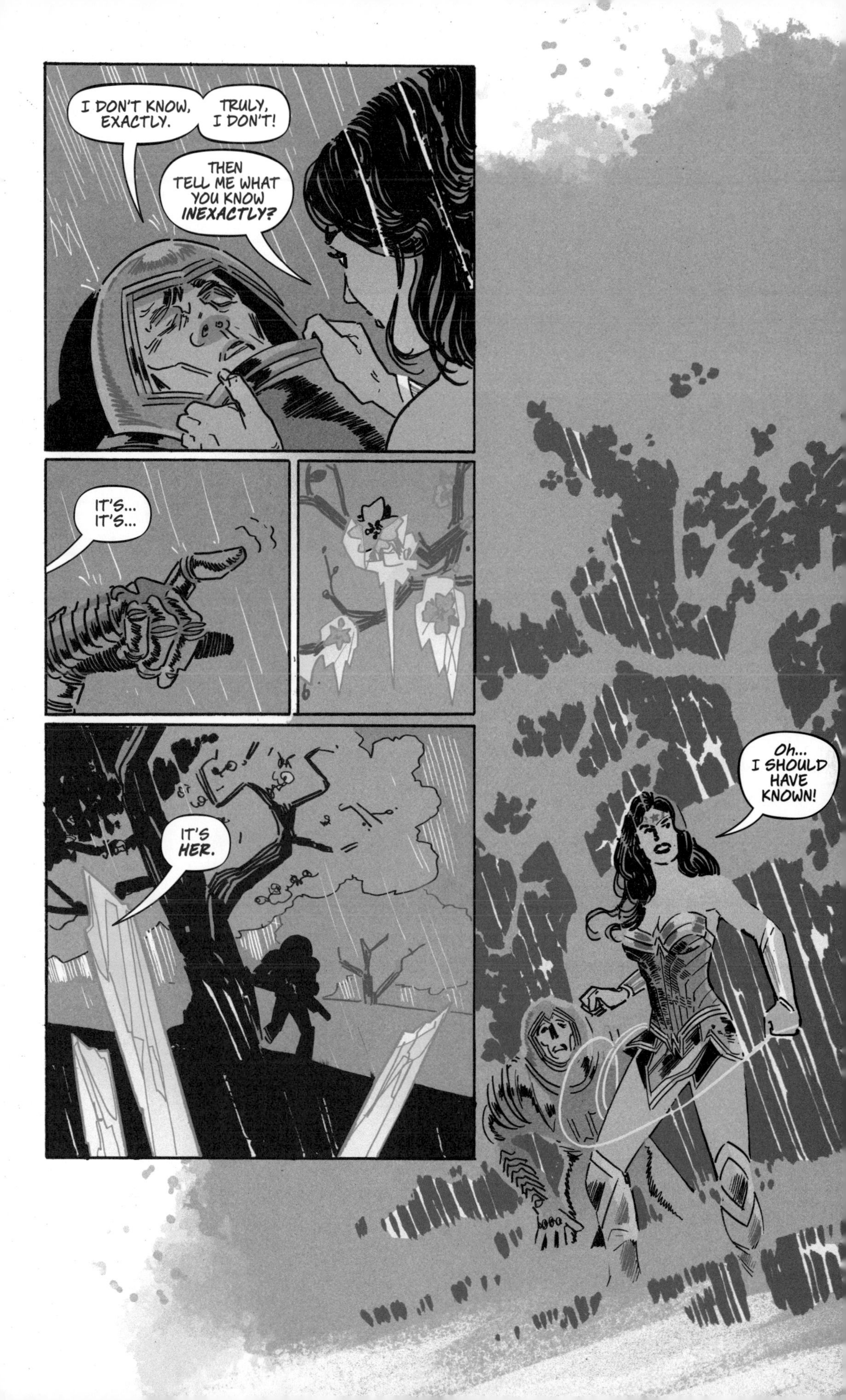
I DON'T KNOW, EXACTLY.
TRULY, I DON'T!
THEN TELL ME WHAT YOU KNOW *INEXACTLY?*
IT'S... IT'S...
IT'S *HER.*
Oh... I SHOULD HAVE KNOWN!

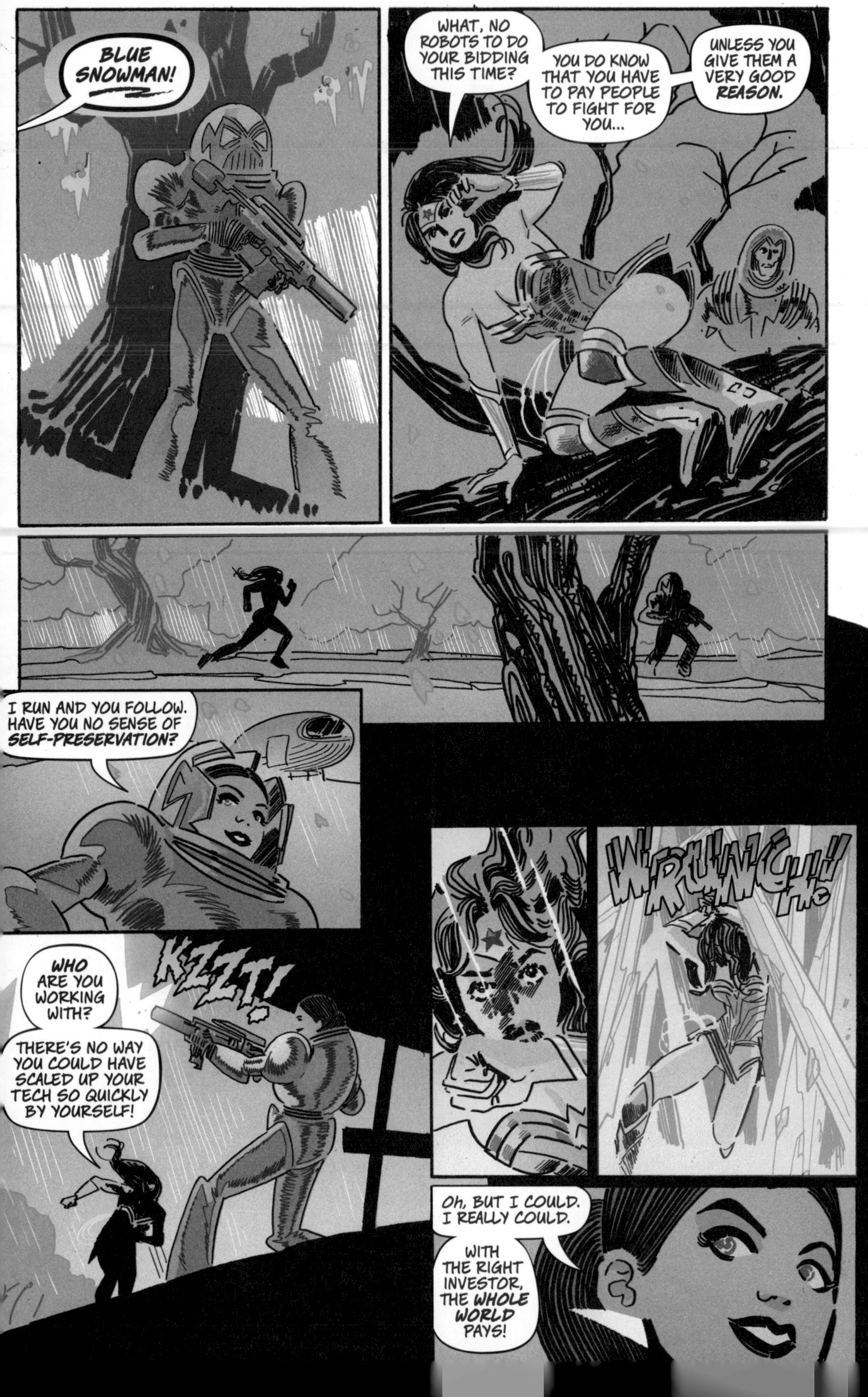
BLUE SNOWMAN!
WHAT, NO ROBOTS TO DO YOUR BIDDING THIS TIME?
YOU DO KNOW THAT YOU HAVE TO PAY PEOPLE TO FIGHT FOR YOU...
UNLESS YOU GIVE THEM A VERY GOOD REASON.
I RUN AND YOU FOLLOW. HAVE YOU NO SENSE OF SELF-PRESERVATION?
WHO ARE YOU WORKING WITH?
THERE'S NO WAY YOU COULD HAVE SCALED UP YOUR TECH SO QUICKLY BY YOURSELF!
KZZT!
WRUNCH!
Oh, BUT I COULD. I REALLY COULD.
WITH THE RIGHT INVESTOR, THE WHOLE WORLD PAYS!

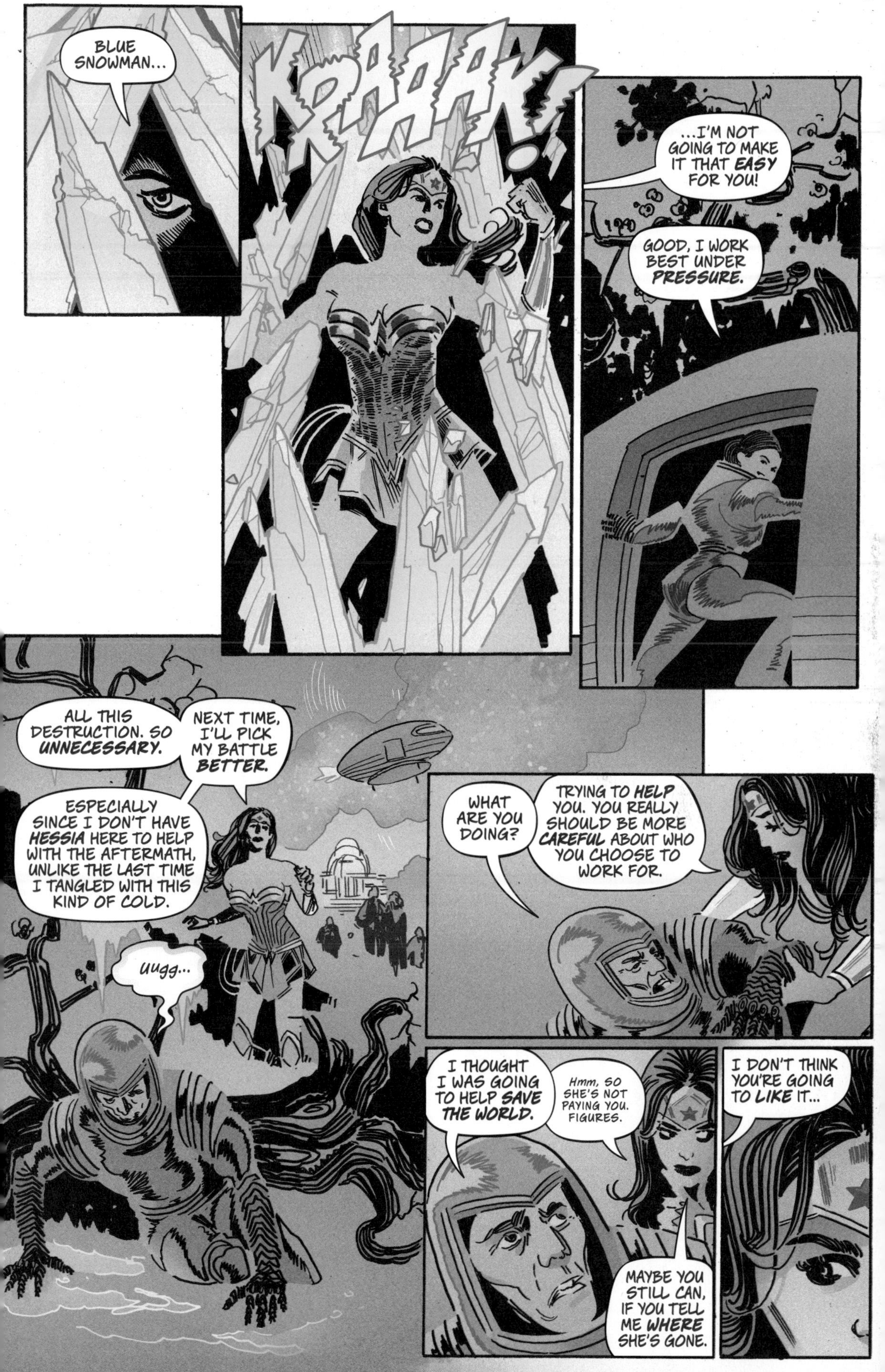
BLUE SNOWMAN...
KRAAAK!
...I'M NOT GOING TO MAKE IT THAT EASY FOR YOU!
GOOD, I WORK BEST UNDER PRESSURE.
ALL THIS DESTRUCTION. SO UNNECESSARY.
NEXT TIME, I'LL PICK MY BATTLE BETTER.
ESPECIALLY SINCE I DON'T HAVE HESSIA HERE TO HELP WITH THE AFTERMATH, UNLIKE THE LAST TIME I TANGLED WITH THIS KIND OF COLD.
uugg...
WHAT ARE YOU DOING?
TRYING TO HELP YOU. YOU REALLY SHOULD BE MORE CAREFUL ABOUT WHO YOU CHOOSE TO WORK FOR.
I THOUGHT I WAS GOING TO HELP SAVE THE WORLD.
Hmm, SO SHE'S NOT PAYING YOU. FIGURES.
MAYBE YOU STILL CAN, IF YOU TELL ME WHERE SHE'S GONE.
I DON'T THINK YOU'RE GOING TO LIKE IT...

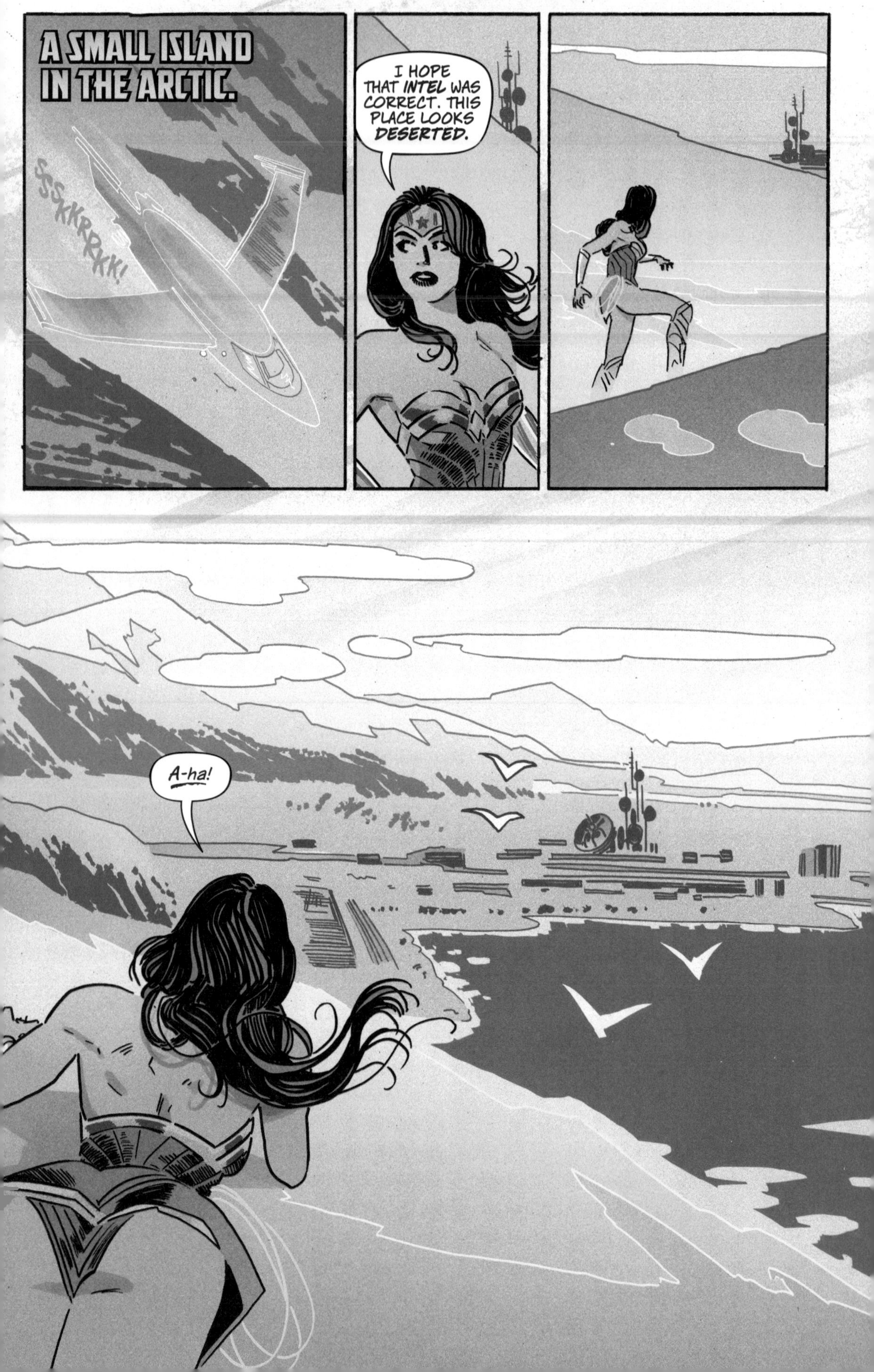
A SMALL ISLAND IN THE ARCTIC.
SSSKKRRKK!
I HOPE THAT INTEL WAS CORRECT. THIS PLACE LOOKS DESERTED.
A-ha!

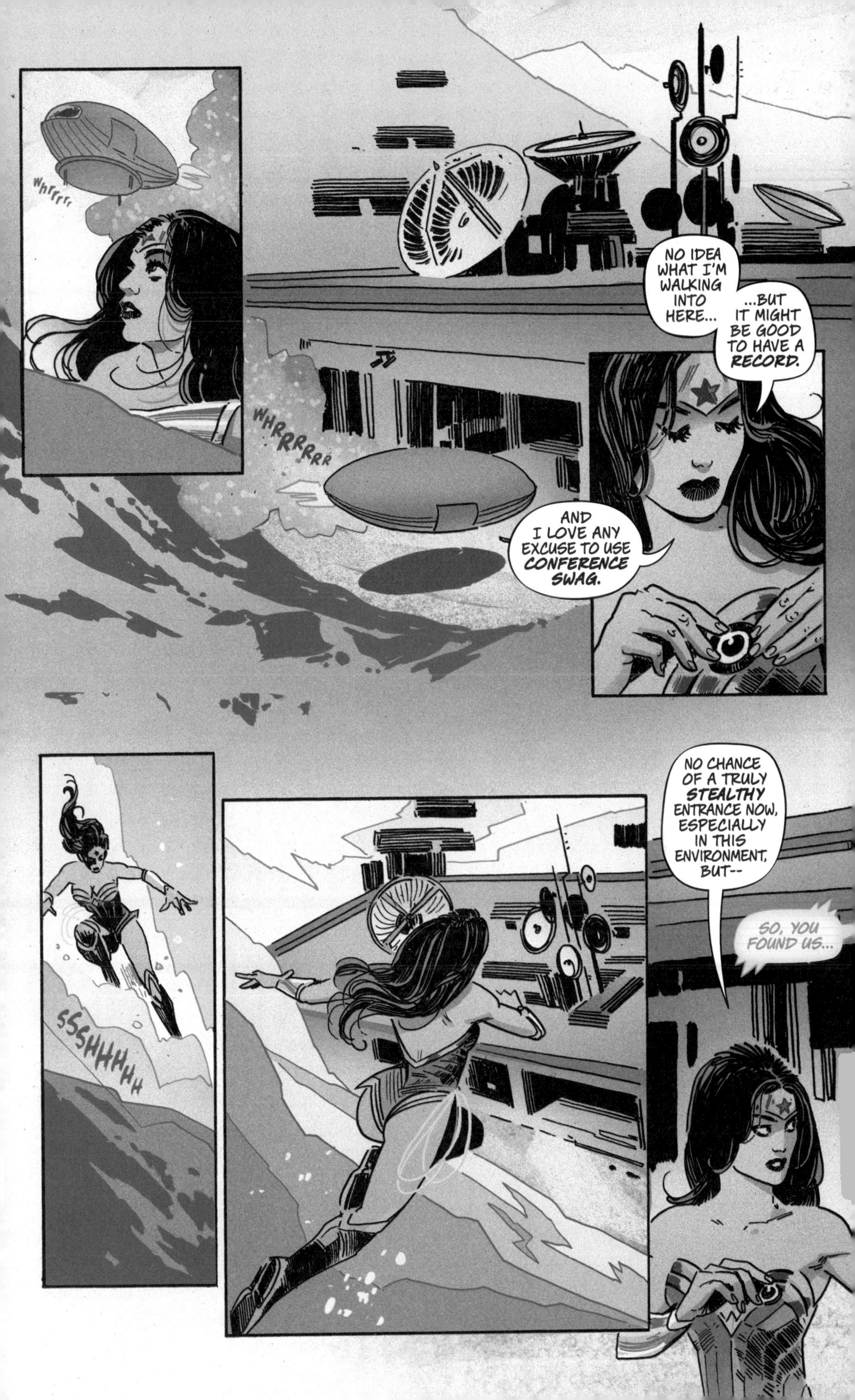
Whrrrrr
WHRRRRRR
NO IDEA WHAT I'M WALKING INTO HERE...
...BUT IT MIGHT BE GOOD TO HAVE A RECORD.
AND I LOVE ANY EXCUSE TO USE CONFERENCE SWAG.
SSSHHHHH
NO CHANCE OF A TRULY STEALTHY ENTRANCE NOW, ESPECIALLY IN THIS ENVIRONMENT, BUT--
SO, YOU FOUND US...

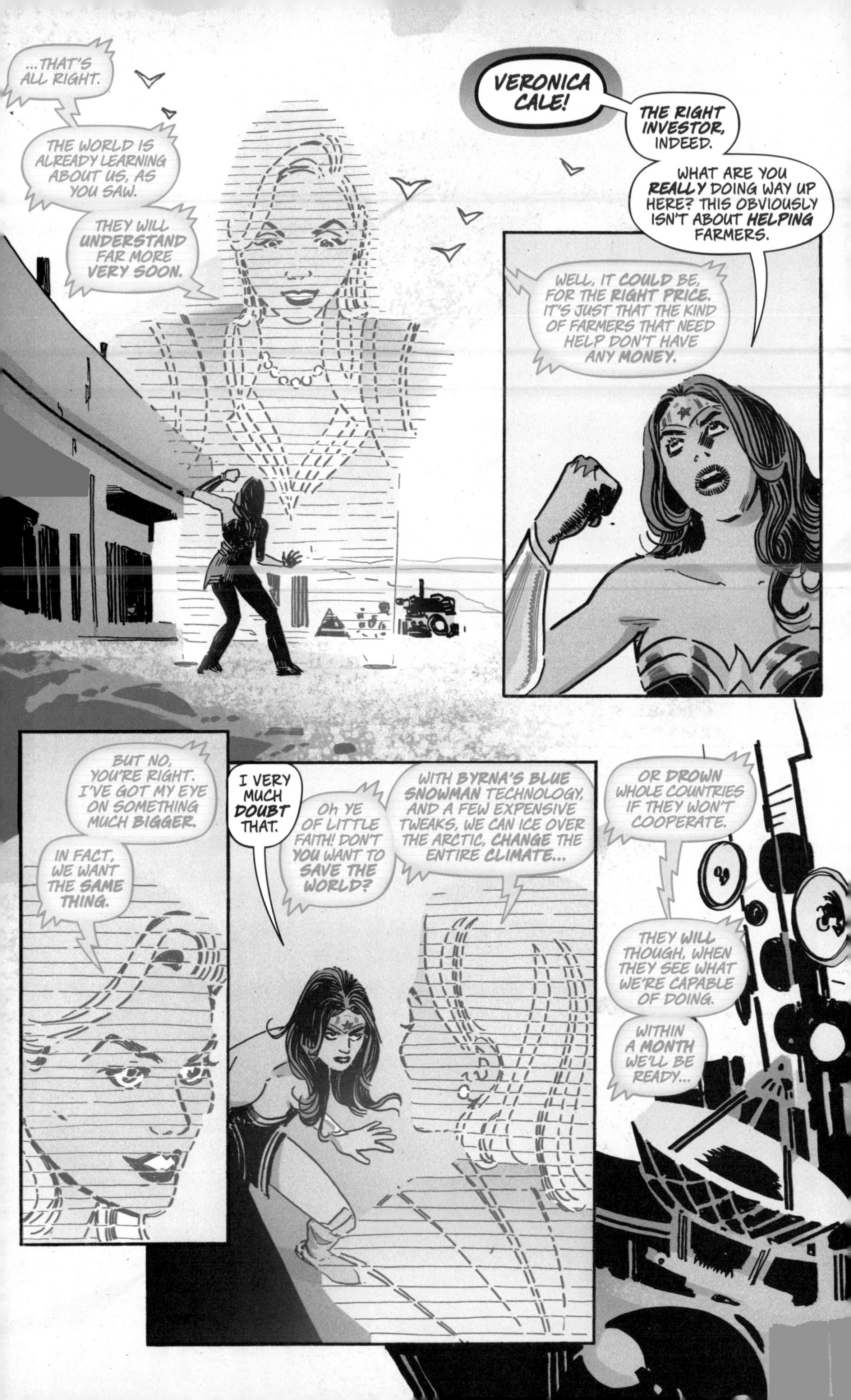
...THAT'S ALL RIGHT.
THE WORLD IS ALREADY LEARNING ABOUT US, AS YOU SAW.
THEY WILL UNDERSTAND FAR MORE VERY SOON.
VERONICA CALE!
THE RIGHT INVESTOR, INDEED.
WHAT ARE YOU REALLY DOING WAY UP HERE? THIS OBVIOUSLY ISN'T ABOUT HELPING FARMERS.
WELL, IT COULD BE, FOR THE RIGHT PRICE. IT'S JUST THAT THE KIND OF FARMERS THAT NEED HELP DON'T HAVE ANY MONEY.
BUT NO, YOU'RE RIGHT. I'VE GOT MY EYE ON SOMETHING MUCH BIGGER.
IN FACT, WE WANT THE SAME THING.
I VERY MUCH DOUBT THAT.
Oh YE OF LITTLE FAITH! DON'T YOU WANT TO SAVE THE WORLD?
WITH BYRNA'S BLUE SNOWMAN TECHNOLOGY, AND A FEW EXPENSIVE TWEAKS, WE CAN ICE OVER THE ARCTIC, CHANGE THE ENTIRE CLIMATE...
OR DROWN WHOLE COUNTRIES IF THEY WON'T COOPERATE.
THEY WILL THOUGH, WHEN THEY SEE WHAT WE'RE CAPABLE OF DOING.
WITHIN A MONTH WE'LL BE READY...

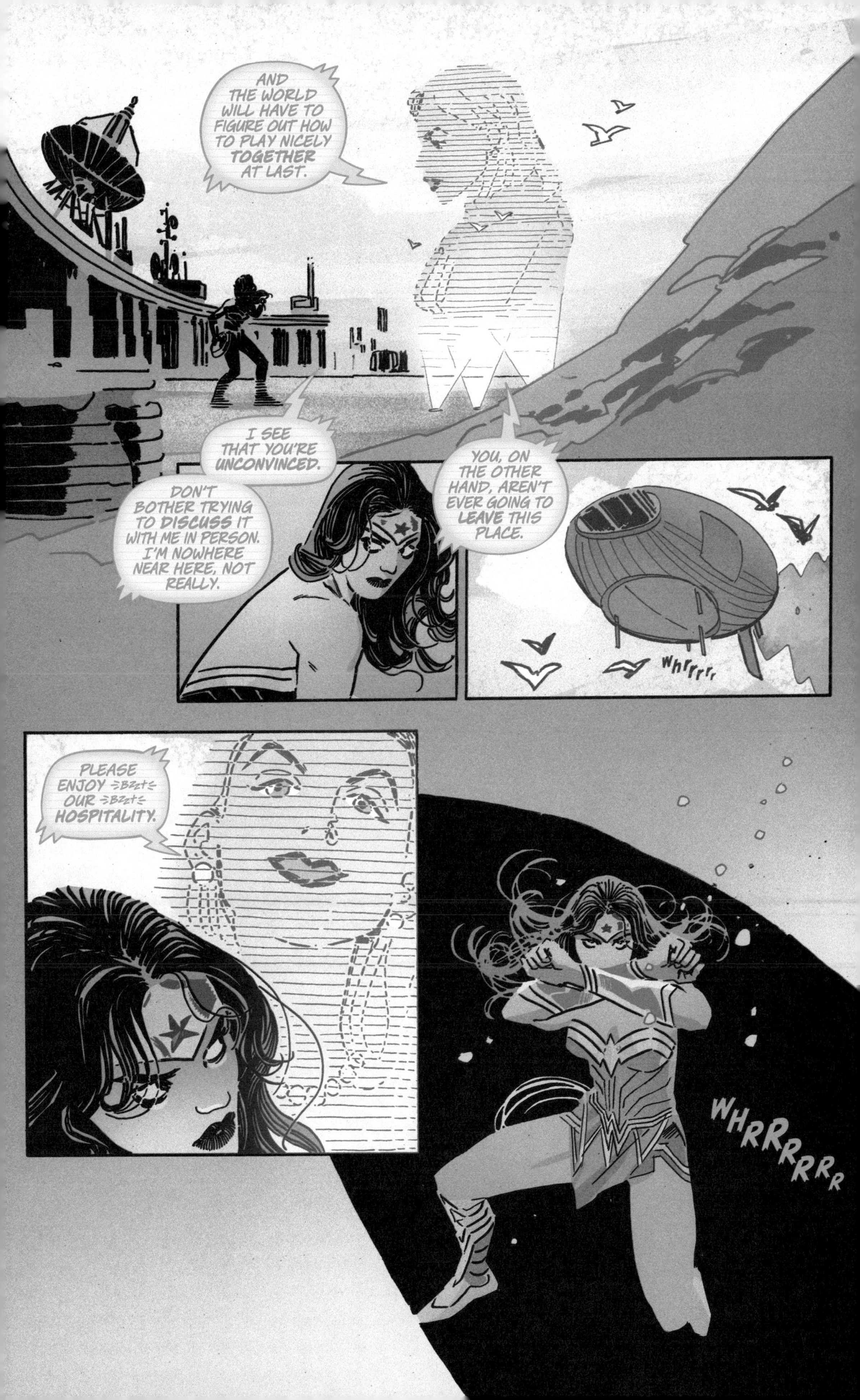
AND THE WORLD WILL HAVE TO FIGURE OUT HOW TO PLAY NICELY TOGETHER AT LAST.
I SEE THAT YOU'RE UNCONVINCED.
DON'T BOTHER TRYING TO DISCUSS IT WITH ME IN PERSON. I'M NOWHERE NEAR HERE, NOT REALLY.
YOU, ON THE OTHER HAND, AREN'T EVER GOING TO LEAVE THIS PLACE.
Whrrrrr
PLEASE ENJOY =BZZT= OUR =BZZT= HOSPITALITY.
WHRRRRRR

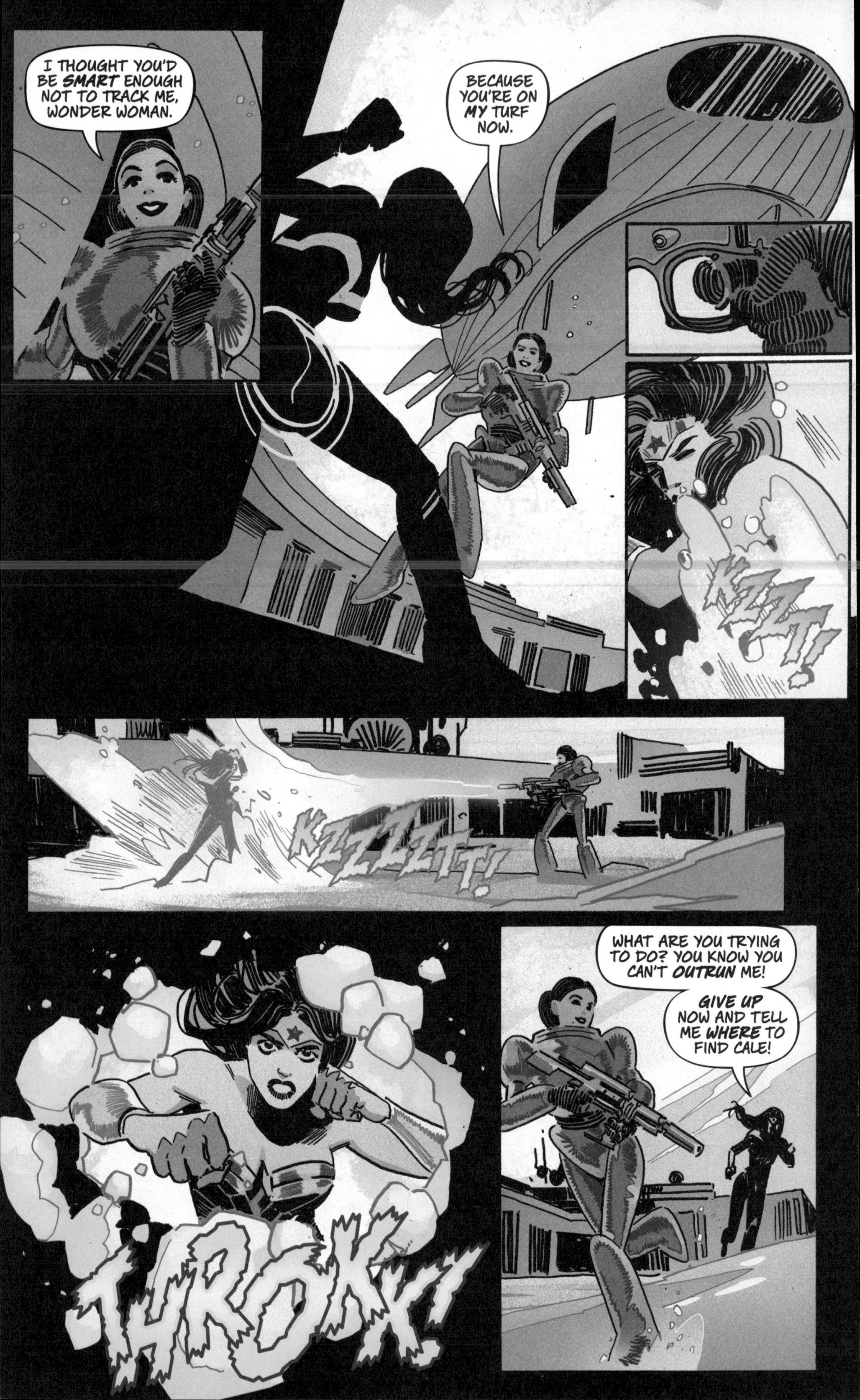
I THOUGHT YOU'D BE SMART ENOUGH NOT TO TRACK ME, WONDER WOMAN.
BECAUSE YOU'RE ON MY TURF NOW.
KZZZT!
KZZZZTTT!
THROK!
WHAT ARE YOU TRYING TO DO? YOU KNOW YOU CAN'T OUTRUN ME!
GIVE UP NOW AND TELL ME WHERE TO FIND CALE!

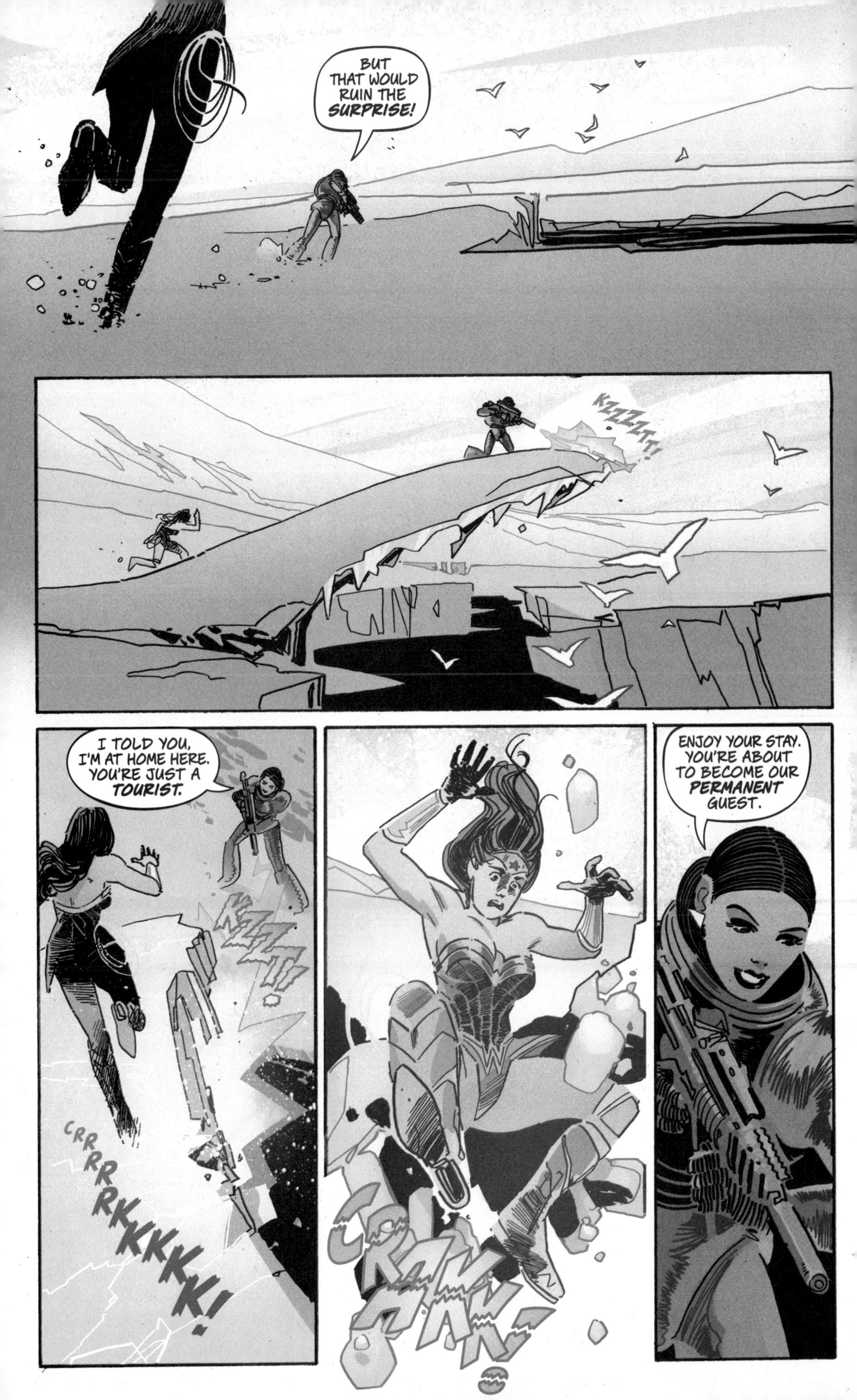
BUT THAT WOULD RUIN THE SURPRISE!
I TOLD YOU, I'M AT HOME HERE. YOU'RE JUST A TOURIST.
ENJOY YOUR STAY. YOU'RE ABOUT TO BECOME OUR PERMANENT GUEST.

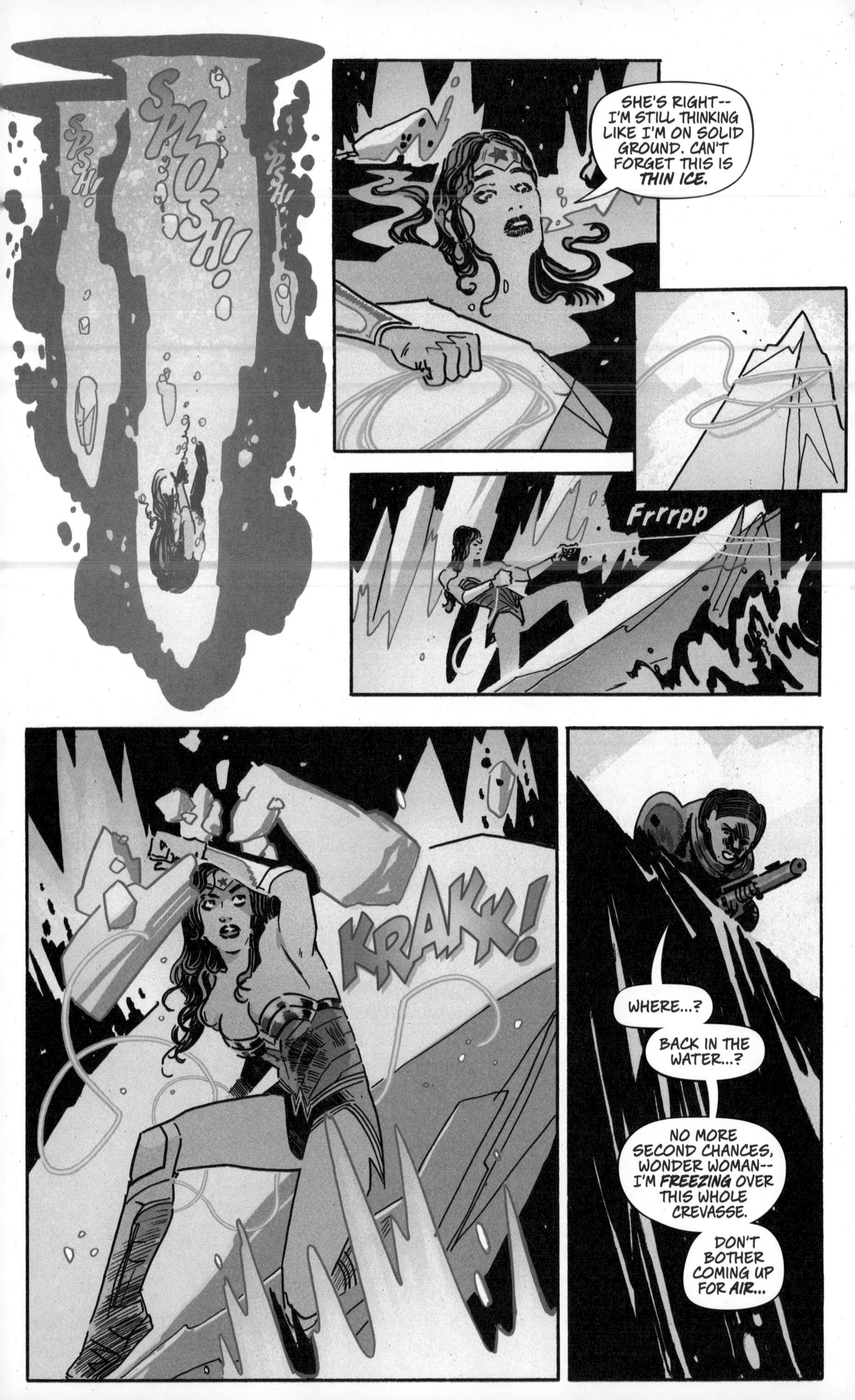
SPSH!
SPLOOSH!
SPSH!
SHE'S RIGHT-- I'M STILL THINKING LIKE I'M ON SOLID GROUND. CAN'T FORGET THIS IS THIN ICE.
Frrrpp
KRAKK!
WHERE...?
BACK IN THE WATER...?
NO MORE SECOND CHANCES, WONDER WOMAN-- I'M FREEZING OVER THIS WHOLE CREVASSE.
DON'T BOTHER COMING UP FOR AIR...

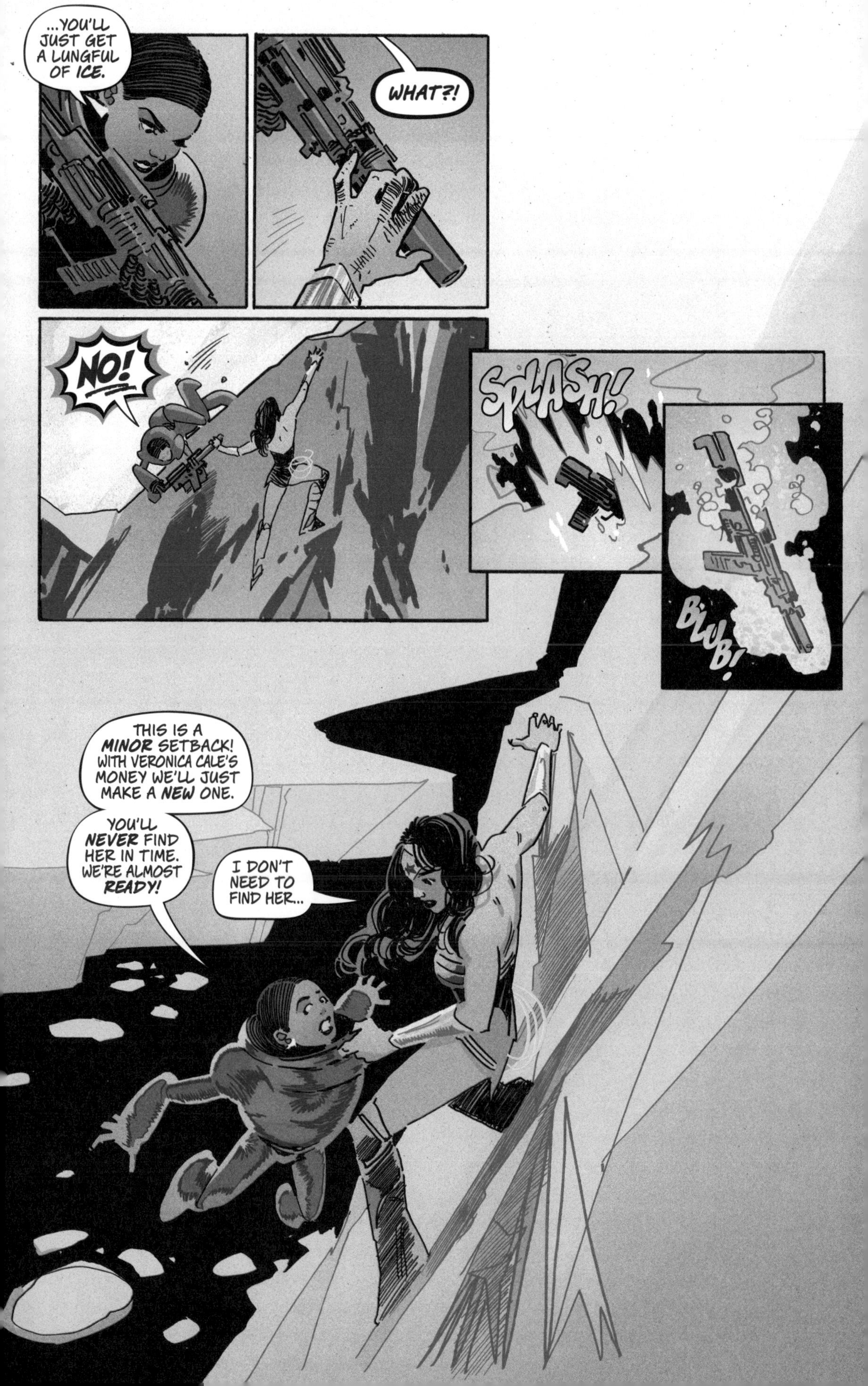
...YOU'LL JUST GET A LUNGFUL OF ICE.
WHAT?!
NO!
SPLASH!
BLUB!
THIS IS A MINOR SETBACK! WITH VERONICA CALE'S MONEY WE'LL JUST MAKE A NEW ONE.
YOU'LL NEVER FIND HER IN TIME. WE'RE ALMOST READY!
I DON'T NEED TO FIND HER...

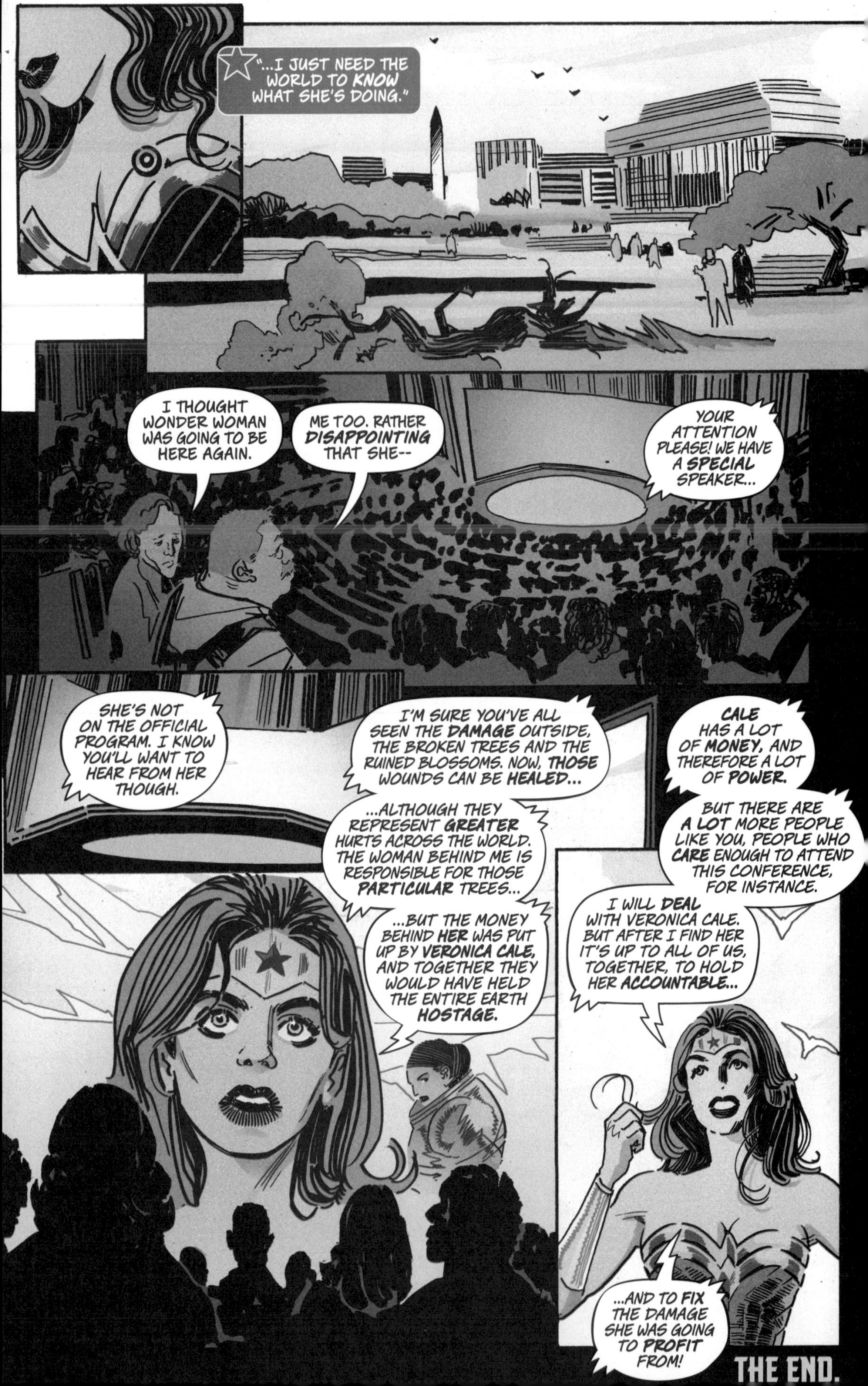
"...I JUST NEED THE WORLD TO KNOW WHAT SHE'S DOING."
I THOUGHT WONDER WOMAN WAS GOING TO BE HERE AGAIN.
ME TOO. RATHER DISAPPOINTING THAT SHE--
YOUR ATTENTION PLEASE! WE HAVE A SPECIAL SPEAKER...
SHE'S NOT ON THE OFFICIAL PROGRAM. I KNOW YOU'LL WANT TO HEAR FROM HER THOUGH.
I'M SURE YOU'VE ALL SEEN THE DAMAGE OUTSIDE, THE BROKEN TREES AND THE RUINED BLOSSOMS. NOW, THOSE WOUNDS CAN BE HEALED...
...ALTHOUGH THEY REPRESENT GREATER HURTS ACROSS THE WORLD. THE WOMAN BEHIND ME IS RESPONSIBLE FOR THOSE PARTICULAR TREES...
...BUT THE MONEY BEHIND HER WAS PUT UP BY VERONICA CALE, AND TOGETHER THEY WOULD HAVE HELD THE ENTIRE EARTH HOSTAGE.
CALE HAS A LOT OF MONEY, AND THEREFORE A LOT OF POWER.
BUT THERE ARE A LOT MORE PEOPLE LIKE YOU, PEOPLE WHO CARE ENOUGH TO ATTEND THIS CONFERENCE, FOR INSTANCE.
I WILL DEAL WITH VERONICA CALE. BUT AFTER I FIND HER IT'S UP TO ALL OF US, TOGETHER, TO HOLD HER ACCOUNTABLE...
...AND TO FIX THE DAMAGE SHE WAS GOING TO PROFIT FROM!
THE END.

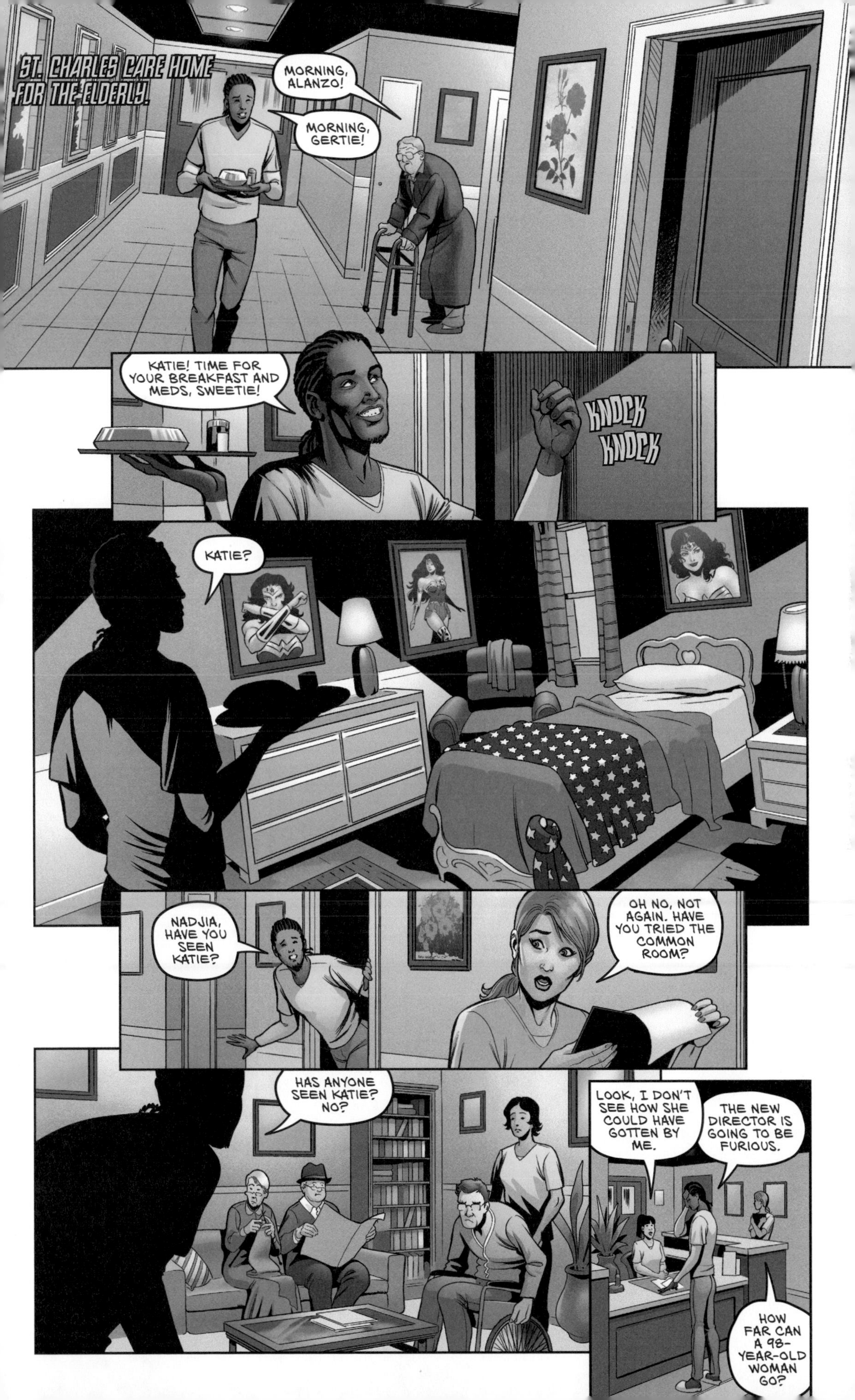
ST. CHARLES CARE HOME FOR THE ELDERLY.
MORNING, ALANZO!
MORNING, GERTIE!
KATIE! TIME FOR YOUR BREAKFAST AND MEDS, SWEETIE!
KNOCK KNOCK
KATIE?
NADJIA, HAVE YOU SEEN KATIE?
OH NO, NOT AGAIN. HAVE YOU TRIED THE COMMON ROOM?
HAS ANYONE SEEN KATIE? NO?
LOOK, I DON'T SEE HOW SHE COULD HAVE GOTTEN BY ME.
THE NEW DIRECTOR IS GOING TO BE FURIOUS.
HOW FAR CAN A 98-YEAR-OLD WOMAN GO?

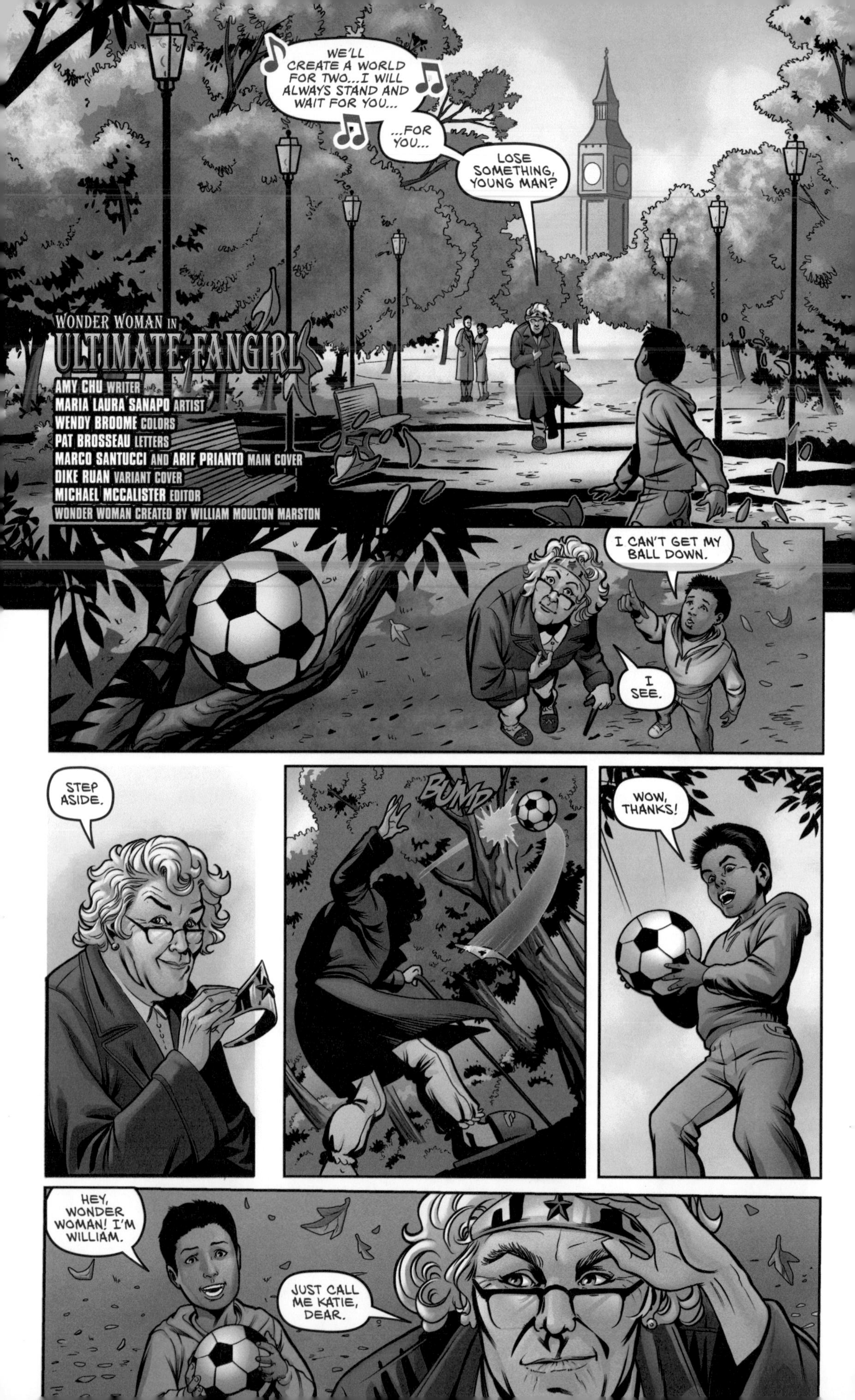
WE'LL CREATE A WORLD FOR TWO...I WILL ALWAYS STAND AND WAIT FOR YOU...
...FOR YOU...
LOSE SOMETHING, YOUNG MAN?
WONDER WOMAN IN
ULTIMATE FANGIRL
AMY CHU WRITER
MARIA LAURA SANAPO ARTIST
WENDY BROOME COLORS
PAT BROSSEAU LETTERS
MARCO SANTUCCI AND ARIF PRIANTO MAIN COVER
DIKE RUAN VARIANT COVER
MICHAEL MCCALISTER EDITOR
WONDER WOMAN CREATED BY WILLIAM MOULTON MARSTON
I CAN'T GET MY BALL DOWN.
I SEE.
STEP ASIDE.
BUMP
WOW, THANKS!
HEY, WONDER WOMAN! I'M WILLIAM.
JUST CALL ME KATIE, DEAR.

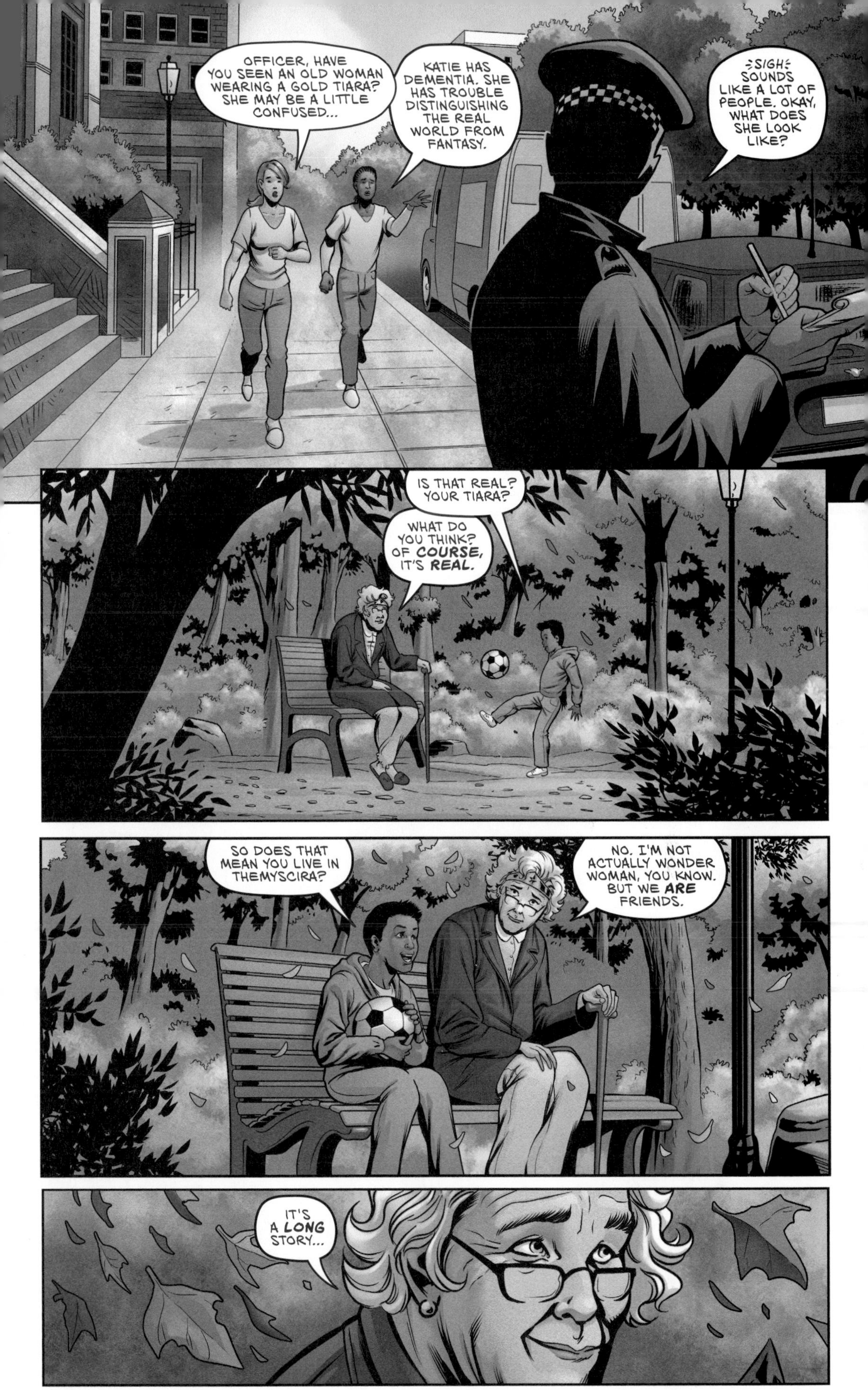
OFFICER, HAVE YOU SEEN AN OLD WOMAN WEARING A GOLD TIARA? SHE MAY BE A LITTLE CONFUSED...
KATIE HAS DEMENTIA. SHE HAS TROUBLE DISTINGUISHING THE REAL WORLD FROM FANTASY.
SIGH SOUNDS LIKE A LOT OF PEOPLE. OKAY, WHAT DOES SHE LOOK LIKE?
IS THAT REAL? YOUR TIARA?
WHAT DO YOU THINK? OF COURSE, IT'S REAL.
SO DOES THAT MEAN YOU LIVE IN THEMYSCIRA?
NO. I'M NOT ACTUALLY WONDER WOMAN, YOU KNOW. BUT WE ARE FRIENDS.
IT'S A LONG STORY...

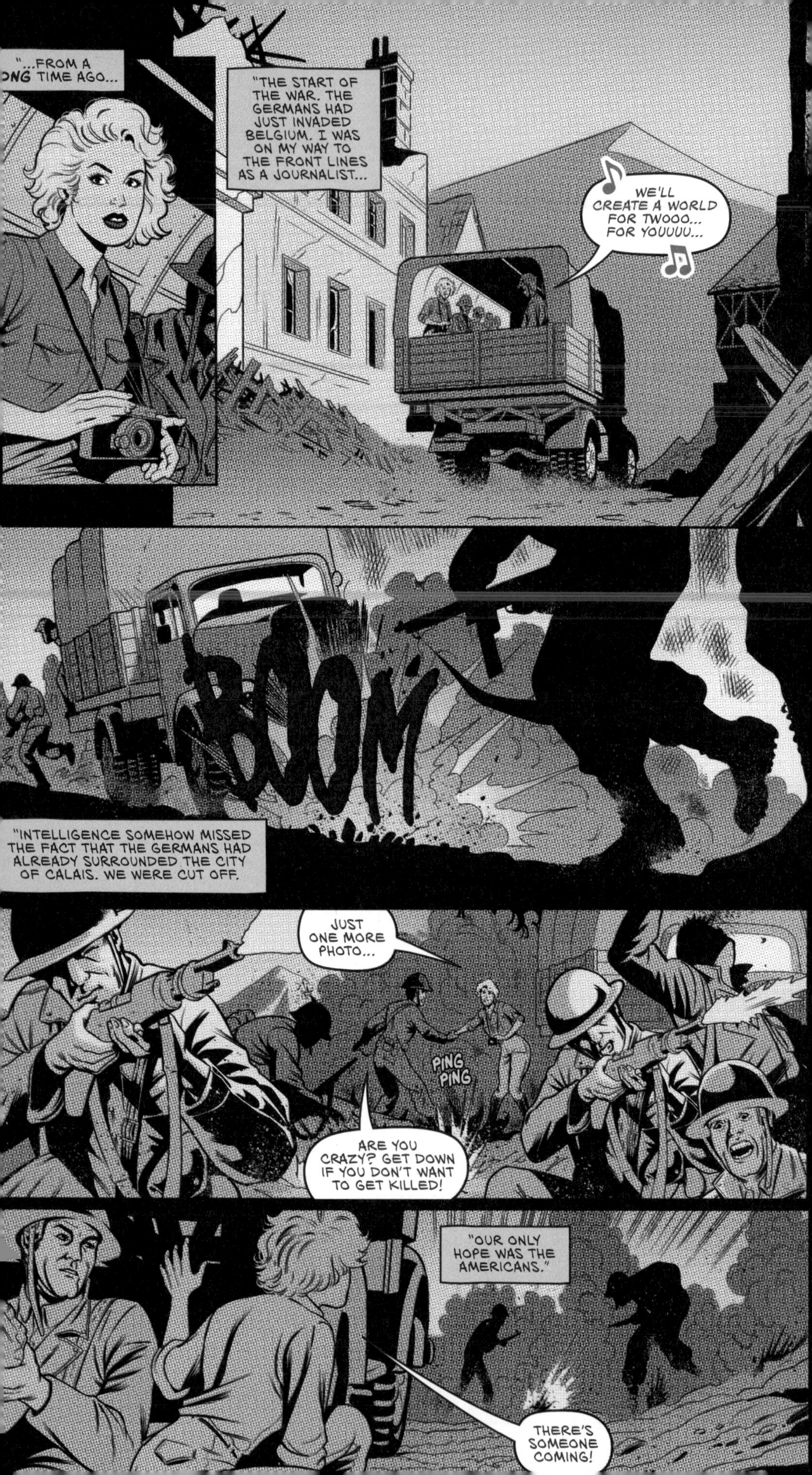
"...FROM A
ONG TIME AGO...
"THE START OF THE WAR. THE GERMANS HAD JUST INVADED BELGIUM. I WAS ON MY WAY TO THE FRONT LINES AS A JOURNALIST...
WE'LL CREATE A WORLD FOR TWOOO... FOR YOUUUU...
BOOM
"INTELLIGENCE SOMEHOW MISSED THE FACT THAT THE GERMANS HAD ALREADY SURROUNDED THE CITY OF CALAIS. WE WERE CUT OFF.
JUST ONE MORE PHOTO...
PING PING
ARE YOU CRAZY? GET DOWN IF YOU DON'T WANT TO GET KILLED!
"OUR ONLY HOPE WAS THE AMERICANS."
THERE'S SOMEONE COMING!

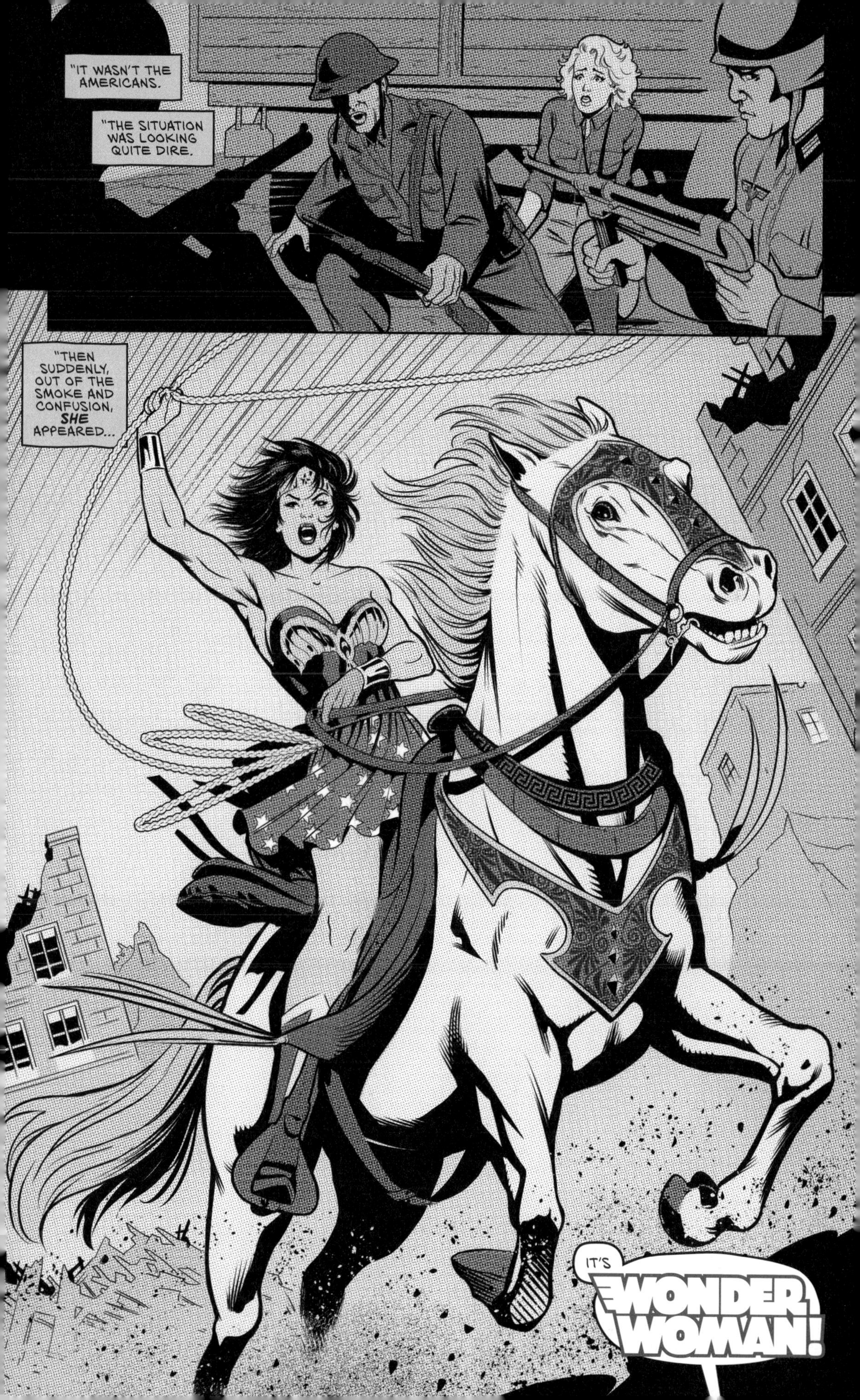
"IT WASN'T THE AMERICANS.
"THE SITUATION WAS LOOKING QUITE DIRE.
"THEN SUDDENLY, OUT OF THE SMOKE AND CONFUSION, SHE APPEARED...
IT'S WONDER WOMAN!

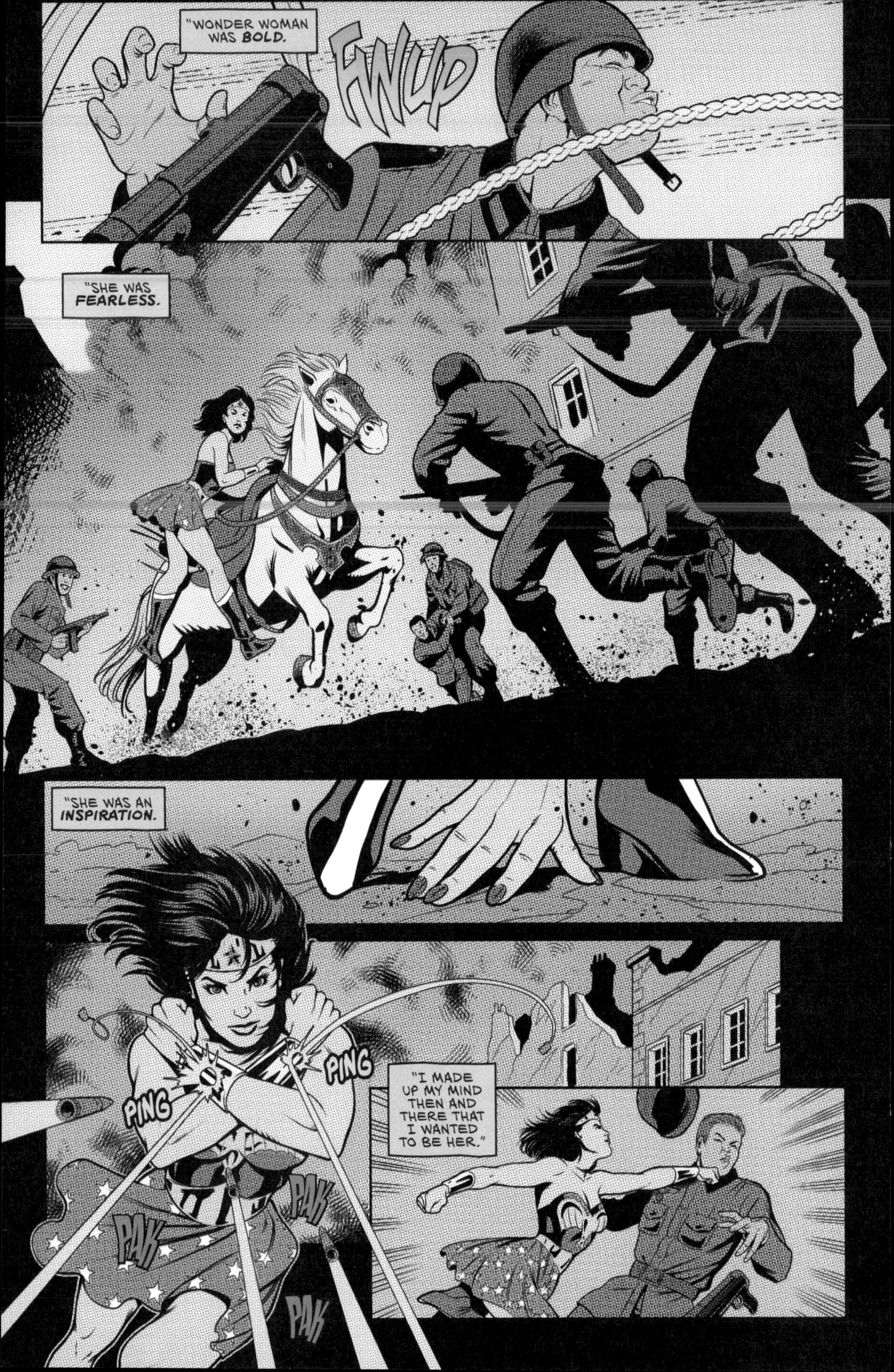
"WONDER WOMAN WAS BOLD.
FWUP
"SHE WAS FEARLESS.
"SHE WAS AN INSPIRATION.
PING
PING
PAK
PAK
PAK
"I MADE UP MY MIND THEN AND THERE THAT I WANTED TO BE HER."

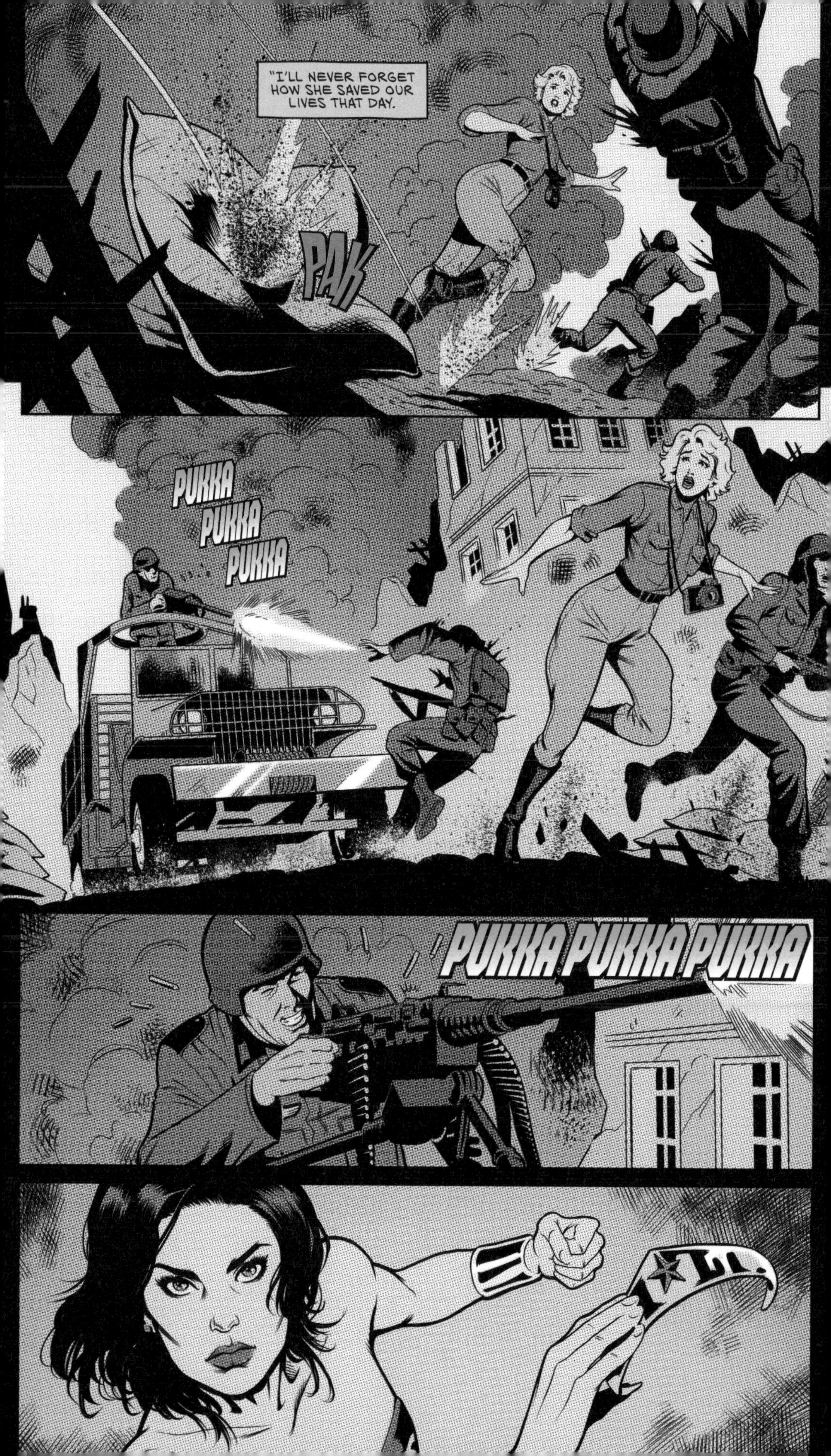
"I'LL NEVER FORGET
HOW SHE SAVED OUR
LIVES THAT DAY.
PAK
PUKKA
PUKKA
PUKKA
PUKKA PUKKA PUKKA

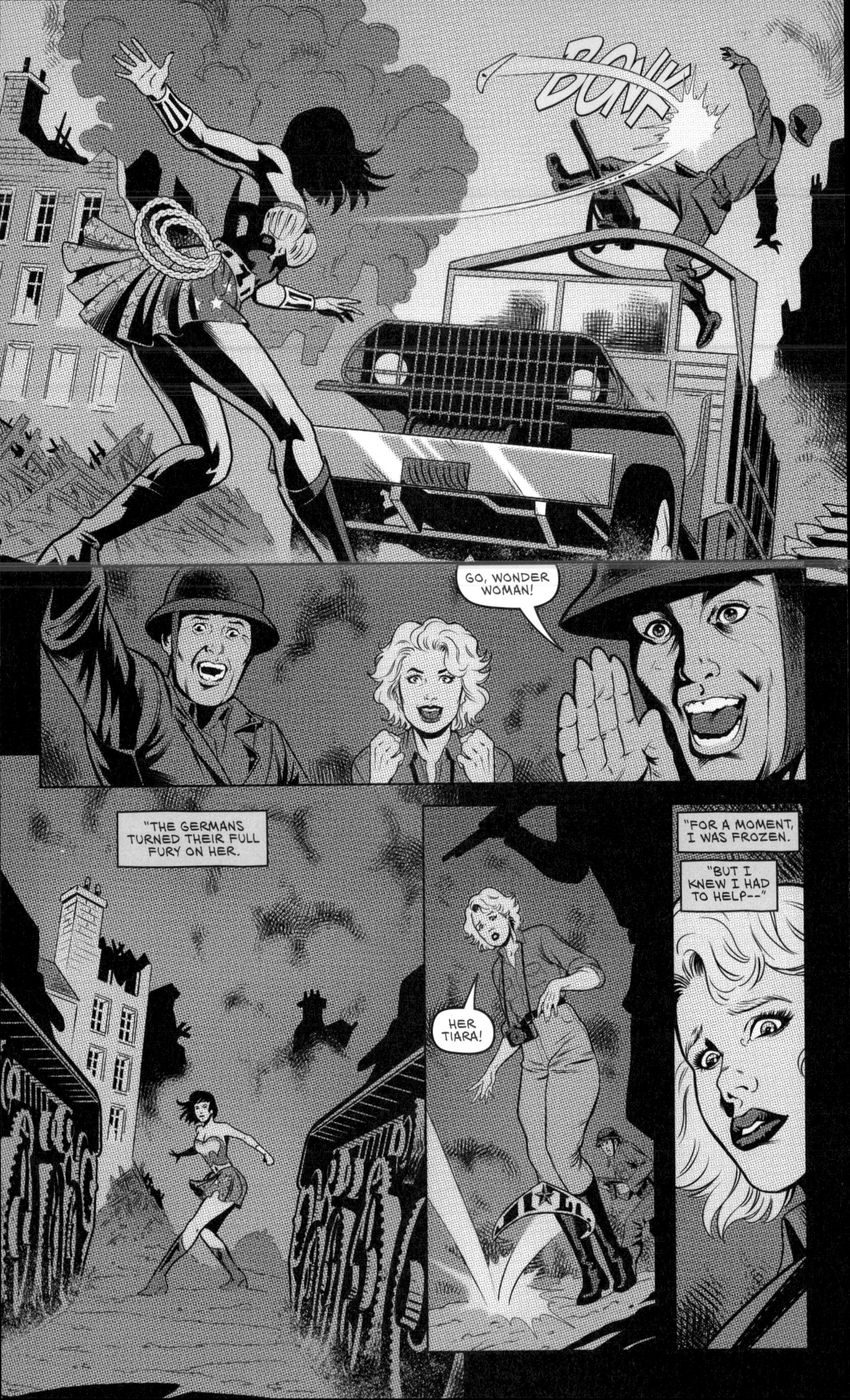
BONK
BONK
GO, WONDER WOMAN!
"THE GERMANS TURNED THEIR FULL FURY ON HER.
HER TIARA!
"FOR A MOMENT, I WAS FROZEN.
"BUT I KNEW I HAD TO HELP--"

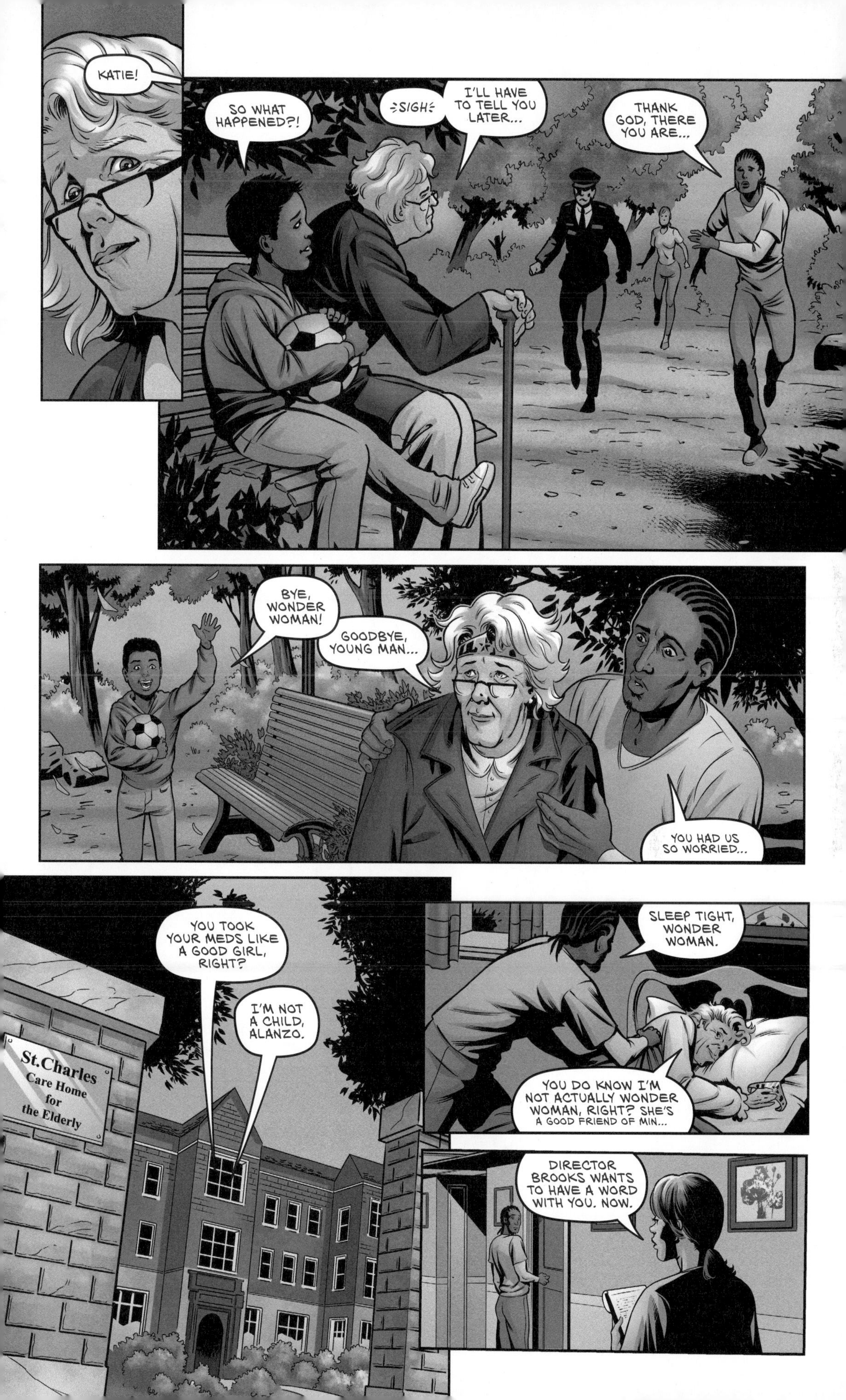
KATIE!
SO WHAT HAPPENED?!
SIGH
I'LL HAVE TO TELL YOU LATER...
THANK GOD, THERE YOU ARE...
BYE, WONDER WOMAN!
GOODBYE, YOUNG MAN...
YOU HAD US SO WORRIED...
St. Charles Care Home for the Elderly
YOU TOOK YOUR MEDS LIKE A GOOD GIRL, RIGHT?
I'M NOT A CHILD, ALANZO.
SLEEP TIGHT, WONDER WOMAN.
YOU DO KNOW I'M NOT ACTUALLY WONDER WOMAN, RIGHT? SHE'S A GOOD FRIEND OF MIN...
DIRECTOR BROOKS WANTS TO HAVE A WORD WITH YOU. NOW.

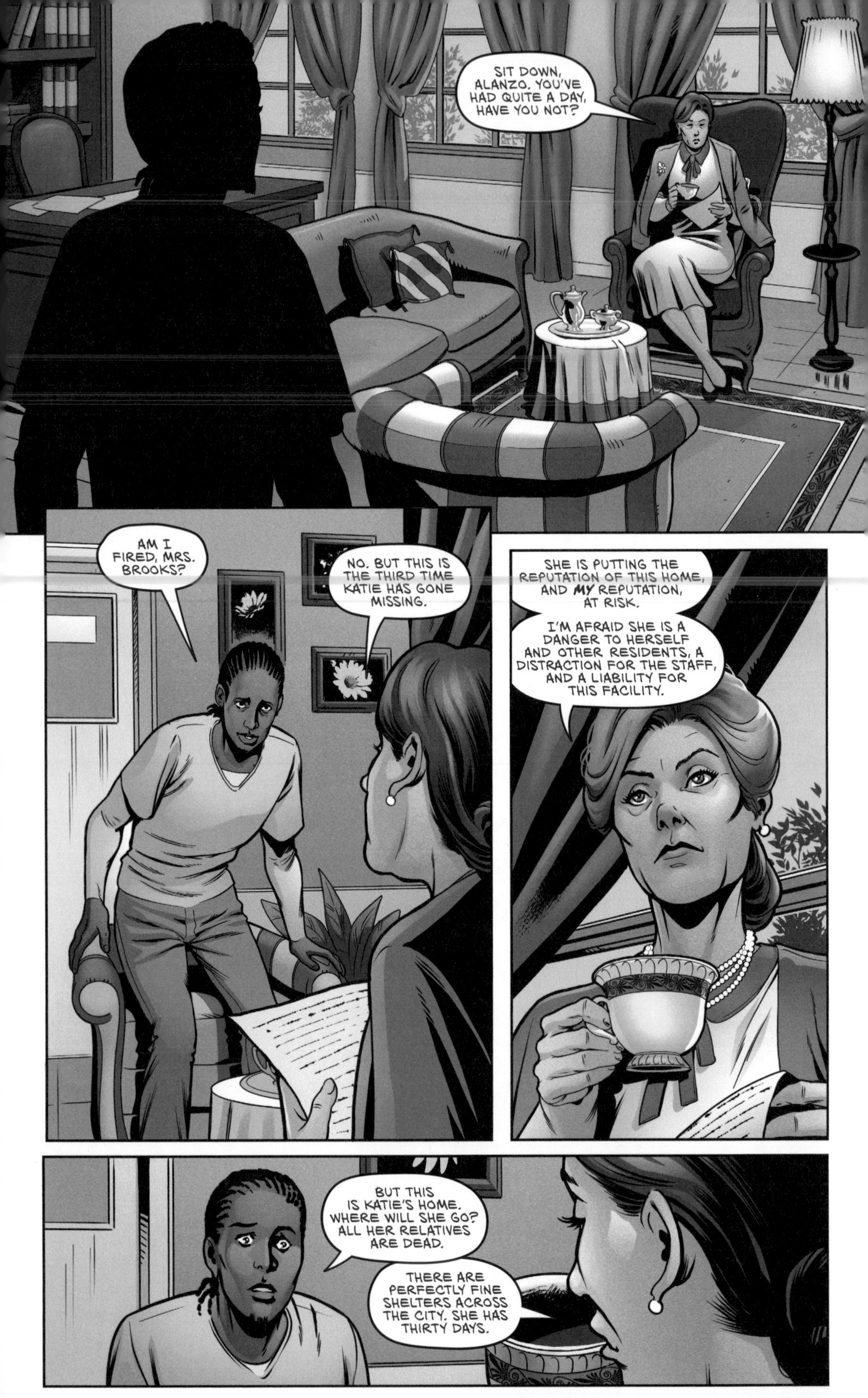
SIT DOWN, ALANZO. YOU'VE HAD QUITE A DAY, HAVE YOU NOT?
AM I FIRED, MRS. BROOKS?
NO. BUT THIS IS THE THIRD TIME KATIE HAS GONE MISSING.
SHE IS PUTTING THE REPUTATION OF THIS HOME, AND MY REPUTATION, AT RISK.
I'M AFRAID SHE IS A DANGER TO HERSELF AND OTHER RESIDENTS, A DISTRACTION FOR THE STAFF, AND A LIABILITY FOR THIS FACILITY.
BUT THIS IS KATIE'S HOME. WHERE WILL SHE GO? ALL HER RELATIVES ARE DEAD.
THERE ARE PERFECTLY FINE SHELTERS ACROSS THE CITY. SHE HAS THIRTY DAYS.

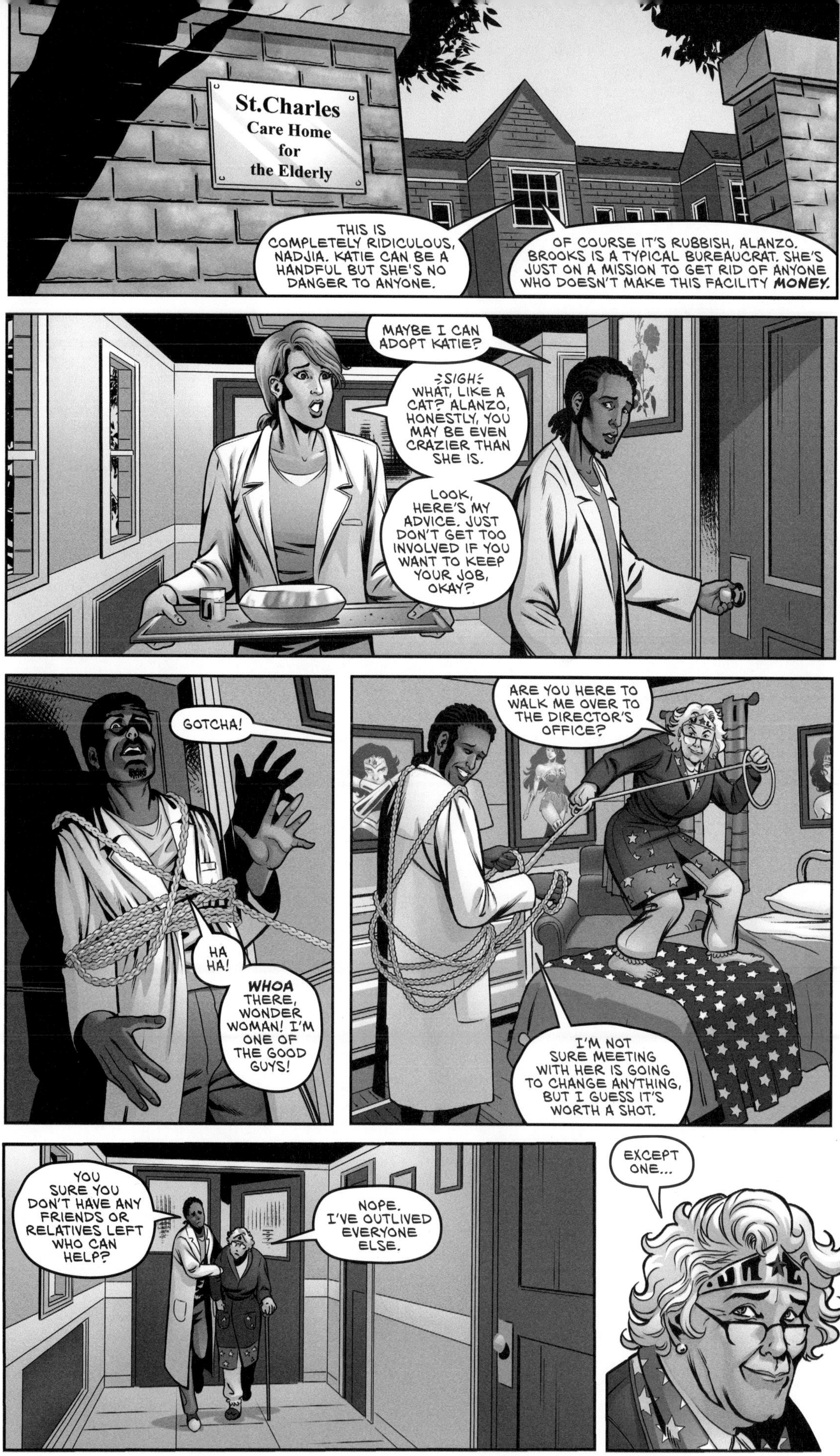
St.Charles
Care Home
for
the Elderly
THIS IS COMPLETELY RIDICULOUS, NADJIA. KATIE CAN BE A HANDFUL BUT SHE'S NO DANGER TO ANYONE.
OF COURSE IT'S RUBBISH, ALANZO. BROOKS IS A TYPICAL BUREAUCRAT. SHE'S JUST ON A MISSION TO GET RID OF ANYONE WHO DOESN'T MAKE THIS FACILITY MONEY.
MAYBE I CAN ADOPT KATIE?
SIGH WHAT, LIKE A CAT? ALANZO, HONESTLY, YOU MAY BE EVEN CRAZIER THAN SHE IS.
LOOK, HERE'S MY ADVICE. JUST DON'T GET TOO INVOLVED IF YOU WANT TO KEEP YOUR JOB, OKAY?
GOTCHA!
HA HA!
WHOA THERE, WONDER WOMAN! I'M ONE OF THE GOOD GUYS!
ARE YOU HERE TO WALK ME OVER TO THE DIRECTOR'S OFFICE?
I'M NOT SURE MEETING WITH HER IS GOING TO CHANGE ANYTHING, BUT I GUESS IT'S WORTH A SHOT.
YOU SURE YOU DON'T HAVE ANY FRIENDS OR RELATIVES LEFT WHO CAN HELP?
NOPE. I'VE OUTLIVED EVERYONE ELSE.
EXCEPT ONE...

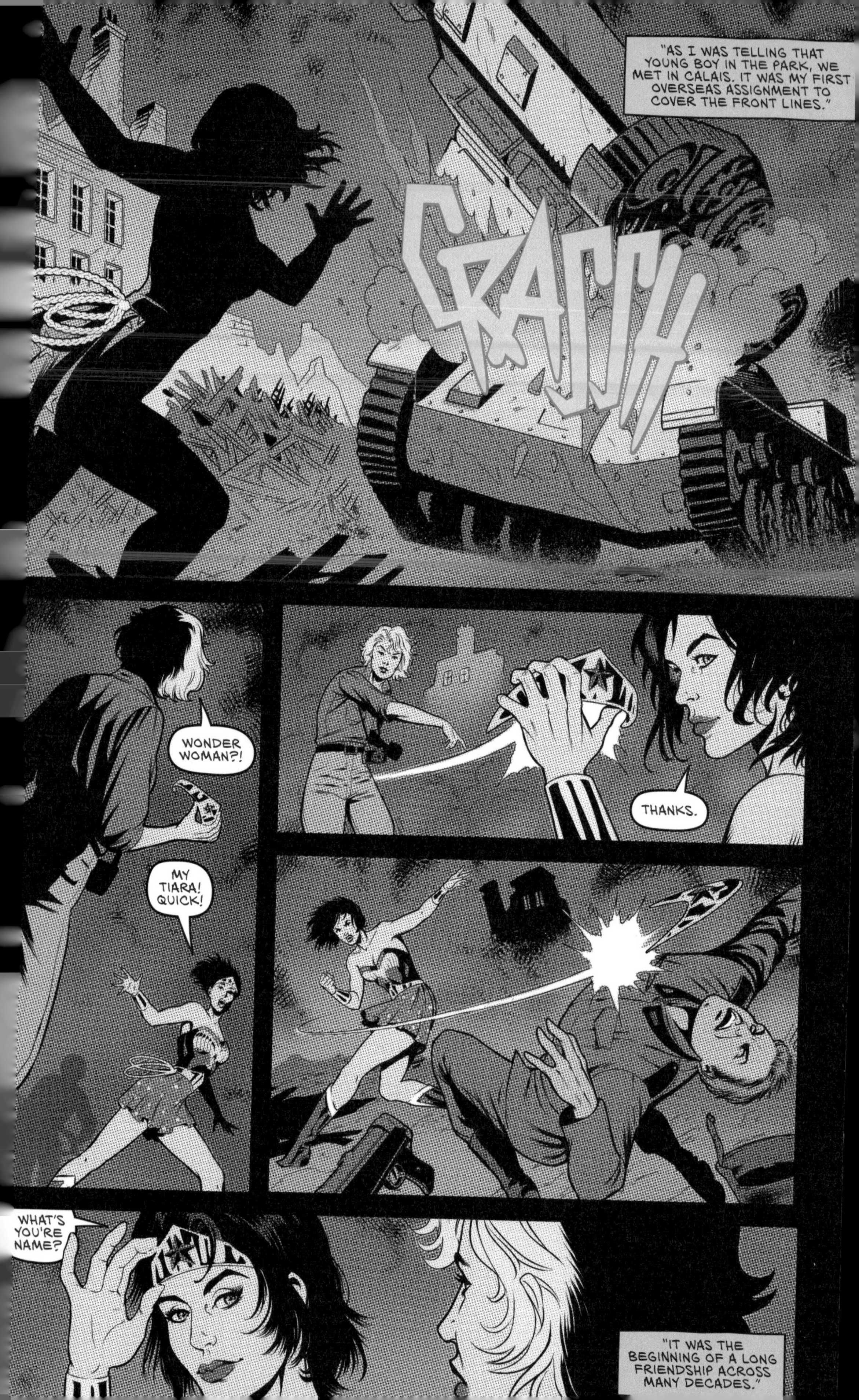
"AS I WAS TELLING THAT YOUNG BOY IN THE PARK, WE MET IN CALAIS. IT WAS MY FIRST OVERSEAS ASSIGNMENT TO COVER THE FRONT LINES."
CRASH
WONDER WOMAN?!
MY TIARA! QUICK!
THANKS.
WHAT'S YOU'RE NAME?
"IT WAS THE BEGINNING OF A LONG FRIENDSHIP ACROSS MANY DECADES."

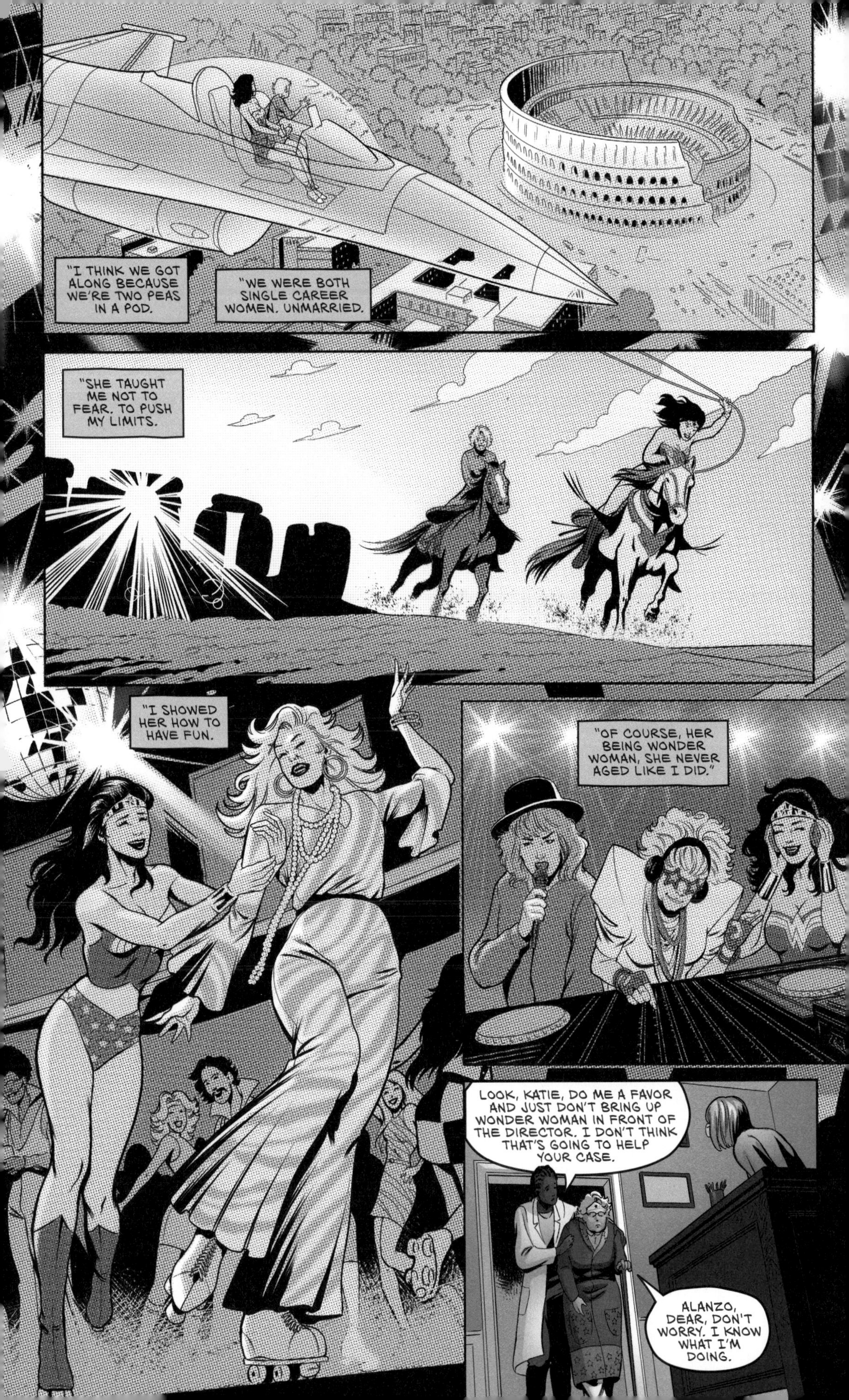
"I THINK WE GOT ALONG BECAUSE WE'RE TWO PEAS IN A POD.
"WE WERE BOTH SINGLE CAREER WOMEN. UNMARRIED.
"SHE TAUGHT ME NOT TO FEAR. TO PUSH MY LIMITS.
"I SHOWED HER HOW TO HAVE FUN.
"OF COURSE, HER BEING WONDER WOMAN, SHE NEVER AGED LIKE I DID."
LOOK, KATIE, DO ME A FAVOR AND JUST DON'T BRING UP WONDER WOMAN IN FRONT OF THE DIRECTOR. I DON'T THINK THAT'S GOING TO HELP YOUR CASE.
ALANZO, DEAR, DON'T WORRY. I KNOW WHAT I'M DOING.

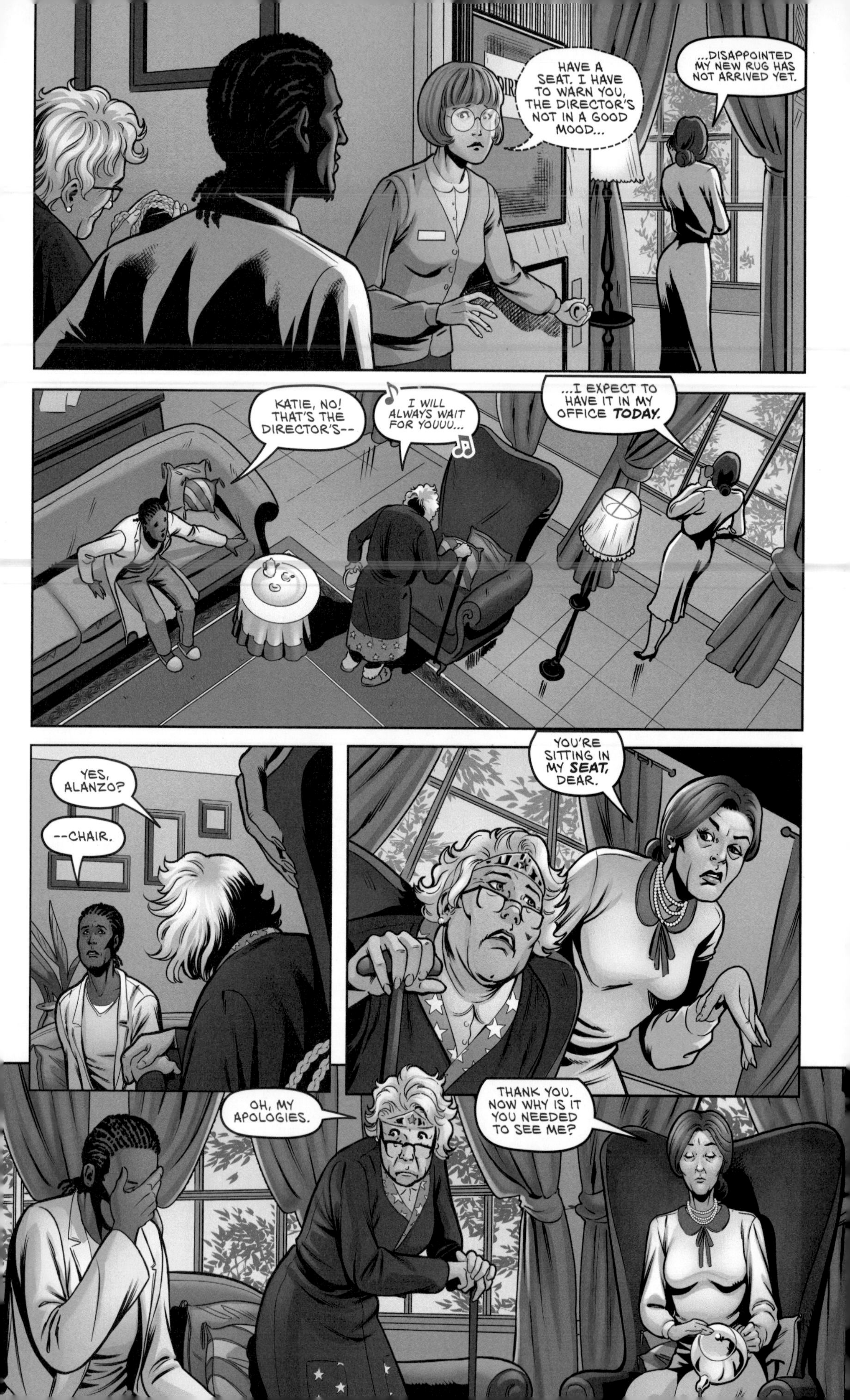
HAVE A SEAT. I HAVE TO WARN YOU, THE DIRECTOR'S NOT IN A GOOD MOOD...
...DISAPPOINTED MY NEW RUG HAS NOT ARRIVED YET.
KATIE, NO! THAT'S THE DIRECTOR'S--
I WILL ALWAYS WAIT FOR YOUUU...
...I EXPECT TO HAVE IT IN MY OFFICE TODAY.
YES, ALANZO?
--CHAIR.
YOU'RE SITTING IN MY SEAT, DEAR.
OH, MY APOLOGIES.
THANK YOU. NOW WHY IS IT YOU NEEDED TO SEE ME?

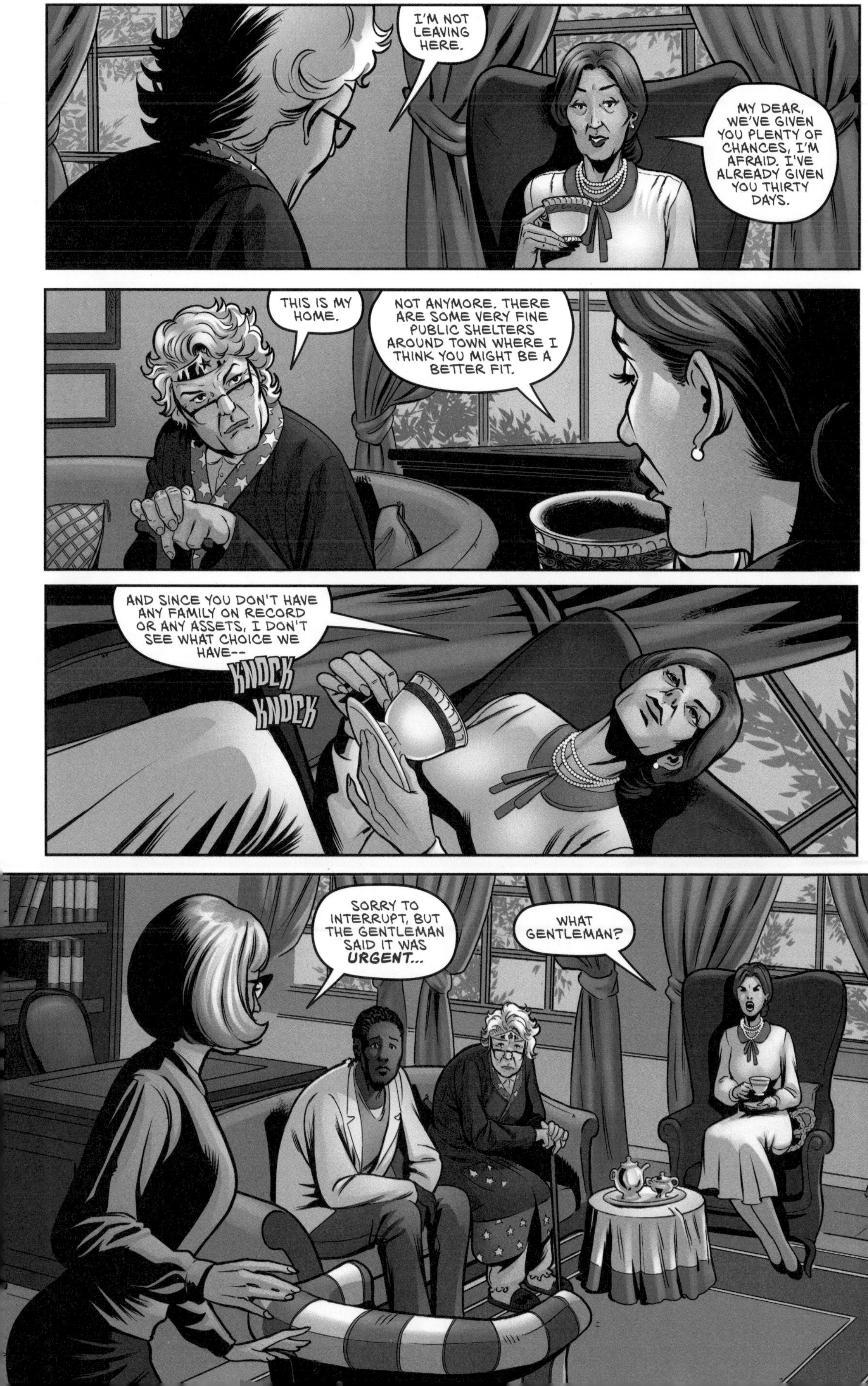
I'M NOT LEAVING HERE.
MY DEAR, WE'VE GIVEN YOU PLENTY OF CHANCES, I'M AFRAID. I'VE ALREADY GIVEN YOU THIRTY DAYS.
THIS IS MY HOME.
NOT ANYMORE. THERE ARE SOME VERY FINE PUBLIC SHELTERS AROUND TOWN WHERE I THINK YOU MIGHT BE A BETTER FIT.
AND SINCE YOU DON'T HAVE ANY FAMILY ON RECORD OR ANY ASSETS, I DON'T SEE WHAT CHOICE WE HAVE--
KNOCK
KNOCK
SORRY TO INTERRUPT, BUT THE GENTLEMAN SAID IT WAS **URGENT...**
WHAT GENTLEMAN?

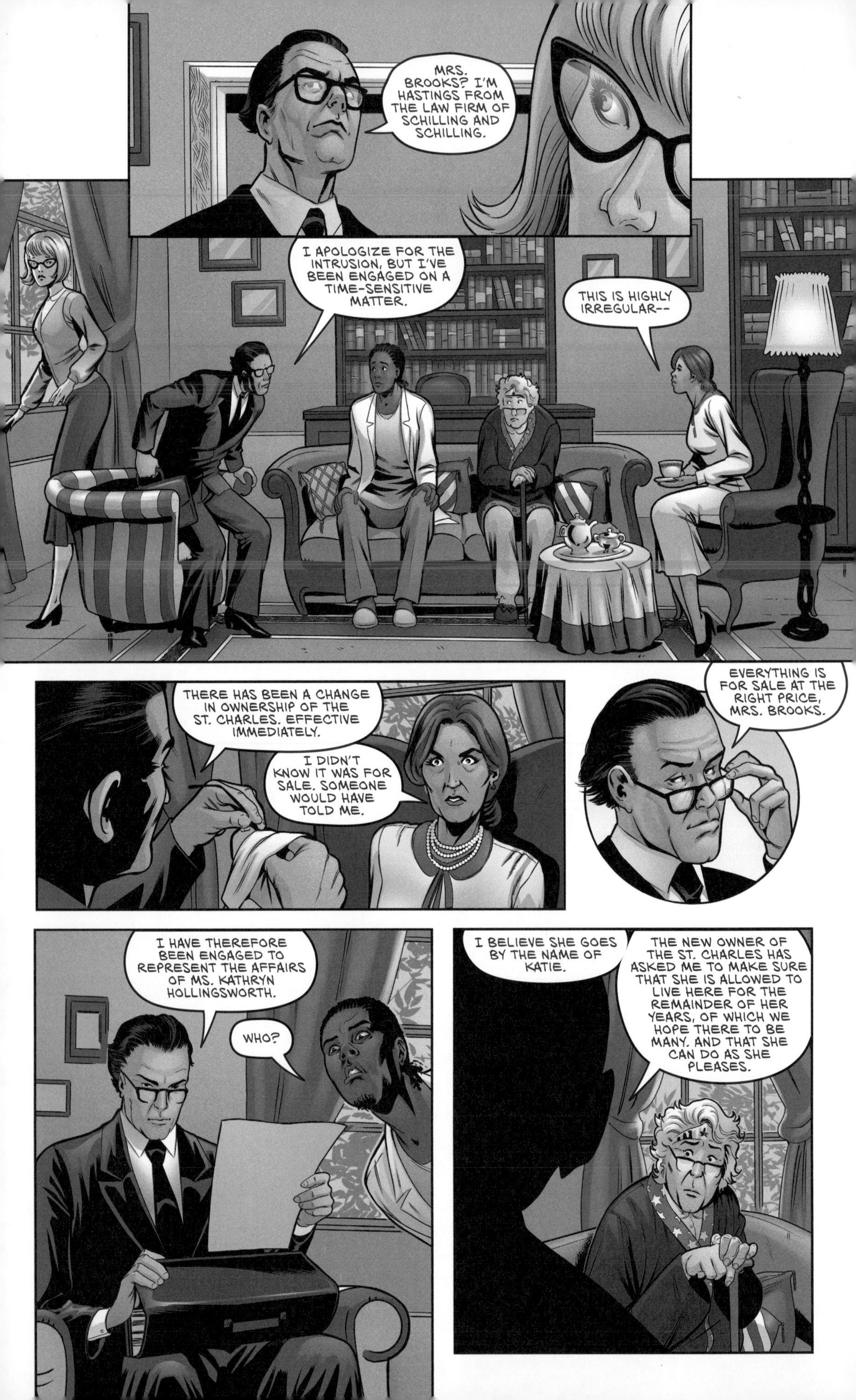
MRS. BROOKS? I'M HASTINGS FROM THE LAW FIRM OF SCHILLING AND SCHILLING.
I APOLOGIZE FOR THE INTRUSION, BUT I'VE BEEN ENGAGED ON A TIME-SENSITIVE MATTER.
THIS IS HIGHLY IRREGULAR--
THERE HAS BEEN A CHANGE IN OWNERSHIP OF THE ST. CHARLES. EFFECTIVE IMMEDIATELY.
I DIDN'T KNOW IT WAS FOR SALE. SOMEONE WOULD HAVE TOLD ME.
EVERYTHING IS FOR SALE AT THE RIGHT PRICE, MRS. BROOKS.
I HAVE THEREFORE BEEN ENGAGED TO REPRESENT THE AFFAIRS OF MS. KATHRYN HOLLINGSWORTH.
WHO?
I BELIEVE SHE GOES BY THE NAME OF KATIE.
THE NEW OWNER OF THE ST. CHARLES HAS ASKED ME TO MAKE SURE THAT SHE IS ALLOWED TO LIVE HERE FOR THE REMAINDER OF HER YEARS, OF WHICH WE HOPE THERE TO BE MANY. AND THAT SHE CAN DO AS SHE PLEASES.

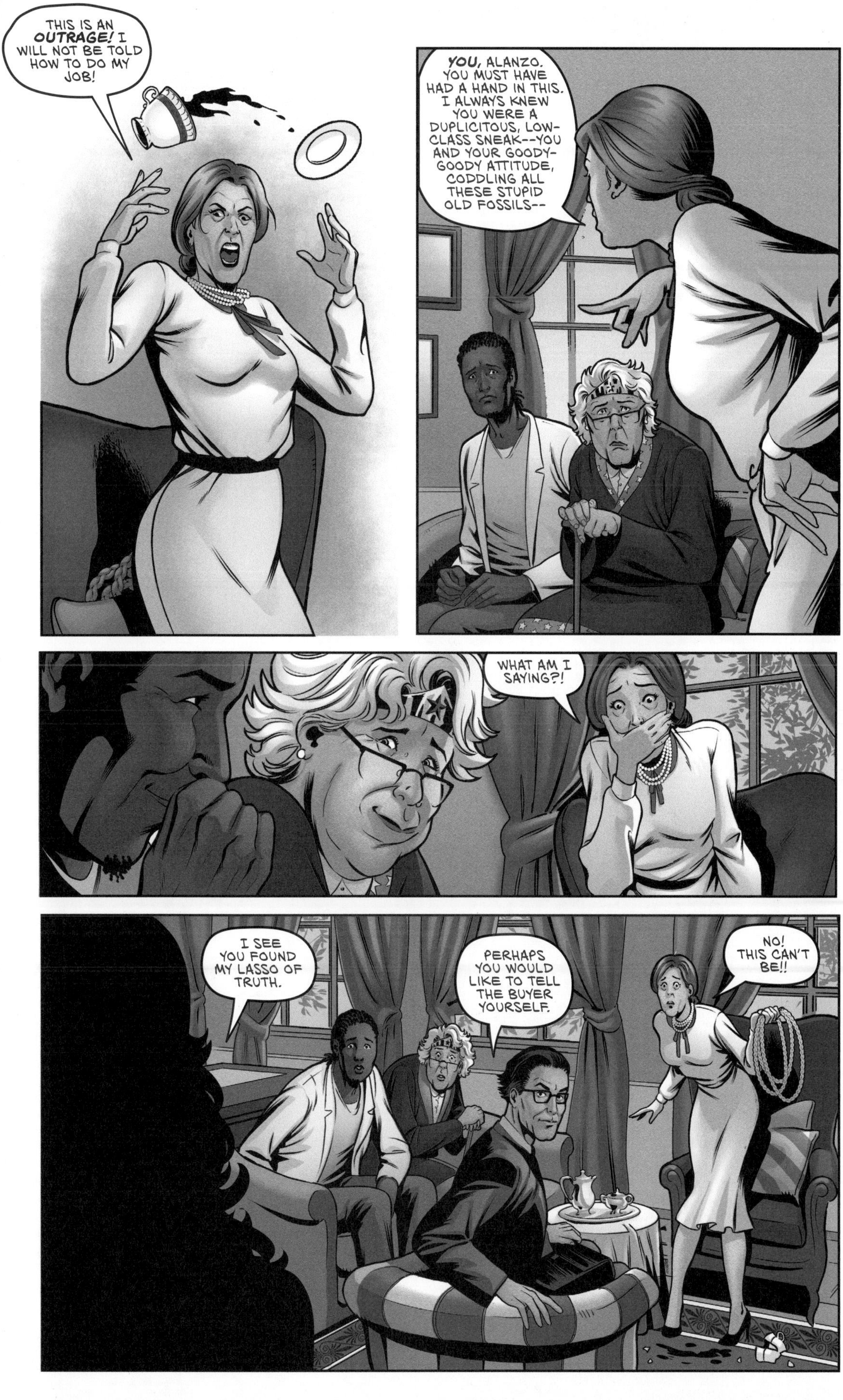
THIS IS AN OUTRAGE! I WILL NOT BE TOLD HOW TO DO MY JOB!
YOU, ALANZO. YOU MUST HAVE HAD A HAND IN THIS. I ALWAYS KNEW YOU WERE A DUPLICITOUS, LOW-CLASS SNEAK--YOU AND YOUR GOODY-GOODY ATTITUDE, CODDLING ALL THESE STUPID OLD FOSSILS--
WHAT AM I SAYING?!
I SEE YOU FOUND MY LASSO OF TRUTH.
PERHAPS YOU WOULD LIKE TO TELL THE BUYER YOURSELF.
NO! THIS CAN'T BE!!

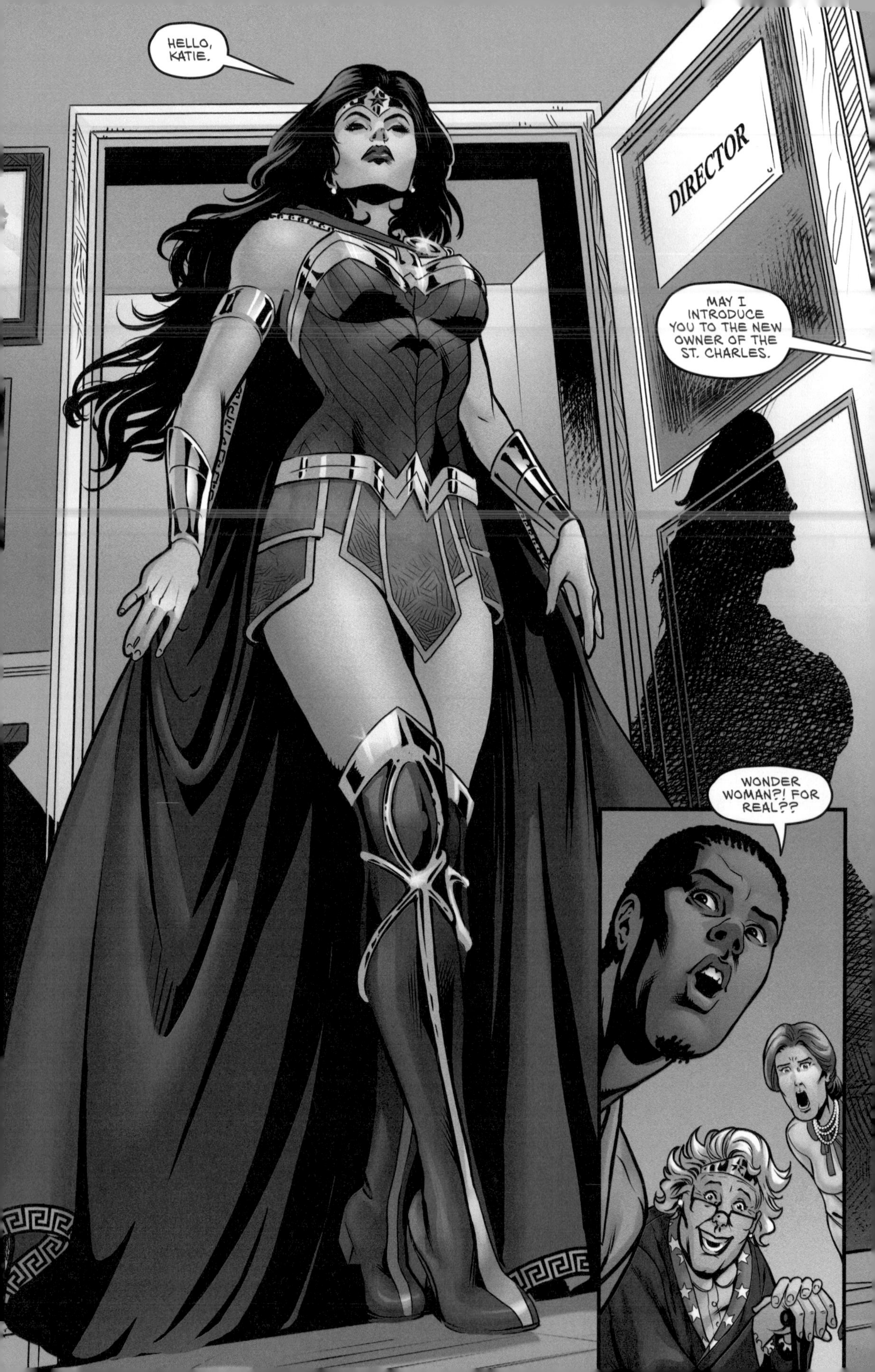
HELLO, KATIE.
DIRECTOR
MAY I INTRODUCE YOU TO THE NEW OWNER OF THE ST. CHARLES.
WONDER WOMAN?! FOR REAL??

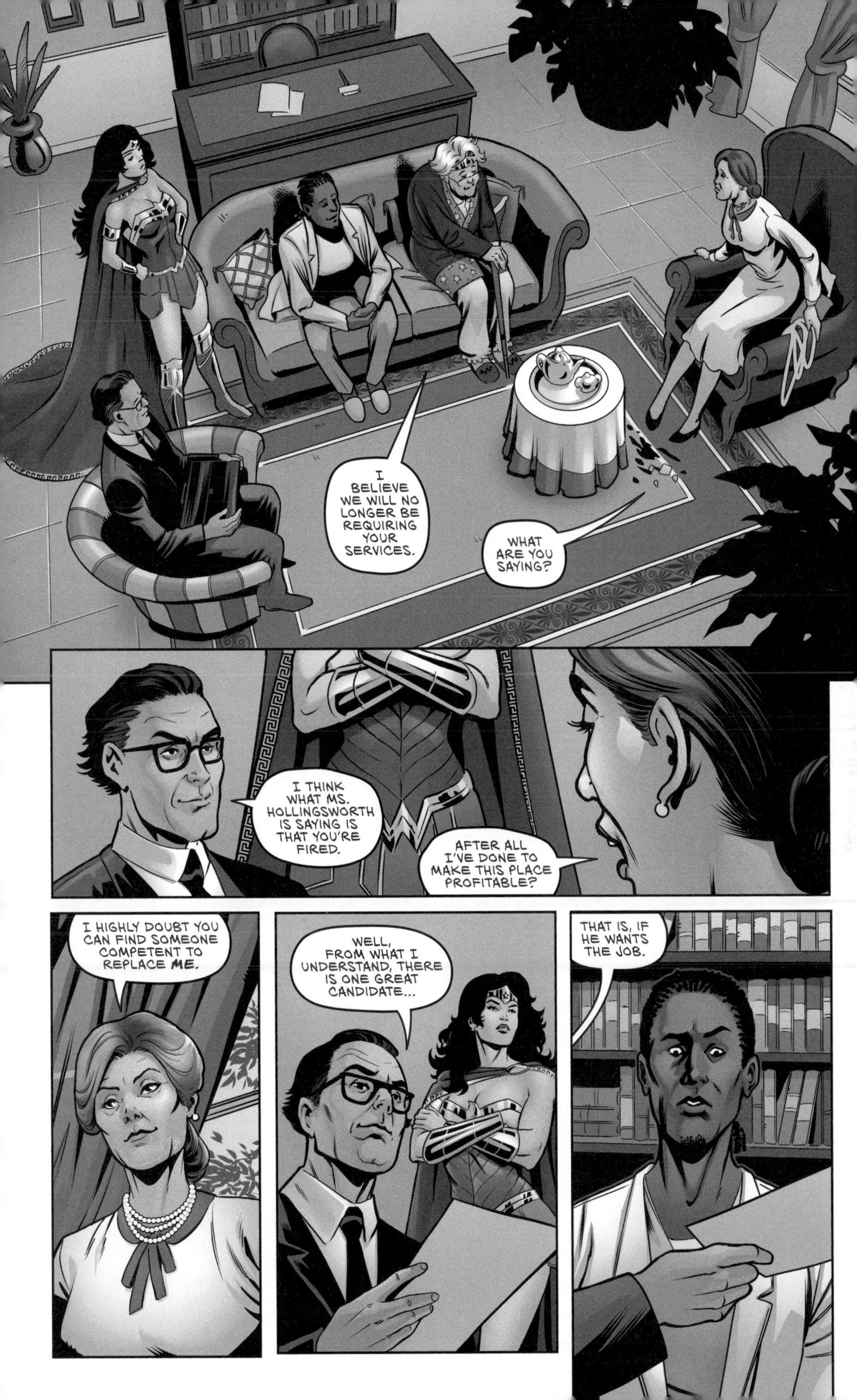
I BELIEVE WE WILL NO LONGER BE REQUIRING YOUR SERVICES.
WHAT ARE YOU SAYING?
I THINK WHAT MS. HOLLINGSWORTH IS SAYING IS THAT YOU'RE FIRED.
AFTER ALL I'VE DONE TO MAKE THIS PLACE PROFITABLE?
I HIGHLY DOUBT YOU CAN FIND SOMEONE COMPETENT TO REPLACE **ME.**
WELL, FROM WHAT I UNDERSTAND, THERE IS ONE GREAT CANDIDATE...
THAT IS, IF HE WANTS THE JOB.

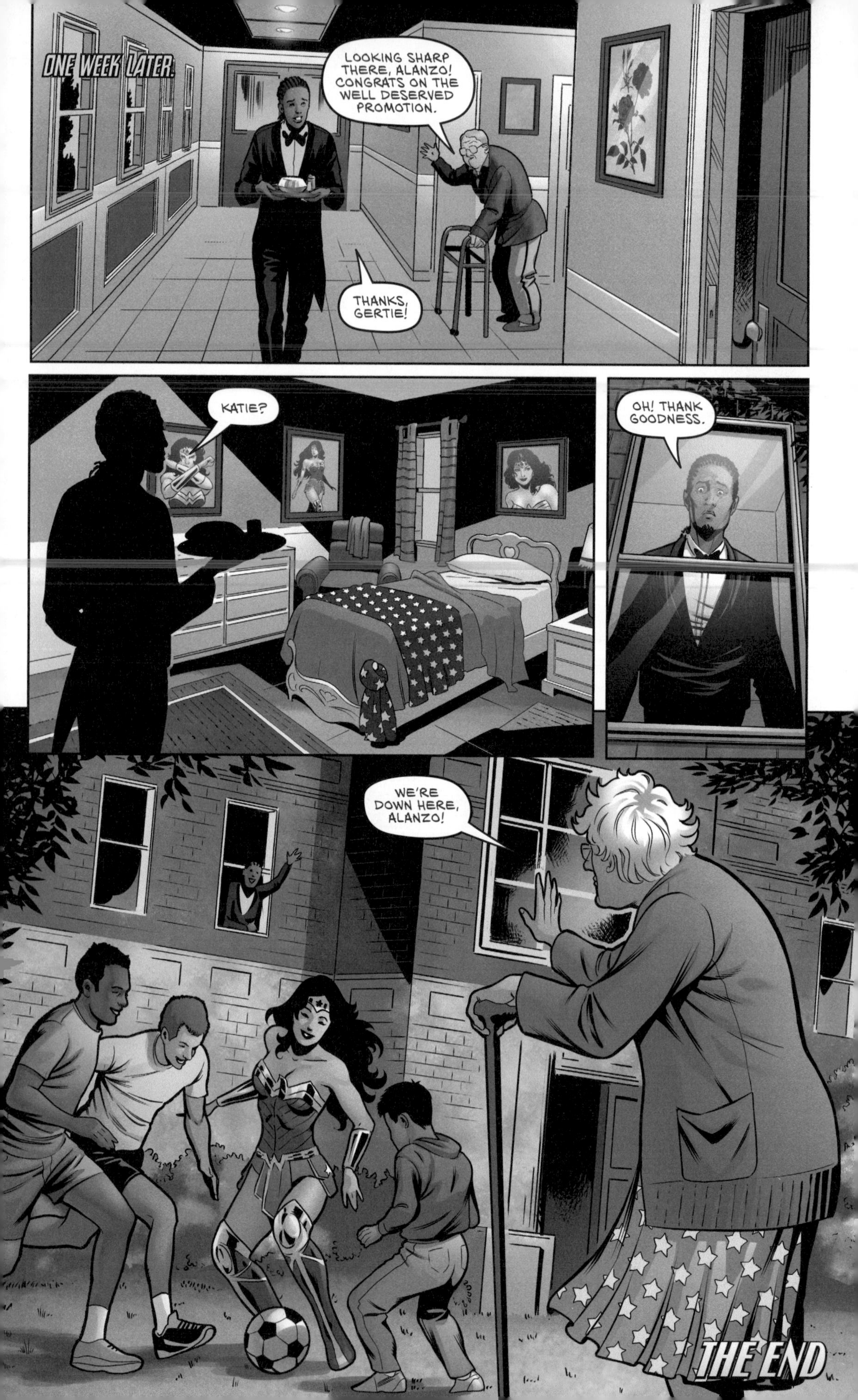
ONE WEEK LATER:
LOOKING SHARP THERE, ALANZO! CONGRATS ON THE WELL DESERVED PROMOTION.
THANKS, GERTIE!
KATIE?
OH! THANK GOODNESS.
WE'RE DOWN HERE, ALANZO!
THE END

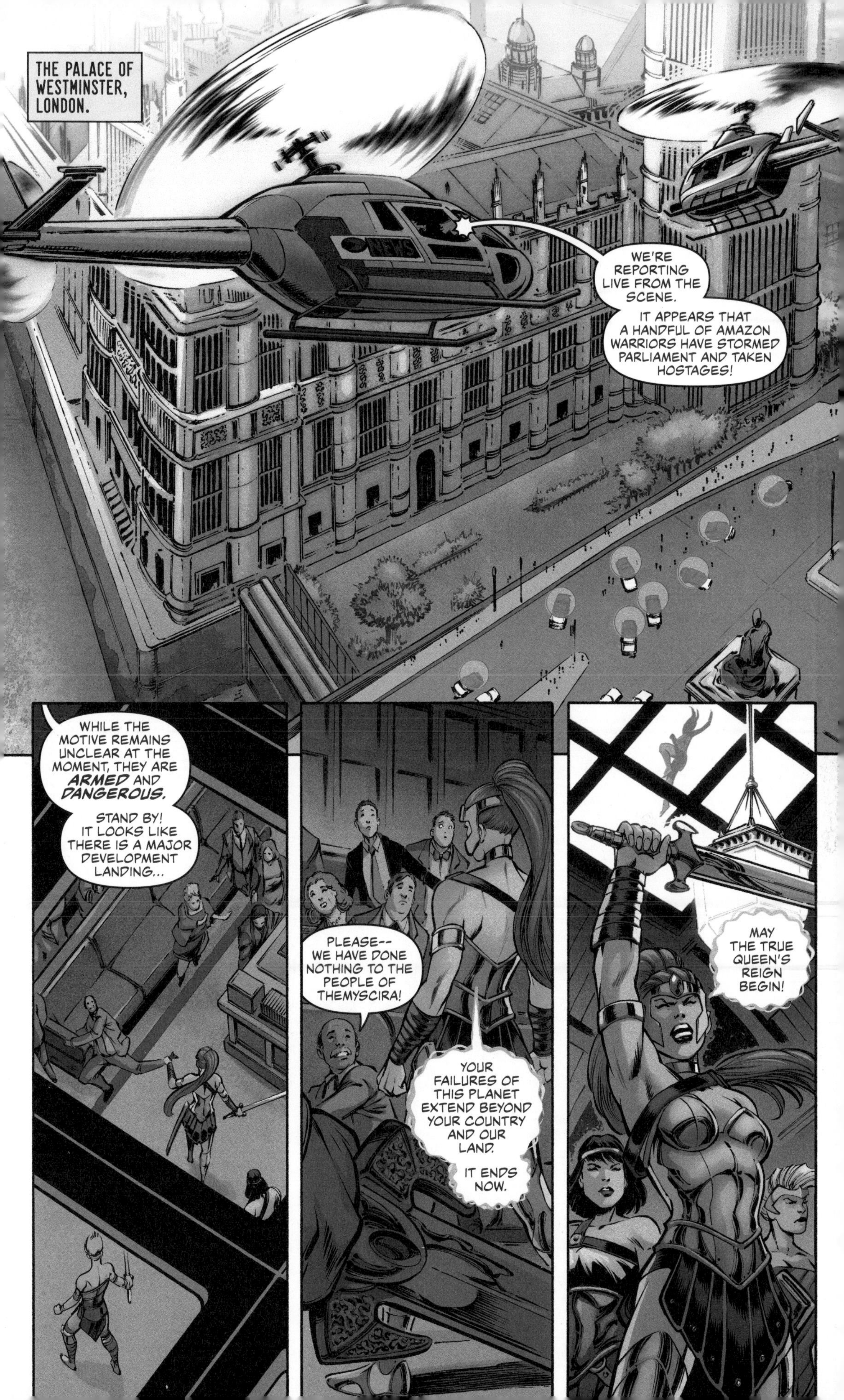
THE PALACE OF WESTMINSTER, LONDON.
NEWS
WE'RE REPORTING LIVE FROM THE SCENE.
IT APPEARS THAT A HANDFUL OF AMAZON WARRIORS HAVE STORMED PARLIAMENT AND TAKEN HOSTAGES!
WHILE THE MOTIVE REMAINS UNCLEAR AT THE MOMENT, THEY ARE ARMED AND DANGEROUS.
STAND BY! IT LOOKS LIKE THERE IS A MAJOR DEVELOPMENT LANDING...
PLEASE-- WE HAVE DONE NOTHING TO THE PEOPLE OF THEMYSCIRA!
YOUR FAILURES OF THIS PLANET EXTEND BEYOND YOUR COUNTRY AND OUR LAND.
IT ENDS NOW.
MAY THE TRUE QUEEN'S REIGN BEGIN!

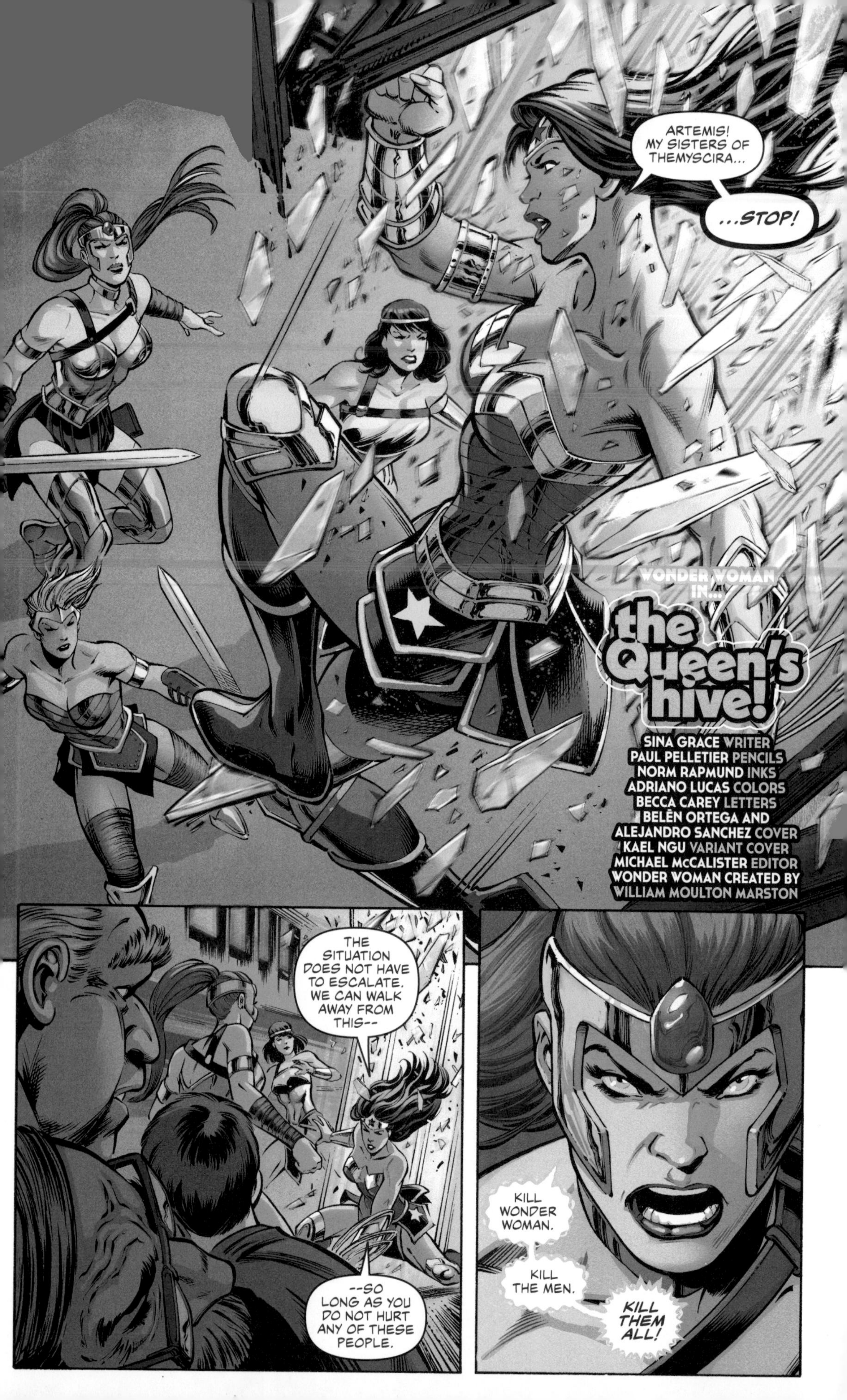

ARTEMIS! MY SISTERS OF THEMYSCIRA...
...STOP!
WONDER WOMAN IN...
the Queen's hive!
SINA GRACE WRITER
PAUL PELLETIER PENCILS
NORM RAPMUND INKS
ADRIANO LUCAS COLORS
BECCA CAREY LETTERS
BELÉN ORTEGA AND ALEJANDRO SANCHEZ COVER
KAEL NGU VARIANT COVER
MICHAEL McCALISTER EDITOR
WONDER WOMAN CREATED BY WILLIAM MOULTON MARSTON
THE SITUATION DOES NOT HAVE TO ESCALATE. WE CAN WALK AWAY FROM THIS--
--SO LONG AS YOU DO NOT HURT ANY OF THESE PEOPLE.
KILL WONDER WOMAN.
KILL THE MEN.
KILL THEM ALL!

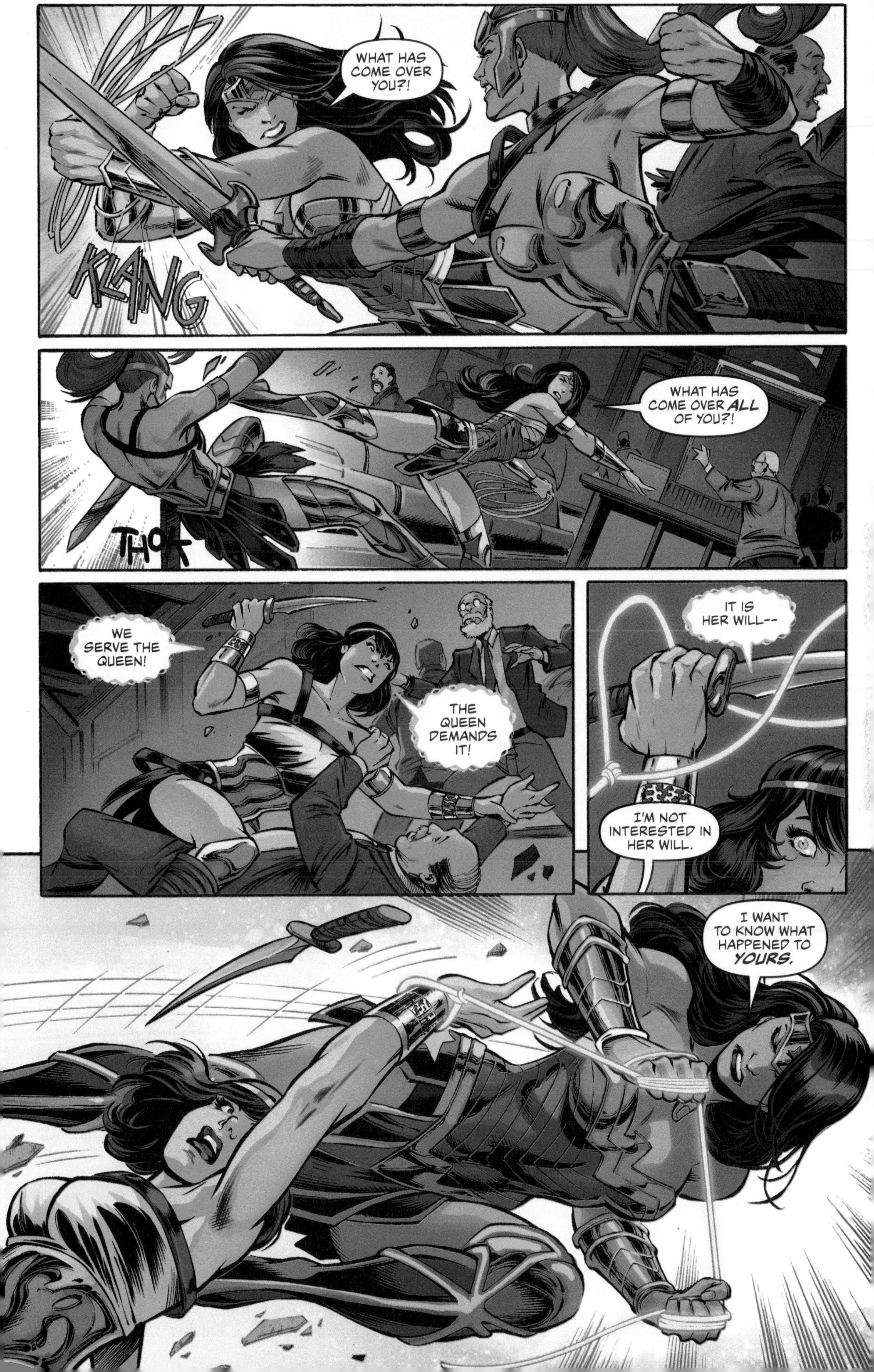
WHAT HAS COME OVER YOU?!
KLANG
WHAT HAS COME OVER **ALL** OF YOU?!
THOK
WE SERVE THE QUEEN!
THE QUEEN DEMANDS IT!
IT IS HER WILL--
I'M NOT INTERESTED IN HER WILL.
I WANT TO KNOW WHAT HAPPENED TO ***YOURS.***

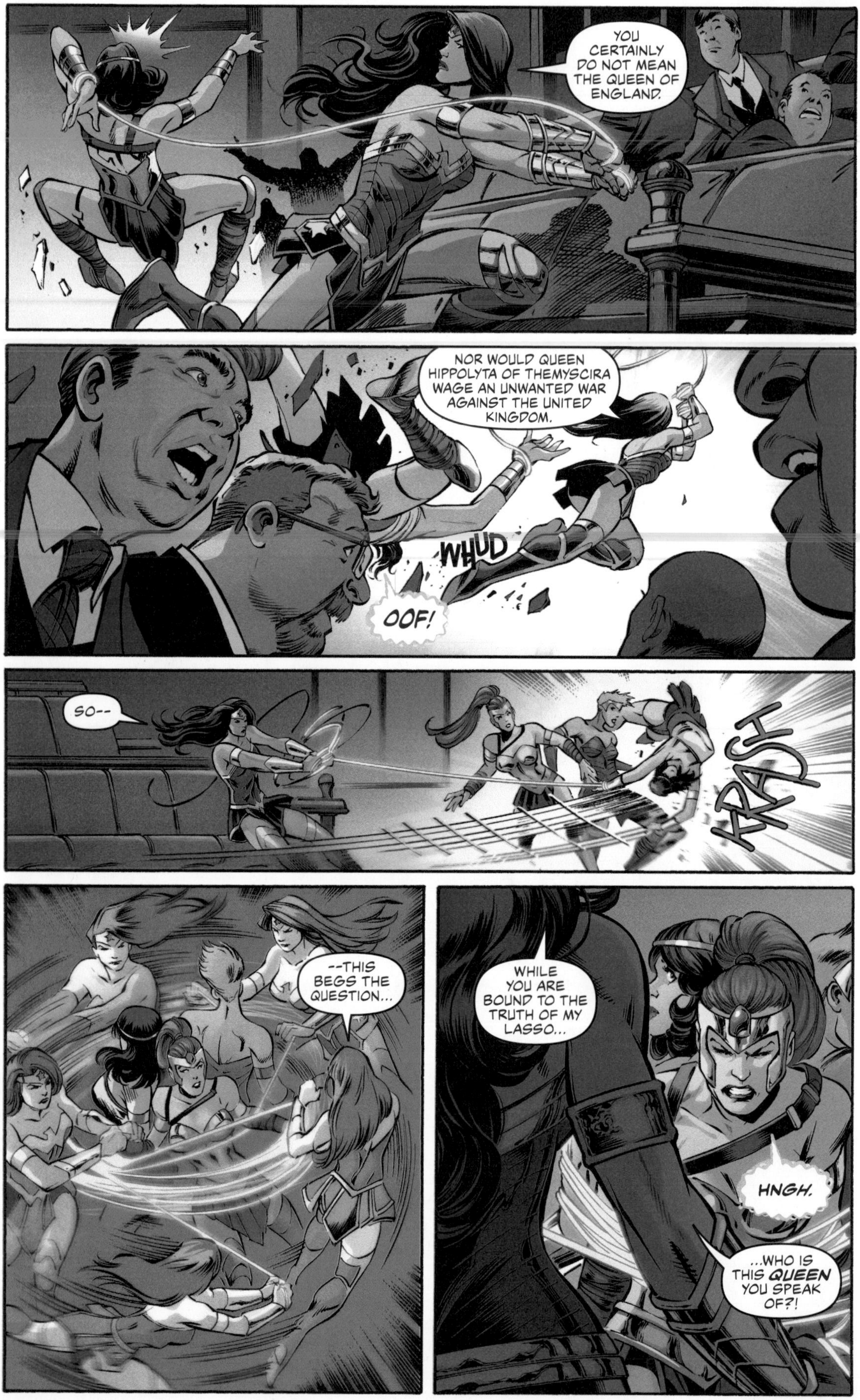
YOU CERTAINLY DO NOT MEAN THE QUEEN OF ENGLAND.
NOR WOULD QUEEN HIPPOLYTA OF THEMYSCIRA WAGE AN UNWANTED WAR AGAINST THE UNITED KINGDOM.
WHUD
OOF!
SO--
KRASH
--THIS BEGS THE QUESTION...
WHILE YOU ARE BOUND TO THE TRUTH OF MY LASSO...
HNGH.
...WHO IS THIS QUEEN YOU SPEAK OF?!

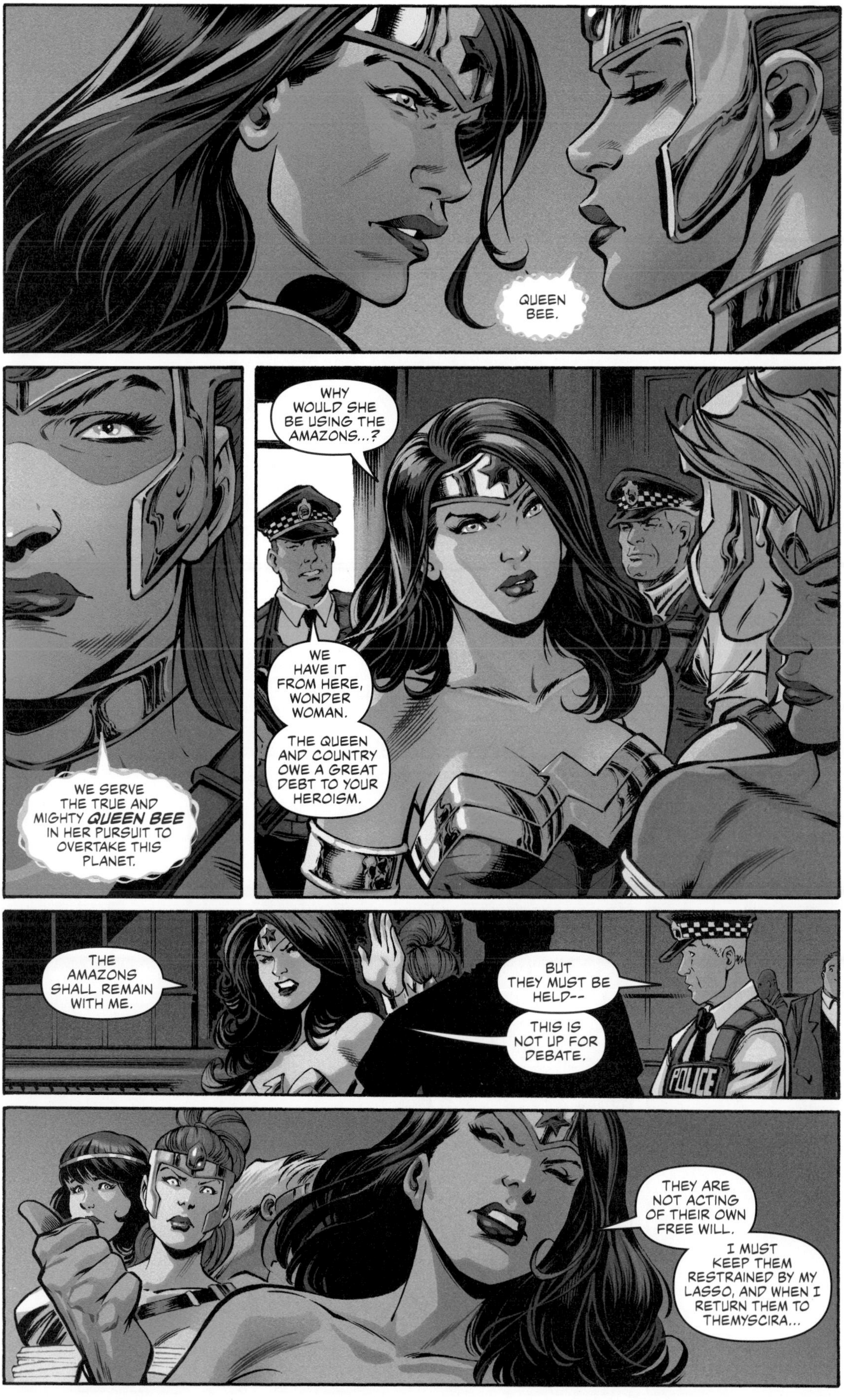

QUEEN BEE.
WE SERVE THE TRUE AND MIGHTY QUEEN BEE IN HER PURSUIT TO OVERTAKE THIS PLANET.
WHY WOULD SHE BE USING THE AMAZONS...?
WE HAVE IT FROM HERE, WONDER WOMAN.
THE QUEEN AND COUNTRY OWE A GREAT DEBT TO YOUR HEROISM.
THE AMAZONS SHALL REMAIN WITH ME.
BUT THEY MUST BE HELD--
THIS IS NOT UP FOR DEBATE.
POLICE
THEY ARE NOT ACTING OF THEIR OWN FREE WILL.
I MUST KEEP THEM RESTRAINED BY MY LASSO, AND WHEN I RETURN THEM TO THEMYSCIRA...

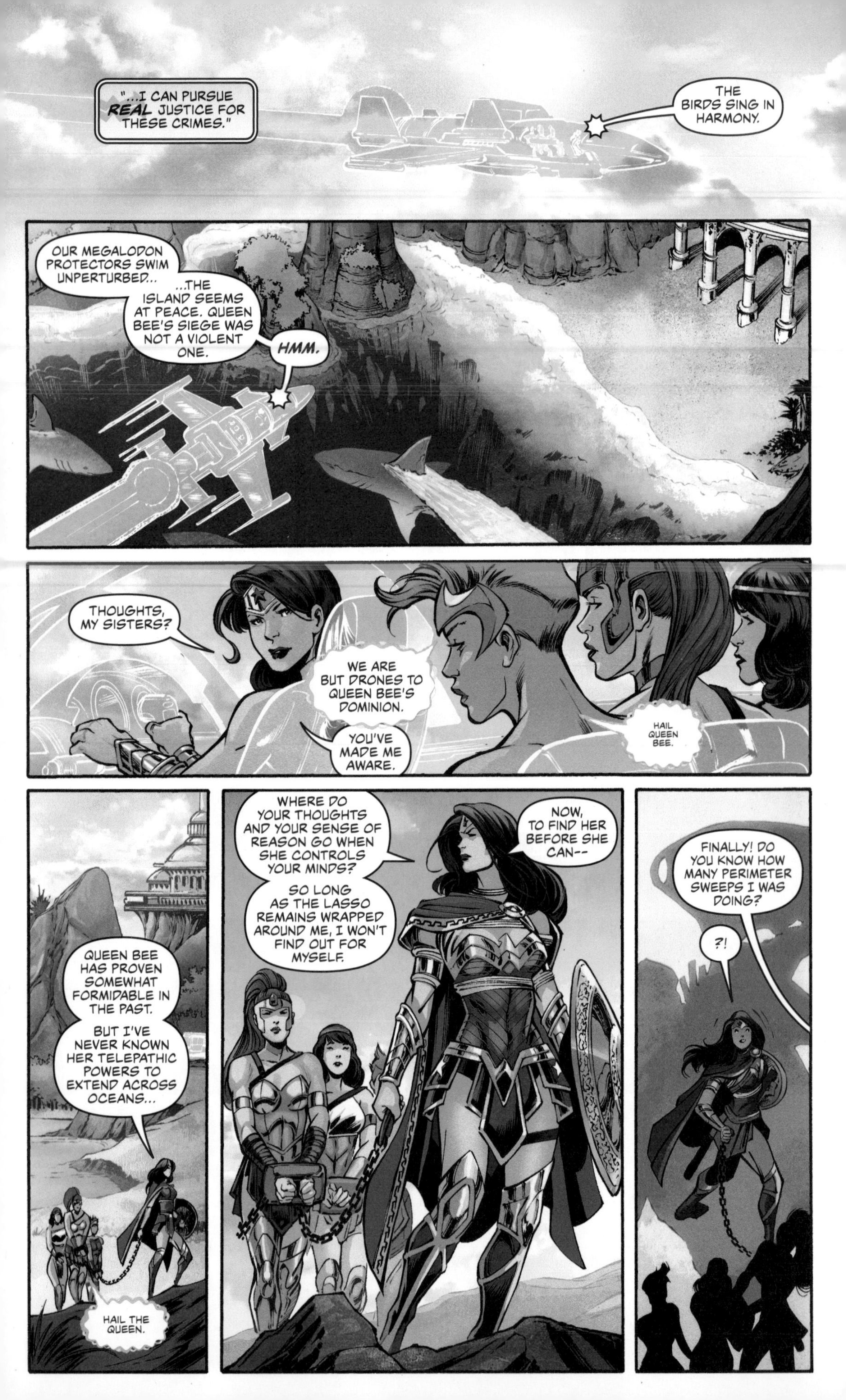
"...I CAN PURSUE REAL JUSTICE FOR THESE CRIMES."
THE BIRDS SING IN HARMONY.
OUR MEGALODON PROTECTORS SWIM UNPERTURBED...
...THE ISLAND SEEMS AT PEACE. QUEEN BEE'S SIEGE WAS NOT A VIOLENT ONE.
HMM.
THOUGHTS, MY SISTERS?
WE ARE BUT DRONES TO QUEEN BEE'S DOMINION.
YOU'VE MADE ME AWARE.
HAIL QUEEN BEE.
QUEEN BEE HAS PROVEN SOMEWHAT FORMIDABLE IN THE PAST.
BUT I'VE NEVER KNOWN HER TELEPATHIC POWERS TO EXTEND ACROSS OCEANS...
HAIL THE QUEEN.
WHERE DO YOUR THOUGHTS AND YOUR SENSE OF REASON GO WHEN SHE CONTROLS YOUR MINDS?
SO LONG AS THE LASSO REMAINS WRAPPED AROUND ME, I WON'T FIND OUT FOR MYSELF.
NOW, TO FIND HER BEFORE SHE CAN--
FINALLY! DO YOU KNOW HOW MANY PERIMETER SWEEPS I WAS DOING?
?!

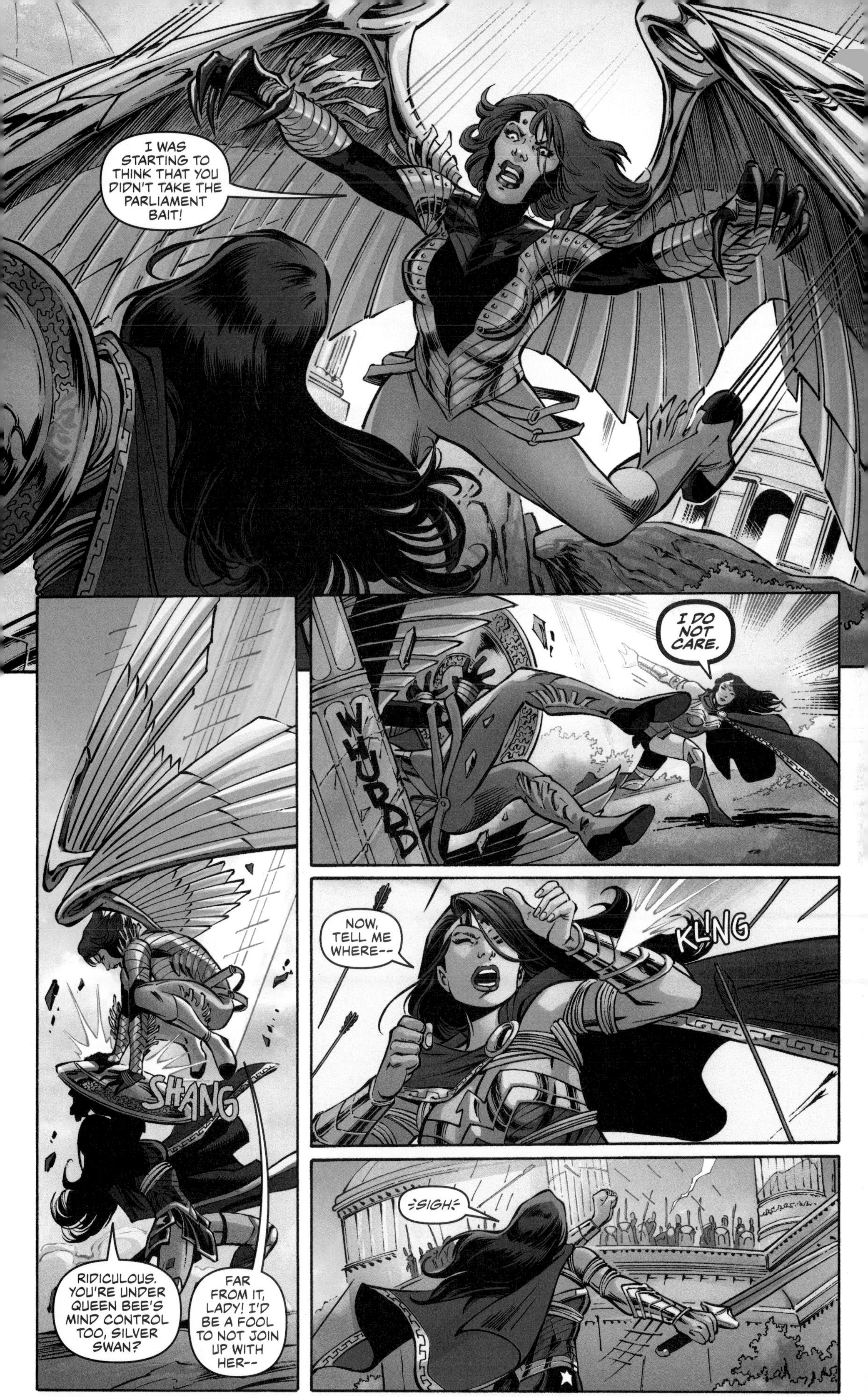
I WAS STARTING TO THINK THAT YOU DIDN'T TAKE THE PARLIAMENT BAIT!
I DO NOT CARE.
WHUDD
SHANG
RIDICULOUS. YOU'RE UNDER QUEEN BEE'S MIND CONTROL TOO, SILVER SWAN?
FAR FROM IT, LADY! I'D BE A FOOL TO NOT JOIN UP WITH HER--
NOW, TELL ME WHERE--
KLING
SIGH

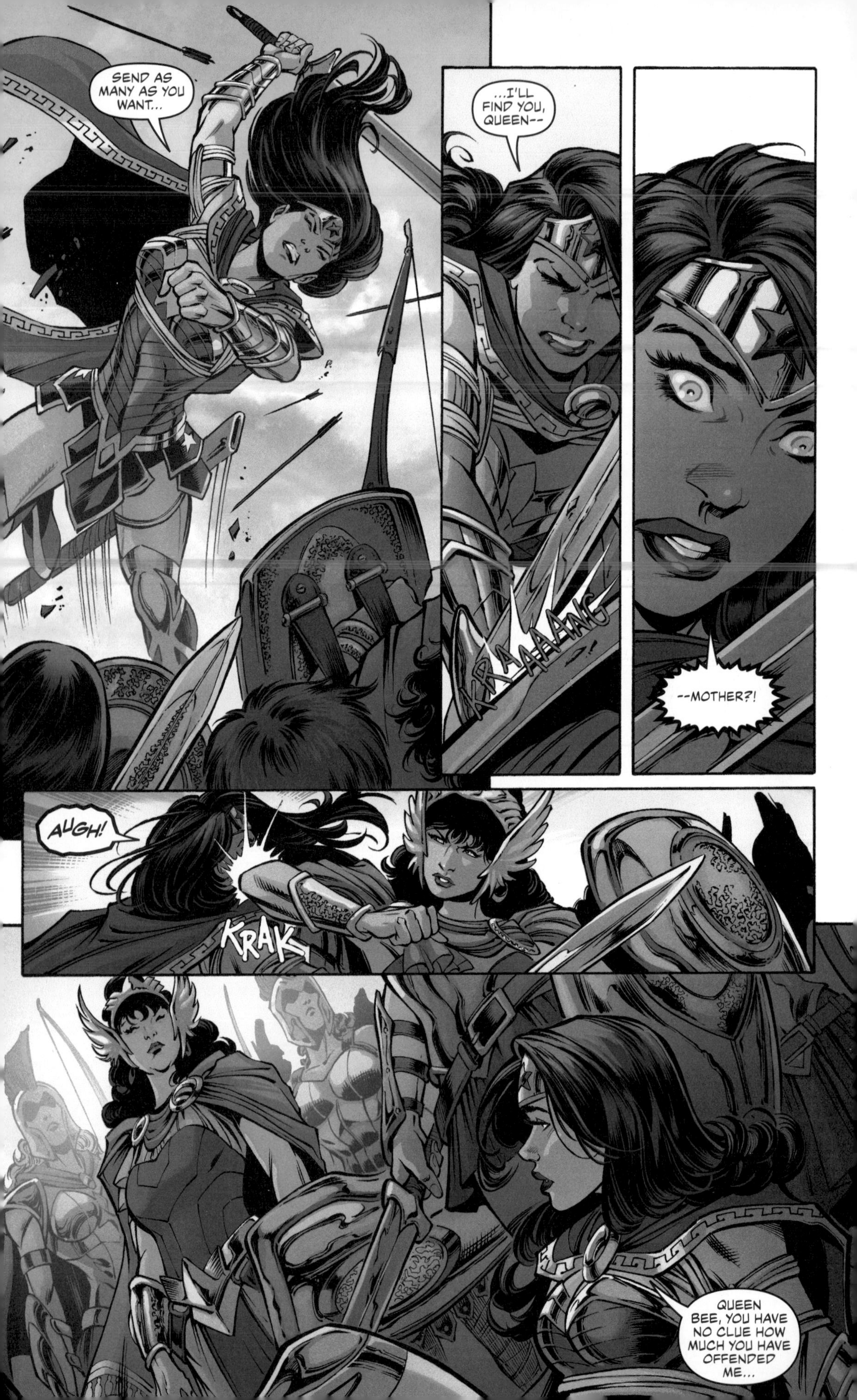

SEND AS MANY AS YOU WANT...
...I'LL FIND YOU, QUEEN--
KRAAAANG
--MOTHER?!
AUGH!
KRAK
QUEEN BEE, YOU HAVE NO CLUE HOW MUCH YOU HAVE OFFENDED ME...

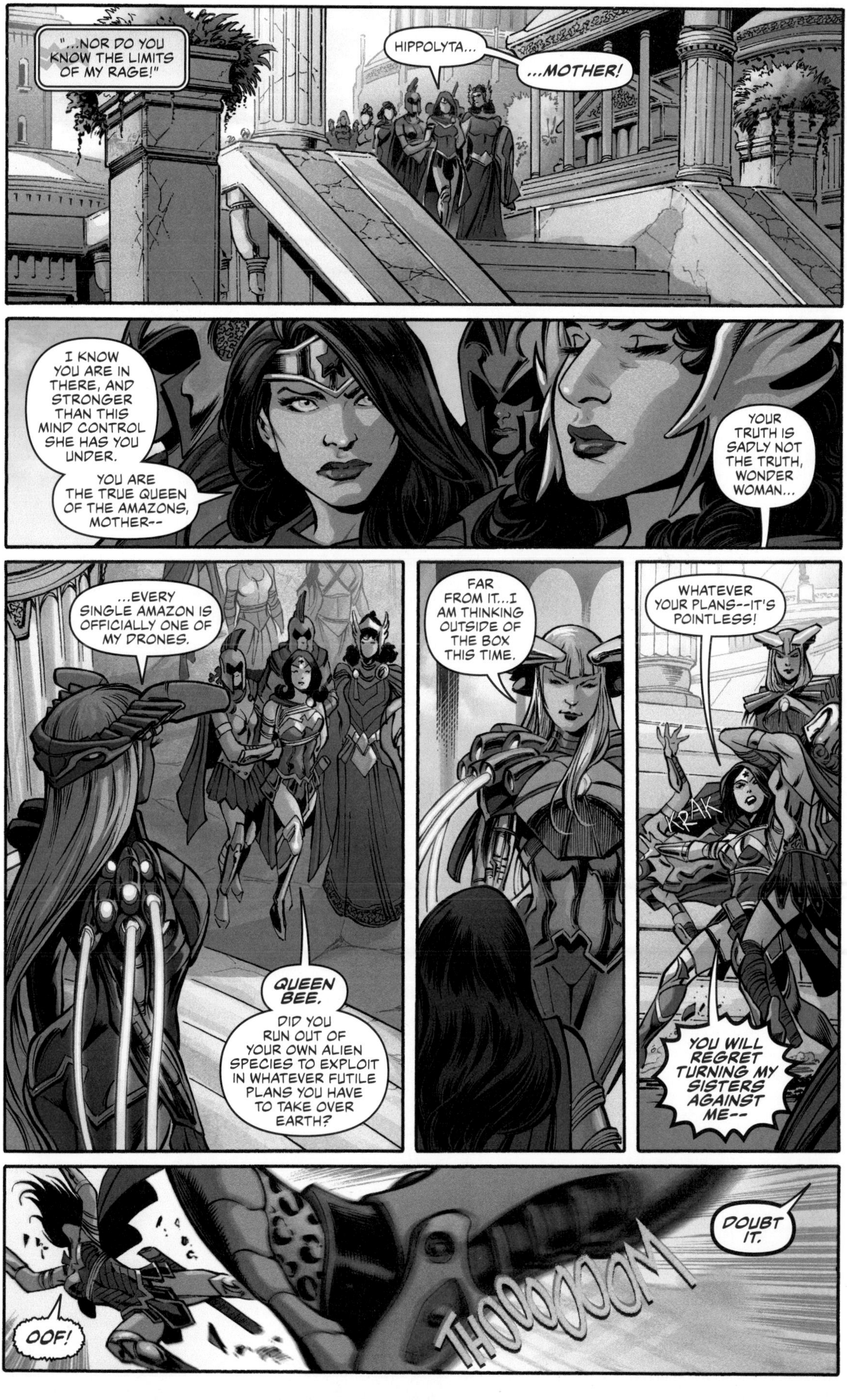
"...NOR DO YOU KNOW THE LIMITS OF MY RAGE!"
HIPPOLYTA...
...MOTHER!
I KNOW YOU ARE IN THERE, AND STRONGER THAN THIS MIND CONTROL SHE HAS YOU UNDER.
YOU ARE THE TRUE QUEEN OF THE AMAZONS, MOTHER--
YOUR TRUTH IS SADLY NOT THE TRUTH, WONDER WOMAN...
...EVERY SINGLE AMAZON IS OFFICIALLY ONE OF MY DRONES.
QUEEN BEE.
DID YOU RUN OUT OF YOUR OWN ALIEN SPECIES TO EXPLOIT IN WHATEVER FUTILE PLANS YOU HAVE TO TAKE OVER EARTH?
FAR FROM IT...I AM THINKING OUTSIDE OF THE BOX THIS TIME.
WHATEVER YOUR PLANS--IT'S POINTLESS!
KRAK
YOU WILL REGRET TURNING MY SISTERS AGAINST ME--
DOUBT IT.
THOOOOOOM
OOF!

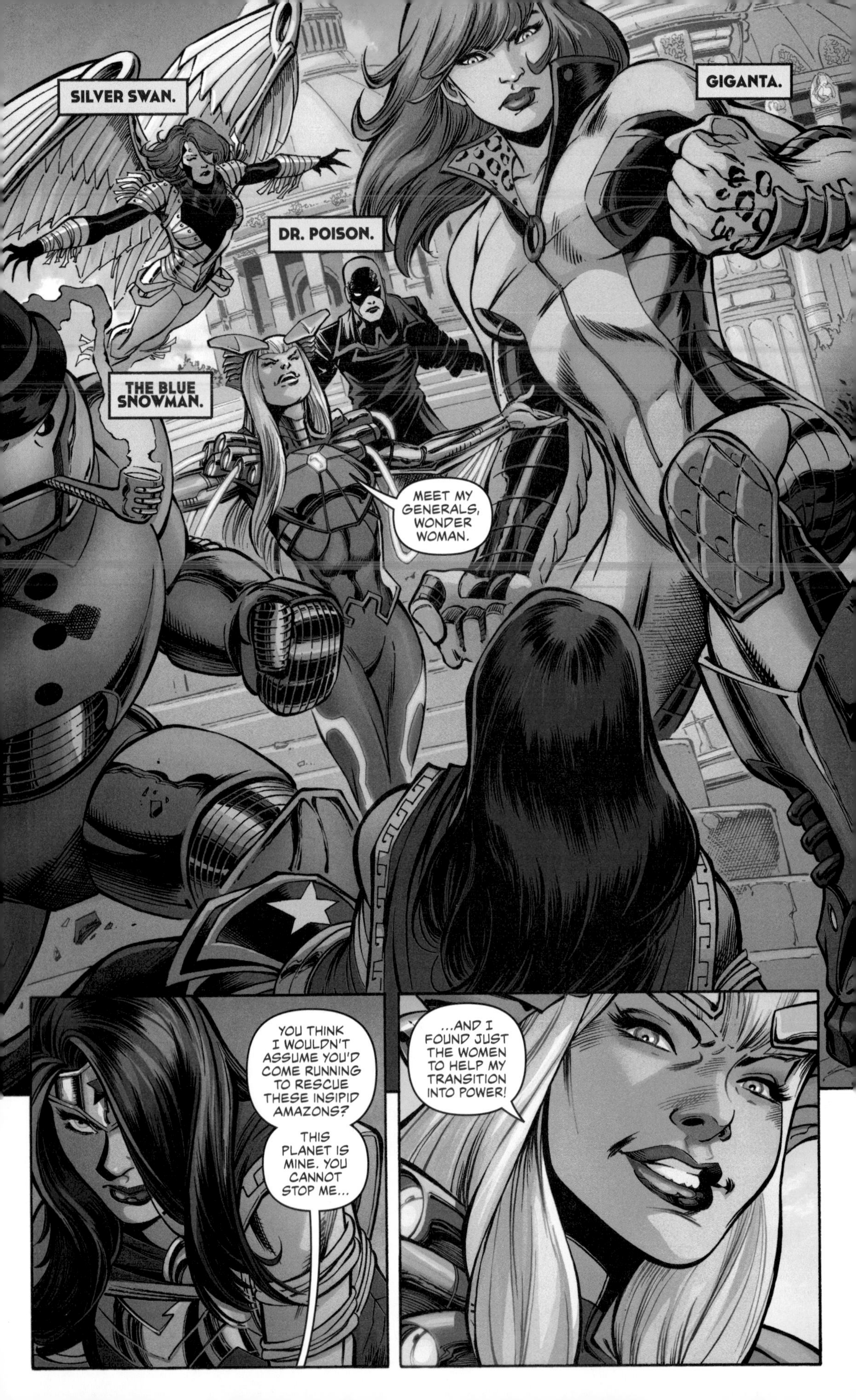
SILVER SWAN.
DR. POISON.
GIGANTA.
THE BLUE SNOWMAN.
MEET MY GENERALS, WONDER WOMAN.
YOU THINK I WOULDN'T ASSUME YOU'D COME RUNNING TO RESCUE THESE INSIPID AMAZONS?
THIS PLANET IS MINE. YOU CANNOT STOP ME...
...AND I FOUND JUST THE WOMEN TO HELP MY TRANSITION INTO POWER!

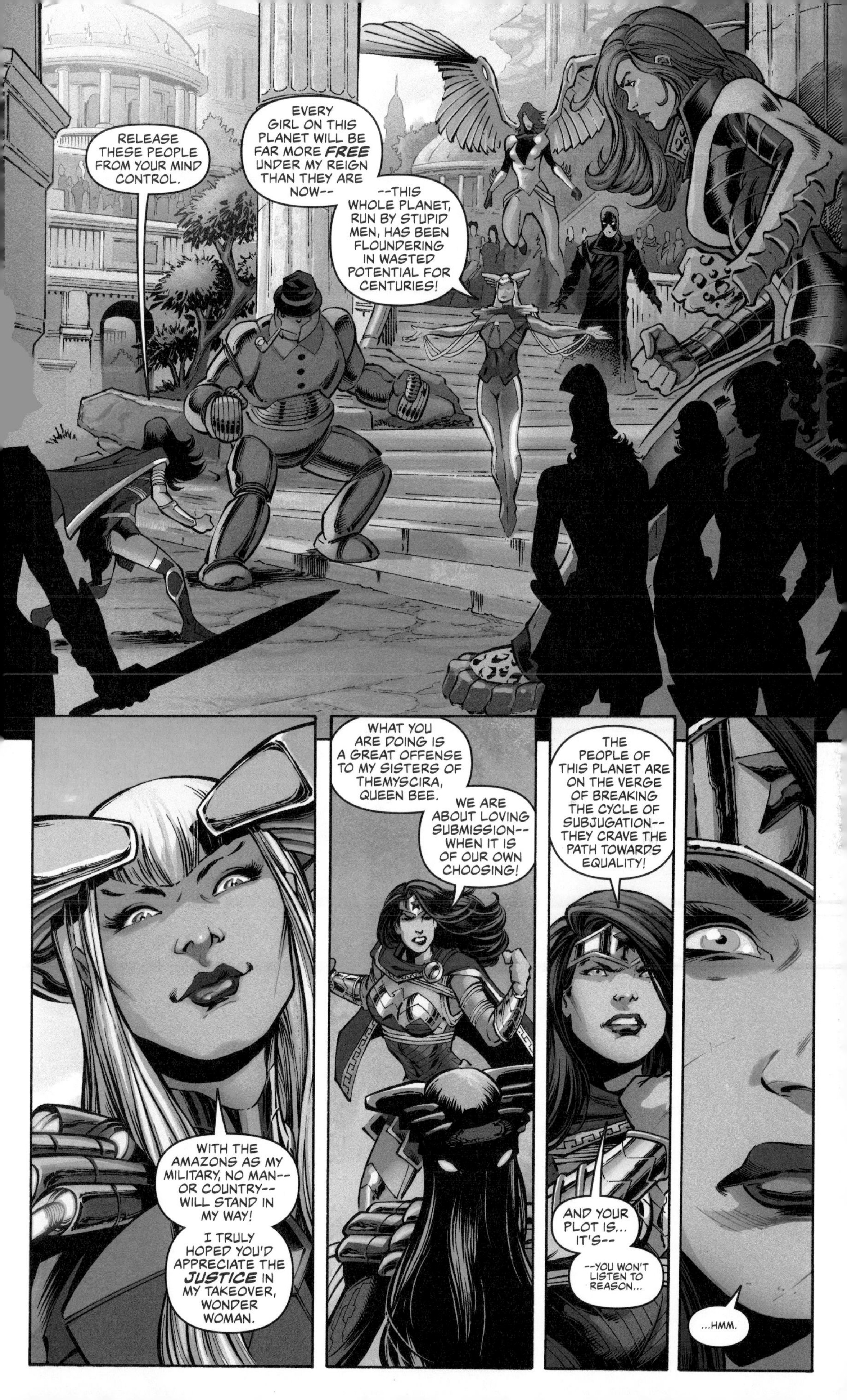
RELEASE THESE PEOPLE FROM YOUR MIND CONTROL.
EVERY GIRL ON THIS PLANET WILL BE FAR MORE FREE UNDER MY REIGN THAN THEY ARE NOW--
--THIS WHOLE PLANET, RUN BY STUPID MEN, HAS BEEN FLOUNDERING IN WASTED POTENTIAL FOR CENTURIES!
WITH THE AMAZONS AS MY MILITARY, NO MAN--OR COUNTRY--WILL STAND IN MY WAY!
I TRULY HOPED YOU'D APPRECIATE THE JUSTICE IN MY TAKEOVER, WONDER WOMAN.
WHAT YOU ARE DOING IS A GREAT OFFENSE TO MY SISTERS OF THEMYSCIRA, QUEEN BEE.
WE ARE ABOUT LOVING SUBMISSION-- WHEN IT IS OF OUR OWN CHOOSING!
THE PEOPLE OF THIS PLANET ARE ON THE VERGE OF BREAKING THE CYCLE OF SUBJUGATION-- THEY CRAVE THE PATH TOWARDS EQUALITY!
AND YOUR PLOT IS... IT'S--
--YOU WON'T LISTEN TO REASON...
...HMM.

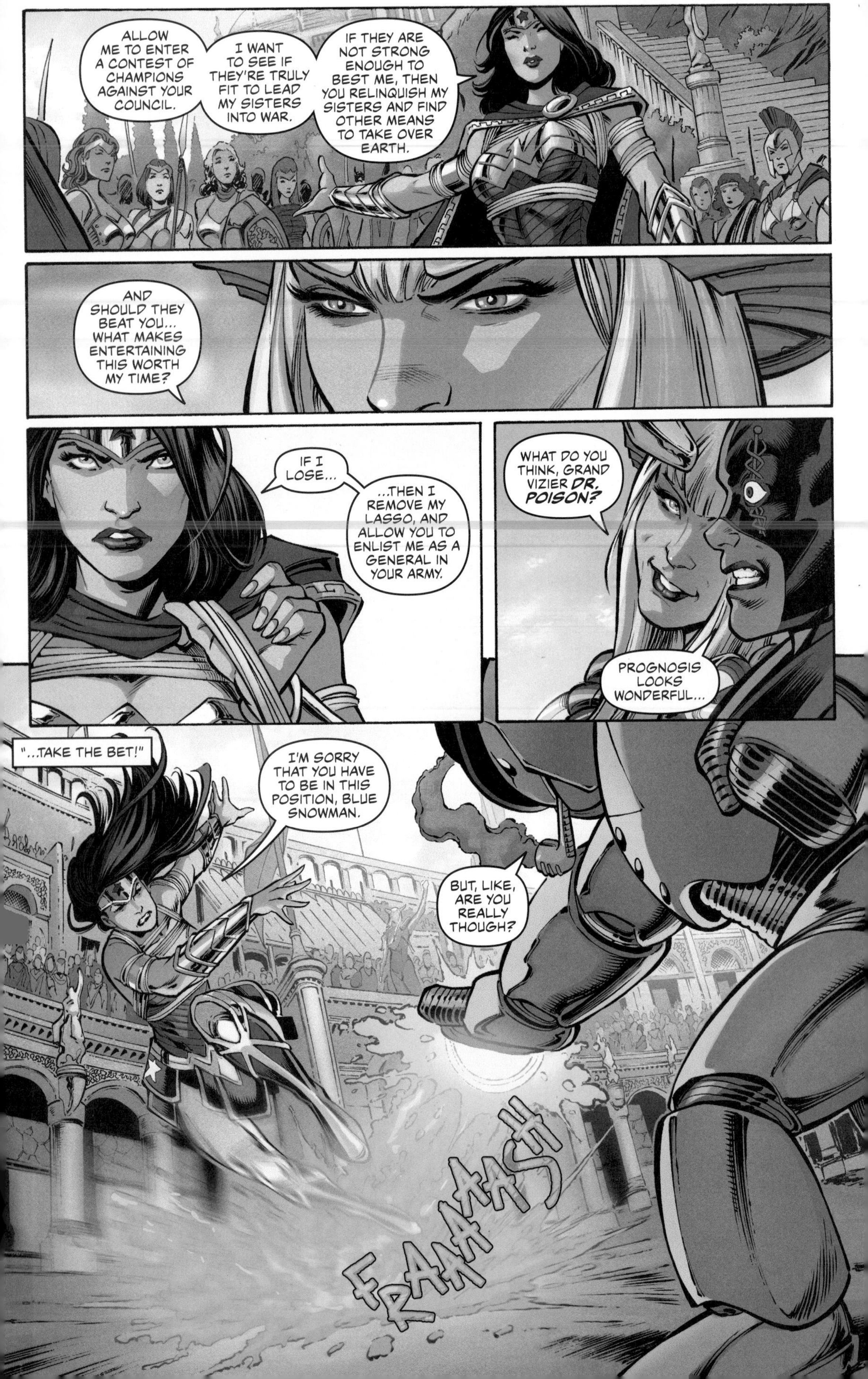
ALLOW ME TO ENTER A CONTEST OF CHAMPIONS AGAINST YOUR COUNCIL.
I WANT TO SEE IF THEY'RE TRULY FIT TO LEAD MY SISTERS INTO WAR.
IF THEY ARE NOT STRONG ENOUGH TO BEST ME, THEN YOU RELINQUISH MY SISTERS AND FIND OTHER MEANS TO TAKE OVER EARTH.
AND SHOULD THEY BEAT YOU... WHAT MAKES ENTERTAINING THIS WORTH MY TIME?
IF I LOSE...
...THEN I REMOVE MY LASSO, AND ALLOW YOU TO ENLIST ME AS A GENERAL IN YOUR ARMY.
WHAT DO YOU THINK, GRAND VIZIER DR. POISON?
PROGNOSIS LOOKS WONDERFUL...
"...TAKE THE BET!"
I'M SORRY THAT YOU HAVE TO BE IN THIS POSITION, BLUE SNOWMAN.
BUT, LIKE, ARE YOU REALLY THOUGH?
FRAAAAASH

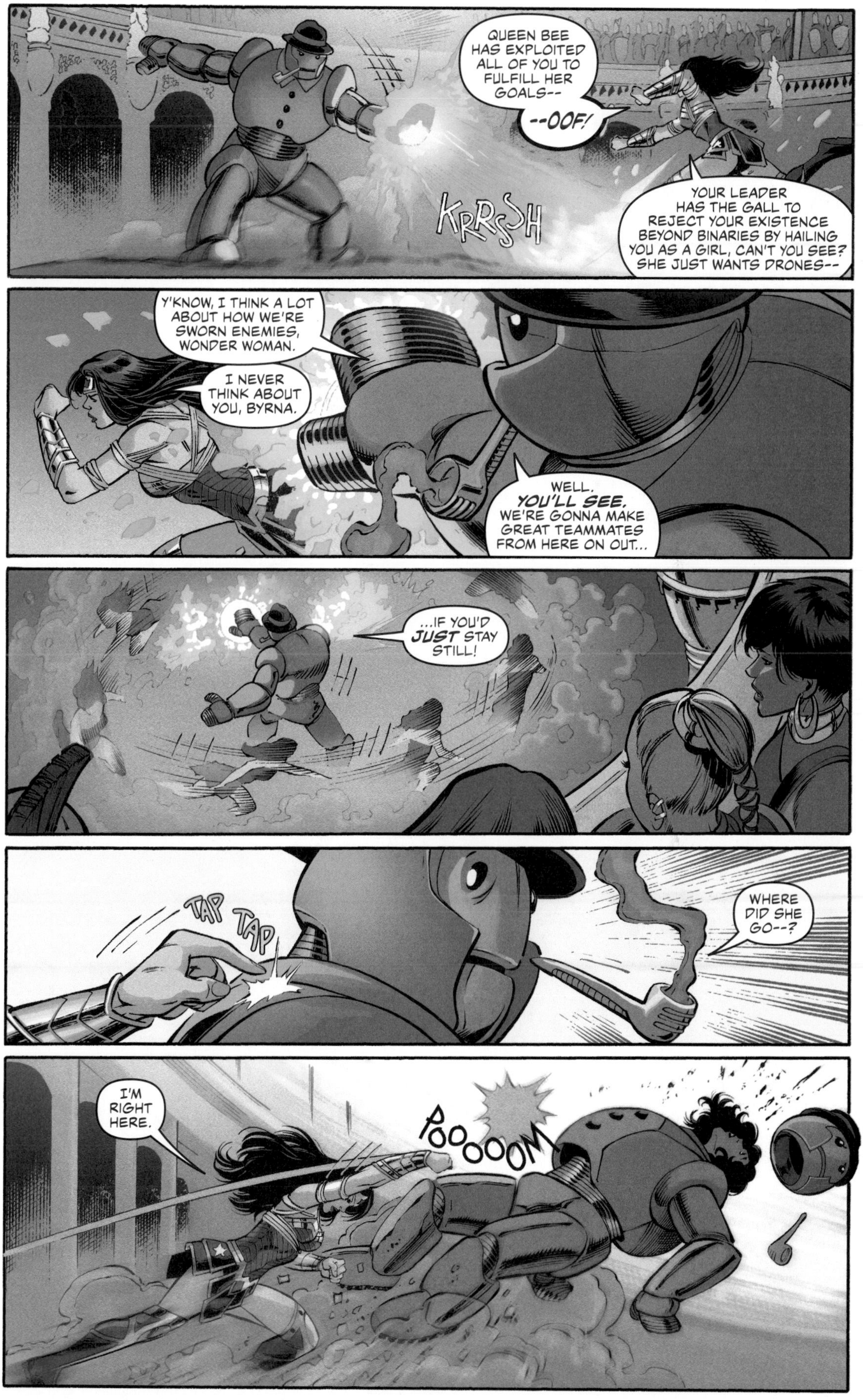
QUEEN BEE HAS EXPLOITED ALL OF YOU TO FULFILL HER GOALS--
--OOF!
KRRSSH
YOUR LEADER HAS THE GALL TO REJECT YOUR EXISTENCE BEYOND BINARIES BY HAILING YOU AS A GIRL, CAN'T YOU SEE? SHE JUST WANTS DRONES--
Y'KNOW, I THINK A LOT ABOUT HOW WE'RE SWORN ENEMIES, WONDER WOMAN.
I NEVER THINK ABOUT YOU, BYRNA.
WELL. YOU'LL SEE. WE'RE GONNA MAKE GREAT TEAMMATES FROM HERE ON OUT...
...IF YOU'D JUST STAY STILL!
TAP TAP
WHERE DID SHE GO--?
I'M RIGHT HERE.
POOOOOM

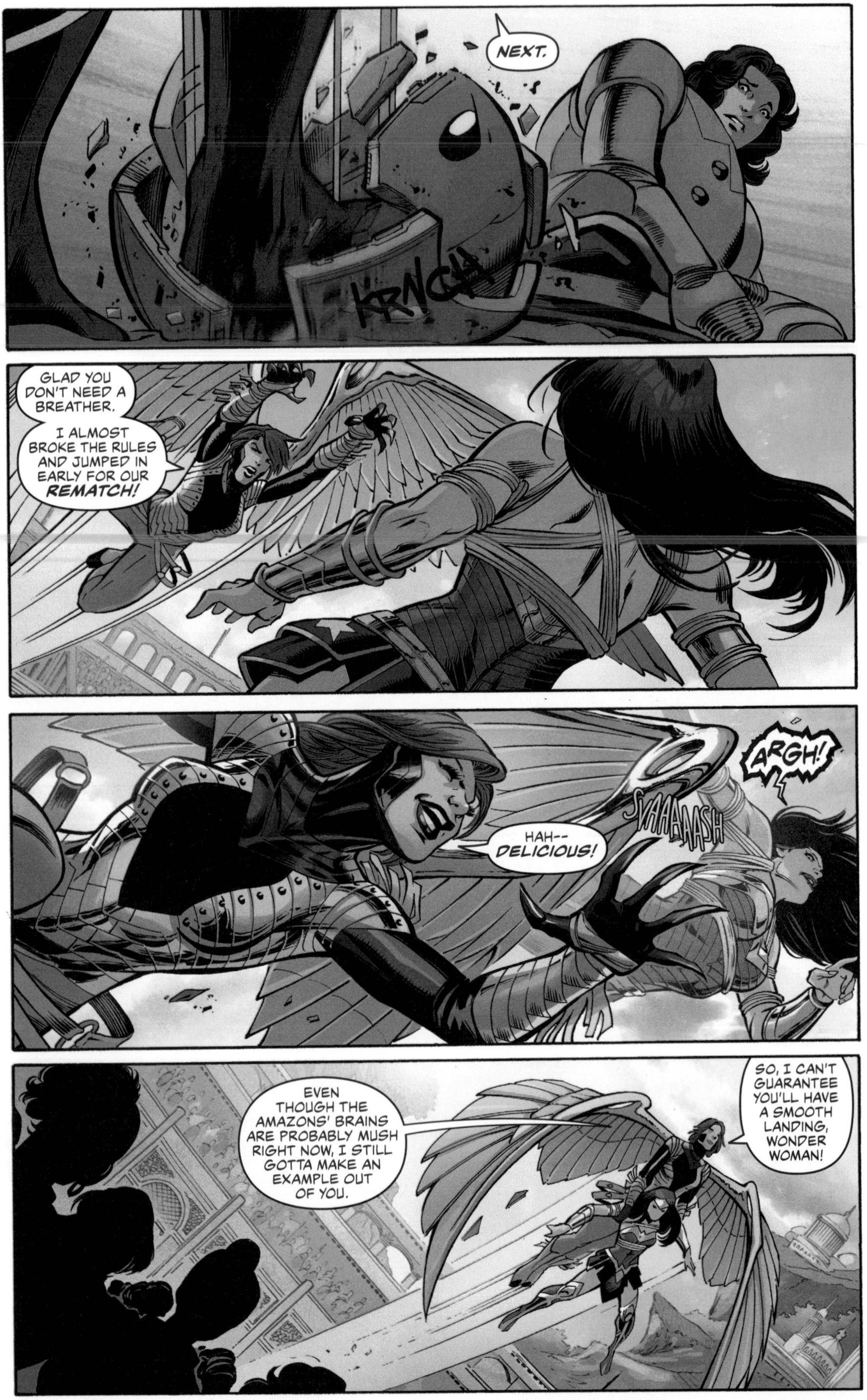
NEXT.
KRNCH
GLAD YOU DON'T NEED A BREATHER.
I ALMOST BROKE THE RULES AND JUMPED IN EARLY FOR OUR REMATCH!
ARGH!
HAH-- DELICIOUS!
SVAAAAASH
EVEN THOUGH THE AMAZONS' BRAINS ARE PROBABLY MUSH RIGHT NOW, I STILL GOTTA MAKE AN EXAMPLE OUT OF YOU.
SO, I CAN'T GUARANTEE YOU'LL HAVE A SMOOTH LANDING, WONDER WOMAN!

NOR I, VANESSA.

NNG.

YOU WERE A FOOL TO JOIN FORCES WITH A FAILED DESPOT.

EVEN MORE FOOLISH THINKING YOU'D FARE BETTER IN A REMATCH WITHOUT THE ELEMENT OF SURPRISE!

JUST.

WHUD

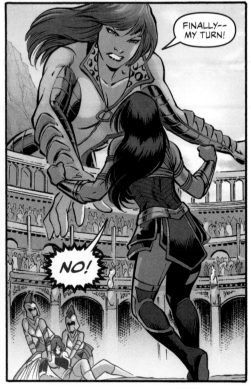

FINALLY-- MY TURN!

NO!

FOOLISHNESS.

WHUDD

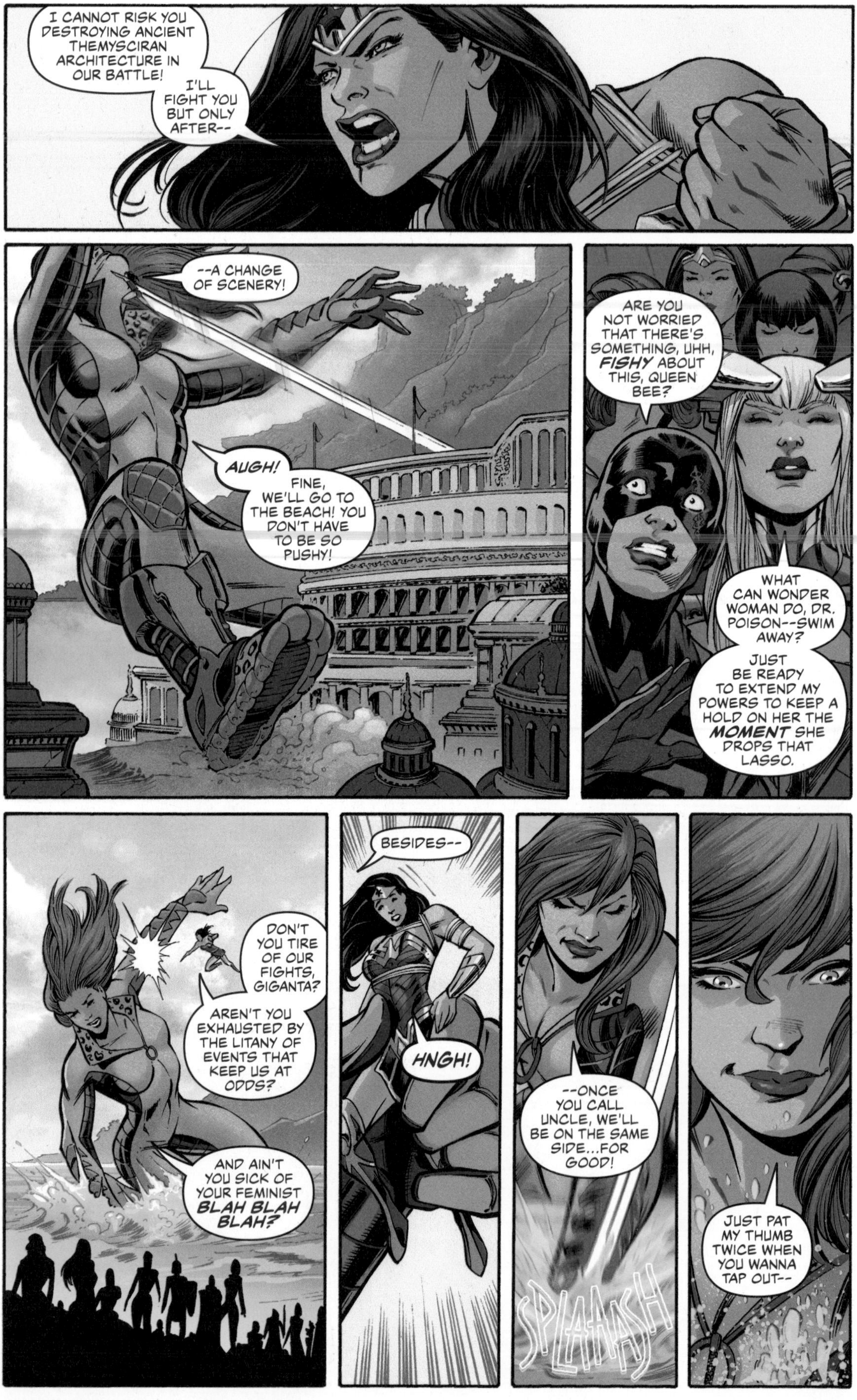
I CANNOT RISK YOU DESTROYING ANCIENT THEMYSCIRAN ARCHITECTURE IN OUR BATTLE!
I'LL FIGHT YOU BUT ONLY AFTER--
--A CHANGE OF SCENERY!
AUGH! FINE, WE'LL GO TO THE BEACH! YOU DON'T HAVE TO BE SO PUSHY!
ARE YOU NOT WORRIED THAT THERE'S SOMETHING, UHH, FISHY ABOUT THIS, QUEEN BEE?
WHAT CAN WONDER WOMAN DO, DR. POISON--SWIM AWAY?
JUST BE READY TO EXTEND MY POWERS TO KEEP A HOLD ON HER THE MOMENT SHE DROPS THAT LASSO.
DON'T YOU TIRE OF OUR FIGHTS, GIGANTA?
AREN'T YOU EXHAUSTED BY THE LITANY OF EVENTS THAT KEEP US AT ODDS?
AND AIN'T YOU SICK OF YOUR FEMINIST BLAH BLAH BLAH?
BESIDES--
HNGH!
--ONCE YOU CALL UNCLE, WE'LL BE ON THE SAME SIDE...FOR GOOD!
SPLAAASH
JUST PAT MY THUMB TWICE WHEN YOU WANNA TAP OUT--

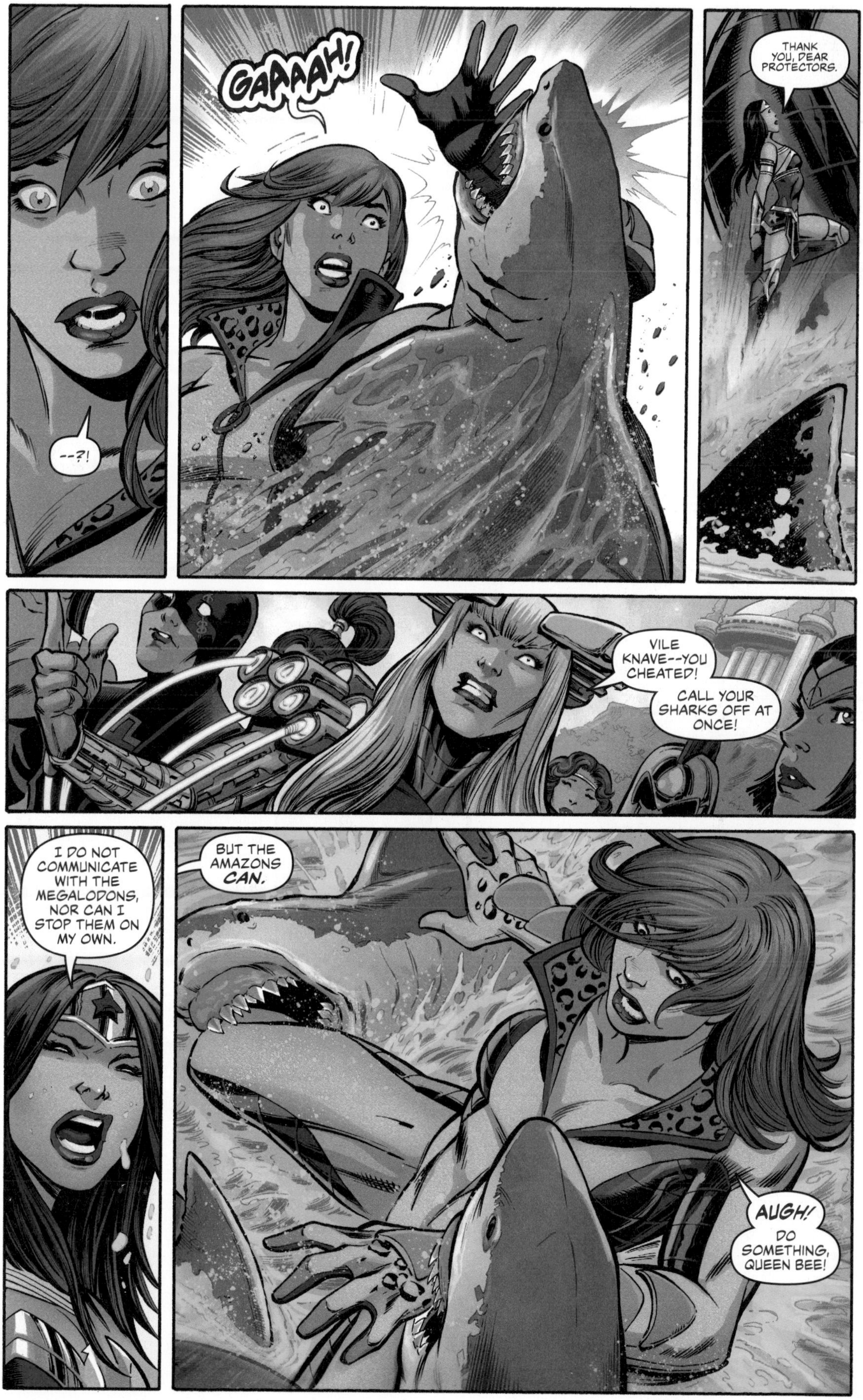
--?!
GAAAAH!
THANK YOU, DEAR PROTECTORS.
VILE KNAVE--YOU CHEATED!
CALL YOUR SHARKS OFF AT ONCE!
I DO NOT COMMUNICATE WITH THE MEGALODONS, NOR CAN I STOP THEM ON MY OWN.
BUT THE AMAZONS CAN.
AUGH!
DO SOMETHING, QUEEN BEE!

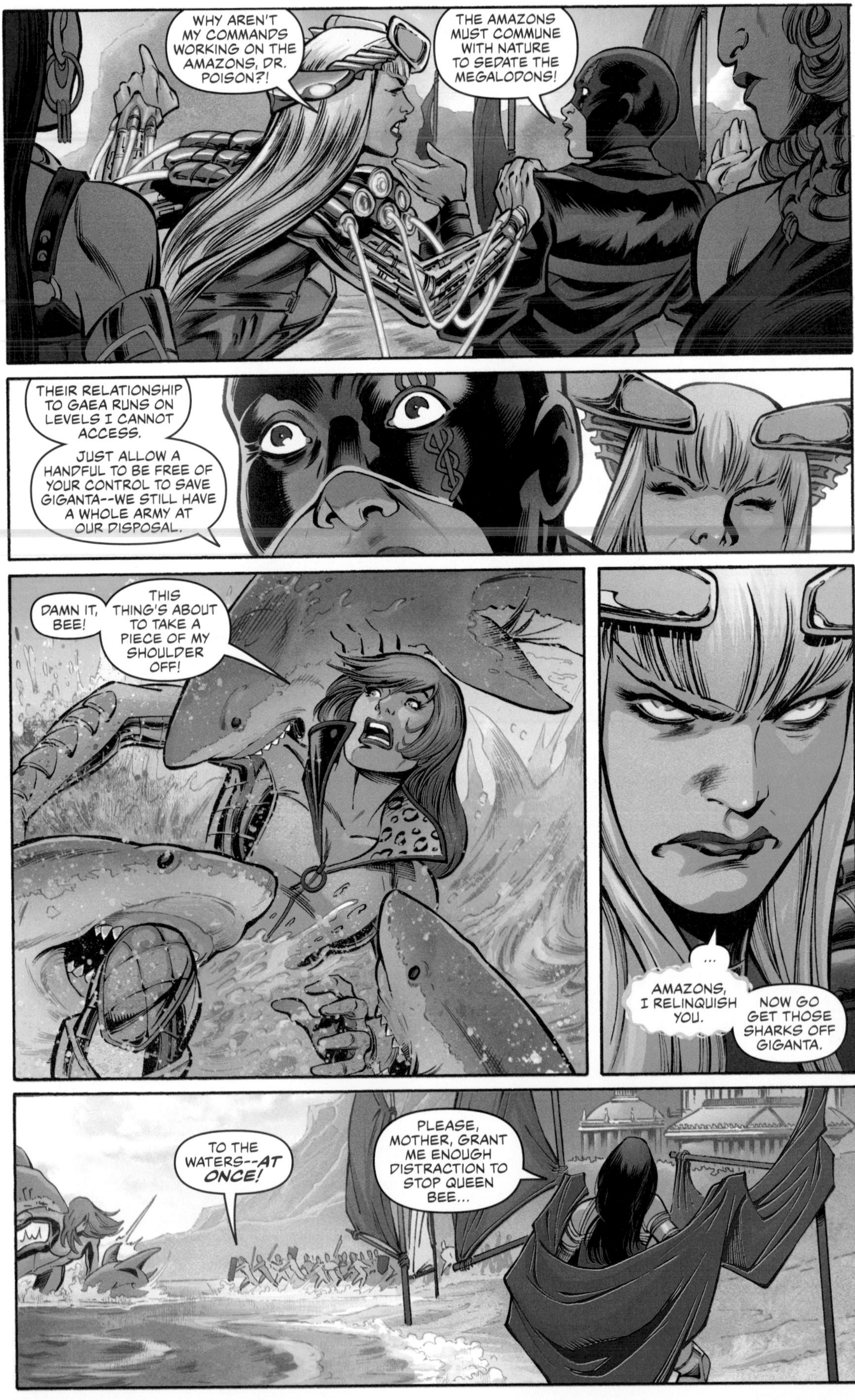
WHY AREN'T MY COMMANDS WORKING ON THE AMAZONS, DR. POISON?!
THE AMAZONS MUST COMMUNE WITH NATURE TO SEDATE THE MEGALODONS!
THEIR RELATIONSHIP TO GAEA RUNS ON LEVELS I CANNOT ACCESS.
JUST ALLOW A HANDFUL TO BE FREE OF YOUR CONTROL TO SAVE GIGANTA--WE STILL HAVE A WHOLE ARMY AT OUR DISPOSAL.
DAMN IT, BEE!
THIS THING'S ABOUT TO TAKE A PIECE OF MY SHOULDER OFF!
...
AMAZONS, I RELINQUISH YOU.
NOW GO GET THOSE SHARKS OFF GIGANTA.
TO THE WATERS--*AT ONCE!*
PLEASE, MOTHER, GRANT ME ENOUGH DISTRACTION TO STOP QUEEN BEE...

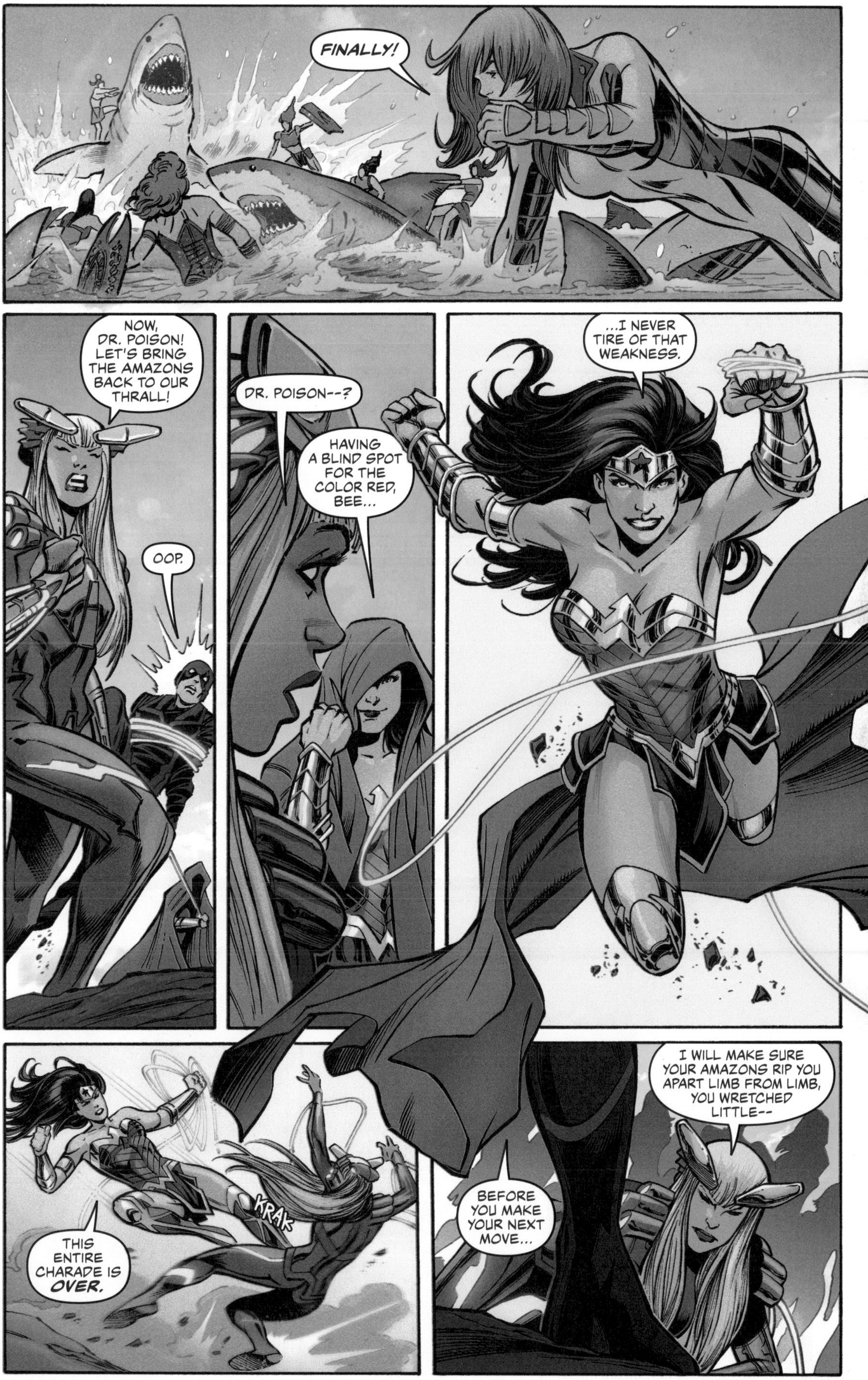
FINALLY!
NOW, DR. POISON! LET'S BRING THE AMAZONS BACK TO OUR THRALL!
OOP.
DR. POISON--?
HAVING A BLIND SPOT FOR THE COLOR RED, BEE...
...I NEVER TIRE OF THAT WEAKNESS.
THIS ENTIRE CHARADE IS *OVER.*
KRAK
I WILL MAKE SURE YOUR AMAZONS RIP YOU APART LIMB FROM LIMB, YOU WRETCHED LITTLE--
BEFORE YOU MAKE YOUR NEXT MOVE...

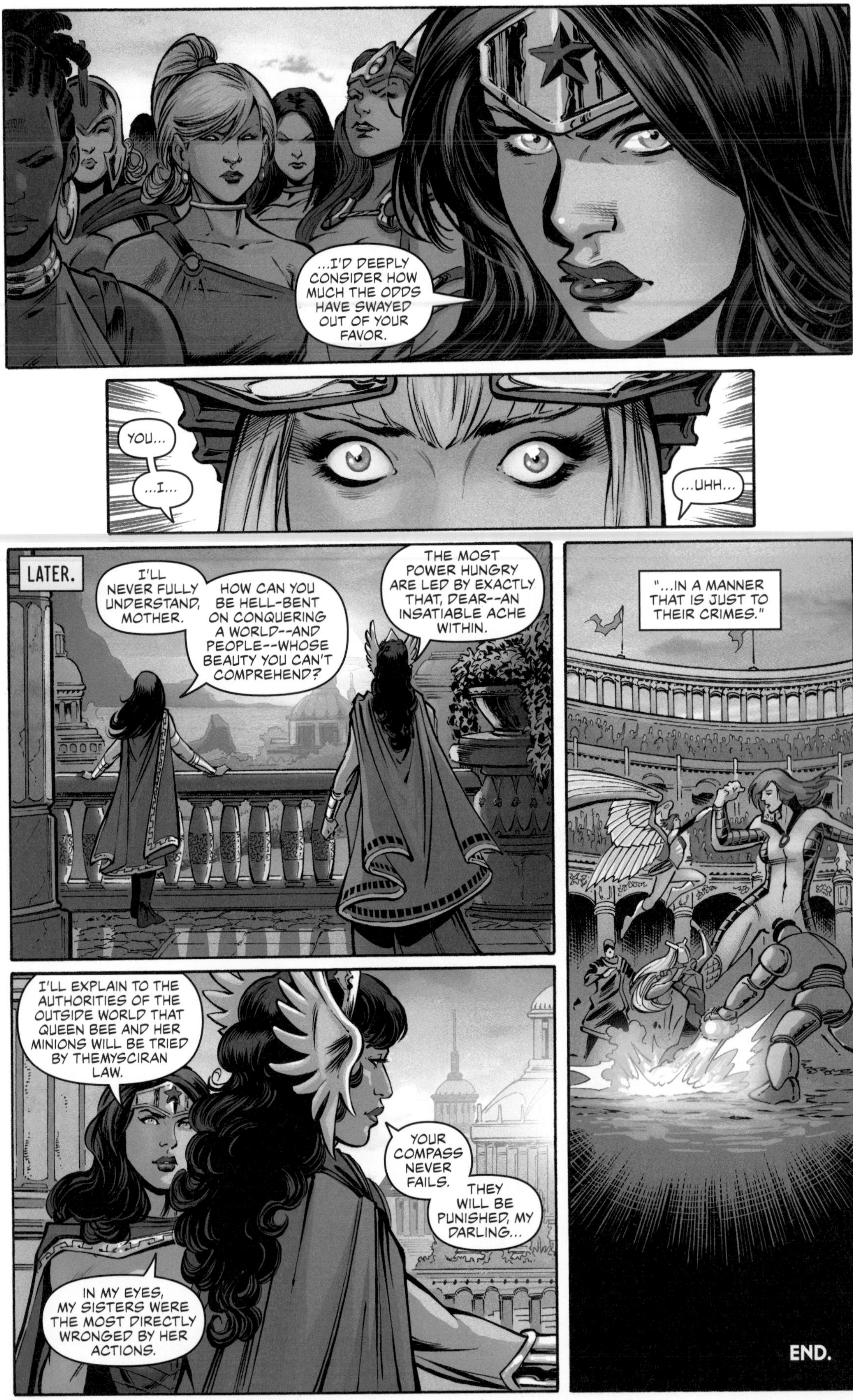

...I'D DEEPLY CONSIDER HOW MUCH THE ODDS HAVE SWAYED OUT OF YOUR FAVOR.
YOU...
...I...
...UHH...
LATER.
I'LL NEVER FULLY UNDERSTAND, MOTHER.
HOW CAN YOU BE HELL-BENT ON CONQUERING A WORLD--AND PEOPLE--WHOSE BEAUTY YOU CAN'T COMPREHEND?
THE MOST POWER HUNGRY ARE LED BY EXACTLY THAT, DEAR--AN INSATIABLE ACHE WITHIN.
I'LL EXPLAIN TO THE AUTHORITIES OF THE OUTSIDE WORLD THAT QUEEN BEE AND HER MINIONS WILL BE TRIED BY THEMYSCIRAN LAW.
IN MY EYES, MY SISTERS WERE THE MOST DIRECTLY WRONGED BY HER ACTIONS.
YOUR COMPASS NEVER FAILS.
THEY WILL BE PUNISHED, MY DARLING...
"...IN A MANNER THAT IS JUST TO THEIR CRIMES."
END.

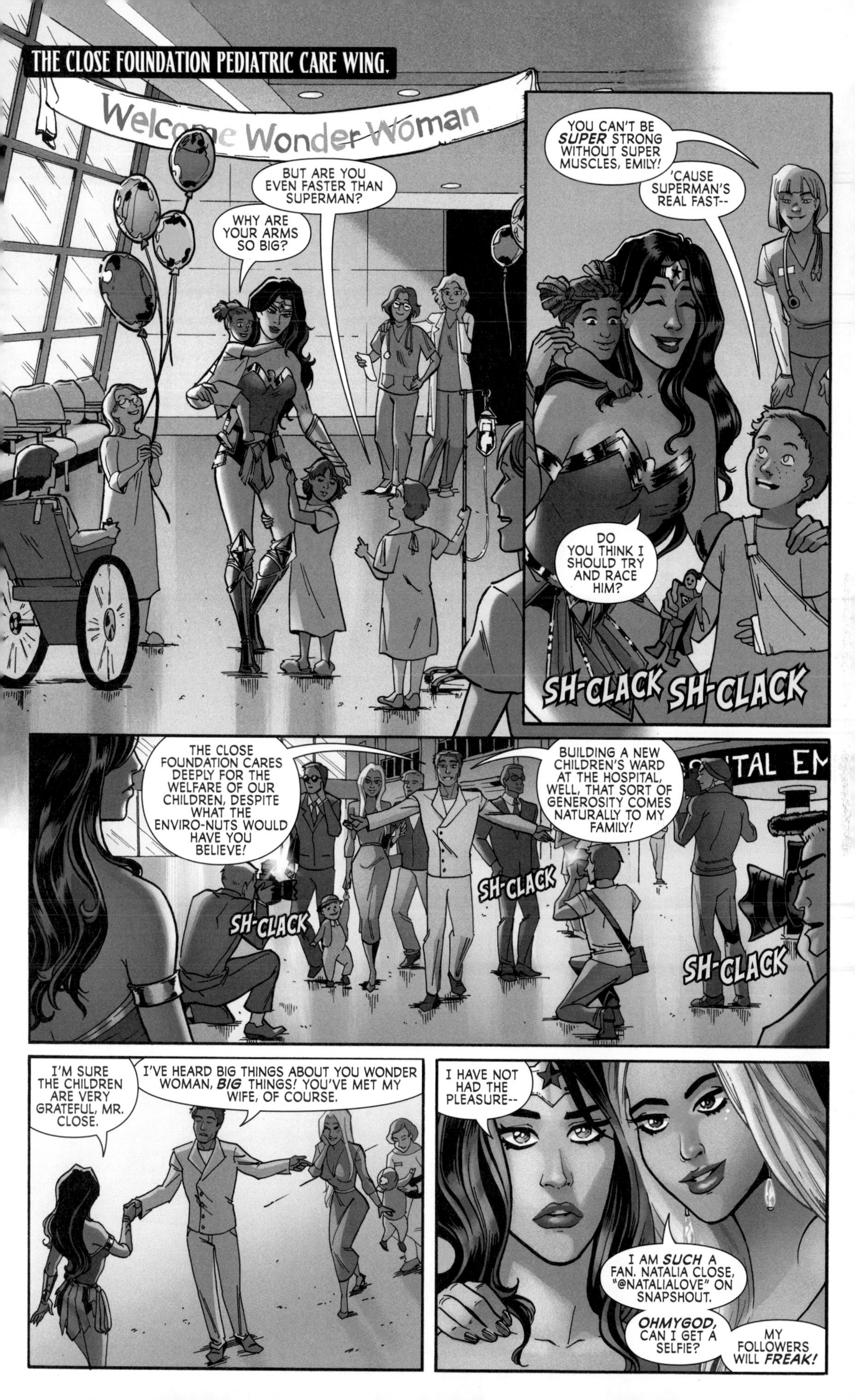

THE CLOSE FOUNDATION PEDIATRIC CARE WING.
Welcome Wonder Woman
BUT ARE YOU EVEN FASTER THAN SUPERMAN?
WHY ARE YOUR ARMS SO BIG?
YOU CAN'T BE SUPER STRONG WITHOUT SUPER MUSCLES, EMILY!
'CAUSE SUPERMAN'S REAL FAST--
DO YOU THINK I SHOULD TRY AND RACE HIM?
SH-CLACK SH-CLACK
THE CLOSE FOUNDATION CARES DEEPLY FOR THE WELFARE OF OUR CHILDREN, DESPITE WHAT THE ENVIRO-NUTS WOULD HAVE YOU BELIEVE!
BUILDING A NEW CHILDREN'S WARD AT THE HOSPITAL, WELL, THAT SORT OF GENEROSITY COMES NATURALLY TO MY FAMILY!
TAL EM
SH-CLACK
SH-CLACK
SH-CLACK
I'M SURE THE CHILDREN ARE VERY GRATEFUL, MR. CLOSE.
I'VE HEARD BIG THINGS ABOUT YOU WONDER WOMAN, BIG THINGS! YOU'VE MET MY WIFE, OF COURSE.
I HAVE NOT HAD THE PLEASURE--
I AM SUCH A FAN. NATALIA CLOSE, "@NATALIALOVE" ON SNAPSHOUT.
OHMYGOD, CAN I GET A SELFIE?
MY FOLLOWERS WILL FREAK!

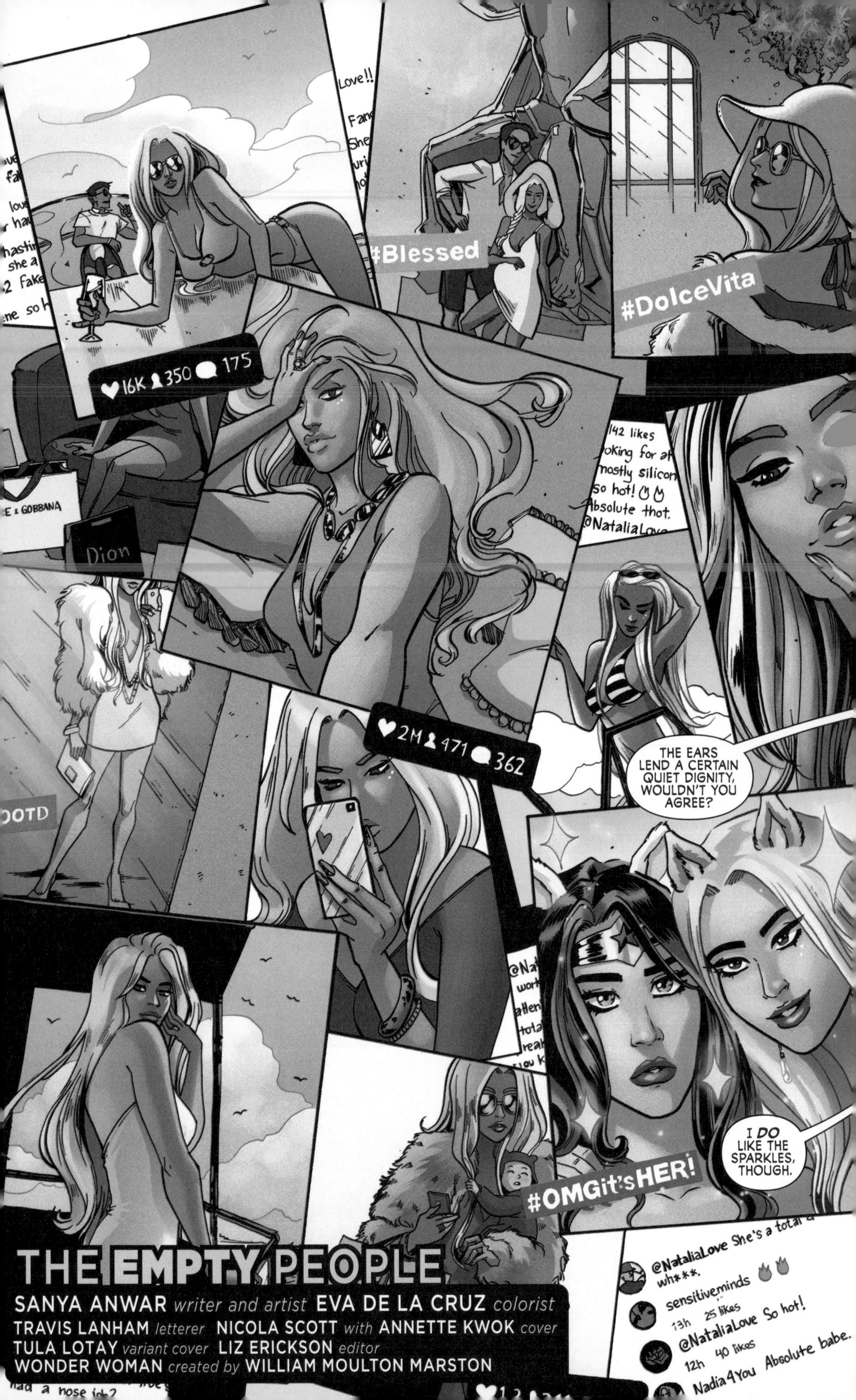
#Blessed
#DolceVita
16K 350 175
142 likes
so hot!
Absolute thot.
Dion
2M 471 362
THE EARS LEND A CERTAIN QUIET DIGNITY, WOULDN'T YOU AGREE?
I DO LIKE THE SPARKLES, THOUGH.
#OMGit'sHER!
sensitiveminds
13h 25 likes
@NataliaLove So hot!
12h 40 likes
Nadia4You Absolute babe.
THE EMPTY PEOPLE
SANYA ANWAR writer and artist EVA DE LA CRUZ colorist
TRAVIS LANHAM letterer NICOLA SCOTT with ANNETTE KWOK cover
TULA LOTAY variant cover LIZ ERICKSON editor
WONDER WOMAN created by WILLIAM MOULTON MARSTON

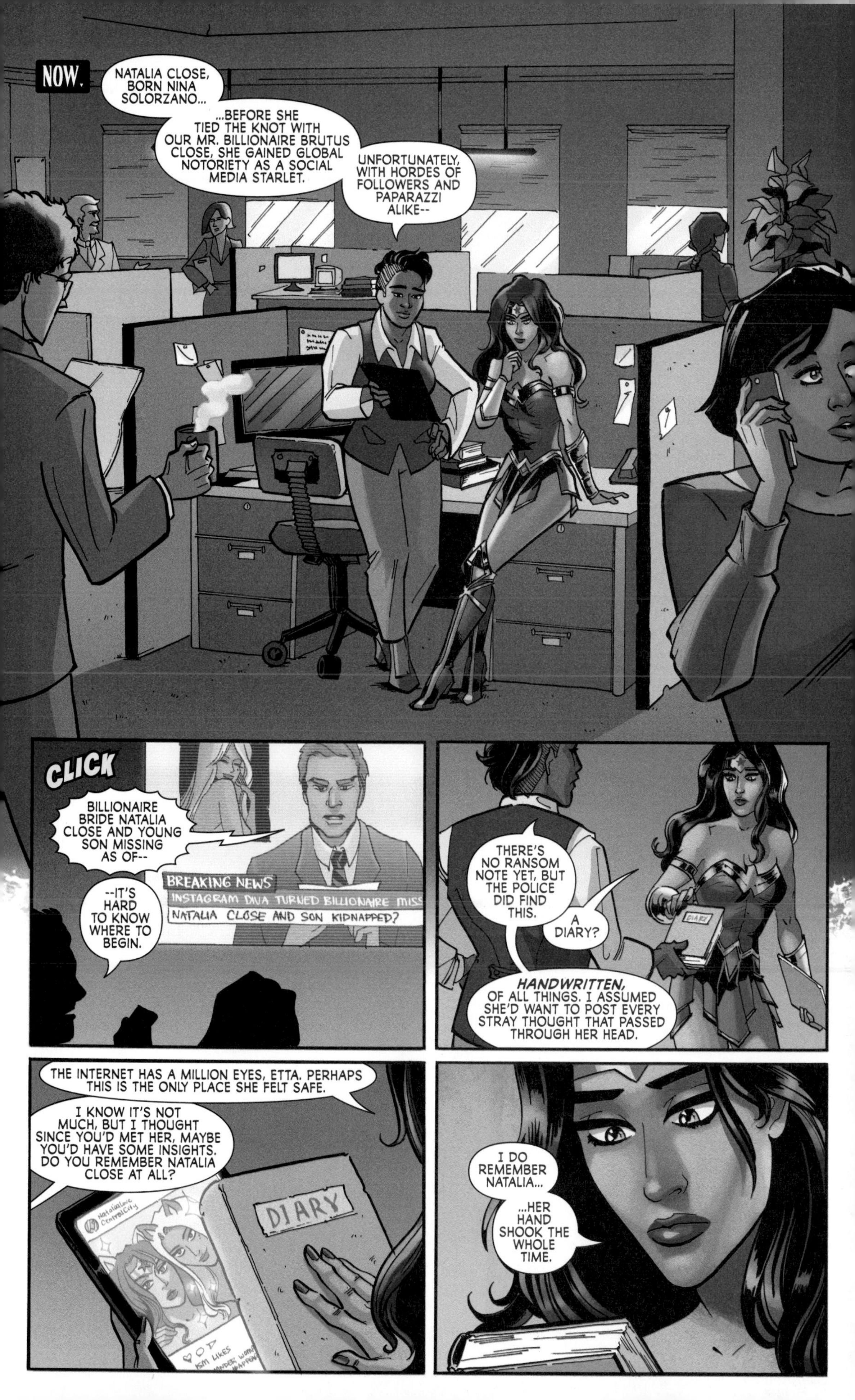

NOW.
NATALIA CLOSE, BORN NINA SOLORZANO...
...BEFORE SHE TIED THE KNOT WITH OUR MR. BILLIONAIRE BRUTUS CLOSE, SHE GAINED GLOBAL NOTORIETY AS A SOCIAL MEDIA STARLET.
UNFORTUNATELY, WITH HORDES OF FOLLOWERS AND PAPARAZZI ALIKE--
CLICK
BILLIONAIRE BRIDE NATALIA CLOSE AND YOUNG SON MISSING AS OF--
BREAKING NEWS
INSTAGRAM DIVA TURNED BILLIONAIRE MISS
NATALIA CLOSE AND SON KIDNAPPED?
--IT'S HARD TO KNOW WHERE TO BEGIN.
THERE'S NO RANSOM NOTE YET, BUT THE POLICE DID FIND THIS.
A DIARY?
DIARY
HANDWRITTEN, OF ALL THINGS. I ASSUMED SHE'D WANT TO POST EVERY STRAY THOUGHT THAT PASSED THROUGH HER HEAD.
THE INTERNET HAS A MILLION EYES, ETTA. PERHAPS THIS IS THE ONLY PLACE SHE FELT SAFE.
I KNOW IT'S NOT MUCH, BUT I THOUGHT SINCE YOU'D MET HER, MAYBE YOU'D HAVE SOME INSIGHTS. DO YOU REMEMBER NATALIA CLOSE AT ALL?
DIARY
I DO REMEMBER NATALIA...
...HER HAND SHOOK THE WHOLE TIME.

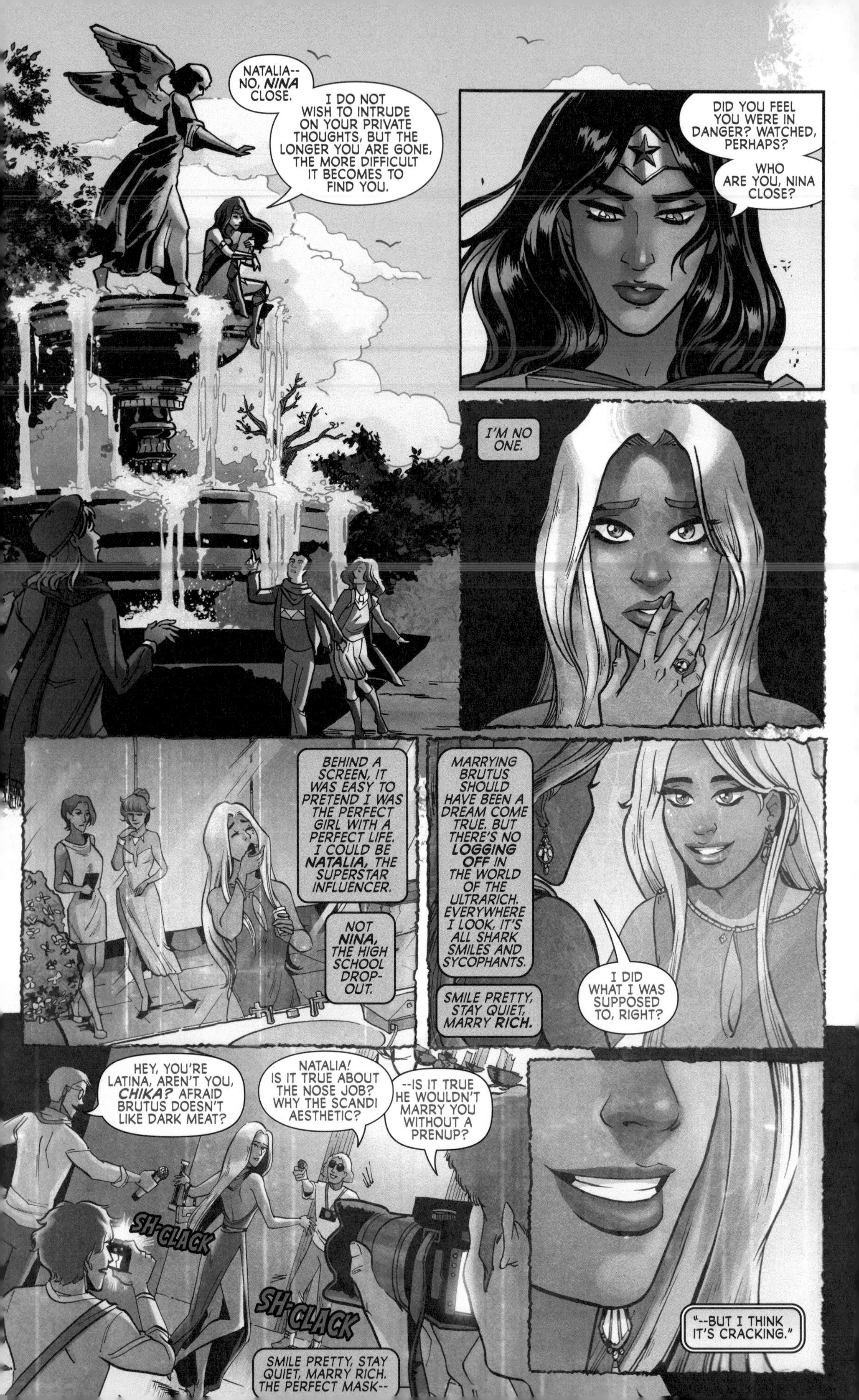
NATALIA-- NO, NINA CLOSE.
I DO NOT WISH TO INTRUDE ON YOUR PRIVATE THOUGHTS, BUT THE LONGER YOU ARE GONE, THE MORE DIFFICULT IT BECOMES TO FIND YOU.
DID YOU FEEL YOU WERE IN DANGER? WATCHED, PERHAPS?
WHO ARE YOU, NINA CLOSE?
I'M NO ONE.
BEHIND A SCREEN, IT WAS EASY TO PRETEND I WAS THE PERFECT GIRL WITH A PERFECT LIFE. I COULD BE NATALIA, THE SUPERSTAR INFLUENCER.
NOT NINA, THE HIGH SCHOOL DROP-OUT.
MARRYING BRUTUS SHOULD HAVE BEEN A DREAM COME TRUE. BUT THERE'S NO LOGGING OFF IN THE WORLD OF THE ULTRARICH. EVERYWHERE I LOOK, IT'S ALL SHARK SMILES AND SYCOPHANTS.
SMILE PRETTY, STAY QUIET, MARRY RICH.
I DID WHAT I WAS SUPPOSED TO, RIGHT?
HEY, YOU'RE LATINA, AREN'T YOU, CHIKA? AFRAID BRUTUS DOESN'T LIKE DARK MEAT?
NATALIA! IS IT TRUE ABOUT THE NOSE JOB? WHY THE SCANDI AESTHETIC?
--IS IT TRUE HE WOULDN'T MARRY YOU WITHOUT A PRENUP?
SH-CLACK
SH-CLACK
SMILE PRETTY, STAY QUIET, MARRY RICH. THE PERFECT MASK--
"--BUT I THINK IT'S CRACKING."

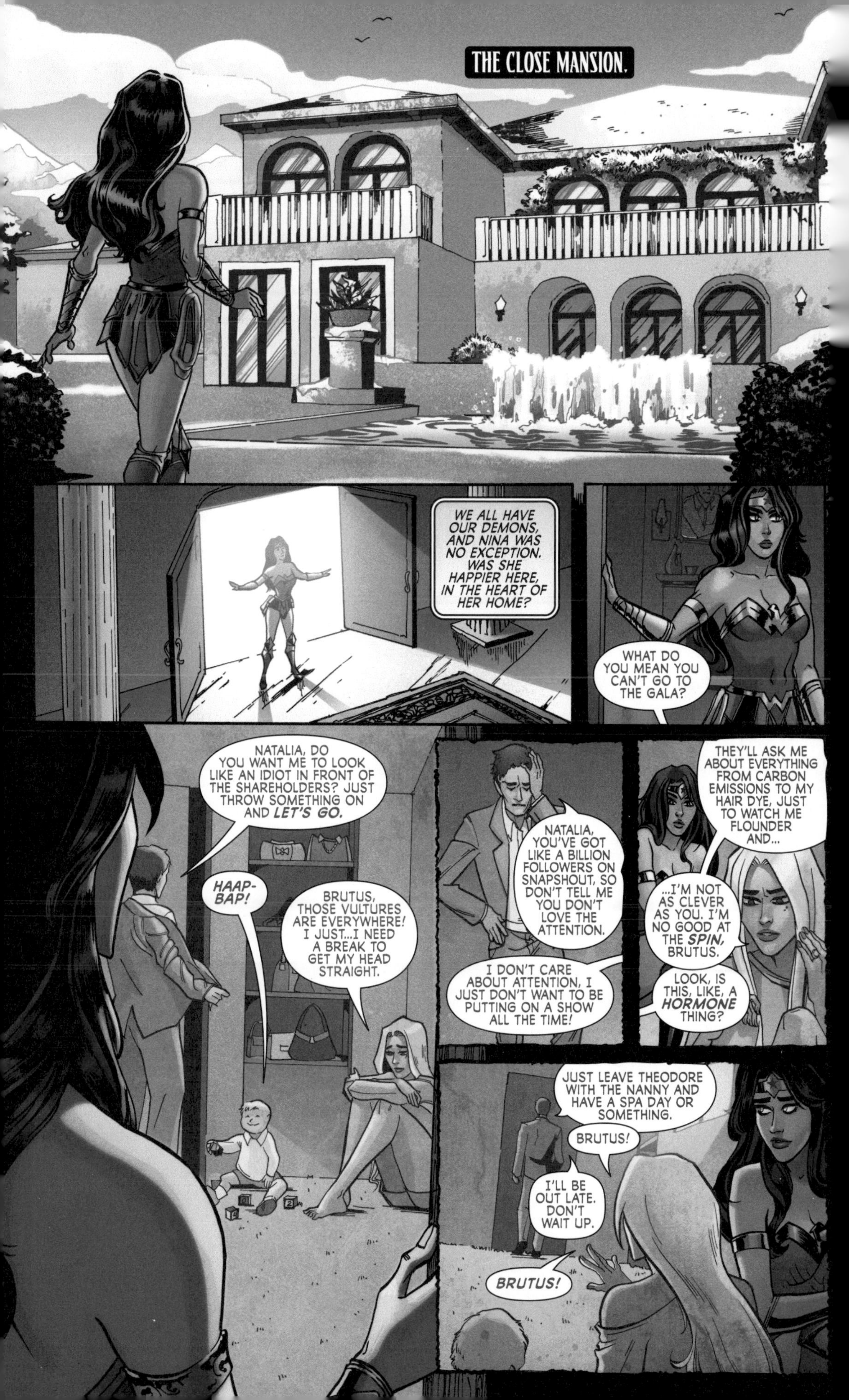
THE CLOSE MANSION.
WE ALL HAVE OUR DEMONS, AND NINA WAS NO EXCEPTION. WAS SHE HAPPIER HERE, IN THE HEART OF HER HOME?
WHAT DO YOU MEAN YOU CAN'T GO TO THE GALA?
NATALIA, DO YOU WANT ME TO LOOK LIKE AN IDIOT IN FRONT OF THE SHAREHOLDERS? JUST THROW SOMETHING ON AND LET'S GO.
HAAP-BAP!
BRUTUS, THOSE VULTURES ARE EVERYWHERE! I JUST...I NEED A BREAK TO GET MY HEAD STRAIGHT.
NATALIA, YOU'VE GOT LIKE A BILLION FOLLOWERS ON SNAPSHOUT, SO DON'T TELL ME YOU DON'T LOVE THE ATTENTION.
I DON'T CARE ABOUT ATTENTION, I JUST DON'T WANT TO BE PUTTING ON A SHOW ALL THE TIME!
THEY'LL ASK ME ABOUT EVERYTHING FROM CARBON EMISSIONS TO MY HAIR DYE, JUST TO WATCH ME FLOUNDER AND...
...I'M NOT AS CLEVER AS YOU. I'M NO GOOD AT THE SPIN, BRUTUS.
LOOK, IS THIS, LIKE, A HORMONE THING?
JUST LEAVE THEODORE WITH THE NANNY AND HAVE A SPA DAY OR SOMETHING.
BRUTUS!
I'LL BE OUT LATE. DON'T WAIT UP.
BRUTUS!

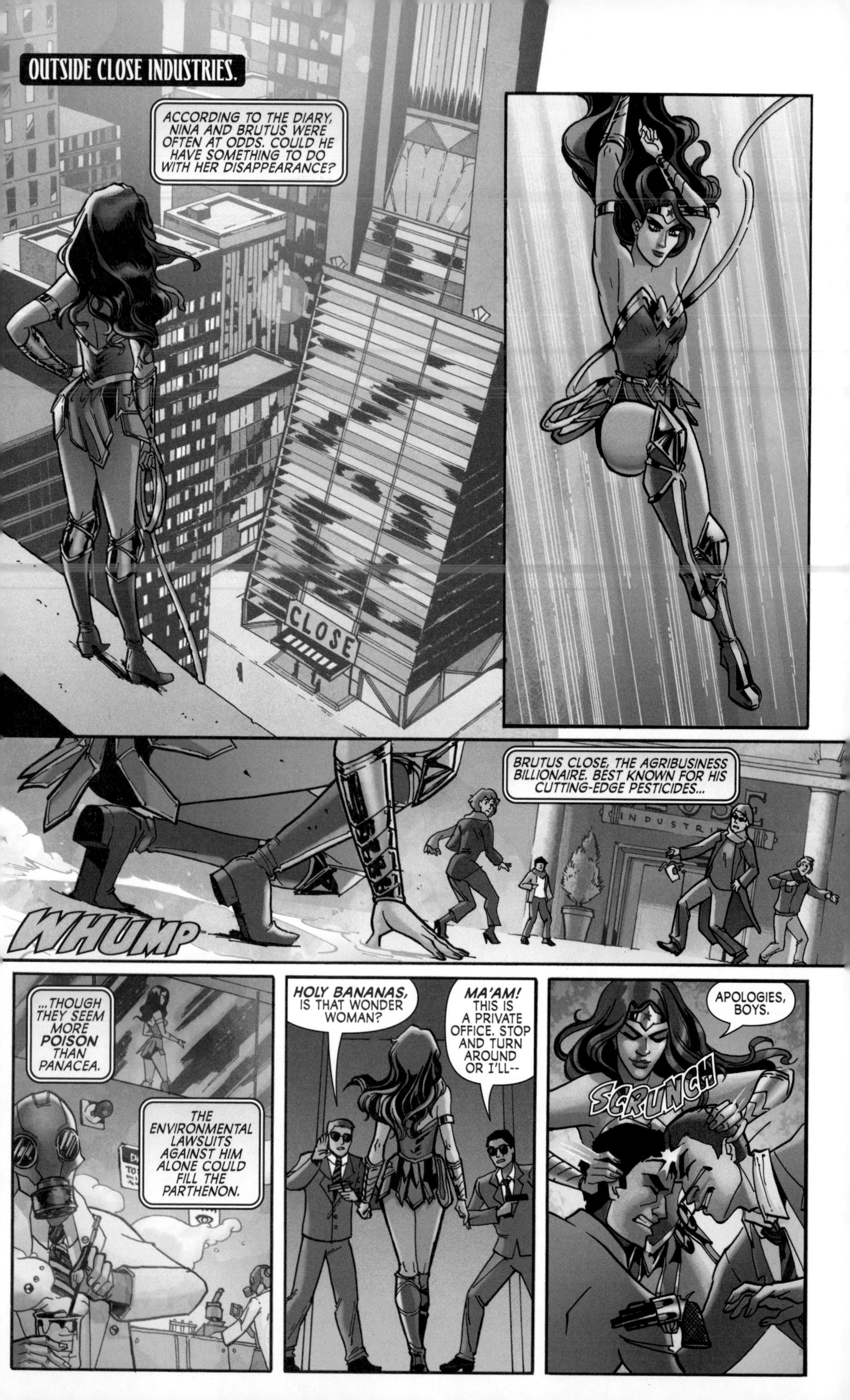
OUTSIDE CLOSE INDUSTRIES.
ACCORDING TO THE DIARY, NINA AND BRUTUS WERE OFTEN AT ODDS. COULD HE HAVE SOMETHING TO DO WITH HER DISAPPEARANCE?
CLOSE
BRUTUS CLOSE, THE AGRIBUSINESS BILLIONAIRE. BEST KNOWN FOR HIS CUTTING-EDGE PESTICIDES...
INDUSTRI
WHUMP
...THOUGH THEY SEEM MORE **POISON** THAN PANACEA.
THE ENVIRONMENTAL LAWSUITS AGAINST HIM ALONE COULD FILL THE PARTHENON.
HOLY BANANAS, IS THAT WONDER WOMAN?
MA'AM! THIS IS A PRIVATE OFFICE. STOP AND TURN AROUND OR I'LL--
APOLOGIES, BOYS.
SCRUNCH

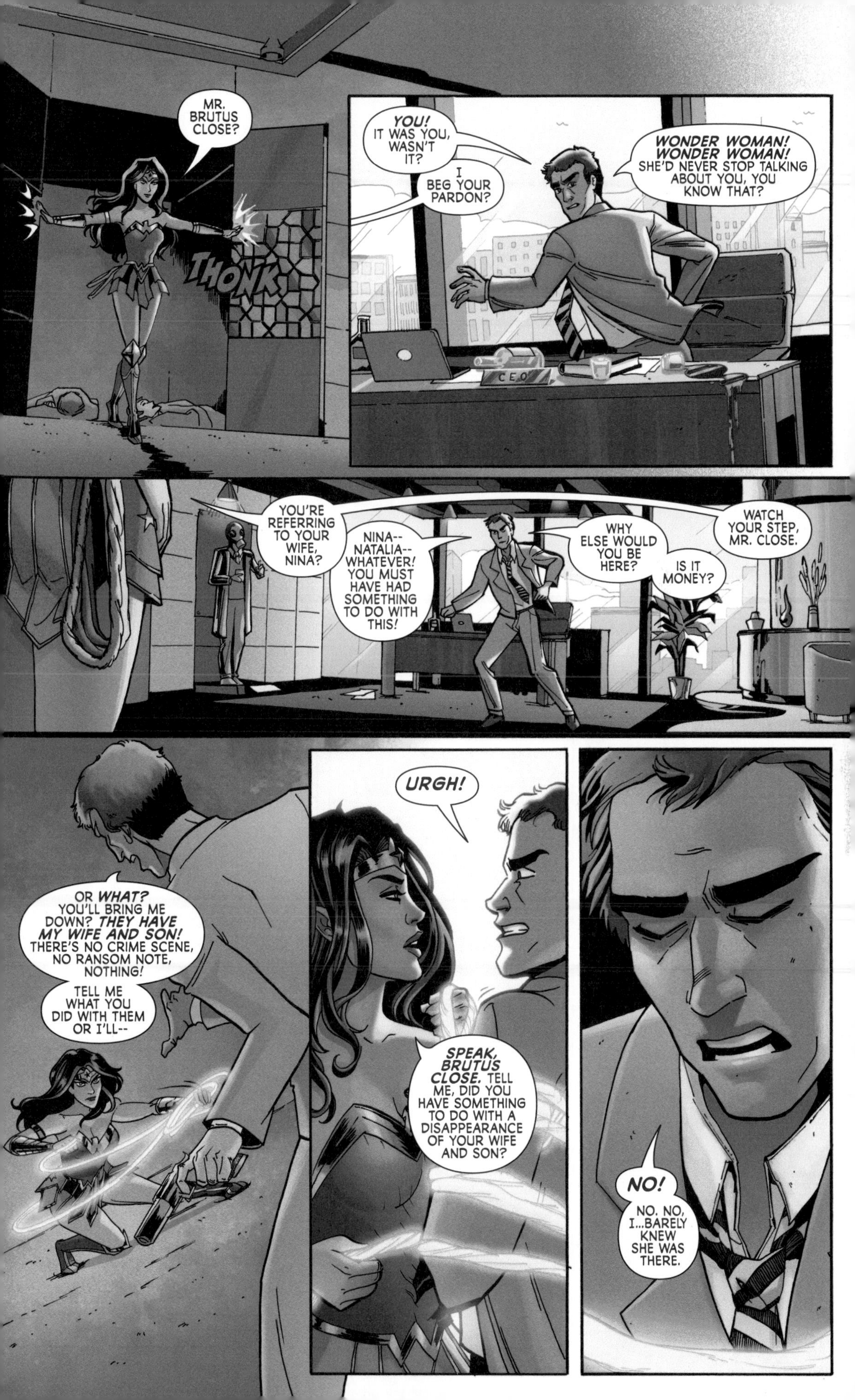
MR. BRUTUS CLOSE?
THONK
YOU! IT WAS YOU, WASN'T IT?
I BEG YOUR PARDON?
WONDER WOMAN! WONDER WOMAN! SHE'D NEVER STOP TALKING ABOUT YOU, YOU KNOW THAT?
YOU'RE REFERRING TO YOUR WIFE, NINA?
NINA-- NATALIA-- WHATEVER! YOU MUST HAVE HAD SOMETHING TO DO WITH THIS!
WHY ELSE WOULD YOU BE HERE?
IS IT MONEY?
WATCH YOUR STEP, MR. CLOSE.
OR WHAT? YOU'LL BRING ME DOWN? THEY HAVE MY WIFE AND SON! THERE'S NO CRIME SCENE, NO RANSOM NOTE, NOTHING!
TELL ME WHAT YOU DID WITH THEM OR I'LL--
URGH!
SPEAK, BRUTUS CLOSE. TELL ME, DID YOU HAVE SOMETHING TO DO WITH A DISAPPEARANCE OF YOUR WIFE AND SON?
NO!
NO. NO, I...BARELY KNEW SHE WAS THERE.
CEO

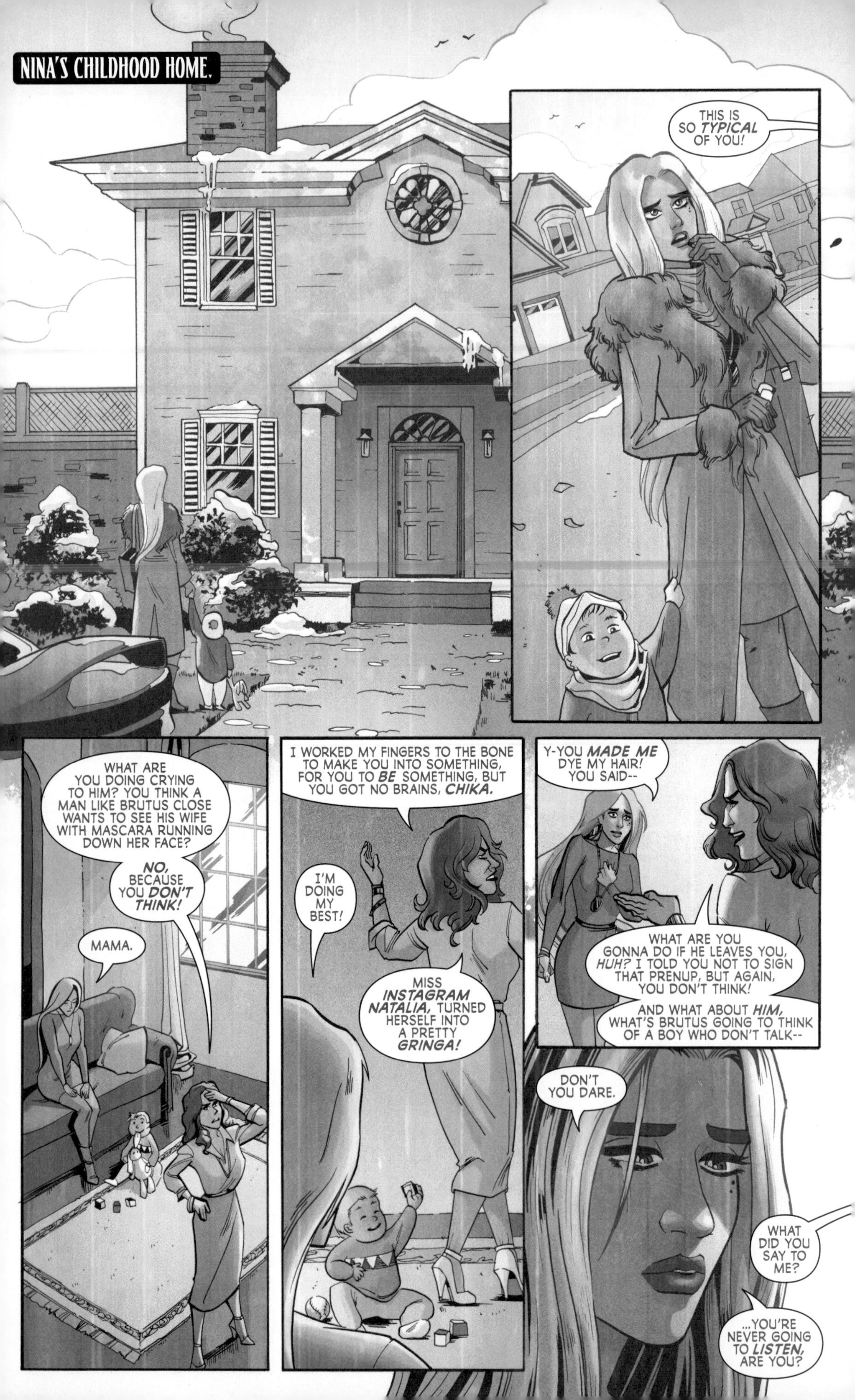
NINA'S CHILDHOOD HOME.
THIS IS SO TYPICAL OF YOU!
WHAT ARE YOU DOING CRYING TO HIM? YOU THINK A MAN LIKE BRUTUS CLOSE WANTS TO SEE HIS WIFE WITH MASCARA RUNNING DOWN HER FACE?
NO, BECAUSE YOU DON'T THINK!
MAMA.
I WORKED MY FINGERS TO THE BONE TO MAKE YOU INTO SOMETHING, FOR YOU TO BE SOMETHING, BUT YOU GOT NO BRAINS, CHIKA.
I'M DOING MY BEST!
MISS INSTAGRAM NATALIA, TURNED HERSELF INTO A PRETTY GRINGA!
Y-YOU MADE ME DYE MY HAIR! YOU SAID--
WHAT ARE YOU GONNA DO IF HE LEAVES YOU, HUH? I TOLD YOU NOT TO SIGN THAT PRENUP, BUT AGAIN, YOU DON'T THINK!
AND WHAT ABOUT HIM, WHAT'S BRUTUS GOING TO THINK OF A BOY WHO DON'T TALK--
DON'T YOU DARE.
WHAT DID YOU SAY TO ME?
...YOU'RE NEVER GOING TO LISTEN, ARE YOU?

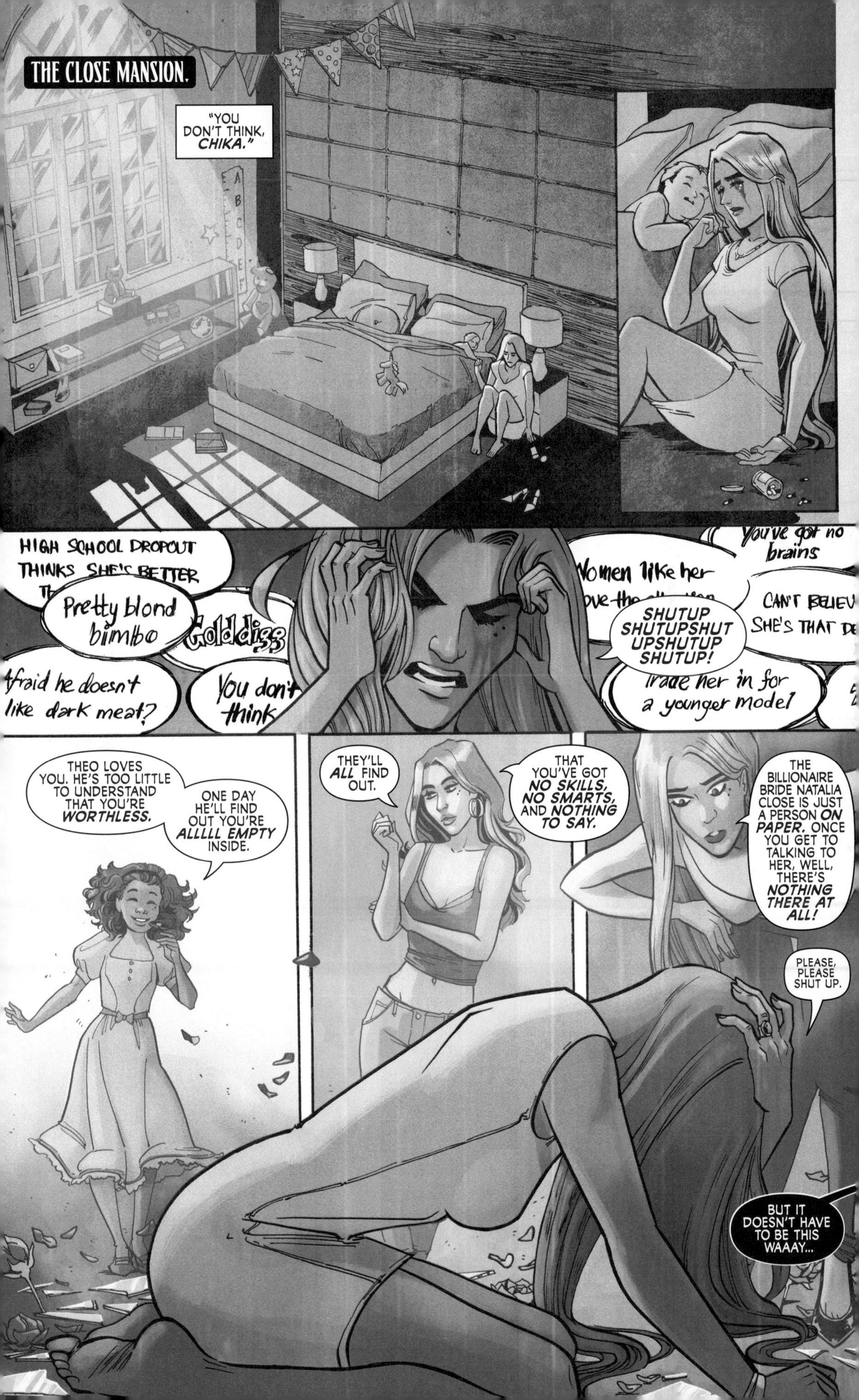
THE CLOSE MANSION.
"YOU DON'T THINK, CHIKA."
HIGH SCHOOL DROPOUT THINKS SHE'S BETTER
Pretty blond bimbo
Golddigg
Afraid he doesn't like dark meat?
You don't think
You've got no brains
Women like her
CAN'T BELIEV SHE'S THAT D
SHUTUP SHUTUPSHUT UPSHUTUP SHUTUP!
Trade her in for a younger model
THEO LOVES YOU. HE'S TOO LITTLE TO UNDERSTAND THAT YOU'RE WORTHLESS.
ONE DAY HE'LL FIND OUT YOU'RE ALLLLL EMPTY INSIDE.
THEY'LL ALL FIND OUT.
THAT YOU'VE GOT NO SKILLS, NO SMARTS, AND NOTHING TO SAY.
THE BILLIONAIRE BRIDE NATALIA CLOSE IS JUST A PERSON ON PAPER. ONCE YOU GET TO TALKING TO HER, WELL, THERE'S NOTHING THERE AT ALL!
PLEASE, PLEASE SHUT UP.
BUT IT DOESN'T HAVE TO BE THIS WAAAY...

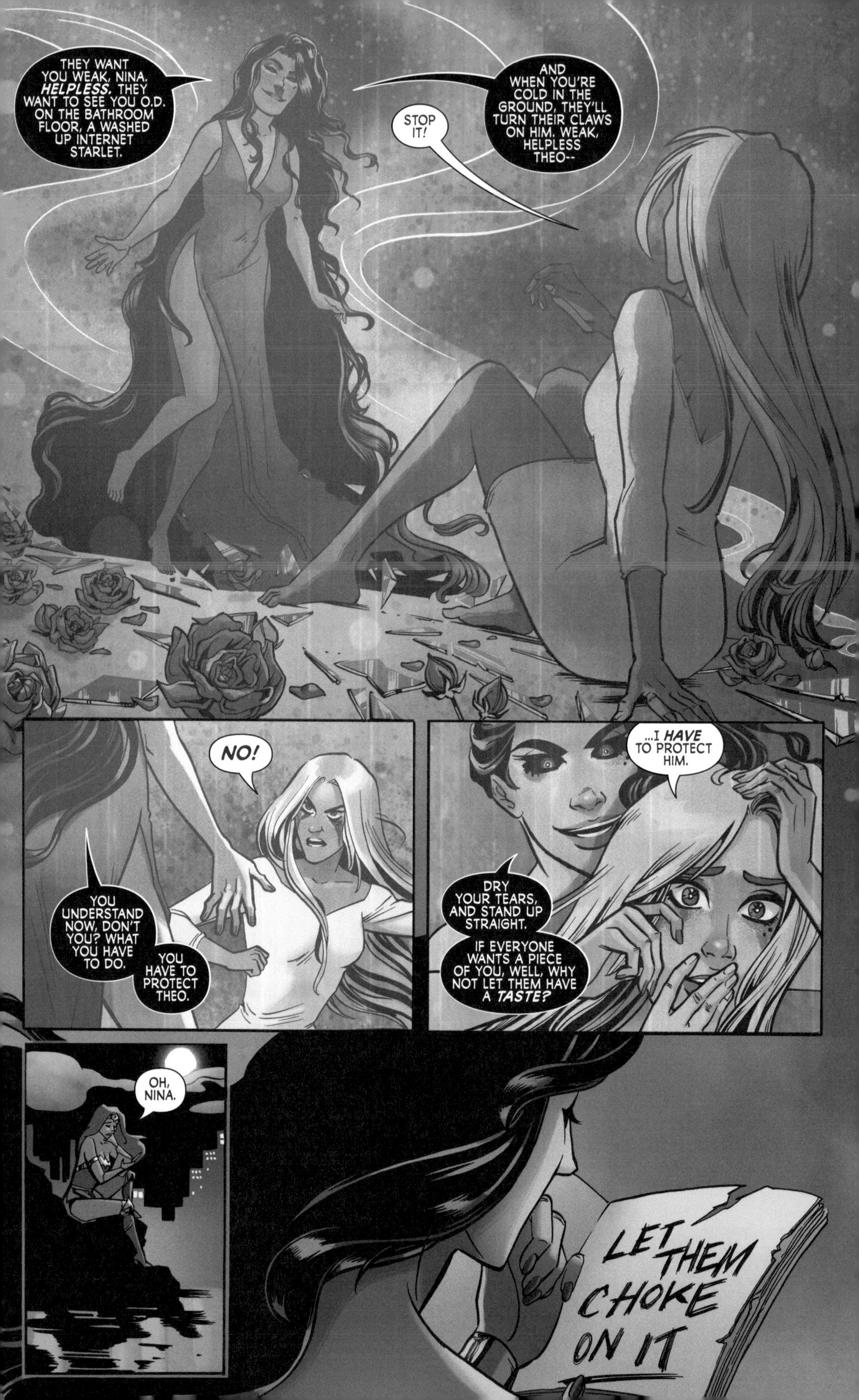
THEY WANT YOU WEAK, NINA. ***HELPLESS.*** THEY WANT TO SEE YOU O.D. ON THE BATHROOM FLOOR, A WASHED UP INTERNET STARLET.
STOP IT!
AND WHEN YOU'RE COLD IN THE GROUND, THEY'LL TURN THEIR CLAWS ON HIM. WEAK, HELPLESS THEO--
NO!
YOU UNDERSTAND NOW, DON'T YOU? WHAT YOU HAVE TO DO.
YOU HAVE TO PROTECT THEO.
...I *HAVE* TO PROTECT HIM.
DRY YOUR TEARS, AND STAND UP STRAIGHT.
IF EVERYONE WANTS A PIECE OF YOU, WELL, WHY NOT LET THEM HAVE A *TASTE?*
OH, NINA.
LET THEM CHOKE ON IT

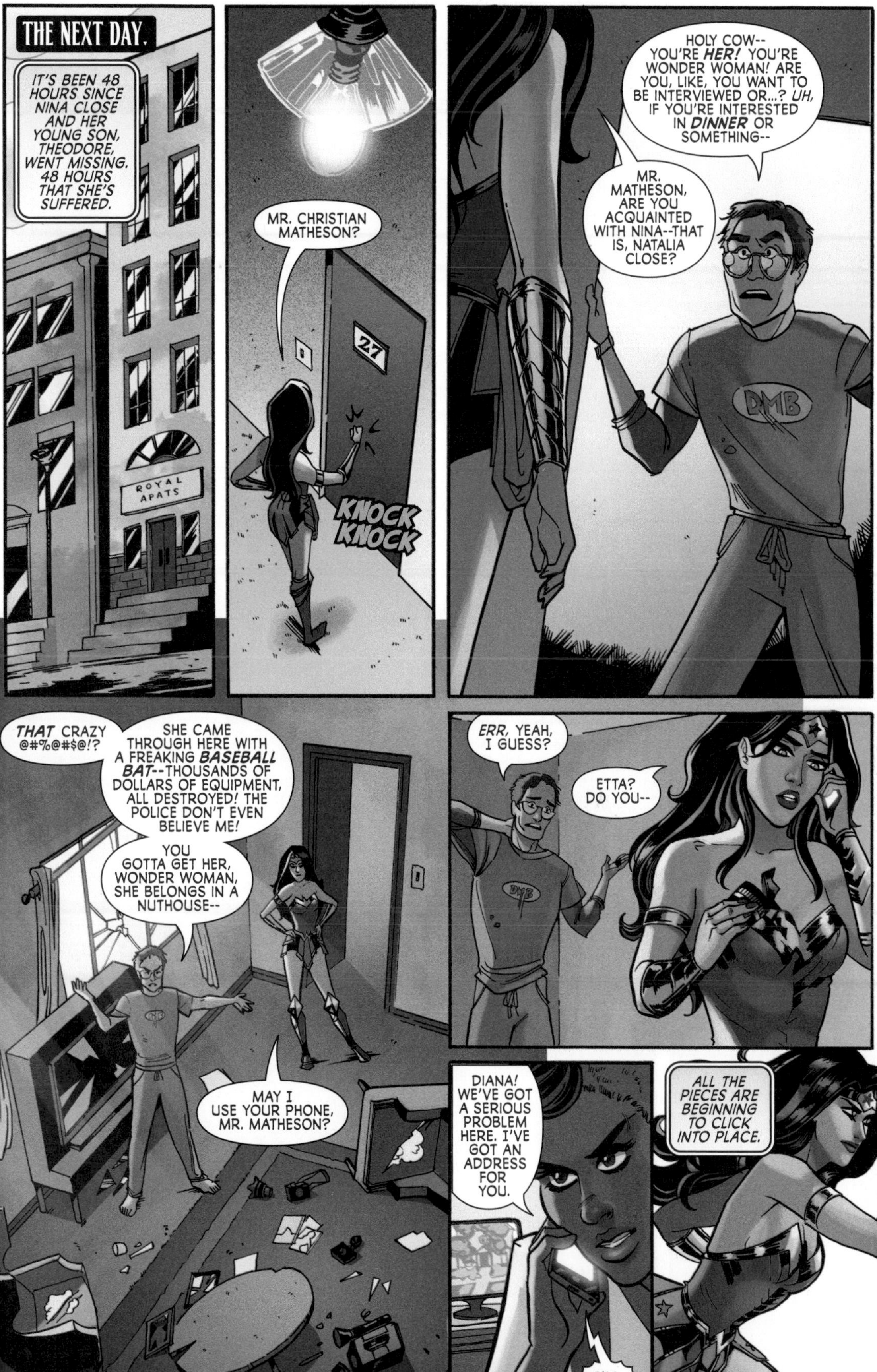
THE NEXT DAY.
IT'S BEEN 48 HOURS SINCE NINA CLOSE AND HER YOUNG SON, THEODORE, WENT MISSING. 48 HOURS THAT SHE'S SUFFERED.
ROYAL APATS
MR. CHRISTIAN MATHESON?
27
KNOCK KNOCK
HOLY COW-- YOU'RE HER! YOU'RE WONDER WOMAN! ARE YOU, LIKE, YOU WANT TO BE INTERVIEWED OR...? UH, IF YOU'RE INTERESTED IN DINNER OR SOMETHING--
MR. MATHESON, ARE YOU ACQUAINTED WITH NINA--THAT IS, NATALIA CLOSE?
DMB
THAT CRAZY @#%@#$@!?
SHE CAME THROUGH HERE WITH A FREAKING BASEBALL BAT--THOUSANDS OF DOLLARS OF EQUIPMENT, ALL DESTROYED! THE POLICE DON'T EVEN BELIEVE ME!
YOU GOTTA GET HER, WONDER WOMAN, SHE BELONGS IN A NUTHOUSE--
MAY I USE YOUR PHONE, MR. MATHESON?
ERR, YEAH, I GUESS?
ETTA? DO YOU--
DIANA! WE'VE GOT A SERIOUS PROBLEM HERE. I'VE GOT AN ADDRESS FOR YOU.
I'M ON IT.
ALL THE PIECES ARE BEGINNING TO CLICK INTO PLACE.

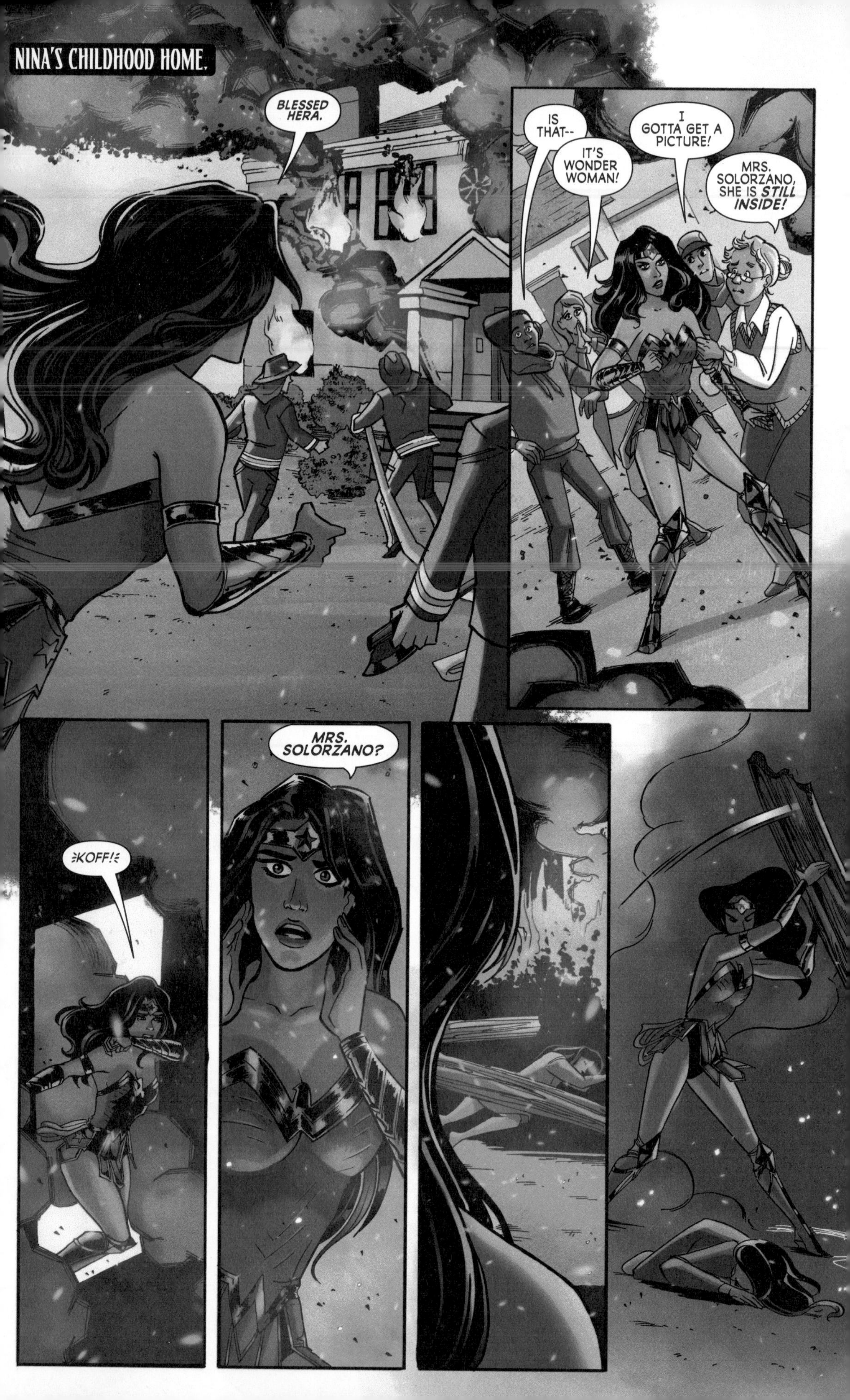
NINA'S CHILDHOOD HOME.
BLESSED HERA.
IS THAT--
IT'S WONDER WOMAN!
I GOTTA GET A PICTURE!
MRS. SOLORZANO, SHE IS STILL INSIDE!
KOFF!
MRS. SOLORZANO?

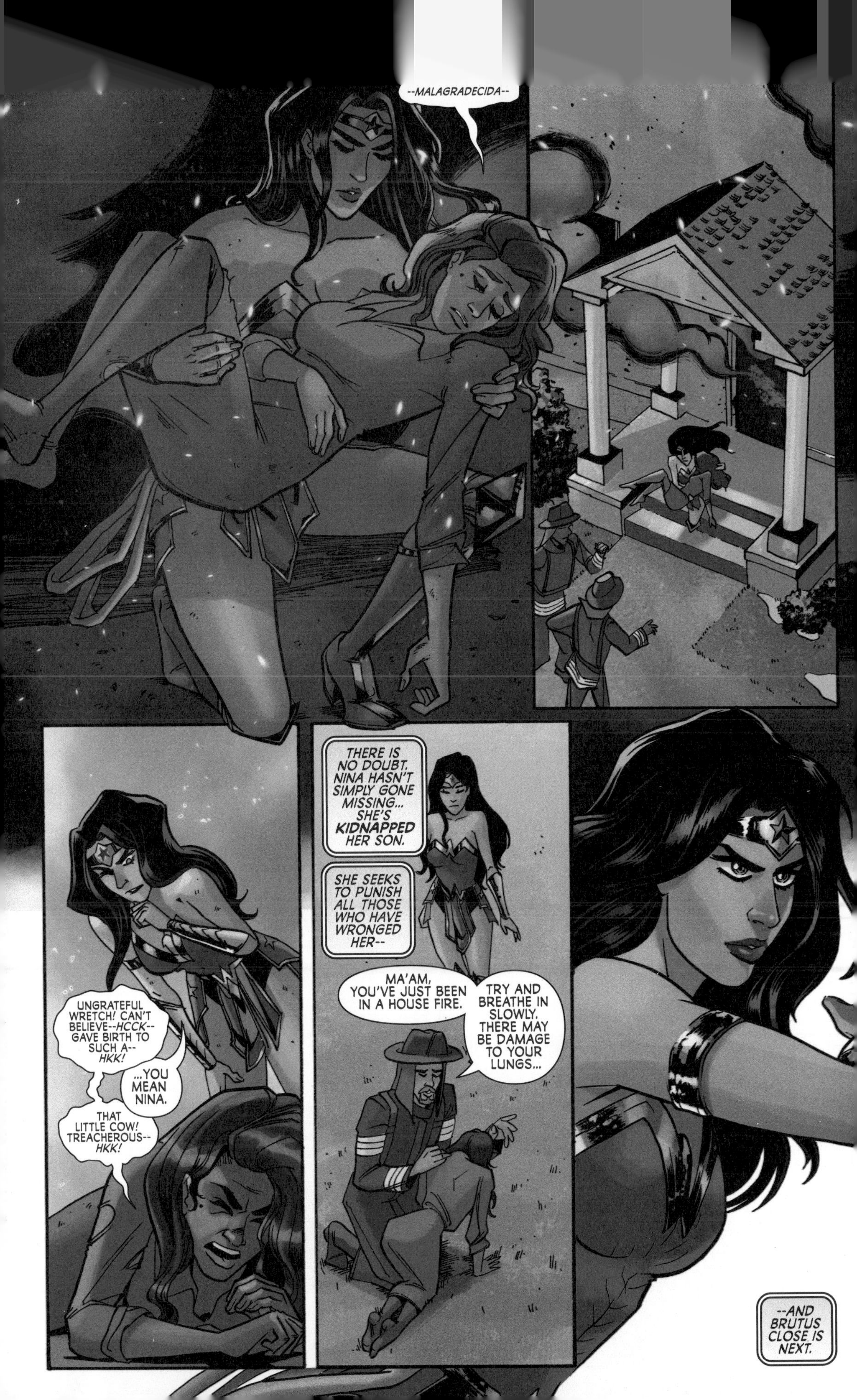
--MALAGRADECIDA--
UNGRATEFUL WRETCH! CAN'T BELIEVE--HCCK--GAVE BIRTH TO SUCH A--HKK!
...YOU MEAN NINA.
THAT LITTLE COW! TREACHEROUS--HKK!
THERE IS NO DOUBT. NINA HASN'T SIMPLY GONE MISSING... SHE'S KIDNAPPED HER SON.
SHE SEEKS TO PUNISH ALL THOSE WHO HAVE WRONGED HER--
MA'AM, YOU'VE JUST BEEN IN A HOUSE FIRE.
TRY AND BREATHE IN SLOWLY. THERE MAY BE DAMAGE TO YOUR LUNGS...
--AND BRUTUS CLOSE IS NEXT.

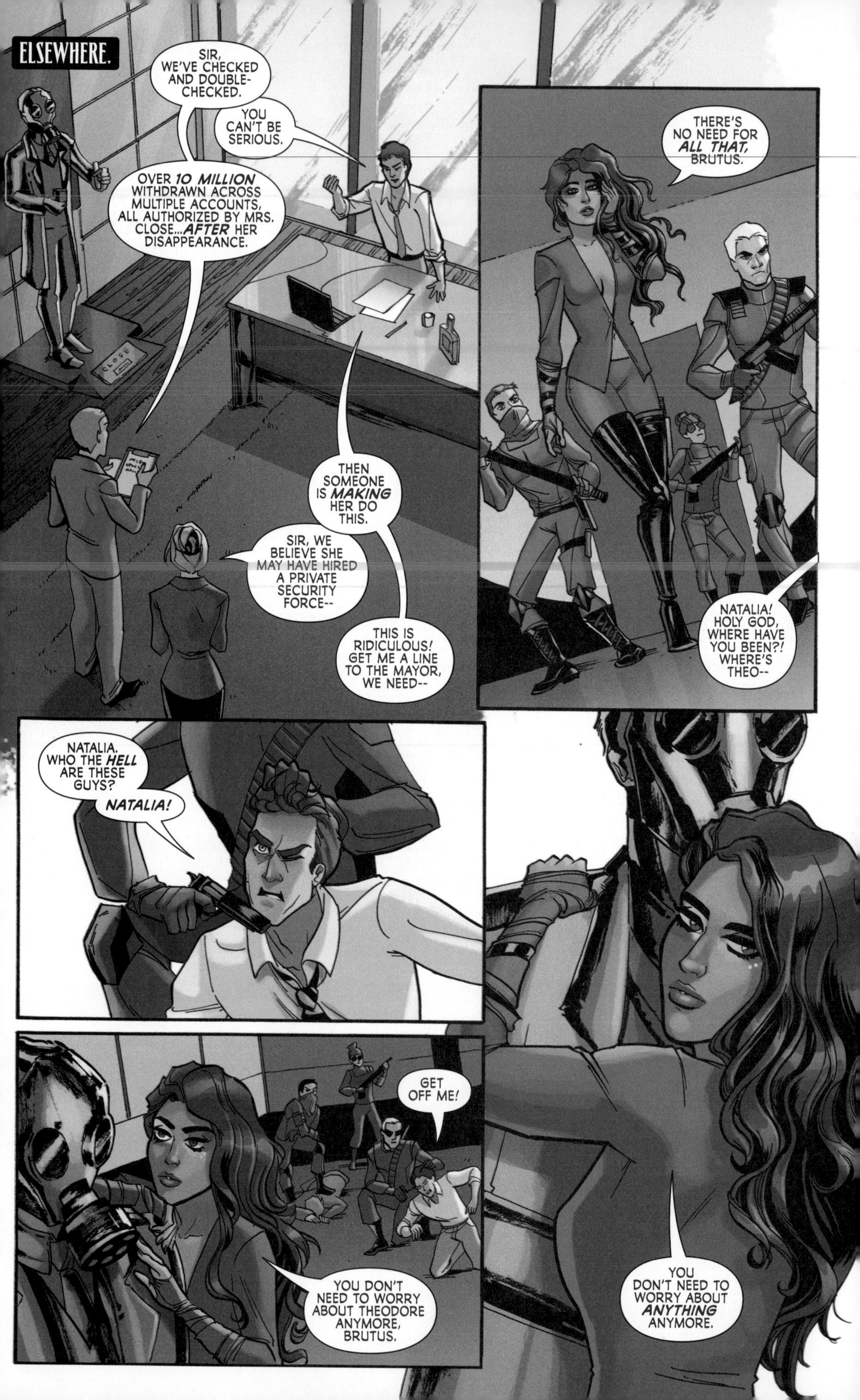
ELSEWHERE.
SIR, WE'VE CHECKED AND DOUBLE-CHECKED.
YOU CAN'T BE SERIOUS.
OVER 10 MILLION WITHDRAWN ACROSS MULTIPLE ACCOUNTS, ALL AUTHORIZED BY MRS. CLOSE...AFTER HER DISAPPEARANCE.
THEN SOMEONE IS MAKING HER DO THIS.
SIR, WE BELIEVE SHE MAY HAVE HIRED A PRIVATE SECURITY FORCE--
THIS IS RIDICULOUS! GET ME A LINE TO THE MAYOR, WE NEED--
THERE'S NO NEED FOR ALL THAT, BRUTUS.
NATALIA! HOLY GOD, WHERE HAVE YOU BEEN?! WHERE'S THEO--
NATALIA. WHO THE HELL ARE THESE GUYS?
NATALIA!
GET OFF ME!
YOU DON'T NEED TO WORRY ABOUT THEODORE ANYMORE, BRUTUS.
YOU DON'T NEED TO WORRY ABOUT ANYTHING ANYMORE.

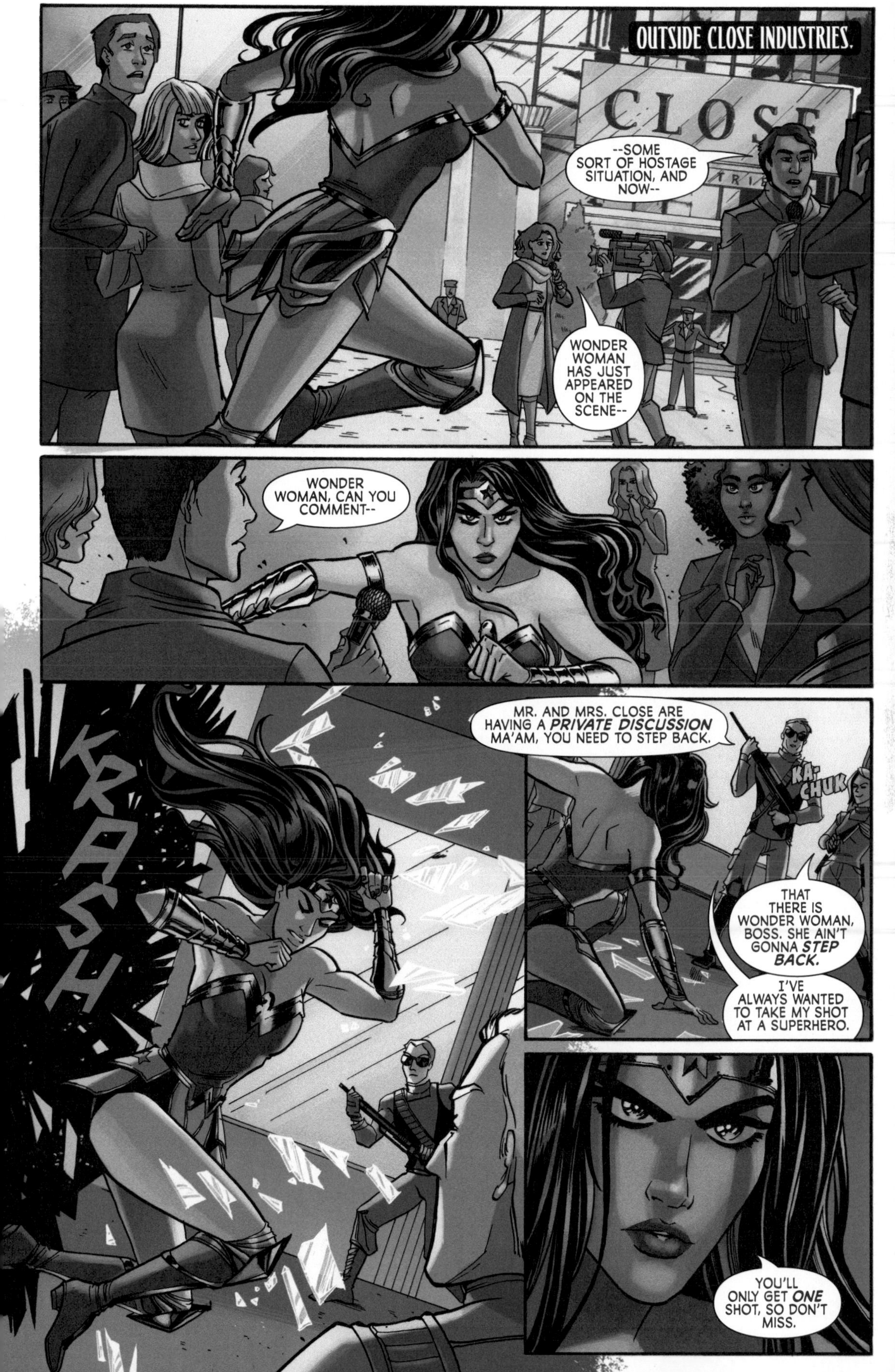

OUTSIDE CLOSE INDUSTRIES.
CLOSE
--SOME SORT OF HOSTAGE SITUATION, AND NOW--
WONDER WOMAN HAS JUST APPEARED ON THE SCENE--
WONDER WOMAN, CAN YOU COMMENT--
KRASH
MR. AND MRS. CLOSE ARE HAVING A *PRIVATE DISCUSSION* MA'AM, YOU NEED TO STEP BACK.
KA-CHUK
THAT THERE IS WONDER WOMAN, BOSS. SHE AIN'T GONNA *STEP BACK.*
I'VE ALWAYS WANTED TO TAKE MY SHOT AT A SUPERHERO.
YOU'LL ONLY GET *ONE* SHOT, SO DON'T MISS.

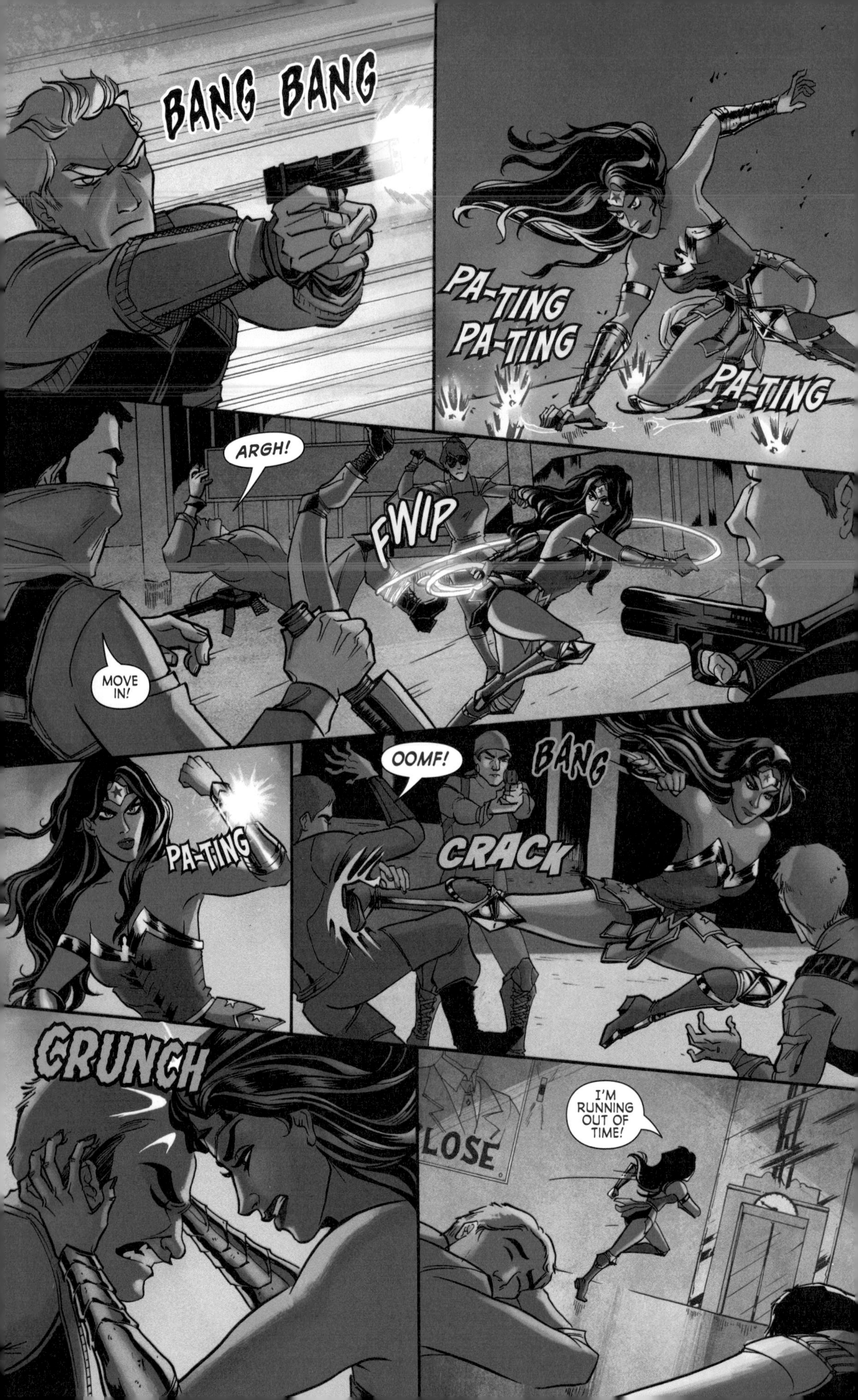
BANG BANG
PA-TING
PA-TING
PA-TING
ARGH!
FWIP
MOVE IN!
PA-TING
OOMF!
BANG
CRACK
CRUNCH
I'M RUNNING OUT OF TIME!
LOSE

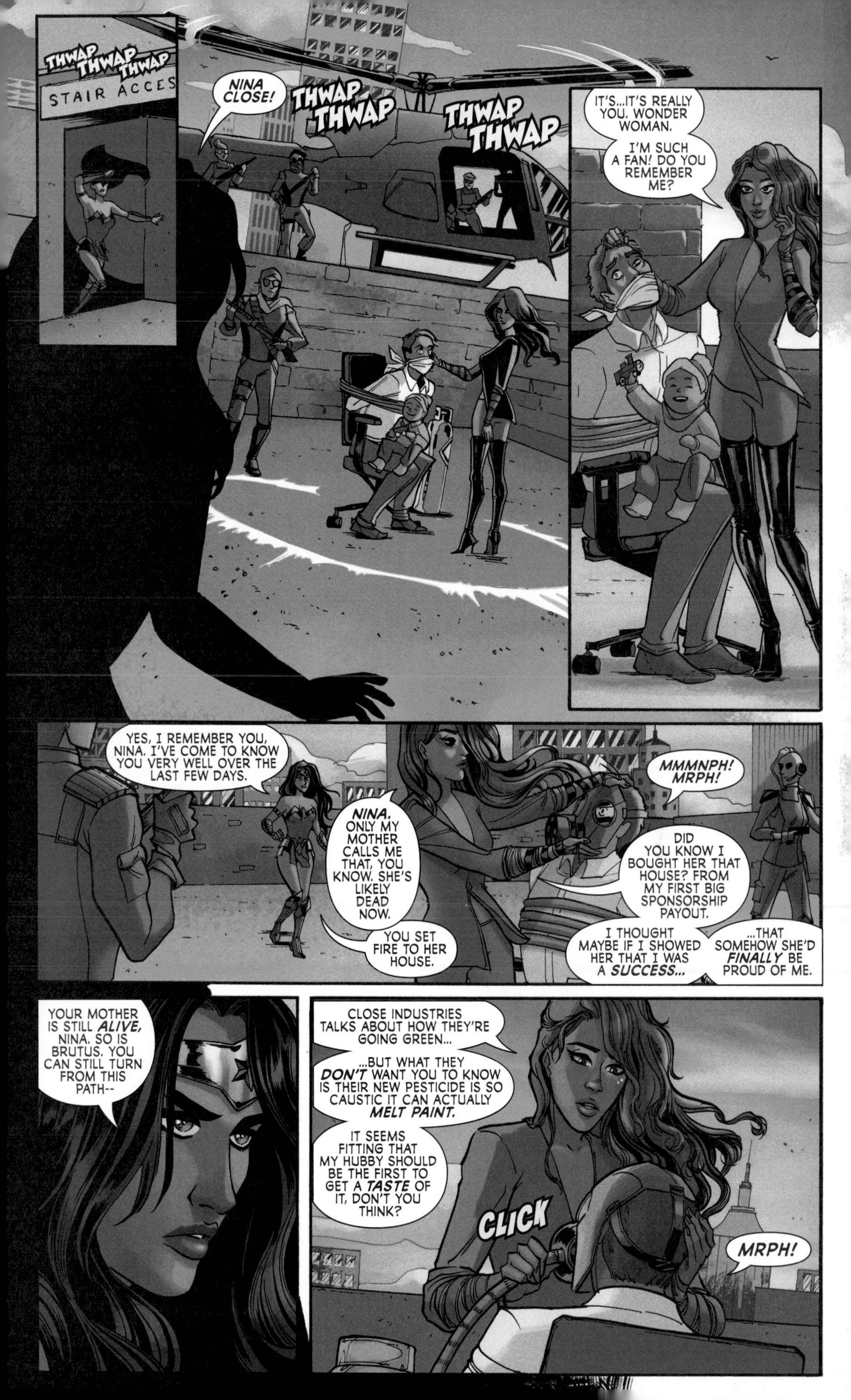
THWAP THWAP THWAP
STAIR ACCES
NINA CLOSE!
THWAP THWAP
THWAP THWAP
IT'S...IT'S REALLY YOU. WONDER WOMAN.
I'M SUCH A FAN! DO YOU REMEMBER ME?
YES, I REMEMBER YOU, NINA. I'VE COME TO KNOW YOU VERY WELL OVER THE LAST FEW DAYS.
NINA. ONLY MY MOTHER CALLS ME THAT, YOU KNOW. SHE'S LIKELY DEAD NOW.
YOU SET FIRE TO HER HOUSE.
MMMNPH! MRPH!
DID YOU KNOW I BOUGHT HER THAT HOUSE? FROM MY FIRST BIG SPONSORSHIP PAYOUT.
I THOUGHT MAYBE IF I SHOWED HER THAT I WAS A SUCCESS...
...THAT SOMEHOW SHE'D FINALLY BE PROUD OF ME.
YOUR MOTHER IS STILL ALIVE, NINA. SO IS BRUTUS. YOU CAN STILL TURN FROM THIS PATH--
CLOSE INDUSTRIES TALKS ABOUT HOW THEY'RE GOING GREEN...
...BUT WHAT THEY DON'T WANT YOU TO KNOW IS THEIR NEW PESTICIDE IS SO CAUSTIC IT CAN ACTUALLY MELT PAINT.
IT SEEMS FITTING THAT MY HUBBY SHOULD BE THE FIRST TO GET A TASTE OF IT, DON'T YOU THINK?
CLICK
MRPH!

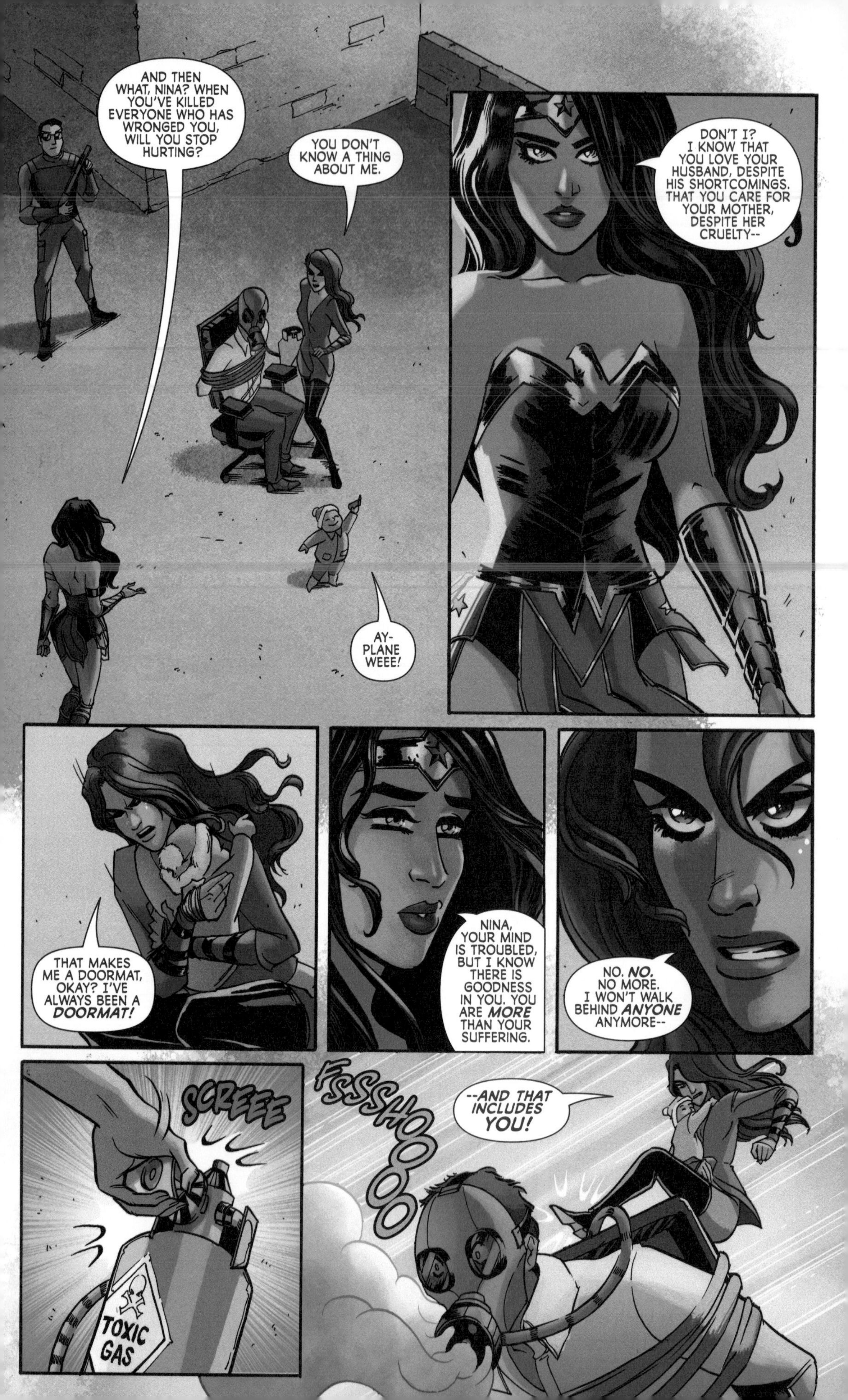

AND THEN WHAT, NINA? WHEN YOU'VE KILLED EVERYONE WHO HAS WRONGED YOU, WILL YOU STOP HURTING?
YOU DON'T KNOW A THING ABOUT ME.
AY-PLANE WEEE!
DON'T I? I KNOW THAT YOU LOVE YOUR HUSBAND, DESPITE HIS SHORTCOMINGS. THAT YOU CARE FOR YOUR MOTHER, DESPITE HER CRUELTY--
THAT MAKES ME A DOORMAT, OKAY? I'VE ALWAYS BEEN A *DOORMAT!*
NINA, YOUR MIND IS TROUBLED, BUT I KNOW THERE IS GOODNESS IN YOU. YOU ARE *MORE* THAN YOUR SUFFERING.
NO. *NO.* NO MORE. I WON'T WALK BEHIND *ANYONE* ANYMORE--
SCREEE
TOXIC GAS
FSSSHOOOO
--AND THAT INCLUDES *YOU!*

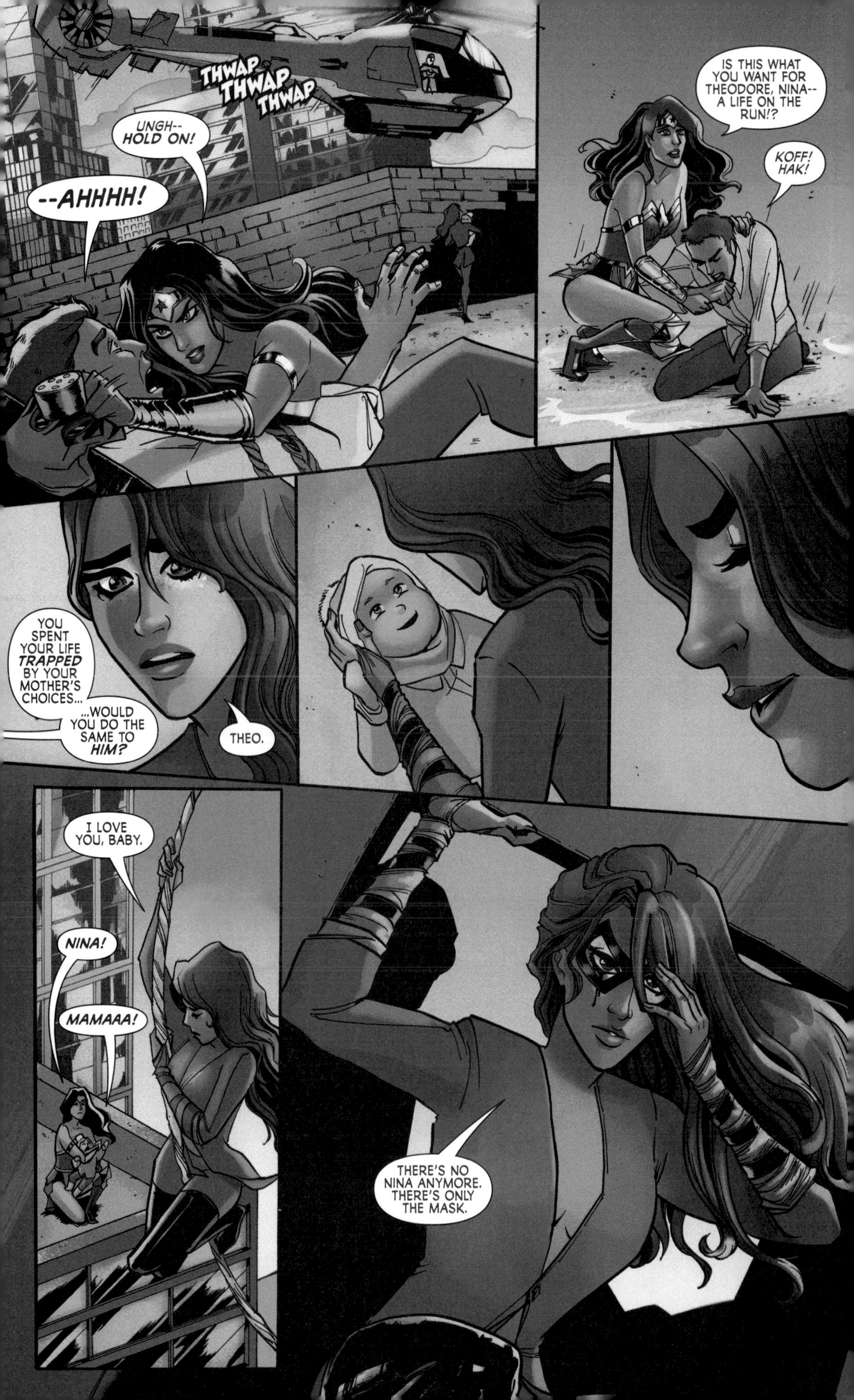
THWAP THWAP THWAP
UNGH-- HOLD ON!
--AHHHH!
IS THIS WHAT YOU WANT FOR THEODORE, NINA-- A LIFE ON THE RUN!?
KOFF! HAK!
YOU SPENT YOUR LIFE TRAPPED BY YOUR MOTHER'S CHOICES...
...WOULD YOU DO THE SAME TO HIM?
THEO.
I LOVE YOU, BABY.
NINA!
MAMAAA!
THERE'S NO NINA ANYMORE. THERE'S ONLY THE MASK.

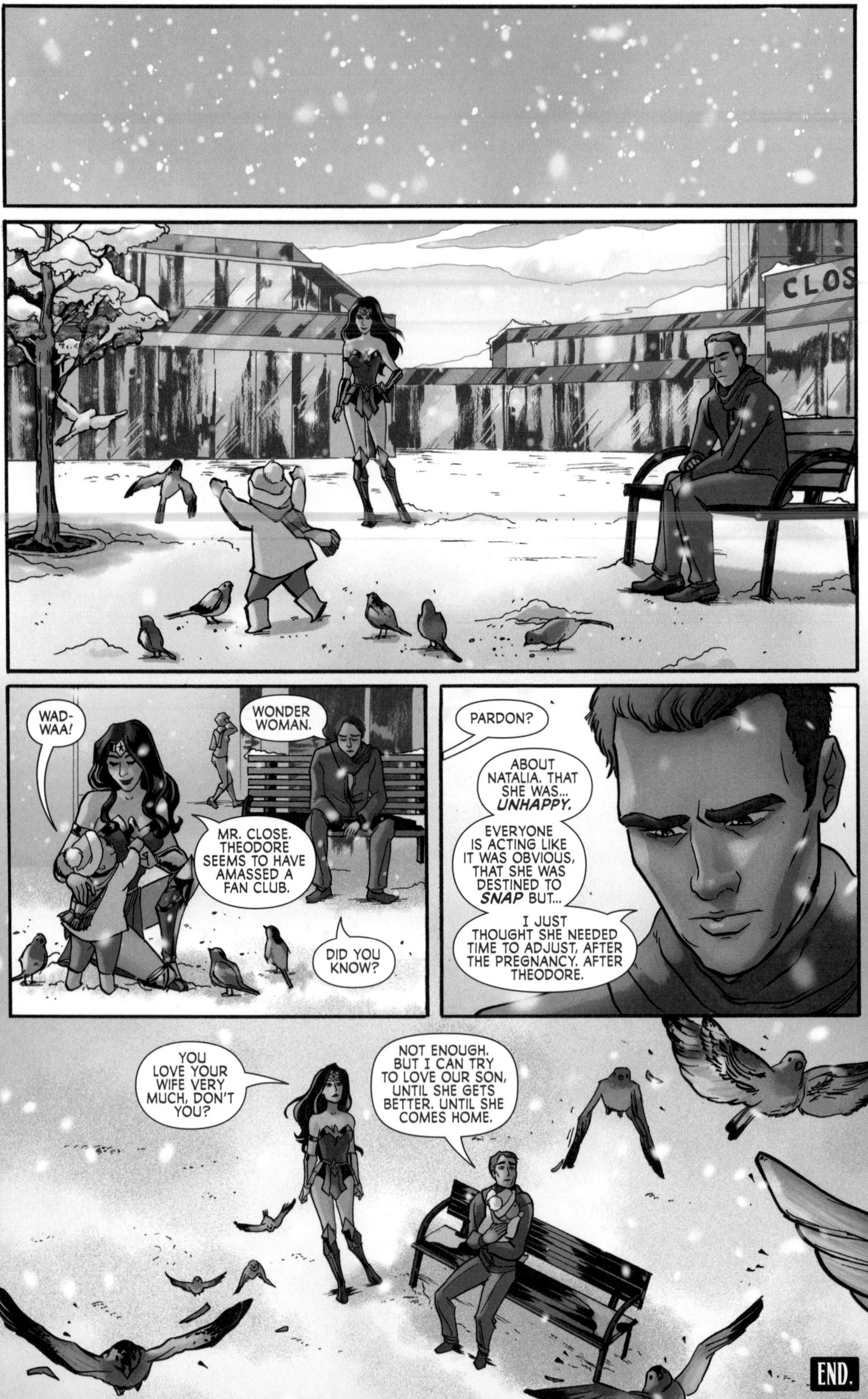
CLOS
WAD-WAA!
WONDER WOMAN.
MR. CLOSE. THEODORE SEEMS TO HAVE AMASSED A FAN CLUB.
DID YOU KNOW?
PARDON?
ABOUT NATALIA. THAT SHE WAS... UNHAPPY.
EVERYONE IS ACTING LIKE IT WAS OBVIOUS, THAT SHE WAS DESTINED TO SNAP BUT...
I JUST THOUGHT SHE NEEDED TIME TO ADJUST, AFTER THE PREGNANCY. AFTER THEODORE.
YOU LOVE YOUR WIFE VERY MUCH, DON'T YOU?
NOT ENOUGH. BUT I CAN TRY TO LOVE OUR SON, UNTIL SHE GETS BETTER. UNTIL SHE COMES HOME.
END.

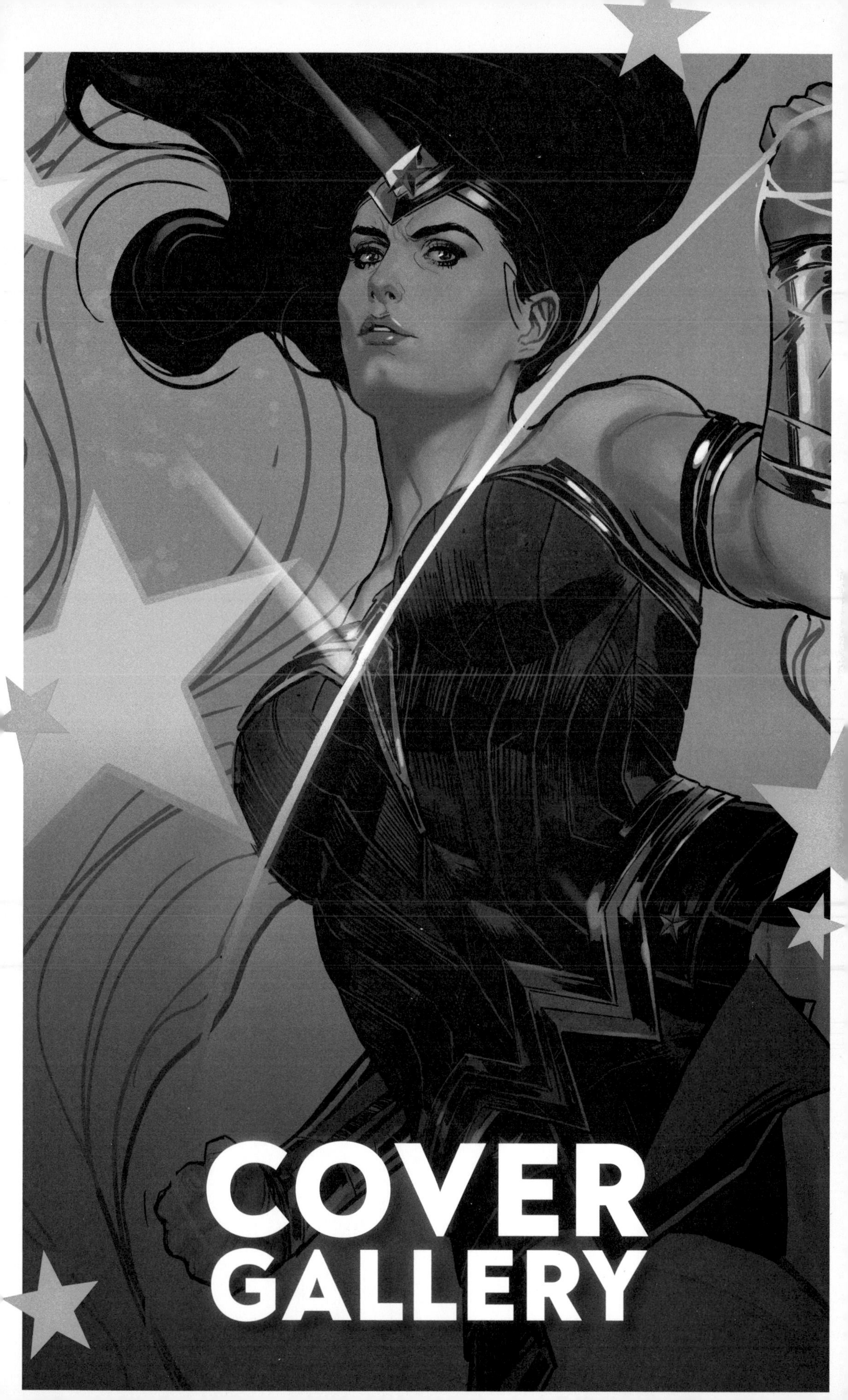
COVER
GALLERY

Issue #1 cover by Yasmine Putri

Issue #1 variant cover by Ejikure

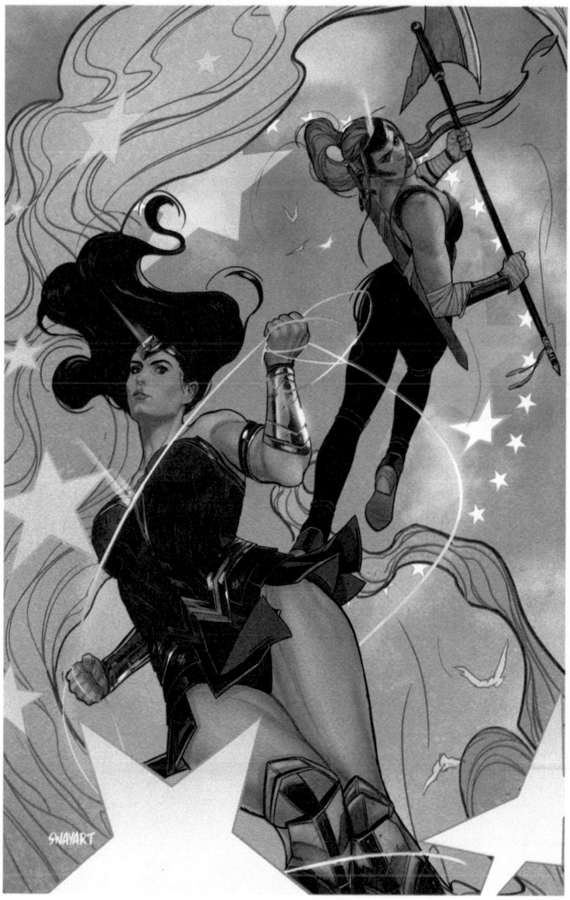
SWAYART

Issue #2 variant cover by Joshua “Sway” Swaby

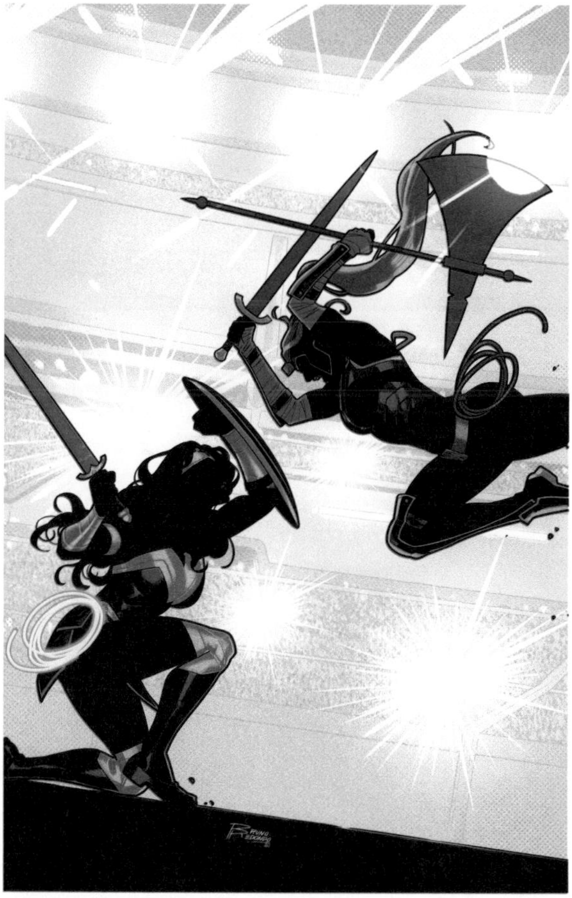

Issue #2 cover by Bruno Redondo

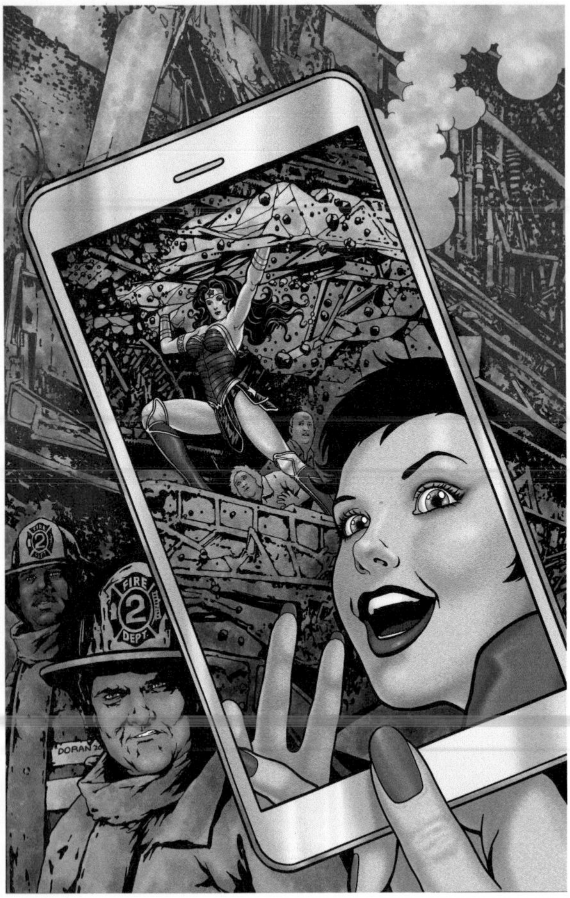
FIRE
2
DEPT.

Issue #3 cover by Colleen Doran

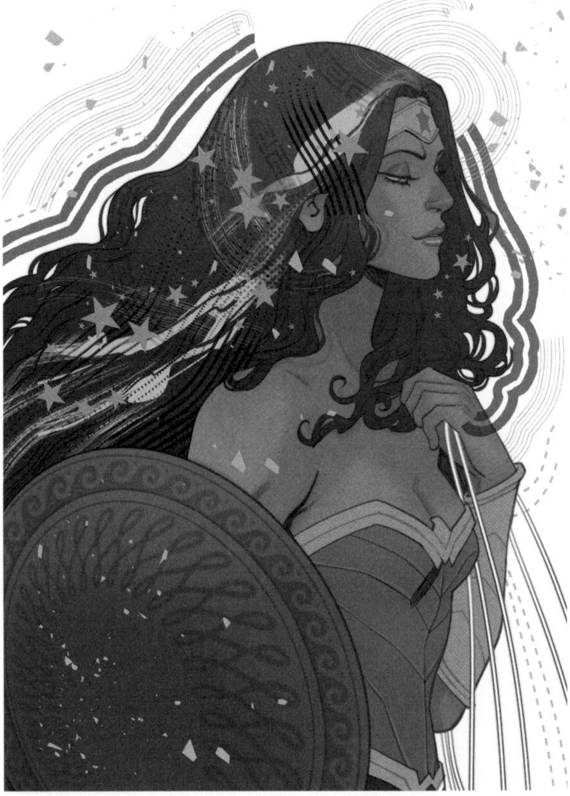

Issue #3 variant cover by Marguerite Sauvage

Issue #4 variant cover by Meghan Hetrick

Issue #4 cover by Dani

Issue #5 cover by Marco Santucci and Arif Prianto

Issue #5 variant cover by Dike Ruan

Issue #6 variant cover by Kael Ngu

Issue #6 cover by Belén Ortega and Alejandro Sanchez

Issue #7 cover by Nicola Scott

Issue #7 variant cover by Tula Lotay